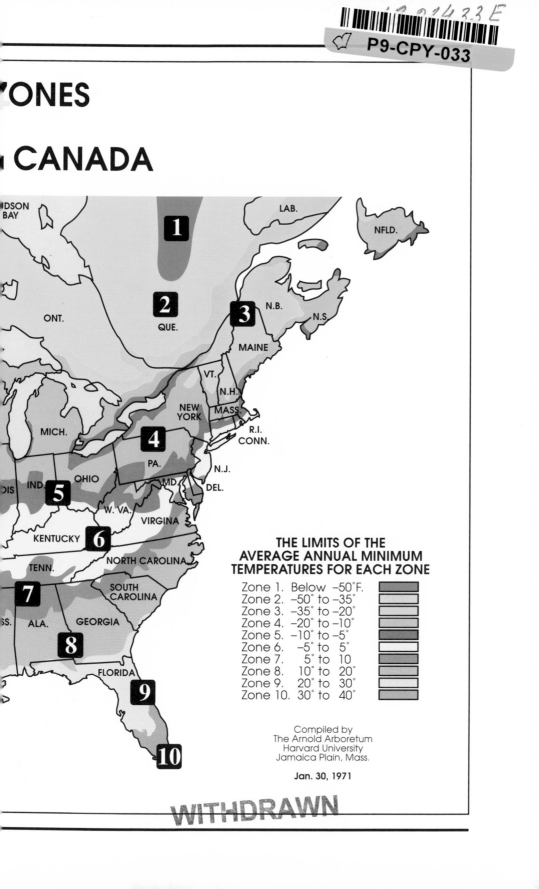

ZONES

CANADA

THE LIMITS OF THE
AVERAGE ANNUAL MINIMUM
TEMPERATURES FOR EACH ZONE

Zone 1. Below −50°F.
Zone 2. −50° to −35°
Zone 3. −35° to −20°
Zone 4. −20° to −10°
Zone 5. −10° to −5°
Zone 6.   −5° to   5°
Zone 7.   5° to 10
Zone 8.   10° to 20°
Zone 9.   20° to 30°
Zone 10. 30° to 40°

Compiled by
The Arnold Arboretum
Harvard University
Jamaica Plain, Mass.

Jan. 30, 1971

TREES
FOR
AMERICAN
GARDENS

⇢≫

TREES
FOR
AMERICAN
GARDENS

THIRD EDITION

→≫

Donald Wyman

MACMILLAN PUBLISHING COMPANY
NEW YORK

COLLIER MACMILLAN CANADA
TORONTO

MAXWELL MACMILLAN INTERNATIONAL
NEW YORK, OXFORD, SINGAPORE, SYDNEY

Macmillan Publishing Company
866 Third Avenue, New York, NY 10022

Collier Macmillan Canada, Inc.
1200 Eglinton Avenue East, Suite 200
Don Mills, Ontario M3C 3N1

Library of Congress Cataloging-in-Publication Data
Wyman, Donald, 1903–
    Trees for American gardens/Donald Wyman.— 3rd ed.
      p.   cm.
    ISBN 0-02-632201-3
      1. Ornamental trees—United States. I. Title.
  SB435.5.W92   1990
  715'.2'0973—dc20   89-13648
                                                      CIP

Macmillan books are available at special discounts for bulk purchases for sales promotions, premiums, fund-raising, or educational use. For details, contact:

    Special Sales Director
    Macmillan Publishing Company
    866 Third Avenue
    New York, NY 10022

10 9 8 7 6 5 4 3 2 1

Printed in the United States of America

Contents

-≫

Foreword

→≫

This is the companion volume to *Shrubs and Vines for American Gardens,* first published in 1949 and subsequently revised and updated in 1969. It is written with the same objectives in mind. Some of the information in that book has necessarily been transferred to this book, especially the Arnold Arboretum Hardiness Map and some of the information on blooming, fruiting, and foliage colors, so that all information pertaining to the growing of ornamental trees will be included in this one volume. Very few plants appear in both volumes merely because they can be grown either as trees or as shrubs. The methods used in describing and evaluating the plants are identical in both volumes.

During the thirty-nine years since this book was first printed, many new trees have become popular in American plantings. As a result, the book has been completely revised and brought up to date. Competition in the nursery industry is such that a premium is always placed on new and valued ornamental trees, so that there is a continuing desire to find or produce worthy new varieties. Some two hundred varieties have been added to those in the first edition, while over a hundred have been judged as not of sufficient merit to grow any longer.

Also during the past twenty-four years a worldwide effort has been broached among the leading botanical and horticultural organizations to obtain agreement on the procedures by which new horticultural varieties (clones or cultivars) are named. As a result an *International Code of Nomenclature for Cultivated Plants* was formulated by the International Union of Biological Sciences and is being adopted by horticultural organizations throughout the world. Adopted in the United States in 1959, this standard of rules for nomenclature and descriptions is therefore definitely followed in this new edition of *Trees for American Gardens.* Those names in single quotations, such as *Acer saccharum* 'Newton's Sentry,' are clones or cultivars and must be propagated asexually, since they will not come true from seed.

In the following pages more than eleven hundred species and varieties of trees now being grown in America are recommended for continued landscape planting. Approximately thirteen hundred additional species and varieties are relegated to a secondary list in which the plants are either inferior to or certainly no better than those in the recommended list. As with the book on shrubs, it is admitted that not everyone will agree with such an arbitrary division, but with the tremendous amount of plant material being grown in this country at present, it is time that someone indicated which plants are superior to others.

There has been a great interest on the part of nurserymen in general to eliminate growing second-rate varieties and to concentrate on growing the better ones. The author has written a series of articles for the trade publication of the commercial growers of the country, *The American Nurseryman.* In these articles the better varieties are recommended, and the poor or mediocre varieties that should no longer be grown are listed. This has stimulated much constructive thought; the Secondary Tree List included at the end of this book is an outgrowth of those articles. Those plants that are recommended have far more stature when compared with the truly large number that have been discarded as mediocre. Although such secondary or discard lists may evoke criticism, the time and effort necessary for their preparation will have been well spent if these lists aid the plant-using public to discriminate wisely when selecting ornamental plants.

It is of interest to note that half the recommended trees are of Asiatic origin, less than half are native to North America, and about one-sixth of the total number are native to Europe.

Most of the pictures have been taken by the author or by Heman A. Howard of the Arnold Arboretum staff. A few are from the extensive photograph files at the Arnold Arboretum. Numerous correspondents all over the country have contributed greatly with valuable information. Special recognition is due to Professor Alfred Rehder, who spent a lifetime on the staff of the Arnold Arboretum, and to his many publications concerning the ornamental woody plants grown in North America. His published information has been drawn on heavily. This book, as well as its immediate predecessor, is the result of an attempt to bring together some of the information accumulated by the Arnold Arboretum and place it before the gardening public in a usable form.

Much credit is due my wife, Florence D. Wyman, for her untiring efforts in the typing and preparation of the first edition. Her help and criticism have made this volume possible. Stella M. Whitehouse helped in many ways with the preparation of the first edition. Typing and assistance given by my daughter, Dorothea W. Thomas, has made this third edition possible, and her valued help in its preparation is gratefully acknowledged.

No acknowledgment would be complete without full credit being given the Arnold Arboretum of Harvard University and its staff. The continued support and assistance the author has received from this world-famous institution during the past fifty years has made the present work possible.

Donald Wyman
Arnold Arboretum
Jamaica Plain, Massachusetts

Introduction

-»»

The trees of any country are the most important plants that can be grown. It is the trees that give shade and beauty to the land, prevent the soil from washing into the sea, and provide shelter to the thousands of different birds and animals.

We should try to know the trees native in our own land better and learn to use them more in landscape planting. They are among the most majestically beautiful plants with which we can possibly work. However, in the following pages of this book it will be noticed that less than half of the trees recommended for landscape use are native to North America. Just about as many are imports from China, Japan, and Korea, and about one-sixth of the total are natives of Europe. Consequently, it becomes important that we know not only our own trees but also those of other temperate regions of the world if we are to make the most of the landscape opportunities available to us now.

When the first European settlers came to these shores, they brought with them small seedlings or seeds of trees from their homes in Europe. In Williamsburg, Virginia, for instance, there are records of such trees as the English yew being planted before 1700. Some of the economically valued trees such as the peach were brought over by the Spaniards a century earlier. It is easy to understand why the early settlers would want some of the plants from their native land in the new. Then, as time went on and they began to realize the tremendous demand in the old country for some of the plants in America, they, too, began to use native plants, especially as the frontier was gradually pushed westward and new plants were discovered.

It was not until about 1850 that the adaptability of the tremendous wealth of material in China and Japan became evident. It was only then that Occidentals had free access to Japan, although many had weathered the trials and tribulations of the rugged travel in China. The climate of Japan and certain parts of China is very similar to that of North America, and as time went on, the ability of Asiatic plants to thrive in North America became an accepted fact. The tree of heaven *(Ailanthus altissima)* is now a weed tree in almost every city on our eastern seaboard. The ginkgo, many of the magnolias, Oriental cherries, and crab apples have now become familiar garden plants to millions of home owners in America.

Exotic trees are not necessarily "better" than our native trees. Nothing can be more beautiful, from a general landscape viewpoint, than our own flowering dogwood *(Cornus florida)* or the white fir *(Abies concolor)* from the Rocky Mountains or the graceful Douglas-fir *(Pseudotsuga menziesii)* of the West Coast.

It must be admitted, however, that Oriental (and European) trees have added a great deal to the general beauty of our landscape plantings and cannot be overlooked in any type of planting in America today. These exotic trees should be accepted on the same basis as our own natives, judged by the same standards, and planted in the same gardens and along the same highways. The intelligent horticulturist will learn about these plants and use them.

The evaluation of trees, that is, the determining of their monetary value, is a controversial subject. It becomes important after a fire, hurricane, or severe storm in which the tree has been damaged or blown over and the property owner has to replace it and figure the amount of depreciation to his property for income tax purposes. Professional arborists throughout the country have at least nine methods of figuring these depreciation values.

It is evident that the real value of a tree must vary with the species—a red oak would be more valuable than a silver maple; with the location—a 25-inch white oak shading the front part of a house would be worth more than the same white oak hidden in the woods; with the condition of the tree, and with land value. A 13-inch red maple has been judged by each one of the nine systems used at one time or another, and the value of the tree comes out anywhere from $115.00 to $489.85—a variation that is much too great to prove any one method reliable.

It is impossible to discuss here all these methods and their merits. Suffice it to say that most trees in landscape plantings, especially the larger trees, are worth more than a simple replacement cost merely because in many cases it is impossible to replace a tree the size and shape of the one destroyed. Estimates are made by reliable arborists after damage has been done, and many of these are sufficiently accurate to be accepted by the Bureau of Internal Revenue. The knowledge, experience, and fairness of the person preparing the evaluation usually determines the accuracy of the resulting estimate.

With the publication of the first edition of *Shrubs and Vines for American Gardens* in 1949, I started a precedent in publishing the names of a long list of shrubs and vines that might be considered to be of only secondary ornamental importance, probably no better than—and many inferior to—those plants recommended in the main part of the book. The same procedure is followed in this companion book on trees.

This practice does not find unanimous approval, but it is an excellent method of pointing out those plants that in the opinion of one individual have little to add to the landscape picture. The better plants, recommended on pages 103–461 of this book, should be given primary consideration. Those in the secondary list (pages 463–78) might be overlooked entirely by most gardeners and considered for use only in trial plantings or by those who wish to experiment in their own situation. No list of recommended plants is worth much unless those that have been eliminated are also listed.

In order to have all the material for the study of trees between two covers, the Arnold Arboretum Hardiness Map (see endpapers), published in the book on shrubs, together with much of the discussion on hardiness and order of bloom, is reproduced in this book; otherwise the material on the following pages deals only with trees.

A tree is usually considered to be a tall, woody plant that normally grows with one main trunk. It is difficult, however, to define precisely the difference between a tall shrub and a small tree. For the purposes of this book, and to reduce to a minimum the number of plants concerned, a tree is considered to be a plant that can be grown with a single trunk and is over 20 feet in height. There are some plants that normally are considered shrubs but that can be grown with a single trunk, such as *Viburnum prunifolium, V. sieboldii, Chionanthus virginicus,* and *Magnolia stellata.* Some of these plants are included in this discussion on trees.

Any list of "the best" plants is always open to criticism and will never be complete, especially when it is made by one individual. Such a list is offered here, however, in the hope that it will considerably aid those who use trees for landscape purposes. It should be pointed out that most (although not all) of the hardy trees have been grown side by side in the Arnold Arboretum where there has been an excellent opportunity to compare them. This does not mean that such a trial proves satisfactory for all the diversified growing conditions throughout the country. Far from it! Such trials are continually going on, at other arboretums and botanical gardens situated at many other places, and the experiences of these institutions have been drawn on heavily in order to make this list of recommended trees.

As an example, the double-flowered Oriental cherries are a group with hundreds of trees, many of them highly exploited in this country. Some have flowers that are very fragrant, some do not. Other things being equal (that is, size and color of flowers, height of tree, hardiness, and so forth), why grow the trees with flowers that are not fragrant?

The same is true of the ornamental crab apples. Over 250 are available from commercial sources in America, yet there is a great similarity among them. Even now there are over fifty recommended flowering crab apples in the lists following, representing plants of all heights, varying degrees of double flowers, sizes, and colors of flowers and fruits, habits, and leaf color. New crab apples are appearing almost every year, but it is highly important that they have some quality superior to the qualities of varieties already available (or discarded) in order to be kept as worthwhile additions to the group.

So often when discussing a plant it is difficult to know whether it actually exists. Taxonomic botanists have a disconcerting habit of describing something that is long since dead and represented only by a dried specimen in a herbarium. All plants mentioned in the following recommended list are probably growing in the United States, and locations for most of them are known.

In response to the increasing demand of the non-Latin student, scientific names have been simplified. All specific names are written without capital letters. A slight degree of accuracy has been sacrificed in order to simplify the scientific or true names of plants as much as possible. Clonal or English varietal names are given in single quotation marks. Thus *Malus* 'Dorothea' is very definitely a clone and must be propagated asexually. Botanical varietal names *(Malus baccata mandshurica)* indicates a group of plants that, if they have the same characteristics, are all given the same name, regardless of whether they are propagated sexually by seed or asexually by cuttings or grafts. All this is in conformity with the *International Code of Nomenclature for Cultivated Plants* now being adopted by all horticultural and botanical organizations throughout the world. It will be noted that in this edition the *ii* endings of certain specific names have been used, necessitated (unfortunately) to conform with the same code, which went into effect in January 1959.

The plants discussed are for all parts of Canada and the United States, except the subtropical areas. There are parts of southern California, the Gulf states, and Florida where the climate is such that hundreds of subtropical and even tropical trees can be grown. This very definitely is a special subject in itself, of interest to people living in a very small portion of this great country. Only a very few subtropical trees are considered here, but many of the plants that are listed can be grown very well in these areas. Consequently, although not covered thoroughly, some planting information can be gleaned from the following lists for these areas.

Something should be said here about plant patents. At the present time there is no minute check on the plants coming up for patenting to ensure that they are "different" from something that has gone before. Many specific instances should be cited of patented plants that are almost identical with older, established varieties. The patent does protect the commercial grower who has something different, and for that reason has merit. The point in mentioning this here is to caution the plant-buying public that merely because a plant is patented does not mean that it is "superior," "different," or even "better" ornamentally than something that has been grown previously. Since there is no authoritative check on this, patented plants should merely be considered at their face value until thoroughly tried out. It is hoped that someday sufficient checks will be adopted so that when a patented plant bears that label it will be decidedly different from everything else. Until that time comes, the general public should not give more attention to a patented plant than any other; it may well be no better than an old, established variety whose qualities are well known.

Extensive plant disease and insect scourges have swept this country in the past half century. The chestnut blight, the gypsy moth and Japanese beetle, the Dutch elm disease, and phloem necrosis of elms have done serious damage. The oak wilt is beginning to threaten certain areas, and the pear thrip is seriously damaging all sugar maple trees. There are many ornamental trees available for all kinds of purposes, and merely because one tree is seriously infested (the American elm, for example) is no reason to throw up our hands in despair. Other trees, although they may not have the majestic habit of growth of the American elm, may have ornamental qualities that are superior—interesting flowers and fruit—and be less susceptible to insect troubles at the same time.

The planting of street trees is becoming increasingly important in light of the elm troubles. It used to be that the American elm was the only street tree. After a century of growth, it is true that it reaches majestic heights, but at the same time the removal of a large number of diseased trees can quickly drain the budget of any city forestry department. Might there not be food for thought in the idea of using smaller trees for planting city streets, which admittedly would not live to the great age of the elm or reach its great height but which would not cost a fortune to remove?

Park executives, town foresters, landscape architects, nurserymen, and just plain gardeners can do well to learn more about the fifteen hundred native and exotic trees in the following recommended lists. It is these that should be considered first in making landscape plantings, for they include the best trees growing in North America today.

ONE

Hardiness

→≫

The ability of a plant or tree to grow in a certain area is usually closely associated with its hardiness. Palm trees do not live outdoors in New England, although the native flowering dogwood *(Cornus florida)* will thrive in the southeastern United States where palms grow. The park superintendent or town forester is familiar with trees that are suitable for highway planting in his area, but the proverbial question about a new plant is always: "Is it hardy in our area?" It would be convenient for everyone if a complete list of plants could be given with minute hardiness data so that one would merely have to glance at the list to know whether or not any one plant would be hardy in any particular location. Such a list is not available, for hardiness is a highly complex matter. It is essential to understand a few things about it in order to be able to make the decision as to whether or not a new plant might grow in a given location.

Hardiness is closely associated with three things—temperature, rainfall, and soil—probably in that order of importance. When three variable factors such as these are combined to give one result, it can become most confusing to keep track of simple fundamentals. The United States Department of Agriculture has studied this problem for some time and has issued maps of the United States on which are superimposed twenty-three "climatic provinces," thirty-two "plant growth regions," and fifty "important soil regions." Such information is most valuable for those who can assimilate it, but it can be most confusing to the lay person. It would seem, after years of thorough study of this topic, that a hardiness map based entirely on simple temperature fluctuations would be sufficiently indicative for most horticulturists, provided, of course, that its limitations were thoroughly understood. Alfred Rehder adopted this principle in his first volume, *Manual of Cultivated Trees and Shrubs* (Macmillan, 1927). For further details see page 10. Consequently, the Arnold Arboretum Hardiness Map in this book is based on this principle and is identical with the one used in *Shrubs and Vines for American Gardens* (Macmillan, 1969).

A tree can grow in one situation for centuries, hence the type of soil in which it does best is an important point in planting. In small areas or on highly priced land, the soil can be modified by excavation and the introduction of completely new soil. Continual modification is sometimes possible with the use of mulches and fertilizers. The modification of soil in this way can become very expensive, however, especially in the growing of trees. It is far better to select at the start the kind of tree that will do well in the soil already on the site rather than to plant a tree of known soil preferences other than those available, and then plan to modify the soil throughout the life of the tree.

The same thing can be said about rainfall. If the rainfall is low in a certain area, and moisture-loving plants are used, they can be watered as long as there is water and the willingness to do the extra work. Usually in dry areas the plants that must be watered continually are so burdensome that they are eventually discarded. There is little that can be done about an overabundance of moisture or rain. Consequently, as far as this phase of hardiness is concerned, it is best to select trees at the start that are known to survive in the area concerned, especially in areas with long summer (or winter) droughts. Recently I saw a chart of the average rainfall worked out on a statewide basis. It meant little, for in each state the rainfall can vary widely—sufficiently to make such a chart of little help in planting. It was of interest to know, however, that the rainfall in the United States varies from an annual average of under 10 inches in most of Nevada to 60 inches on the coast of Oregon and Washington, three hundred miles away. It goes without saying that many of the trees perfectly "hardy" on the West Coast would have a very difficult time in most parts of Nevada, due solely to lack of sufficient moisture.

A study of the rainfall over North America will show that, by and large, the greatest centers of population (that is, where gardening and tree planting are greatest) are in areas considered to have "normal" amounts of rainfall, where most plants will live and thrive without too much additional watering. There are always populated centers in the midst of areas susceptible to prolonged droughts, such as the Great Plains, but when the extent of the horticultural activity in areas like northern Illinois or Ohio or the eastern seaboard is compared with the little-populated drought areas of the Southwest, it will be admitted that the greatest horticultural areas have sufficient rainfall. Hence, a simplified hardiness map, of use to the greatest number of planters, need not include data on rainfall.

Temperature, usually minimum temperature, is the most important single factor governing hardiness in the heavily populated areas of North America. These are the records that anyone can obtain merely by noting the daily minimum temperature on a thermometer placed out of doors.

Injury caused by fluctuations in temperature may occur in several ways.

It may result from a sudden, out-of-season freeze, a sudden drop in temperature, or a long period of very low temperatures. Considerable investigation has shown that very low temperature is the chief factor in killing plant tissue. Pomologists have been very interested in the "sun scald" of fruit tree trunks, a killing of the living tissue usually on the southwest side (in northern orchards). A sudden drop in temperature may do this killing in one night. If a sunny, slightly warm afternoon is followed immediately by a sudden drop in temperature after sunset—possibly to 10°F—this may kill the living tissues of some fruit tree varieties. The temperature gradient will be steepest on the side exposed to the warm afternoon sun, hence the "sun scald" of trunks on the southwest side. On the other hand, a gradual drop in temperature to this same point over a period of several hours might have no harmful effects whatsoever.

Temperature records in the Arnold Arboretum in Boston have yielded valuable data. There was severe winter injury during the winters of 1933–34, 1935, and 1942–43, during which periods there were no more than eight days when the minimum temperature went to zero or below. It is of interest to note that it was only in these three winters that plants suffered severe winter injury and in only a few winters since 1943 have minimum temperatures reached zero. This does not mean that all plants suffer with a minimum temperature of zero. Far from it! There are, however, so many tender varieties of plants growing in the Arnold Arboretum that, from the evidence, when zero temperatures are reached, rather widespread damage on some of them can be expected. This, then, is a killing of tissue done mostly at low temperature.

There is evidence to prove that the tissues of some plants may not be injured by low temperatures if the drop to those temperatures is gradual and not sudden. Just what these temperatures are and how long they can be withstood by certain plants can be ascertained only by careful experimentation.

Soil moisture enters the hardiness picture to this extent: evergreens, particularly, are giving off a certain amount of water from their leaves throughout the entire winter. Deciduous plants give off some from their twigs but not nearly as much as the evergreens. When winter winds are high, this causes the plants to give off a larger amount of water than they normally would. If the ground is frozen, as it usually is in the winter, the plant roots are unable to absorb additional soil moisture, so there comes a time, if high winds continue, when the evergreen needles or leaves give off too much water and the living tissue is injured, resulting in the characteristic browning or "burning" of the evergreens so common in late February and March.

This same injury can be caused when unseasonably warm days in late winter occur with high air temperatures but do not last sufficiently long to thaw out the ground and allow the roots to take up additional moisture. Because of this, it is important that the soil around all evergreens have plenty of water prior to the time the ground freezes in the fall. Mulching with all kinds of materials—snow included—proves helpful in keeping the ground unfrozen for the longest possible time. Burlap screens and protection with evergreen boughs also are helpful in reducing water loss due to high winds or unseasonable, warm sunshine while the ground is still frozen. The same principles hold for all areas of the country where the ground freezes in the winter or where winter droughts are pronounced.

Lack of winter hardiness is evident, of course, only after the damage has been done. The plant may die completely. A few of the more vigorous branches may be killed, indicating that those branches may have made a late active growth and not had sufficient time in the fall to harden or mature properly. Then there are the many cases of flower buds being killed. Flowering dogwood, magnolias, and many of the fruit trees all suffer in this respect. Flower buds are more susceptible to cold than leaf buds, and frequently there is a varietal difference of considerable economic importance. Some peach tree varieties ('Veteran' and 'Marigold' are two examples) are notably more flower-bud resistant to cold than others and hence are better adapted for planting in the colder parts of the country.

In recent years the flowering dogwood has suffered injury frequently in the North. Sometimes the cold is of sufficient intensity to kill the flower buds completely; at other times only the two outside flower bracts are injured and the so-called flower appears as a peculiar freak with only two white bracts developed, and sometimes even these are deformed.

The hardiness map on the inside covers of this book is based solely on average annual minimum temperatures. Most of the data were taken and summarized by the United States Weather Bureau over a forty-year period; hence the map is based on sound fact. Data for Canada were supplied by the Meteorological Division, Department of Transport of the Canadian government. The United States and Canada are arbitrarily divided into ten zones, nine of which are in the United States. (Alfred Rehder adopted this principle in his *Manual of Cultivated Trees and Shrubs,* but at that time the United States Department of Agriculture Weather Bureau data were not available.) These zones are based on 5-, 10-, or 15-degree differences in the average annual minimum temperatures. Slight variations were made in the map as taken from the Weather Bureau records, in accord with known variations in plant performance on the eastern seaboard. Incidentally, part of this map was first published in my book *Hedges, Screens and Windbreaks* (McGraw-Hill, 1938) and later used and augmented by Alfred Rehder in the second edition of his *Manual* (1940).

On a small-scale map such as this, it is impossible to show all the minute climatic variations within the limits of each zone. The Grand Canyon, for example, appears in the hardiness map in one zone; yet, due to variations in altitude alone, there are at least four climatic zones, each with a different flora, in this one canyon. Plants grow in the bottom of the canyon that also thrive on the Mexican deserts, yet on the North Rim (5,700 feet above the canyon floor) plants are found that are native to southern Canada.

Local hardiness studies are being undertaken by certain of the state agricultural experiment stations—New York, for example. Information has been collected and assessed over a period of many years, and a hardiness map has been issued showing considerably more detail than is possible on the small-scale map in this book. Such studies are decidedly worthwhile because altitude and nearness to large bodies of water do make marked changes in hardiness for certain plants, and it is valued information for the planting public to have available.

Consequently, many local variations in the small map submitted are to be expected. In the list following, a plant is usually listed in the coldest zone where it will grow normally, while at the same time it can be expected to grow in many of the warmer zones. Maximum temperatures and drought conditions would prove the major limiting factors. The following trees, common in many gardens, are listed in the coldest zones in which they will

This is the common canoe birch (Betula papyrifera), *noted for its excellent white bark and golden yellow autumn color.*

normally grow. These should prove reliable indicators for the type of plant material it is possible to grow in each zone.

ZONE 2
Acer ginnala
Alnus incana
Betula papyrifera
Elaeagnus angustifolia
Juniperus virginiana

ZONE 3
Acer pensylvanicum
Aesculus hippocastanum
Chamaecyparis obtusa
Fagus grandifolia
Pinus strobus

ZONE 4
Abies concolor
Amelanchier laevis
Cornus florida
Liriodendron tulipifera
Tsuga canadensis

ZONE 5
Betula albo-sinensis
Chamaecyparis lawsoniana
Ilex opaca
Magnolia soulangiana
Picea asperata

ZONE 6
Acer macrophyllum
Broussonetia papyrifera

Davidia involucrata
Salix babylonica
Sequoiadendron giganteum

ZONE 7
Cedrus deodara
Cornus nuttallii
Ilex cassine
Magnolia grandiflora
M. veitchii

ZONE 8
Arbutus unedo
Cornus capitata
Euonymus japonica
Pinus canariensis
Prosopis glandulosa

ZONE 9
Acer barbatum floridanum
Cinnamomum camphora
Eucalyptus species
Quercus agrifolia

ZONE 10
Acacia longifolia floribunda
Araucaria heterophylla
Ceiba pentandra
Delonix regia
Jacaranda acutifolia

TWO

Order of Bloom

→≫

Indiscriminate planting of trees and shrubs without a knowledge of when they flower is certainly not the best way to create a beautiful landscape picture. Best results are naturally obtained when one has a knowledge of the time trees bloom, which ones bloom together, and which ones can be depended upon to bloom in sequence. The actual day on which a certain plant first opens its flowers may vary from year to year according to the vagaries of the weather, but certain species and varieties can always be depended upon to bloom together.

After a careful study of the blooming dates of woody plants over wide areas of the United States, compared with carefully kept notes for long periods in the Arnold Arboretum in Boston, Massachusetts, where nearly seven thousand different kinds of woody plants are growing together in the same soil and climate, certain facts concerning the sequence of bloom have become evident. It will be of interest to most horticulturists to note some of the following facts about this phenomenon of nature.

The sequence of bloom proves a most interesting study, for it can include the bloom of wild flowers and perennials as well as trees and shrubs. The blooming period of annuals is on a somewhat different basis since the time they flower can be modified by the time they are "set out" or by the size to which they are grown in the greenhouse before they are planted outdoors. Trees, shrubs, vines, perennials, and wild flowers growing in one locality fairly unprotected from the weather all work themselves into a definite sequence of bloom that does not vary to any appreciable extent from one year to the next. The sequence of bloom in Boston, Massachusetts, will be the same as the sequence in Augusta, Georgia, provided the same plants are normally grown out of doors in those localities.

The length of bloom or the amount of time the plants remain ornamentally effective while in flower does vary. It varies with the kind of plant and with the season. A double-flowering cherry such as the variety 'Kwanzan' may remain in flower for a full three weeks, and so it can be used effectively with other blooming trees and shrubs. It is reasonable to expect all double-flowered trees to make a longer show while in flower than will varieties with single flowers. Take as another example the shadblow or *Amelanchier*. These have single flowers and may remain in flower a week, if the weather is cold, or may drop their flower petals only three days later after they open if the weather is unusually warm. In 1944, *Magnolia heptapeta* first opened its flowers in the Arnold Arboretum on May 2. Unseasonably warm weather occurred during the next few days so that most of the petals of this tree had fallen by May 5. Normally the petals would have remained on the plant at least a week. This same year *M. stellata* remained colorful five days longer than *M. heptapeta* merely because it had many more petals.

Hence the amount of time the flowers of trees and shrubs remain in good condition varies a great deal. Length of bloom is not considered here because it is highly unpredictable, but individual gardeners who are interested in this subject could keep notes of their own observations from year to year to show just how much these periods vary in their own localities.

The specific day of the year on which a certain plant first opens its flowers varies with two things. These are important. The first is the location in which the particular plant is growing. The second is the variation of temperature in the particular year (and often in the particular location) in question.

The Yoshino cherry (Prunus yedoensis) *is the most prominent species of flowering cherry around the Tidal Basin in Washington, D.C.*

⇥ *BLOOMING DATES VARY WITH LOCATION*

All plants bloom on an earlier date when grown in the South than they do when grown in the North. Magnolias, dogwoods, crab apples, and lindens can be seen blooming in northern Florida at least eight weeks before they start to bloom in New England. Hence there is a very marked difference in blooming dates due to differences in latitude.

There are also marked differences due to altitude. Shadblow or *Amelanchier* species, as an example, will bloom at the higher altitudes in the Great Smokies of Tennessee at nearly the same time they will in Maine. Certainly the differences are marked in many, many places throughout the land where flowers high up on the mountains bloom considerably later than they do in the lowlands close by.

Differences in blooming dates due to latitude alone can be graphically shown on maps in a general way so that they can be easily understood. However, variations due to differences in altitude are extremely difficult to portray except on highly complicated maps. For the purposes of this discussion, suffice it to say that differences in blooming dates due to variations in altitude do exist. In many cases they are very marked and are usually of such a local nature that they can be easily worked out and depended upon from one year to the next.

It must be admitted that even in the same locality there may be differences in time of bloom not due to altitude. Forsythia grown next to the foundation of a warm building will bloom days earlier than a plant of the same variety grown a hundred feet away but in an exposed situation. In New England, for instance, a very early blooming shrub such as *Rhododendron mucronulatum,* if grown in a warm, sunny location, blooms sufficiently early so that its flower buds may be badly nipped by late frosts, whereas if it is grown in a shaded situation with a northern exposure, the opening of the flowers is often retarded for a sufficient number of days to escape such frost injury.

Variations in blooming dates due to latitude are easily portrayed. The march of spring from south to north can be clearly depicted on a map. In adapting this map to show the advance of blooming dates and of spring in general, it is not implied that all plants are anxiously awaiting the time of the last killing frost in order to burst into bloom! A study of this map would show, however, that the last killing frost in northern Florida is usually expected about the first of March, while in the vicinity of Boston, about the first of May. The difference between these two is eight weeks, the exact difference in the time of bloom of certain plants such as *Cornus florida* or *Kalmia latifolia* or *Philadelphus coronarius* when grown in these two areas.

The actual blooming dates of many trees have been noted in widely separated areas in the United States. In general, the differences in actual bloom of specific plants in any area when compared with Boston are the same as the differences between the date of the last killing frost of that particular place and Boston. Once the sequence of bloom has been established (see pages 18–23) and approximate blooming dates for a specific area listed (in this case Boston), one can easily obtain an approximate estimate of when the same species will bloom in any other area of the country where they are located.

Like the hardiness map, a map depicting the "advance of spring" is fallible and should be used under the same consideration as the hardiness map (inside cover). It does, however, give an unmistakable picture of the gradual advance of spring from south to north—and it is sufficiently accurate to bear real study. Actual blooming dates of *Cornus florida* for different areas are given below merely to show how this collected information definitely shows an advance of blooming dates.

Glen St. Mary, Florida	Mid-February
Augusta, Georgia	Late March
St. Louis, Missouri	Early April
Asheville, North Carolina	Mid-April
Washington, D.C.	Late April
Lexington, Kentucky	Late April
Columbus, Ohio	Early May
Philadelphia, Pennsylvania	Early May
London, England	Early May
Chicago, Illinois	Mid-May
Detroit, Michigan	Mid-May
Rochester, New York	Mid-May
Boston, Massachusetts	Mid-May
Seattle, Washington	Mid-May
Portland, Maine	Late May
Southern Ontario, Canada	Late May

⇶ BLOOMING DATES VARY WITH ANNUAL WEATHER FLUCTUATIONS

The other factor causing a variance in the specific blooming date of a particular plant is really a series of factors that might be termed "the vagaries of the weather" or the "earliness" or "lateness" of the season. We speak of spring being "early" this year, or "late," meaning the forsythias or lilacs or azaleas or violets or narcissi are not blooming at the "normal" time. They are blooming earlier if the weather has been unseasonably mild or later if the weather has been unseasonably cold. Every locality in the country has its own peculiarities in this respect. Take as an example the blooming date of the Oriental cherries planted around the Tidal Basin in Washington, D.C. Hundreds of thousands of people flock to Washington to see this beautiful sight annually. Over a thirty-five-year period the date of the opening of these 'Yoshino' cherries in Washington has been from March 20 to April 16. That of the double-flowered 'Kwanzan' cherries during the same period has been from April 1 to May 2, about a month's spread in both cases, depending on the weather.

The Arnold Arboretum has kept a very interesting series of figures showing how these annual weather variations affect widely different species of plants over a period of years. One year may be "early" from start to finish, another may be unusually "early" at the beginning, only to be brought back to "normal" by a prolonged cold spell. It should be emphasized in this respect that in some localities in the United States, especially in Montana and parts of the South, this "catching up" process can even be depended upon annually.

Such figures merely prove what everyone knows—that actual blooming dates in one locality do vary from year to year. An unusual cold spell in the early spring followed by a warm spell may bring forsythia and lilac into bloom at the same time. This happened in many places in 1945. Normally, forsythia has finished blooming when lilac begins. Other variations may hold other groups in flower longer, causing a telescoping of an otherwise protracted bloom period.

Sometimes a very cold spell in the spring will greatly retard all the earlier-blooming shrubs. Such was the case during the spring of 1962. Until April 28 there were no plants showing any green leaves at all and very few plants in bloom. Then April 29, 30, and May 1 were unseasonably warm in New England, with temperatures in the upper sixties and seventies. This seemed to be the spark needed for all the retarded flowers, and the following ten plants are examples of many that came into full bloom suddenly for the first time that year on May 2.

	NORMAL BLOOMING PERIOD
Acer saccharum	Early May
Prunus sargentii	Late April
Prunus subhirtella autumnalis	Late April
Forsythia species	Mid-April
Prunus tomentosa	Late April
Prunus armeniaca	Late April
Lindera benzoin	Mid-April
Magnolia heptapeta	Late April
Magnolia stellata	Late April
Rhododendron mucronulatum	Mid-April

It is interesting to keep a few notes on the advance of spring each year. I have noticed a particular weeping willow tree from my office window for a number of years. It has the unique habit of turning green overnight when weather conditions are just right. A few days prior to this time the buds are undoubtedly swelling, but as soon as they burst and the tiny leaf blades first appear, then the tree seems suddenly to turn green when viewed from a distance. The dates for this over a twenty-six-year period have varied from April 1 to May 1.

≫≫ SOME TREES LISTED IN THEIR ORDER OF BLOOM IN THE ARNOLD ARBORETUM, BOSTON, MASSACHUSETTS

In this listing some common perennials are included as well since they are useful in orienting the time other plants bloom. The list is made up from a long series of notes kept by the author during the 1940s as well as notes kept by Professor J. G. Jack of the Arboretum staff between the years 1887 and 1893. Since 1936 additional records have been kept annually in the Arboretum so that the sequence has been checked and rechecked many times. A tree is listed only for the particular date when its bloom is first of value from a landscape point of view, although its flower buds may be conspicuous for several days before full bloom. Some trees are included, merely for the record, with flowers that are of little ornamental significance.

It should be stressed that some of the trees will remain in bloom longer than others and hence can be used effectively in gardens with plants that bloom later. Still others are effective in flower bud and might be planted with varieties blooming earlier. Local studies along this line should prove of great interest to individual gardeners.

The following order of bloom is applicable in localities other than New England. If local blooming dates of a few key plants are noted and the differences checked with those given in the following sequence, then all the dates can be correspondingly shifted and the sequence can be thus adapted to local climatic conditions.

⇥⟫ ORDER OF BLOOM

(All trees in the following lists are growing in the Arnold Arboretum under practically the same soil and climatic conditions and have bloomed together in the following sequence.)

MARCH
Acer saccharinum
Corylus species
Salix species

EARLY APRIL
Acer rubrum
Alnus incana
A. rugosa
Cornus mas
C. officinalis
Populus species
Prunus davidiana
Ulmus americana

MID-APRIL
Acer negundo
Betula species
Cercidiphyllum japonicum

LATE APRIL
Acer circinatum
A. diabolicum purpurascens
A. dieckii
A. leucoderme
A. platanoides
Amelanchier canadensis
A. laevis
A. spicata
Buxus microphylla
B. sempervirens
Carpinus species
Magnolia heptapeta
M. kobus
M. kobus borealis
M. loebneri
M. proctoriana
M. salicifolia
M. stellata
Malus baccata mandshurica
Ostrya species
Poncirus trifoliata
Prunus apetala

P. armeniaca
P. canescens
P. cerasifera
P. concinna
P. cyclamina
P. dasycarpa
P. domestica
P. fenzliana
P. hillieri 'Spire'
P. incisa and varieties
P. juddii
P. mandshurica
P. nipponica
P. persica and varieties
P. sargentii
P. simonii
P. subhirtella and varieties
P. yedoensis

EARLY MAY
Acer campestre
A. circinatum
A. japonicum
A. mandshuricum
A. mono
A. saccharum nigrum
A. pseudoplatanus
A. pseudo-sieboldianum
A. saccharum
A. schirasawanum
A. triflorum
Amelanchier florida
A. grandiflora
A. intermedia
A. oblongifolia
A. sanguinea
A. sera
Carpinus species
Crataegus arnoldiana
Exochorda giraldii
Malus arnoldiana
M. atrosanguinea
M. baccata

M. 'Bob White'
M. 'Dolgo'
M. 'Flame'
M. floribunda
M. halliana and varieties
M. hartwigii
M. 'Hopa'
M. hupehensis
M. kansuensis
M. 'Katherine'
M. magdeburgensis
M. 'Makamik'
M. micromalus
M. prunifolia and varieties
M. pumila
M. purpurea and varieties
M. robusta and varieties
M. scheideckeri
M. soulangiana and varieties
M. soulardii
M. spectabilis and varieties
M. sublobata
M. sylvestris
M. zumi and varieties
Nemopanthus mucronatus
Ostrya species
Prunus alleghaniensis
P. americana
P. avium
P. avium 'Plena'
P. blireiana and varieties
P. domestica
P. dunbarii
P. gigantea
P. glandulosa and varieties
P. 'Hally Jolivette'
P. hortulana
P. incana
P. instititia
P. japonica nakai
P. kansuensis
P. munsoniana
P. padus and varieties
P. pensylvanica
P. pumila susquehanae
P. salicina
P. schmittii

P. serrulata and varieties
(Many double-flowered forms
starting to bloom and continuing
for two weeks at least, depending
on the variety, some being slightly
earlier than others)
P. sieboldii
P. spinosa
Pyrus betulaefolia
P. calleryana
P. communis and varieties
P. pyrifolia
P. serrulata
P. ussuriensis
Sorbopyrus auriculiformis
Syringa oblata dilatata
Zanthoxylum americanum

MID-MAY
Abies species
Acer palmatum
A. pensylvanicum
A. rufinerve
Aesculus carnea
A. glabra
A. hippocastanum
Amelanchier amabilis
Amelasorbus jackii
Caragana arborescens
Cercis canadensis and varieties
Cornus florida and varieties
Cydonia oblonga
Davidia involucrata
Enkianthus campanulatus
Exochorda korolkowii
E. macrantha
E. racemosa
Fagus species
Fraxinus ornus
Halesia carolina
H. monticola
Magnolia fraseri
Malus bracteata
M. dawsoniana
M. 'Dorothea'
M. glaucescens
M. ioensis
M. 'Marshall Oyama'

The tea crab apple (Malus hupehensis) *has a vase-shaped habit. It was introduced by the Arnold Arboretum in 1900.*

M. *sargentii*
M. *sieboldii* and varieties
M. 'Tanner'
Paulownia tomentosa
Prunus cerasus
P. *maackii*
P. *maritima*
P. *virginiana*
Quercus species

LATE MAY
Acer ginnala
A. *heldreichii*
A. *miyabei*
A. *trautvetteri*
A. *zoeschense*
Asimina triloba
Cornus alternifolia
C. *controversa*
Crataegus crus-galli
C. *laevigata*

C. *monogyna* and varieties
C. *nitida*
C. *pinnatifida*
C. *pruinosa*
C. *punctata*
C. *sorbifolia*
C. *succulenta*
Juglans sieboldiana
Laburnum species
Magnolia acuminata
M. *cordata*
M. *soulangiana* 'Lennei'
M. *tripetala*
M. *virginiana*
M. *watsonii*
Malus angustifolia
M. *coronaria*
M. *coronaria* 'Charlottae'
M. *honanensis*
M. *ioensis* 'Plena'
M. 'Prince Georges'

M. toringoides
Photinia villosa
Prunus laucheana
P. maximowiczii
Rhamnus cathartica
Robinia slavinii
Sorbaronia jackii
Sorbus species
Symplocos paniculata
Viburnum lentago
V. prunifolium
V. rufidulum
V. sieboldii
Xanthoceras sorbifolium

EARLY JUNE
Chionanthus retusus
C. virginicus
Cladrastis lutea
Cornus kousa
Cotinus coggygria
Decaisnea fargesii
Elaeagnus angustifolia
Euonymus bungeana
Idesia polycarpa
Ilex opaca
Magnolia hypoleuca
M. sieboldii
Malus lancifolia
M. transitoria
Phellodendron species
Rhamnus davurica
R. frangula
Robinia hartwigii
R. 'Idaho'
R. kelseyi
R. pseudoacacia
Sassafras albidum
Sophora viciifolia
Styrax japonica
S. obassia

MID-JUNE
Cornus coreana
C. macrophylla
Cotinus americanus
Crataegus calpodendron

C. phaenopyrum
Diospyros virginiana
Euonymus bungeana
E. europaea
Gymnocladus dioicus
Ilex laevigata
I. montana
Ligustrum ibolium
L. ovalifolium
L. vulgare
Liriodendron tulipifera
Syringa pekinensis
S. reticulata

LATE JUNE
Ailanthus altissima
Catalpa speciosa
Cladrastis platycarpa
Ehretia thyrsiflora
Ilex crenata
Rhododendron maximum
Rhus glabra
R. typhina
Tilia americana
T. amurensis
T. platyphyllos

EARLY JULY
Castanea species
Catalpa bignonioides
C. hybrida
Cornus dunbarii
Ilex pedunculosa
Maackia amurensis
Stewartia koreana
S. monadelpha
S. pseudo-camellia
Tilia cordata
T. dasystyla
T. euchlora
T. flavescens
T. mandshurica
T. maximowicziana
T. moltkei
T. monticola
T. neglecta

Lagerstroemia indica
'*Peppermint Lace,*' a
variety of crape-myrtle.
Photograph courtesy of
Monrovia Nursery
Company.

MID-JULY
Albizia julibrissin 'E. H. Wilson'
Hydrangea paniculata praecox
Koelreuteria paniculata
Oxydendrum arboreum
Stewartia ovata
Tilia floridana
T. heterophylla
T. insularis
T. japonica
T. nuda
T. oliveri
T. petiolaris
T. tomentosa
T. venulosa

LATE JULY
Aralia spinosa
Clethra acuminata
C. barbinervis

Kalopanax pictus
Sorbaria arborea

AUGUST
Aralia chinensis
A. elata
Bumelia lanuginosa
Clerodendron trichotomum
Evodia daniellii
Hydrangea paniculata grandiflora
Lagerstroemia indica
Sophora japonica

SEPTEMBER
Franklinia alatamaha

OCTOBER
Hamamelis virginiana

THREE

Ornamental Fruits

↬

The fruits of trees are not nearly as important ornamentally as are the fruits of shrubs. In the first place, trees are taller, hence their fruits are usually borne above the level of the eye, often so high up in the tree that sometimes one hardly knows they are present. Because of this they must be borne in great profusion to be effective. There are perhaps less than a dozen genera with large numbers of species bearing bright-colored fruits, including such effective landscape plants as the hollies, crab apples, dogwoods, junipers, and hawthorns.

Then there is a large group of plants bearing cone fruits that are interesting when they are borne, but this unfortunately occurs only at irregular intervals. Some years are "poor" cone years, when evergreens over wide areas bear few if any fruit. Other years they are borne in great profusion and are of considerable interest on the trees for months at a time. The important point to remember is that profuse cone production is not an annual occurrence, hence such trees should not be planted for their fruits alone.

A third and very large group of trees bears uninteresting fruits. The elms, oaks, and lindens are examples. Even though these fruits may appear in large numbers every year, they are not particularly colorful or of much ornamental value on the trees. Certainly these trees have many other meritorious attributes, but if color or effectiveness of fruit is desired, such trees can be overlooked.

There is a sequence in fruiting just as there is a sequence in blooming. This is of interest, and some of it is recorded in the following pages. It is of value to know, for instance, that the fruits of some of the crab apples color in late August and then quickly drop, while the fruits of others may not color until late September but will remain on the tree for weeks and even months. The length of time that the fruits remain colorful is important, for in most cases it is considerably longer than the period of time that the flowers are conspicuous. It varies, of course, with the season, the amount of rainfall, and the type of soil. In the lists given on pages 29–32 the sequence has been plotted for the fruiting of many trees as it has been observed in the Arnold Arboretum.

It is important to understand some of the factors affecting the amount of fruit produced on a certain tree. Good rainfall at the proper time and good soil may result in excellent fruits, while little rainfall and poor soil may result in poorly colored, dried-up fruits.

"Alternate bearing" is a physiological phenomenon resulting in excellent fruit production one year and little the next. Some trees are notoriously "alternate bearing." The crab apple 'Katherine' is one example, for it is literally covered with fruits one year and has practically none the next. On the other hand, the crab apple 'Dorothea' is apparently annual bearing, having splendid crops of fruits annually, provided the weather conditions are just right. Commercial orchardists the country over have to put up with this natural phenomenon, more evident in some varieties of fruit trees than in others. There is little that can be done with ornamentals to vary this alteration if it is a hereditary trait.

⇥≫ *INCLEMENT WEATHER*

The fertilization necessary for the production of fruit is carried out in several different ways. For instance, there are the perfect flowers of the crab apples; the pollen borne on the stamens of one flower can fertilize the pistil of the same flower. Then there are plants such as the apricots, the pistils of the flowers on one plant apparently needing pollen produced by the stamens of another plant of different parentage in order to "set" proper fruit. There are many plants like the hollies with sexes separate, that is, with the staminate flowers being borne on one plant and the pistillate flowers on another so that plants of both sexes must be present to ensure fruiting.

Then the means by which the pollen is spread from one plant to the flowers of another plant varies. With some plants, such as hollies, this may be the wind, but with many plants multitudinous insects feed on the pollen and nectar of the flowers and do the greater part of the fertilization. Bees are outstanding in this respect, but there are other insects that are also important pollen carriers.

Weather plays a very important part in the pollination of most plants, and we notice the result of favorable (or unfavorable) weather conditions months after that fertilization period has come and gone. Take, for example, the peculiar conditions necessary for holly, which has its sexes separate. Both wind or air circulation and the presence of many insects are necessary. If the weather is rainy during the time the pollen is ripe, there may be little opportunity for either wind pollinization or insect flight. On the other hand, if the weather is very cold during the time the pollen of a certain plant is ripe, then insect activity is at a low ebb and a plant such as the viburnum, for instance, would have to depend primarily on wind pollination. If the weather is very cold and rainy with little wind during the time of ripe pollen formation, then all these conditions combine to make fertilization of many kinds of shrubs extremely difficult.

The commercial orchardist knows these things because he has studied them in relation to his fruit production for years. He finds it necessary to interplant certain varieties of fruits producing just the right type of pollen for his main crop. He puts hives of bees in his orchards to aid in the general pollen carrying, and he manipulates the hives so that they will be at maximum activity when the flowers are mature.

There is little we can do about modifying the weather on a large scale, but if we have a few plants in our garden on which we want good fruit each year, we could study their optimum needs during the time when pollen is ripe and endeavor to aid pollen carriers in every way.

⇥≫ *SEXES SEPARATE*

As has been mentioned, some groups of plants are dioecious, that is, they bear staminate flowers on one plant and pistillate flowers on the other. The staminate plants will never bear fruit, of course, but neither will the pistillate plants (there are a few exceptions) unless the right pollen-bearing plant is within a reasonable distance. Just what the "reasonable distance" is, we do not know, for many things enter into an understanding of this problem, and few studies have been made concerning the type of pollen carriers required. Certainly, the closer the sexes are together, the more reasonable it is to expect the pistillate plant to produce a good supply of fruit.

⇥≫ GENERA WITH FLOWERS DIOECIOUS

(Female or pistillate flowers on one plant and male or pollen-bearing flowers on another plant)

Acer	*Baccharis*
Actinidia	*Broussonetia*
Ailanthus	*Carica*
Aucuba	*Celastrus*

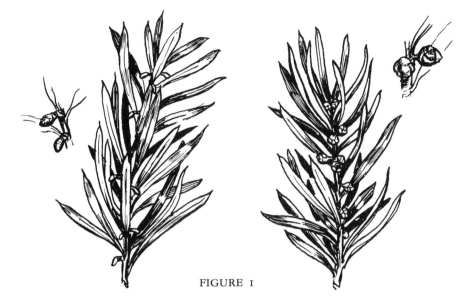

FIGURE I

Female flower buds of the yew.   *Male flower buds of the yew.*

Cephalotaxus	*Nemopanthus*
Cercidiphyllum	*Orixa*
Chionanthus	*Phellodendron*
Comptonia	*Podocarpus*
Cotinus	*Populus*
Diospyros	*Rhus*
Eucommia	*Ribes*
Garrya	*Ruscus*
Ginkgo	*Salix*
Helwingia	*Schisandra*
Hippophae	*Securinega*
Idesia	*Shepherdia*
Ilex	*Skimmia*
Juniperus	*Smilax*
Leitneria	*Taxus*
Lindera	*Torreya*
Maclura	*Vitis*
Morus	*Zanthoxylum*
Myrica	

The hollies *(Ilex),* bittersweets *(Celastrus),* and yews *(Taxus)* are perhaps the most important plants in this group—at least from the viewpoint of landscaping, for which they are highly valued. They should be propagated commercially by cuttings, budding, or grafting so that there is no question at all about their sex. It is particularly difficult to distinguish one sex from the other in the hollies unless they are in flower or fruit. Nurseries that propagate the hollies asexually and keep the sexes clearly marked are the ones to patronize; only then can plants of known sex be obtained.

In planting any of the trees in this group, especially for fruit production, it is advisable to have a pollen-bearing plant in close proximity to the fruiting plant. The exact distance is not known, but certainly the closer the two are, the better the chances for profuse annual fruit production. These trees are even more dependent on the weather for good fruiting than some of the others. Since their pollen must be either wind- or insect-borne, weather conditions must be at an optimum for the very short period the flowers are open.

Sometimes there may be a single plant in this dioecious group that will have a few male and female flowers on the same plant, but this is most unusual and should not be counted on when selecting male and female plants for the garden.

There is another large group of trees, including all the conifers, that has two kinds of flowers (male and female) but both appear on the same tree. The birches and alders and even the walnuts and oaks are common examples; only one type of flower, the long, pollen-bearing catkin, is really conspicuous in the spring of the year, but it cannot be considered very ornamental. Close examination of fir trees in the spring sometimes will show the truly beautiful, young, reddish pistillate flowers that mature into the cones later. The following genera are of this class:

→≫ MALE AND FEMALE FLOWERS SEPARATE BUT ON SAME TREE

Abies	*Libocedrus*
Alnus	*Ostrya*
Betula	*Picea*
Carpinus	*Pinus*
Carya	*Platanus*
Castanea	*Pseudolarix*
Cedrus	*Pseudotsuga*
Chamaecyparis	*Pterocarya*
Corylus	*Quercus*
Cryptomeria	*Sciadopitys*
Cunninghamia	*Sequoia*
Cupressus	*Sequoiadendron*
Fagus	*Taxodium*
Ficus	*Thuja*
Juglans	*Thujopsis*
Keteleeria	*Tsuga*
Larix	

There are still two more reasons trees will not bear fruit. One of these is age. It takes a ginkgo tree twenty years before it will bear its first fruit; that is, if all other members of this species perform in the same way that they have in the Arnold Arboretum. Some of the magnolias, also, will not bear flowers or fruit until they are nearly the same age. It is unfortunate that we do not have the approximate ages that all trees first bear their fruit, for here is certainly an excellent field for research. We do know, for instance, that some trees bear flowers and fruit very early in life. *Malus* 'Dorothea,' for instance, and *Prunus* 'Hally Jolivette' will bear flowers the second year and sometimes even the first after grafting. Other trees will take considerably longer, and usually the length of this period is specific for the species and hereditary.

Then there are a very few plants such as the plums and the chestnuts that will bear only a very few fruit if a single tree is grown alone. If several seedlings or clones of the same species are growing adjacent to each other, however, fruit production will be very much better. It is well to keep this fact in mind if fruit production is the main objective.

These are a few of the reasons trees will not bear fruit or will not fruit well annually. An understanding of these factors may help in solving individual problems relating to poor fruit production as they arise.

→》》 ORNAMENTAL FRUITS LENGTH OF TIME FRUITS REMAIN EFFECTIVE

	Jan.	Feb.	March	April	May	June	July	Aug.	Sept.	Oct.	Nov.	Dec.
Abies species	•	•	•	•	•	•	———————			•	•	•
Acer ginnala	•	•	•	•	•	•	—————		•	•	•	•
A. griseum	•	•	•	•	•	•	•	———	•	•	•	•
A. negundo	•	•	•	•	•	•	•	—•	•	•	•	•
A. palmatum	•	•	•	•	•	•	•	•	—•	•	•	•
A. pseudoplatanus	•	•	•	•	•	•	————	•	•	•	•	•
A. rubrum	•	•	•	•	———————		•	•	•	•	•	•
A. saccharum	•	•	•	•	———————		•	•	•	•	•	•
A. tataricum	•	•	•	•	•	•	———————		•	•	•	•
Aesculus species	•	•	•	•	•	•	———————		•	•	•	•
Ailanthus altissima	•	•	•	•	•	•	•	——————————			•	•
Amelanchier canadensis	•	•	•	•	•	•	—•	•	•	•	•	•
A. grandiflora	•	•	•	•	•	•	—•	•	•	•	•	•
A. laevis	•	•	•	•	•	•	—•	•	•	•	•	•
Aralia elata	•	•	•	•	•	•	•	•	—————	•	•	•
Asimina triloba	•	•	•	•	•	•	•	•	—•	•	•	•

	Jan.	Feb.	March	April	May	June	July	Aug.	Sept.	Oct.	Nov.	Dec.
Carpinus species	•	•	•	•	•	•	•	——	——	•	•	•
Castanea mollissima	•	•	•	•	•	•	•	•	——	•	•	•
Cedrus libani	——	——	——	——	——	——	——	——	——	——	——	——
Chamaecyparis species	——	——	——	•	•	•	——	——	——	——	——	——
Cladrastis lutea	•	•	•	•	•	•	•	•	——	•	•	•
Cornus controversa	•	•	•	•	•	•	•	•	——	•	•	•
C. florida and varieties	•	•	•	•	•	•	•	•	——	——	•	•
C. kousa and varieties	•	•	•	•	•	•	•	•	——	•	•	•
C. kousa chinensis	•	•	•	•	•	•	•	•	——	•	•	•
C. macrophylla	•	•	•	•	•	•	•	•	——	——	•	•
C. mas	•	•	•	•	•	•	•	•	——	——	•	•
C. mas flava	•	•	•	•	•	•	•	•	——	•	•	•
Crataegus arnoldiana	•	•	•	•	•	•	•	•	——	•	•	•
C. coccinioides	•	•	•	•	•	•	•	•	——	——	•	•
C. crus-galli	——	•	•	•	•	•	•	•	——	——	——	——
C. laevigata	•	•	•	•	•	•	•	•	——	——	——	——
C. lavallei	•	•	•	•	•	•	•	•	•	•	——	——
C. mollis	•	•	•	•	•	•	•	•	——	•	•	•
C. monogyna	•	•	•	•	•	•	•	•	——	——	——	•
C. nitida	——	•	•	•	•	•	•	•	——	——	——	——
C. phaenopyrum	——	——	——	•	•	•	•	•	•	•	•	——
C. pinnatifida	•	•	•	•	•	•	•	•	•	——	•	•
C. prunifolia	•	•	•	•	•	•	•	•	•	•	——	——
C. punctata	•	•	•	•	•	•	•	•	——	——	•	•
C. succulenta	•	•	•	•	•	•	•	•	——	——	•	•
C. viridis	——	•	•	•	•	•	•	•	——	——	——	——
Diospyros virginiana	•	•	•	•	•	•	•	•	——	——	•	•
Euonymus species	•	•	•	•	•	•	•	•	——	——	——	——
Evodia daniellii	•	•	•	•	•	•	•	•	——	——	——	——
Gleditsia triacanthos	•	•	•	•	•	•	•	——	——	——	——	•
Gymnocladus dioicus	•	•	•	•	•	•	•	——	——	——	——	•
Halesia monticola	•	•	•	•	•	•	——	——	——	——	——	——
Hippophae rhamnoides	•	•	•	•	•	•	•	•	——	——	•	•
Ilex aquifolium	——	——	——	•	•	•	•	——	——	——	——	——
I. montana	•	•	•	•	•	•	•	——	——	——	——	——
I. opaca	——	——	——	•	•	•	•	•	——	——	——	——
I. pedunculosa	•	•	•	•	•	•	•	•	——	——	——	——
Juniperus chinensis	——	——	——	•	•	——	——	——	——	——	——	——
J. scopulorum	——	——	——	•	•	•	•	——	——	——	——	——
J. virginiana	——	——	——	•	•	——	——	——	——	——	——	——
Kalopanax pictus	•	•	•	•	•	•	•	•	——	——	•	•
Koelreuteria paniculata	•	•	•	•	•	•	•	•	——	•	•	•
Larix decidua	——	——	——	——	——	——	——	——	——	——	——	——
Liquidambar styraciflua	•	•	•	•	•	•	•	•	——	•	•	•
Magnolia species	•	•	•	•	•	•	•	•	——	•	•	•

	Jan.	Feb.	March	April	May	June	July	Aug.	Sept.	Oct.	Nov.	Dec.
Malus 'Adams'	•	•	•	•	•	•	•	•	—	—	•	•
M. arnoldiana	•	•	•	•	•	•	•	•	—	—	•	•
M. atrosanguinea	•	•	•	•	•	•	•	•	—	—	•	•
M. baccata	•	•	•	•	•	•	•	•	—	—	•	•
M. baccata gracilis	•	•	•	•	•	•	•	•	—	—	•	•
M. baccata 'Jackii'	•	•	•	•	•	•	•	•	—	—	—	—
M. baccata mandshurica	•	•	•	•	•	•	•	•	—	•	•	•
M. 'Bob White'	—	—	•	•	•	•	•	•	—	—	—	—
M. dawsoniana	•	•	•	•	•	•	•	•	—	—	—	•
M. 'Dolgo'	•	•	•	•	•	•	•	•	—	•	•	•
M. 'Dorothea'	•	•	•	•	•	•	•	•	—	—	•	•
M. 'Flame'	•	•	•	•	•	•	•	•	—	—	•	•
M. floribunda	•	•	•	•	•	•	•	•	—	•	•	•
M. halliana parkmanii	•	•	•	•	•	•	•	•	—	—	•	•
M. halliana spontanea	•	•	•	•	•	•	•	•	—	—	•	•
M. hartwigii	•	•	•	•	•	•	•	•	—	—	•	•
M. 'Henry F. DuPont'	•	•	•	•	•	•	•	•	—	—	•	•
M. 'Hopa'	•	•	•	•	•	•	•	•	—	•	•	•
M. hupehensis	•	•	•	•	•	•	•	•	—	—	•	•
M. 'Katherine'	•	•	•	•	•	•	•	•	—	—	—	•
M. 'Makamik'	•	•	•	•	•	•	•	•	—	—	—	—
M. 'Ormiston Roy'	—	—	•	•	•	•	•	•	•	•	—	—
M. purpurea 'Aldenhamensis'	•	•	•	•	•	•	•	•	—	—	•	•
M. purpurea 'Lemoinei'	•	•	•	•	•	•	•	•	—	—	•	•
M. 'Red Jade'	•	•	•	•	•	•	•	•	—	—	•	•
M. robusta	•	•	•	•	•	•	•	•	—	—	•	•
M. robusta 'Persicifolia'	•	•	•	•	•	•	•	•	—	—	—	—
M. sargentii	•	•	•	•	•	•	•	•	—	—	—	—
M. sieboldii arborescens	•	•	•	•	•	•	•	•	—	—	•	•
M. spectabilis 'Riversii'	•	•	•	•	•	•	•	•	—	•	•	•
M. 'Tanner'	—	—	•	•	•	•	•	•	•	—	—	—
M. toringoides	•	•	•	•	•	•	•	•	—	—	—	•
M. 'Winter Gold'	•	•	•	•	•	•	•	•	•	—	—	•
M. zumi calocarpa	—	—	•	•	•	•	•	•	—	—	—	—
Morus species	•	•	•	•	•	•	•	—	•	•	•	•
Ostrya virginiana	•	•	•	•	•	•	—	—	—	•	•	•
Oxydendrum arboreum	•	•	•	•	•	•	•	•	—	—	—	•
Phellodendron species	•	•	•	•	•	•	•	—	—	—	—	—
Picea abies	—	—	•	•	•	•	—	—	—	—	—	—
P. engelmannii	—	—	•	•	•	•	•	—	—	—	—	—
P. glauca	—	—	•	•	•	•	—	—	—	—	—	—
P. omorika	—	—	•	•	•	•	•	—	—	—	—	—
P. orientalis	—	—	•	•	•	•	—	—	—	—	—	—
P. polita	—	—	•	•	•	•	•	—	—	—	—	—
P. pungens	—	—	•	•	•	•	—	—	—	—	—	—

	Jan.	Feb.	March	April	May	June	July	Aug.	Sept.	Oct.	Nov.	Dec.
Pinus banksiana			———	———	———	———	———	———	———	———	———	———
P. bungeana	•	•	•	•	•	•	———	———	———	———	•	•
P. densiflora	———	———	———	———	———	———	———	———	———	———	———	———
P. monticola	———	———	•	•	•	•	———	———	———	———	———	———
P. nigra	•	•	•	•	•	•	———	———	———	———	———	———
P. parviflora	———	———	———	———	———	———	———	———	———	———	———	———
P. pungens	———	———	———	———	———	———	———	———	———	———	———	———
P. resinosa	———	———	———	———	———	———	———	———	———	———	———	———
P. rigida	———	———	———	———	———	———	———	———	———	———	———	———
P. strobus	•	•	•	•	•	•	———	———	———	———	•	•
P. sylvestris	———	———	———	———	———	———	———	———	———	———	———	———
P. thunbergii	———	———	———	———	———	———	———	———	———	———	———	———
P. virginiana	———	———	———	———	———	———	———	———	———	———	———	———
Platanus species	•	•	•	•	•	•		•	———	———	———	•
Prunus avium	•	•	•	•	•	•	—	•	•	•	•	•
P. cerasus	•	•	•	•	•	•	—	•	•	•	•	•
P. padus	•	•	•	•	•	•	•	—	•	•	•	•
P. pensylvanica	•	•	•	•	•	•	•	•	—	•	•	•
P. sargentii	•	•	•	•	•	•	—	•	•	•	•	•
P. serotina	•	•	•	•	•	•	•	•	—	•	•	•
P. subhirtella	•	•	•	•	•	•	—	•	•	•	•	•
P. yedoensis	•	•	•	•	•	•	—	•	•	•	•	•
Pseudolarix kaempferi	•	•	•	•	•	•	•	———	———	———	———	•
Pseudotsuga menziesii	•	•	•	•	•	•	———	———	———	———	———	———
Pterocarya fraxinifolia	•	•	•	•	•	•	•	•	—	•	•	•
Rhamnus davurica	•	•	•	•	•	•	•	•	•	—	•	•
Sorbus alnifolia	•	•	•	•	•	•	•	•	———	———	———	•
S. aria	•	•	•	•	•	•	•	•	———	———	———	•
S. aucuparia	•	•	•	•	•	•	•	•	———	———	———	•
S. decora	•	•	•	•	•	•	•	•	———	———	———	•
S. discolor	•	•	•	•	•	•	•	•	———	———	———	•
Styrax japonica	•	•	•	•	•	•	•	•	———	———	•	•
Symplocos paniculata	•	•	•	•	•	•	•	•	•	—	•	•
Taxus species	•	•	•	•	•	•	•	•	———	———	———	•
Thuja occidentalis	———	———	———	•	•	•	———	———	———	———	———	———
T. orientalis	———	———	•	•	•	•	———	———	———	———	———	———
T. plicata	———	———	———	•	•	•	•	———	———	———	———	———
T. standishii	———	———	———	•	•	•	•	———	———	———	———	———
Tsuga species	———	———	•	•	•	•	———	———	———	———	———	———
Viburnum lentago	•	•	•	•	•	•	•	•	———	———	•	•
V. prunifolium	•	•	•	•	•	•	•	•	———	———	•	•
V. sieboldii	•	•	•	•	•	•	•	•	———	•	•	•

FOUR

Foliage Colors
→>>

Although the leaves of most woody plants are green, at least during the growing season, some plants have leaves that are differently colored. Such plants would be those with variegated foliage; those with permanently red or yellow foliage; and those with colored foliage for a short time in spring or fall. These groups of plants with more or less pronounced variations in foliage color are the materials from which the knowing gardener can fashion colorfully interesting gardens to be enjoyed every season of the year.

Leaves are green because they contain a material called chlorophyll. This is essential to the growth of all plants except the saprophytes and a few parasites, for it is through the action of the chlorophyll that the plant can manufacture the food it requires from crude chemicals in the presence of light and heat. Chlorophyll is a highly complex chemical material being continually manufactured in the leaf and at the same time being continually destroyed. Ordinarily the rate of its breakdown about equals the rate of its manufacture.

There are two general groups of coloring pigments in the leaf with the chlorophyll. These are the carotins (yellow-coloring pigments) and anthocyanin (the red-coloring pigment), both usually omnipresent but masked by chlorophyll. In some plants this delicate balance is upset and the yellows appear in various so-called yellow-leaved varieties. The red leaves of some of the Japanese maples afford an example of red-colored foliage. As the season progresses and more and more chlorophyll is manufactured, some of the plants that have colored foliage earlier in spring are capable of manufacturing sufficient chlorophyll to mask completely what was a good colored leaf. Schwedler's variety of the Norway maple is an example of this. In the very early spring it is most conspicuous for its brilliant red leaves, but as summer advances, the color gradually fades into a dull, reddish green that lasts until the advent of autumn coloration.

It is probable that variations in soil have some effect on leaf color. For

33

instance, a heavy application of a nitrogenous fertilizer will make the leaves of many plants a good dark green. Plenty of moisture will also help. Soil acidity is another factor for, with a low pH, the leaves of some plants, like those of the pin oak, will become deficient in iron and become yellowish, a condition quickly eliminated by feeding the tree soluble ferrous sulphate salts. Consequently, there may be several reasons—physiological, physical, and genetic—that the leaves of certain plants are not green at all times. Let us consider the interesting groups of plants with colored foliage and, possibly, become acquainted with some new ones among them so that we can make our gardens more attractive by using them properly.

⤙≫ I. DECIDUOUS TREES SHOWING THE FIRST FOLIAGE COLORS IN THE SPRING

The changing color of spring foliage can be almost as beautiful as autumn coloration, but usually it is not quite as pronounced and does not last as long. So many other things are of interest in the early spring that few people pay much attention to this interesting phenomenon, but it is there for all to see if they want to look for it. The following trees are among the first to show their new foliage in the vicinity of Boston, Massachusetts, usually during April. About four weeks after these trees first show their leaves, the majority of the rest will have their foliage open also (except the bald cypress, which is one of the last to send out its leaves). The colors of all may change from yellow-green to bronze to dark green in varying shades until June, when most will have taken on their normal green color.

Acer campestre—yellow-green
A. griseum—bronze to reddish
A. negundo—yellow-green
A. platanoides 'Crimson King'—red
A. platanoides 'Schwedleri'—bronze to reddish
A. rubrum—bronze to reddish
Amelanchier canadensis—gray-green
A. laevis—bronze to reddish
Cercidiphyllum japonicum—bronze to reddish

Euonymus europaea—green
E. sanguinea—green
Malus robusta—yellow-green
M. robusta 'Persicifolia'—green
Prunus padus—green
Pyrus ussuriensis—green
Salix alba 'Vitellina'—yellow-green
Tilia platyphyllos—yellow-green

→»» II. SOME DECIDUOUS TREES WITH LEAVES COLORED THROUGHOUT THE GREATER PART OF THE GROWING SEASON

There are some trees with variegated foliage, but few of these are recommended here because usually they are a sickly-looking group. A few do have interest. Much better are some of the trees with gray or bronze or reddish foliage. Some trees do not have foliage of a prominently different color but are just slightly colored—enough to make them of value. A few crab apples, for instance, have foliage that is just slightly reddish, enough to make them of interest when planted in front of a normally green foliage background.

→»» GRAY TO GRAY-GREEN

Acer rubrum and varieties
Elaeagnus angustifolia
Eucalyptus globulus
E. leucoxylon
Hippophae rhamnoides
Leucadendron argenteum
Olea europaea

Populus alba
Salix elaeagnos
Sorbus folgneri
S. sargentiana
Tilia petiolaris—silvery green
T. tomentosa—silvery green

→»» YELLOW TO YELLOW-GREEN

Acer japonicum 'Aureum'
A. negundo 'Auratum'
A. palmatum dissectum
A. palmatum 'Dissectum Flavescens'
A. palmatum 'Dissectum Ornatum'
A. pseudoplatanus 'Worleei'
Alnus incana 'Aurea'
Catalpa bignonioides 'Aurea'

Chamaecyparis, some varieties
Cornus florida 'Hohman's Golden'
Gleditsia triacanthos 'Sunburst'
Populus alba 'Richardii'
Quercus robur 'Concordia'
Sorbus aria 'Aurea'
Tilia platyphyllos aurea

⇶ RED TO REDDISH PURPLE

Acer diabolicum purpurascens
A. palmatum 'Atropurpureum'
A. palmatum 'Burgundy Lace'
A. palmatum 'Nomura-Nishiki'
A. palmatum 'Sanguineum'
A. palmatum 'Yezo-Nishiki'

A. platanoides 'Crimson King'
A. platanoides 'Fassen's Black'
Prunus blireiana
P. cerasifera 'Atropurpurea' (and
    varieties)

⇶ REDDISH GREEN

Malus 'Baskatong'
M. 'Evelyn'
M. 'Oekonmierat Echtermeyer'

M. purpurea 'Lemoinei'
M. 'Red Silver'
M. 'Strathmore'

⇶ BLUISH GREEN

Cupressocyparis leylandii 'Naylor's Blue'
Cupressus sempervirens 'Glauca'

Eucalyptus sideroxylon

⇶ BRONZE

Fagus sylvatica 'Cuprea'

⇶ BRIGHT YELLOW

Chamaecyparis pisifera 'Gold Spangle'

Cupressocyparis leylandii 'Castlewellan'

⇶ PURPLE

Acer platanoides 'Crimson Sentry'
A. pseudoplatanus 'Purpureum'
Fagus sylvatica 'Purpureo-pendula'

F. sylvatica 'Riversii'
F. sylvatica 'Rohanii'
F. sylvatica 'Spaethiana'

Liriodendron tulipifera
'Majestic Beauty,' a
cultivar of L. tulipifera
'Aureo-marginatum.' Both
have yellow markings on
the leaf margin.
Photograph courtesy of
Monrovia Nursery
Company.

❧⟫ GREEN WITH YELLOW MARGIN

Acer negundo aureo-variegatum
Cornus controversa 'Variegata'
C. mas 'Aureo-elegantissima'

Liriodendron tulipifera
  'Aureo-marginatum'

❧⟫ GREEN WITH WHITE MARGIN

Acer negundo 'Variegatum'
Cornus florida 'Welchii'

C. mas 'Variegata'

↣ III. A FEW EVERGREEN TREES WITH FOLIAGE OTHER THAN NORMAL GREEN

Abies concolor—bluish to gray-green
A. magnifica glauca—whitish
A. pinsapo 'Argentea'—silvery
Acacia baileyana—steel blue
A. dealbata—blue to grayish
A. pendula—bluish gray
Callitris preissii—blackish green
Cedrus atlantica 'Argentea'—silvery
C. atlantica glauca—bluish
Chamaecyparis lawsoniana 'Allumii'—steel blue
C. lawsoniana 'Argentea'—silvery
C. lawsoniana 'Triomphe de Boskoop'—steel blue
C. pisifera 'Aurea'—yellow

The white fir (Abies concolor), *a native of Colorado and one of the best firs available for city planning.*

C. *pisifera* 'Boulevard'—steel blue
C. *pisifera* 'Plumosa Aurea'—yellow
C. *pisifera plumosa* 'Cyano-viridis'—steel blue
Ilex aquifolium (and varieties)—silver and yellow
Juniperus scopulorum (varieties)—bluish to silvery
J. *virginiana* 'Burkii'—steel blue
J. *virginiana glauca*—silvery
Myrica californica—bronze-green
Olea europaea—gray-green
Picea engelmannii 'Argentea'—silvery
P. *engelmannii* 'Glauca'—steel blue
P. *orientalis* 'Aurea'—bronzy yellow
P. *pungens* (varieties)—silvery to bluish white
Pinus densiflora 'Oculus-draconis'—yellowish green
P. *parviflora glauca*—silvery blue
P. *strobus glauca*—light bluish green
P. *sylvestris* 'Argentea'—silvery
Pittosporum eugenioides—yellowish green
Pseudotsuga menziesii glauca—bluish green

→≫ *AUTUMN COLOR*

The eastern United States is fortunately located in one of the few regions of the world where brilliant autumn coloration of foliage prevails. There is only one small region of autumn coloration in the Southern Hemisphere, and that is in South America. In the Northern Hemisphere there is a large section of eastern Asia, including central and northern Japan, and a small part of southwestern Europe where brilliant fall coloration can be observed. In North America the region characterized by brilliant autumn foliage extends from the Gulf of St. Lawrence to Florida and westward to the Great Plains, areas that have extensive deciduous forests and considerable rainfall. Here the general climatic conditions are often just what is needed to produce that lovely phenomenon of nature—the autumn coloration of deciduous foliage.

In North America the most brilliant displays of autumn color are, of course, in southeastern Canada, the northeastern United States, and in certain other areas at higher altitudes. The farther south one goes, the less brilliant is the display, particularly in low areas along the seacoast. In the higher altitudes of the South, such as the Blue Ridge Mountains, the color is usually just as spectacular as in the northeastern United States. Many places in western North America are likewise fortunate, with vivid autumn color, especially in the higher altitudes. Autumn color is excellent in the vicinity of Seattle, Portland, and San Francisco.

It is chiefly in areas of predominantly deciduous forests that autumn color displays are best, and these areas occur chiefly in two general regions of the world. Plants growing in deciduous forests in tropical regions usually drop their leaves toward the end of the dry season. Since these leaves usually dry up before they fall (because of lack of water), they do not develop brilliant colors but usually turn brown. In the case of plants growing in deciduous forests in temperate regions—especially in areas with ample rainfall equally distributed throughout the year—the leaves fall at the approach of cold weather, and because the plants have been well supplied with water, leaves of many trees change color before they fall.

In some years the autumn color is much more pronounced than in others. There are always plants whose foliage turns yellow in the fall, but it is the brilliant reds and gorgeous scarlets, in combination with the yellows, that make autumn color of outstanding beauty. It is chiefly the reds and scarlets that are intensified by the right climatic conditions.

⇥≫ WHY LEAVES ARE YELLOW

A certain stage is reached where there is little if any chlorophyll manufactured. Most of the chlorophyll already made is eventually destroyed. This is the reason that leaves are yellow, for the two yellow pigments usually present, carotin and xanthophyll, are continually masked by the chlorophyll. These same coloring materials are present in large quantities in egg yolk, carrots, and in some yellow flowers, and when most of the chlorophyll is destroyed, they become apparent.

This is also the case when green plants are taken into dark places, such as a cellar, or when young shoots are grown in very low light. This is because when light is absent, plants are unable to manufacture new chlorophyll, and the yellow pigments become predominant as soon as the previously manufactured chlorophyll has been utilized.

The gradual cessation of chlorophyll manufacture and the final breakdown of that previously made completes the first stage in autumn coloration, causing certain plants to become yellow. There are other plants, some magnolias for instance, whose leaves do not turn yellow but change from green directly to brown. For some reason the breakdown of chlorophyll does not start soon enough or is not complete enough to result in the appearance of the yellow pigments. The yellow color, however, appears in the foliage of many other plants regardless of the weather conditions, though there is an interesting high degree of individuality in certain species. Red maple, for instance, usually turns a good red in fall, but some may color yellow. The same can be said of sugar maples and several other plants. This is an interesting physiological problem worthy of considerable investigation.

→>>> WHY LEAVES TURN RED

The sassafras, some of the maples, oaks, sumacs, sourwood, tupelo, and other plants are particularly outstanding for their brilliant red autumn color, and the intensity of their color apparently varies from year to year. The red in their leaves is caused by a pigment called anthocyanin, which results from the accumulation of sugars and tannins in the leaf. In some of the maples valued for their sugar production, it is probably the sugars that cause this red color. The oaks, however, probably owe their high autumn coloration to the presence of tannins.

Two factors are necessary in the production of red autumn color. The first is light. There must be warm, bright, sunny days in the fall, during which time the leaves naturally manufacture a great deal of sugar. Second, such days must be followed by cool nights, during which the temperature falls below 45°F. Plant physiologists have shown definitely that, under such conditions, there is little or no translocation of sugars and other materials from the leaf to other parts of the plant. In other words, when cool nights occur, following warm, bright, sunny days, sugars and other materials are "trapped" in the leaves. The accumulation of these products results in the manufacture of the red anthocyanin pigment.

The combination of these factors is well understood when one observes a certain tree that may be red only on the side exposed to the sun. Other leaves not directly in the sun's rays may be green or yellow. It is interesting to note that trees and shrubs growing in swamps and other low places are often among the first to color in the fall simply because it is in such places that cold air first settles on still nights.

With these points in mind, it can be seen easily why there is so much divergence of opinion about autumn color. When plants are located where they receive full sunlight, especially in late afternoons during early fall, they should be expected to show pronounced color if weather conditions have been favorable. On the other hand, if a plant grows in shade where it receives no direct sunlight, it cannot be expected to have marked red autumn color.

One species in the Arnold Arboretum annually demonstrates this point. There is a splendid plant of *Fothergilla monticola* exposed to full sunlight in the lowest spot in the arboretum. In years when the climatic conditions have favored the formation of autumn color, this particular plant is a gorgeous red and yellow—on the western side. On the eastern side, where the foliage is shaded from the late afternoon sun, it is merely yellowish. Fortunately not all plants show such great variation in autumn color when one side is compared with another, but it is a fact that the western side usually has the deepest colored foliage when there has been plenty of sunshine. This point should be kept in mind when planting. Locations and plants should be selected that will show to the best advantage during the period of autumn color.

⇉ DULL AUTUMN COLORATION

A warm, cloudy fall, sometimes with much rain, will restrict the formation of bright colors. With insufficient sunlight the sugar production is greatly reduced, and with warm nights what little sugar has been manufactured in the leaves is readily transported to the trunk and roots where it has no effect on the color of the foliage.

The leaves of many evergreens change color in autumn. Some pine needles may turn yellow, but usually such color lasts only for a short time, the needles quickly turning brown. This is particularly true of those evergreen leaves that are normally shed each year, and although the autumn color may not be conspicuous in many evergreen plants, it is evident on close examination.

All leaves eventually turn brown. This is not an autumn color but merely the result of the death or decay of plant tissue. Sometimes leaves turn brown while on the tree, as in the American beech and some oaks. In other cases, such as the sugar maple and spicebush, leaves drop while still brightly colored and turn brown afterward.

Autumn color is, then, a physiological phenomenon that is very complex. The sugar formation in the leaf, the amount of sunshine received by the plants, and the temperature of the air are three variable factors that to a large degree control autumn coloration.

⇉ TREES WITH VIVID AUTUMN COLOR

The following trees are listed according to their most conspicuous autumn color. As has been explained above, these may change from year to year, depending on climatic conditions. For instance, some years *Cladrastis lutea* will be yellow, other years the same tree will be purplish. The degree of color may also depend on soil conditions, it being a well-known fact that pin oaks, for instance, that have received heavy applications of nitrogenous fertilizers will have a much deeper red color than those grown in poor soils without such fertilizers.

⇉ RED

Acer capillipes
A. circinatum (red to orange)
A. ginnala
A. ginnala 'Flame'

A. japonicum and varieties
A. mandshuricum
A. maximowiczianum
A. palmatum and varieties

A. platanoides 'Crimson King'
A. platanoides 'Fassen's Black'
A. rubrum
A. rubrum 'October Glory'
A. saccharum (and yellow)
A. saccharum nigrum 'Slavin's Upright'
A. spicatum (orange and scarlet)
A. tataricum (red to yellow)
A. triflorum
Amelanchier canadensis (yellow to red)
A. laevis (yellow to red)
Betula pendula 'Purpurea' (purplish to red)
Carpinus caroliniana (orange to red)
C. japonica
C. orientalis
Cercidiphyllum japonicum (yellow to scarlet)
Cornus florida
C. mas
C. nuttallii (red to yellow)
Cotinus americanus (scarlet to orange)
Crataegus lavallei (bronze-red)
C. nitida (orange to red)
C. phaenopyrum
Franklinia alatamaha (orange to red)

Liquidambar formosana
L. styraciflua and varieties
Malus dawsoniana (red and yellow)
Nyssa sylvatica
Oxydendrum arboreum
Parrotia persica (red to yellow)
Pistacia chinensis (red to orange)
Prunus maximowiczii
P. nipponica (yellow to red)
P. pensylvanica
P. sargentii
Pyrus calleryana
P. ussuriensis
Quercus coccinea
Q. palustris
Q. rubra
Q. velutina
Sassafras albidum (orange to scarlet)
Sorbus alnifolia
S. aucuparia
S. cashmiriana
S. discolor
S. folgneri
Stewartia koreana (orange to red)
Viburnum species
Zelkova carpinifolia

→≫ YELLOW

Acer davidii (and purple)
A. glabrum
A. japonicum 'Itayo'
A. japonicum 'Junshitoe'
A. macrophyllum
A. pensylvanicum
A. platanoides
A. saccharum 'Goldspire'
A. tschonoskii
Aesculus glabra (orange)
Amelanchier grandiflora (yellow to orange)
A. laevis
Asimina triloba
Betula species
Carya species
Castanea crenata

C. mollissima (yellow to bronze)
Cercis species
Chionanthus virginicus
Cladrastis lutea (orange to yellow)
Fagus grandifolia (golden bronze)
F. sylvatica (golden bronze)
Fraxinus americana (purple to yellow)
F. velutina glabra
Ginkgo biloba
Gleditsia triacanthos 'Autumn Gold'
Magnolia stellata (bronze)
Nyssa sinensis
Populus species
Pseudolarix kaempferi
Quercus alba (purplish)
Q. imbricaria (russet)
Sorbus alnifolia (orange to scarlet)

⇥⟫ NO AUTUMN COLOR

Acer campestre
A. negundo
A. pseudoplatanus
Aesculus hippocastanum
Ailanthus altissima
Albizia julibrissin
Alnus glutinosa
Carpinus betulus
Cedrela sinensis
Corylus colurna
Crataegus laevigata
C. monogyna
Elaeagnus angustifolia

Fraxinus excelsior
Juglans species
Laburnum species
Magnolia species
Malus, many species
Quercus robur
Robinia species
Sophora japonica
Syringa reticulata
Tilia cordata
T. euchlora
T. europaea

FIVE

Trees for Various Purposes

➤➤➤

Park superintendents, landscape gardeners, and amateur horticulturists frequently are at a loss to think of more than two or three trees for a particular situation. Some of the common questions we receive concern substitutes for the American elm. What are these substitutes and how might they be used? How many of them are there? What are the "low maintenance" trees? Which trees have merit in seashore gardens or in difficult growing conditions? The more particular the growing conditions, or the more specific the requirements for the trees to fill the situation, the more difficult it becomes to make the proper selection. This should not be done haphazardly by the simple means of trial and error; it should be done intelligently from lists in which a major number of the possibilities are included so that trees can be considered without omitting any.

Lists prove helpful to the experienced park superintendent as well as the amateur, for it is much easier to make a proper selection from a complete list of trees known to meet certain specific growing requirements than to select more or less unknown plants at random, without detailed information concerning their individual qualifications.

The following trees are grouped in various suggested lists. The experienced planter realizes there are situations sufficiently difficult that it is almost impossible to force any tree to grow in them, and the first step is to try to overcome such situations rather than select the trees and hope they succeed. After considering the trees suggested in the following lists, the planter will be much better prepared to make proper selections and to gauge the possibilities for success of other plants to be added to these lists as the result of personal experiences. These are not offered as being "complete" by any means, but they are offered as worthy suggestions that the individual can augment in considering his or her own growing conditions and experiences.

45

⤙≫ SMALL TREES THAT WITHSTAND SHADE

Very few trees require shaded conditions in which to grow. Some will withstand such conditions, but the deeper the shade the more difficult for any tree to grow properly. Certainly trees will not flower and fruit as well as in full sunlight, and usually there is also considerable root competition from other trees.

Acer circinatum
A. pensylvanicum
A. spicatum
Amelanchier species
Cercis canadensis
Cornus florida

Ilex species
Prunus pensylvanica
Rhododendron maximum
Thuja occidentalis
Tsuga species

⤙≫ TREES FOR MOIST SOIL

It is usually advisable to drain wet spots, particularly those where water stands for any length of time. The following trees can withstand wet soil conditions better than most:

Acer rubrum
Alnus species
Calocedrus decurrens
Casuarina species
Ilex species
Larix laricina
Liquidambar styraciflua
Magnolia virginiana

Melaleuca leucadendron
Myrica cerifera
Nyssa sylvatica
Quercus bicolor
Salix species
Taxodium distichum
Thuja occidentalis

⤙≫ TREES THAT WITHSTAND DRY OR POOR, STERILE SOILS

It is always risky to recommend any trees for growing in poor, dry soils without knowing just what this means. In a region with 45 inches of annual rainfall, it might mean merely a sandy soil through which an adequate amount of rain filters, always leaving the soil fairly dry. This condition could (and should) be corrected by mixing organic matter with the soil where the tree is to be planted and mulching the soil about the roots of the tree with some good material. Both these methods should aid in assisting to make more of the rainfall available to the tree by holding it until it is used.

The Eastern larch (Larix laricina) *is deciduous.*

On the other hand, dry soils are consistent throughout the Midwest where annual rainfall is very low (20 inches or less in some places). In such areas very few trees will grow.

Then there are the unusually alkaline soils that are also mostly dry, especially in the western part of North America where growing trees is particularly difficult. The following trees will not all grow in any one of these situations, but a few may. There are undoubtedly others, especially those in the list of trees growing at the seashore, which might also be included.

Acer negundo
Ailanthus altissima
Albizia julibrissin
Aralia elata
Bauhinia species
Betula davurica
B. populifolia
Brachychiton species
Broussonetia papyrifera
Casuarina species
Celtis australis
Ceratonia siliqua
Cupressus macrocarpa

Eucalyptus species
Ficus species
Fraxinus americana
F. velutina
Gleditsia species
Grevillea robusta
Juniperus species
Keteleeria fortunei
Koelreuteria paniculata
Leptospermum laevigatum
Maclura pomifera
Melaleuca species
Melia azedarach

Olea europaea
Parkinsonia aculeata
Pinus banksiana
P. canariensis
P. rigida
P. torreyana
P. virginiana
Populus alba
P. fremontii

Prosopis glandulosa
Quercus kelloggii
Q. marilandica
Q. prinus
Robinia species
Sassafras albidum
Schinus molle
Sophora japonica
Ulmus pumila

⇥⟫ TREES FOR SEASHORE PLANTING

Many trees can be grown in gardens near the seashore, especially if the soil is good. As the soil becomes sandier and exposure more pronounced, fewer and fewer trees are able to withstand such conditions year in and year out without some injury. The following trees are well adapted for use in seashore gardens; in fact, some withstand saltwater spray. For really trying seashore conditions, this list of trees should be considered first before any other selections are made:

Acer platanoides
A. pseudoplatanus
Aesculus hippocastanum
Ailanthus altissima
Amelanchier canadensis
Araucaria species
Casuarina equisetifolia
C. stricta
Crataegus crus-galli
Cryptomeria japonica
Cupressus macrocarpa
Elaeagnus angustifolia
Eucalyptus species
Fraxinus velutina
Hippophae rhamnoides
Ilex opaca
Juniperus excelsa 'Stricta'
J. lucayana
J. virginiana
Lagunaria patersonii
Magnolia grandiflora
Maytenus boaria
Melaleuca leucadendron
Morus alba
Nyssa sylvatica

Olea europaea
Picea asperata
P. pungens glauca
Pinus halepensis
P. nigra
P. pinaster
P. radiata
P. rigida
P. sylvestris
P. thunbergii
Pittosporum undulatum
Populus alba
Prunus serotina
Quercus agrifolia
Q. alba
Q. ilex
Q. marilandica
Q. virginiana
Robinia pseudoacacia
Roystonea regia
Sabal palmetto
Schinus molle
S. terebinthifolius
Thuja occidentalis
T. orientalis

Tilia cordata	*U. pumila*
T. euchlora	*Umbellularia californica*
Ulmus parvifolia	*Washingtonia robusta*

→≫ THE HARDIEST TREES

A most interesting study that was carried on for many years by F. L. Skinner of Dropmore, Manitoba, Canada, is the variation in hardiness of different geographic clones of the same species. With winter temperatures of −50°F, he was well situated to study this type of variation. He found that plants of many species grown from seed collected near the center of their known habitats are not hardy, whereas plants grown from seed collected from the northernmost limits of their habitats often proved hardy in his very severe climate. A specific example was a row of *Ulmus pumila* seedlings in his nursery, some of which were grown from seed collected in Harbin, Manchuria, and some from a tree producing seed in southern Manitoba. In September 1942, the temperature went down to zero and later that winter to −55°F. In the spring of 1943, the seedlings from Manchuria were alive out to the tips of the branches; the remainder of the seedlings were killed completely, roots and all.

Several examples of this type of injury have occurred in the Arnold Arboretum to lend proof to this fact that geographic forms are very important when an attempt is being made to establish seedlings in very cold places. Seed collected from plants growing near the northernmost limits of their habitats is likely to give rise to seedlings that will prove hardier than will seedlings grown from seed collected in the milder parts of those habitats.

The following ornamental trees are among those hardy in the coldest parts of settled areas in the United States and Canada:

ZONE 1	*Juniperus virginiana*
Larix laricina	*Larix decidua*
Populus tremuloides	*Malus baccata*
	M. 'Flame'
ZONE 2	M. *ioensis* 'Plena'
Acer ginnala	*Picea abies*
A. negundo	*P. engelmannii*
A. spicatum	*P. glauca*
Alnus incana	*P. pungens*
Betula papyrifera	*Pinus banksiana*
B. pendula	*P. cembra*
Carpinus caroliniana	*P. flexilis*
Elaeagnus angustifolia	*P. resinosa*
Fraxinus pennsylvanica lanceolata	*P. sylvestris*

Populus berolinensis
P. deltoides
P. nigra 'Italica'
P. simonii
P. tacamahaca
Prunus maackii
P. pensylvanica
Pyrus ussuriensis
Rhamnus davurica
Salix alba
Sorbus aucuparia
S. decora
Syringa reticulata
Thuja occidentalis
Tilia cordata
Ulmus americana
Viburnum lentago

ZONE 3
Abies veitchii
Acer pensylvanicum
A. platanoides
A. rubrum
A. saccharum
Aesculus carnea 'Briotii'
A. glabra
A. hippocastanum 'Baumannii'
A. octandra
Alnus glutinosa

Aralia elata
Betula lenta
Chamaecyparis obtusa
C. pisifera
Cladrastis lutea
Crataegus succulenta
Euonymus europaea
Fagus grandifolia
Fraxinus americana
F. excelsior
Hippophae rhamnoides
Malus 'Dolgo'
M. prunifolia rinkii
M. robusta
Pinus koraiensis
P. strobus
Populus alba
Prunus avium
P. cerasifera
P. cerasus
P. padus
P. serotina
Quercus bicolor
Rhododendron maximum
Robinia pseudoacacia
R. viscosa
Tilia europaea
T. platyphyllos
Viburnum prunifolium

➤➤ TREES THAT WITHSTAND CITY CONDITIONS

Vegetation in the city has a very difficult time fighting for existence. Poor soil, insufficient light, insufficient water, and excessive smoke and gas fumes in the air are only a few of the disadvantages. Dust and soot quickly encrust the leaves and restrict the normal entrance of oxygen into them. Serious damage can be expected from the carbon monoxide gas given off by a stream of automobile traffic. The more intense these conditions become, the fewer the plants and trees that can be grown. Evergreens in particular are difficult subjects for growing in the city, especially evergreen trees. The following trees might well be considered first for planting in the city, for they are among the best suited for withstanding these trying conditions:

The Swiss stone pine, Pinus cembra, *is a good ornamental but sometimes disappointing because of its very slow growth.*

Abies concolor
Acer campestre
A. negundo
A. platanoides
A. pseudoplatanus
Aesculus species
Ailanthus altissima
Albizia julibrissin 'E. H. Wilson'
Aralia elata
Catalpa species
Cedrela sinensis
Celtis species
Crataegus laevigata
C. monogyna
C. phaenopyrum
Elaeagnus angustifolia
Euonymus europaea
Fraxinus americana

F. excelsior
F. pennsylvanica lanceolata
Ginkgo biloba
Gleditsia triacanthos
Koelreuteria paniculata
Magnolia grandiflora
M. soulangiana
M. stellata
Malus species
Melia azedarath
Morus alba
Phellodendron amurense
Picea pungens
Platanus species
Populus alba
P. canadensis eugenei
P. nigra 'Italica'
Quercus rubra

Rhamnus davurica
Robinia pseudoacacia
Sophora japonica
Taxus cuspidata
Tilia species

Tsuga caroliniana
Ulmus americana
U. procera
U. pumila

→≫ TREES FREQUENTLY NOT ALLOWED IN NEW STREET PLANTINGS

Some trees may have such a bad record in certain locations that there may be local ordinances prohibiting their use as street trees. This may be caused by the fact that such trees split easily; their wood is brittle and breaks easily; their roots clog drains and sewers; they are unusually susceptible to disease or insect pests; or they have vicious thorns. Regardless of the exact reason for such bans, the following trees have been prohibited as street trees in some localities:

Acer negundo
A. rubrum
A. saccharinum
Aesculus hippocastanum
Carya species
Catalpa species
Crataegus species
Fraxinus species

Gleditsia triacanthos (with thorns)
Juglans nigra
Morus species
Populus species
Prunus species
Robinia species
Salix species
Ulmus species

→≫ TREES WITH THORNY TWIGS
(Barrier Plants When Restrained to Many Stems)

Aralia elata
Crataegus species
Gleditsia triacanthos
Hemiptelea davidii
Hippophae rhamnoides
Kalopanax pictus
Maclura pomifera
Parkinsonia aculeata

Poncirus trifoliata
Prunus cerasifera
Pyrus species
Rhamnus davurica
Robinia species
Xanthoceras species
Ziziphus species

An early introduction to America from Europe, Aesculus hippocastanum, *once very popular, has now been superseded by other trees of greater beauty.*

⇢≫ WINDBREAKS AND SHELTERBELTS

Windbreaks can be very essential elements of home and highway plantings, especially in the colder parts of the country where protection is needed against prevailing winter winds and heavy snows. On the Great Plains of the Midwest, where many a farm home has no planting of trees whatsoever, shelterbelts are frequently essential. Climatic conditions vary considerably, so the selection of the right trees for the windbreak or shelterbelt is very important.

It has been found that trees moderate the effect of the wind on their leeward side for a distance on the ground equal to approximately twenty times their height. This means that the wind is less, soil evaporation is decreased, severely cold temperatures brought by winds in winter are reduced, and snow accumulation, and hence soil water, is increased—reasons enough for planting trees as a shelterbelt on windy plains.

A windbreak can be a single row of deciduous or evergreen trees, but a shelterbelt, to be truly effective, consists of several rows of trees, usually the rows being 6 to 8 feet apart and the trees about 6 feet apart in the row. Sometimes the shelterbelt consists of as many as fifteen rows of trees, bordered on the outside with hardy shrubs such as *Caragana arborescens* and

Elaeagnus angustifolia, or evergreens such as red-cedar, blue spruce or Black Hills spruce, and ponderosa pine. Several species are used in the shelterbelt since soil and climatic conditions vary considerably, and where one species may not do so well, another will. The tallest trees are, of course, planted in the middle rows. Windbreaks in certain parts of South Dakota, for instance, must grow in soil receiving an annual rainfall of only 17 inches, not sufficient for good growth based on the 48-inch rainfall of the northeastern states.

Where rainfall is more plentiful, windbreaks become important only for protecting houses and gardens against prevailing winds, often merely winter winds, and usually one or, at the most, two rows of dense-growing trees are sufficient.

⇢≫ TREES FOR WINDBREAKS

These trees make good windbreaks in areas other than the Great Plains. The best windbreaks are, of course, the evergreens, but since they grow slowly, fast-growing deciduous windbreaks are frequently planted in front of the evergreens and then eventually cut out when the evergreens become large enough to prove effective.

Acer ginnala
A. platanoides
A. pseudoplatanus
A. rubrum
A. saccharum
Carpinus betulus
Cornus mas
Crataegus phaenopyrum
Eucalyptus species
Fagus species
Fraxinus americana
F. pennsylvanica lanceolata
Juniperus species
Ligustrum lucidum
Maclura pomifera
Malus baccata
Picea abies
P. glauca
P. omorika

Pinus nigra
P. resinosa
P. strobus
Populus alba
P. berolinensis
P. nigra 'Italica'
P. simonii
P. tremuloides
Pseudotsuga menziesii
Quercus, many species
Q. imbricaria (one of the best)
Q. phellos (one of the best)
Rhamnus davurica
Syringa reticulata
Thuja species
Tilia species
Tsuga caroliniana
Viburnum prunifolium

⇢≫ TREES FOR SHELTERBELTS IN GREAT PLAINS

These are recommended for the Great Plains area of the Midwest since they will grow and develop very tenacious roots even with comparatively little rainfall. Trees such as the hackberry, honey-locust, and ponderosa pine have roots known to reach 10 to 20 feet deep into the soil.

Acer negundo	*Picea glauca*
A. saccharinum	*P. pungens*
Caragana arborescens	*Pinus ponderosa*
Celtis occidentalis	*Populus* species
Elaeagnus angustifolia	*Prunus americana*
Fraxinus pennsylvanica lanceolata	*P. virginiana*
Gleditsia triacanthos	*Pseudotsuga menziesii*
Juglans nigra	*Quercus macrocarpa*
Juniperus scopulorum	*Salix alba*
J. virginiana	*S. pentandra*
Maclura pomifera	

Poplars being grown in the northeast polder area of Holland as a windbreak.

⇛ TREES OF DIFFERENT HEIGHTS

LOW TREES (20–35 FEET TALL)
Acacia baileyana
A. pendula
Acer argutum
A. buergerianum
A. campestre
A. capillipes
A. carpinifolium
A. circinatum
A. diabolicum purpurascens
A. ginnala
A. glabrum
A. griseum
A. japonicum and varieties
A. mandshuricum
A. monspessulanum
A. palmatum and varieties
A. spicatum
A. tataricum
A. triflorum
A. tschonoskii
Aesculus glabra
Amelanchier grandiflora
Arbutus unedo
Bauhinia variegata
Betula populifolia
Bumelia lanuginosa
Carpinus betulus 'Globosa'
C. orientalis
Carya tomentosa
Cassia fistula
Castanea crenata
Casuarina stricta
Cercis canadensis and varieties
C. racemosa
C. siliquastrum
Chionanthus virginicus
Clethra barbinervis
Cornus kousa
C. mas
Cotinus americanus
Crataegus species
Cupressus bakeri
Elaeagnus angustifolia
Eriobotrya japonica

Erythea armata
Euonymus species
Evodia daniellii
Ficus carica
Franklinia alatamaha
Fraxinus holotricha
F. mariesii
F. ornus
Halesia carolina
Hemiptelea davidii
Hippophae rhamnoides
Hovenia dulcis
Ilex cassine
I. ciliospinosa
I. decidua
I. pedunculosa
I. pernyi
I. vomitoria
Juniperus rigida
Koelreuteria paniculata
Laburnum species
Lagerstroemia indica
Laurus nobilis
Leptospermum laevigatum
Leucadendron argenteum
Ligustrum lucidum
Macadamia ternifolia
Magnolia cordata
M. dawsoniana
M. nitida
M. salicifolia
M. sieboldii
M. soulangiana
M. stellata
M. watsonii
M. wilsonii
Malus, many species
Maytenus boaria
Nyssa sinensis
Olea europaea
Parkinsonia aculeata
Phoenix reclinata
Pinus aristata
P. contorta
Prunus, many species

x *P. hillieri* 'Spire'
Quercus liaotungensis
Q. libani
Q. marilandica
Ravenala madagascariensis
Rhamnus davurica
Rhododendron maximum
Robinia 'Idaho'
S. babylonica
S. caprea
Sorbus decora
S. discolor
S. folgneri
S. tianshanica
S. vilmorinii
Styrax species
Symplocos paniculata
Syringa reticulata
Tecoma stans
Tilia mongolica
Vaccinium arboreum
Viburnum species
Xanthoceras sorbifolium
Ziziphus jujuba

(TREES 35–75 FEET TALL)
Abies koreana
A. pinsapo
Acacia dealbata
A. decurrens mollis
A. pruinosa
Acer barbatum floridanum
A. davidii
A. lobelii
A. maximowiczianum
A. negundo
A. pensylvanicum
Aesculus carnea
Ailanthus altissima
Albizia julibrissin
Alnus cordata
A. incana
A. rhombifolia
A. rubra
Amelanchier canadensis
A. laevis
Aralia elata
Asimina triloba

Betula davurica
B. pendula
B. platyphylla szechuanica
Brachychiton acerifolium
Broussonetia papyrifera
Camellia japonica
Carpinus betulus
C. caroliniana
C. japonica
Castanea mollissima
Castanospermum australe
Casuarina equisetifolia
Catalpa bignonioides
Cedrela sinensis
Celtis bungeana
C. jessoensis
C. sinensis
Ceratonia siliqua
Cercidiphyllum japonicum
Cercis canadensis
C. chinensis
Cinnamomum camphora
Cladrastis lutea
Clethra delavayi
Cornus capitata
C. controversa
C. florida
C. macrophylla
Corylus colurna
Crataegus species
Cunninghamia lanceolata
Cupressus arizonica 'Bonita'
C. macrocarpa
C. sempervirens
Davidia involucrata
Delonix regia
Diospyros kaki
D. virginiana
Eucommia ulmoides
Eugenia paniculata
Ficus macrophylla
Firmiana simplex
Fraxinus ornus
F. pennsylvanica lanceolata
F. velutina
Gordonia lasianthus
Hymenosporum flavum
Ilex aquifolium and varieties

I. cassine

I. chinensis

I. latifolia

I. montana

I. opaca and varieties

I. purpurea

Jacaranda acutifolia

Juglans hindsii

Juniperus chinensis

J. deppeana

J. drupacea

J. excelsa

J. lucayana

J. scopulorum

Koelreuteria bipinnata

Lagunaria patersonii

Larix laricina

Lithocarpus densiflorum

Livistona australis

Maackia amurensis

Maclura pomifera

Magnolia heptapeta

M. fraseri

M. kobus borealis

M. loebneri

M. loebneri 'Merrill'

M. macrophylla

M. rostrata

M. sargentiana

M. sprengeri

M. veitchii

M. virginiana

Malus, many species and varieties

Melaleuca leucadendron

Melia azedarach

Morus alba

Myrica cerifera

Nyssa sinensis

Oxydendrum arboreum

Parrotia persica

Paulownia tomentosa

Phellodendron amurense

Picea asperata

P. glauca densata

P. koyamai

Pinus aristata

P. banksiana

P. bungeana

P. cembra

P. coulteri

P. flexilis

P. halepensis

P. muricata

P. patula

P. peuce

P. radiata

P. resinosa

P. rigida

P. sylvestris

P. torreyana

P. virginiana

Pistacia chinensis

Pittosporum eugeniodes

Podocarpus elongatus

P. macrophyllus

Poncirus trifoliata

Populus lasiocarpa

P. simonii

Prosopis glandulosa

Prunus avium

P. lusitanica

P. maackii

P. maximowiczii

P. padus

P. pensylvanica

P. sargentii

P. yedoensis

Pterostyrax hispida

Pyrus ussuriensis

Quercus acutissima

Q. bicolor

Q. chrysolepis

Q. coccinea

Q. falcata

Q. glandulifera

Q. ilex

Q. imbricaria

Q. laurifolia

Q. nigra

Q. palustris

Q. phellos

Q. rubra

Q. suber

Q. variabilis

Q. virginiana

Q. wislizenii

Quillaja saponaria
Rhododendron maximum
Roystonea regia
Salix alba
S. blanda
S. elaeagnos
S. elegantissima
S. pentandra
Sambucus coerulea
Sapium sebiferum
Sassafras albidum
Schinus molle
S. terebinthifolius
Sorbus alnifolia
S. aria
S. aucuparia
S. cashmiriana
Spathodea campanulata
Stewartia koreana
S. pseudo-camellia
Symplocos paniculata
Taxus baccata
T. cuspidata
T. media
Thuja occidentalis
T. orientalis
T. standishii
Thujopsis dolabrata
Tilia euchlora
Torreya nucifera
Tsuga caroliniana
Ulmus alata
U. parvifolia
U. pumila
Umbellularia californica
Zelkova carpinifolia

TALL TREES—75 FEET OR OVER
Abies procera
A. spectabilis
A. veitchii
Acer macrophyllum
A. platanoides
A. pseudoplatanus
A. rubrum
A. saccharum
Aesculus hippocastanum
A. octandra

Alnus glutinosa
Araucaria araucana
A. heterophylla
Betula albo-sinensis
B. lenta
B. nigra
B. payrifera
Calocedrus decurrens
Carya, most species
Castanopsis chrysophylla
Catalpa speciosa
Cedrus species
Ceiba pentandra
Celtis australis
C. laevigata
Cercidiphyllum japonicum
Chamaecyparis species
Cocos nucifera
Cornus nuttallii
Cryptomeria japonica
Eucalyptus species
Fagus species
Fraxinus americana
F. excelsior
F. oregona
Ginkgo biloba
Gleditsia triacanthos
Grevillea robusta
Gymnocladus dioicus
Halesia monticola
Juglans nigra
J. regia
Juniperus virginiana
Kalopanax pictus
Keteleeria fortunei
Larix decidua
L. kaempferi
Liquidambar styraciflua
Liriodendron tulipifera
Magnolia acuminata
M. campbellii
M. grandiflora
M. hypoleuca
Metasequoia glyptostroboides
Nyssa sylvatica
Ostrya virginiana
Picea abies
P. breweriana

P. engelmannii
P. omorika
P. torano
P. pungens
P. sitchensis
P. smithiana
P. wilsonii
Pinus coulteri
P. densiflora
P. griffithii
P. jeffreyi
P. koraiensis
P. lambertiana
P. monticola
P. nigra
P. parviflora
P. pinaster
P. pinea
P. ponderosa
P. strobus
P. thunbergii
Pittosporum rhombifolium
Platanus species
Populus, most species
Prunus sargentii
P. serotina
Pseudolarix kaempferi
Pseudotsuga menziesii

Pterocarya fraxinifolia
Quercus agrifolia
Q. alba
Q. cerris
Q. garryana
Q. kelloggii
Q. prinus
Q. robur
Q. velutina
Sabal palmetto
Sciadopitys verticillata
Sequoia sempervirens
Sequoiadendron giganteum
Taxodium distichum
Thuja plicata
Tilia cordata
T. europaea
T. platyphyllos
T. tomentosa
Tsuga canadensis
T. diversifolia
T. heterophylla
Ulmus americana
U. carpinifolia
U. glabra
U. procera
Washingtonia robusta
Zelkova serrata

⇢≫ TREES WITH FRAGRANT FLOWERS

Acacia dealbata
A. pendula
A. pruinosa
Acer ginnala
Albizia julibrissin
A. julibrissin 'E. H. Wilson'
Arbutus menziesii
Buxus sempervirens
Chionanthus virginicus
Citrus species
Cladrastis lutea, slightly
Crataegus laevigata

Elaeagnus angustifolia
Eriobotrya japonica
Franklinia alatamaha
Fraxinus ornus
Hymenosporum flavum
Laburnum alpinum
Laurus nobilis
Liriodendron tulipifera
Magnolia acuminata, slightly
M. campbellii
M. grandiflora and varieties
M. heptapeta

M. *hypoleuca*
M. *kobus*
M. *loebneri* 'Ballerina'
M. *macrophylla*
M. *nitida*
M. *sieboldii*
M. *sprengeri*
M. *stellata*
M. *virginiana*
M. *watsonii*
M. *wilsonii*
Malus species
Melia azedarach
Oxydendrum arboreum
Paulownia tomentosa
Poncirus trifoliata
Prunus conradinae 'Semiplena'
P. *mume*
P. *padus*

P. *serrulata* 'Amanogawa'
P. *serrulata* 'Botan-zakura'
P. *serrulata* 'Jo-nioi'
P. *serrulata* 'Shirotae'
P. *serrulata* 'Takasago'
P. *serrulata* 'Taki-nioi'
P. *serrulata* 'Washin-o'
P. *yedoensis*
Pyrus species
Robinia pseudoacacia
Salix alba 'Vitellina'
Sophora japonica
Sorbus species
Styrax japonica
S. *obassia*
Symplocos paniculata
Tilia species
Umbellularia californica
Viburnum lentago

→≫ TREES WITH FRAGRANT LEAVES

Abies balsamea
Cedrus species
Cercidiphyllum japonicum
Cinnamomum camphora (has scented wood)
Davidia involucrata

Eucalyptus species
Ficus species
Myrica species
Pinus species
Thuja species
Tsuga canadensis

→≫ TREES WITH COLORED BARK

The bark of many trees is most interesting, especially on deciduous trees in the winter. Certain characteristics come with mature age. The bark of a young and vigorous oak sapling is quite different from that of a venerable century-old monarch. Many people appreciate the varying colors of the bark of trees and like to have the lower limbs removed primarily to show this to best advantage. Whether this is good practice or not depends on individual preference, but the bark of all trees can be interesting, whether it is smooth or deeply furrowed or exfoliating in strips.

Some trees are superior to others in respect to ornamental bark characteristics. The birches, many of the cherries, and the beeches are all greatly valued primarily for their bark. They are planted in conspicuous places where their trunks can always be seen.

There are some trees that are not used to any great extent yet which have varicolored bark. The mature bark of these trees may be a deep gray (as in the case of stewartias, *Pinus bungeana,* and *Ulmus parvifolia*) and when it peels or flakes off in irregular plates (somewhat like sycamores), it leaves lighter colored bark beneath. This most interesting habit gives the bark of these trees a unique appearance the entire year and makes them excellent subjects for planting in conspicuous places. Usually, the more vigorous the tree, the more colorful the bark.

The following trees are a few with interesting bark of various kinds:

→≫ GRAY

Acer rubrum
Amelanchier species
Carpinus species
Ceiba pentandra
Celtis species (on upper trunk)
Cladrastis lutea
Crataegus, many species
Fagus species
Ilex opaca

Juglans regia
Magnolia acuminata
M. soulangiana
Quercus rubra (on young trunk and branches)
Q. velutina (on young trunk and branches)
Sorbus species
Ulmus carpinifolia

→≫ WHITE

Acer barbatum floridanum (pale gray)
Alnus rhombifolia (whitish- to grayish-brown)
Betula papyrifera
B. pendula

B. populifolia
Populus alba (sometimes greenish white)
P. tremuloides (sometimes greenish white)

→≫ RED

Pinus densiflora
P. resinosa

P. sylvestris

→≫ CORAL-RED

Acer palmatum 'Sango Kaku'

Prunus serrula *is one of the most interesting ornamental trees available because of its shiny red bark that peels off in paper-thin strips.*

→»» RED TO BROWN, CHERRYLIKE

Betula albo-sinensis (almost orange
   colored)
Prunus, several species

P. sargentii (one of the best)
P. serrula (one of the best)
Syringa reticulata

→»» COLORED BRANCHES

Acer capillipes (green and white
   stripes)
A. davidii (white stripes in winter)
A. lobelii (white stripes)
A. palmatum (red)
A. pensylvanicum (green and white
   stripes)
A. pensylvanicum 'Erythrocladum'
   (winter twigs red)

Poncirus trifoliata (green)
Salix alba 'Chermesina' (red)
S. alba 'Tristis' (yellow)
S. alba 'Vitellina' (yellow)
S. blanda (green)
Sophora japonica (green)
Tilia cordata 'Handsworth' (light
   yellow-green)
T. platyphyllos 'Rubra' (red)

→»» CORKY MATURE BARK

Phellodendron amurense
Quercus suber

Q. variabilis

⇶ BARK THAT EXFOLIATES OR FLAKES OFF IN IRREGULAR PLATES

Acer griseum—one of the best, light brown; peels off like birch bark
A. triflorum—sheds off in flakes
Arbutus unedo—inner bark, bright red; outer bark flakes off irregularly
Betula—several species, white, yellow, or reddish; peels off laterally
Carya ovata—stiff older bark breaks off in longitudinal strips
Cornus kousa—flakes off in irregular patches
Elaeagnus angustifolia—shreds off longitudinally
Eucalyptus species—flakes off irregularly
Juniperus scopulorum—shreds off longitudinally
J. virginiana—shreds off longitudinally
Lagerstroemia indica—flakes off in irregular patches, lighter in color beneath bark
Parrotia persica—flakes off in irregular patches, older bark red-brown
Pinus bungeana—flakes off in irregular patches, lighter in color beneath bark
Platanus species—flakes off in irregular patches, lighter in color beneath bark
Stewartia species—flakes off in irregular patches, lighter in color beneath bark
Thuja species—shreds off longitudinally
Ulmus parvifolia—flakes off in irregular patches, yellowish beneath bark
   (apparently not all members of this species have this interesting
   bark characteristic)

⇶ TREES WITH DIFFERENT HABITS

Some trees, such as the Douglas-fir and the American elm, have very definite outlines at maturity; many others are more or less indefinite. The shapes do vary considerably and can be slightly modified by corrective pruning. However, if a rounded specimen is wanted in the middle of a huge expanse of field or lawn, it is well to know that the white oak has just that form and would serve the purpose admirably. The following short lists are not complete by any means but will serve to illustrate these groups of trees and can easily be augmented by the individual observer who takes an interest in tree forms.

⇶ COLUMNAR TREES

Acer platanoides 'Cleveland'
A. platanoides 'Crimson Sentry'
A. platanoides 'Erectum'
A. pseudoplatanus 'Erectum'

A. rubrum 'Columnare'
A. saccharum 'Monumentale'
A. saccharum 'Newton's Sentry'
A. saccharum nigrum 'Slavin's Upright'

Betula pendula 'Fastigiata'
Carpinus betulus 'Columnaris'
C. betulus 'Fastigiata'
Chamaecyparis lawsoniana 'Allumii'
C. lawsoniana 'Erecta'
Crataegus monogyna 'Stricta'
C. phaenopyrum 'Fastigiata'
Cupressus sempervirens 'Stricta'
Fagus sylvatica 'Fastigiata'
Ginkgo biloba fastigiata
Gleditsia triacanthos 'Columnaris'
Juniperus chinensis columnaris
J. chinensis mas
J. scopulorum 'Skyrocket'
J. virginiana pyramidalis
J. virginiana 'Schottii'
Koelreuteria paniculata 'Fastigiata'
Liriodendron tulipifera 'Fastigiatum'
Magnolia salicifolia 'Else Frye'
Malus baccata 'Columnaris'
M. robusta 'Erecta'
M. 'Strathmore'
M. 'Van Eseltine'
Picea orientalis 'Gowdy'
Pinus cembra
P. cembra 'Columnaris'
P. lambertiana
P. strobus 'Fastigiata'
P. sylvestris 'Fastigiata'
Populus alba 'Pyramidalis'
P. simonii 'Fastigiata'
P. tremula erecta
Prunus sargentii 'Columnaris'
P. serrulata 'Amanogawa'
Quercus robur 'Fastigiata'
Sophora japonica 'Fastigiata'
S. japonica 'Princeton Upright'
Sorbus aucuparia 'Fastigiata'
S. hybrida 'Fastigiata'
Taxodium distichum
Taxus baccata stricta
Thuja occidentalis 'Douglasii Pyramidalis'
T. occidentalis fastigiata
Tilia cordata 'Swedish Upright'
T. platyphyllos 'Fastigiata'
Tsuga canadensis 'Kingsville'

TREES WITH WEEPING HABIT

Acacia pendula
Alnus incana 'Pendula'
Betula pendula 'Tristis'
B. pendula 'Youngii'
Carpinus betulus 'Pendula'
Cedrus atlantica glauca 'Pendula'
C. deodara
C. libani 'Pendula'
Cercidiphyllum japonicum 'Pendula'
Chamaecyparis lawsoniana 'Pendula'
C. nootkatensis 'Pendula'
Cornus florida 'Pendula'
Euonymus bungeana 'Pendula'
Fagus sylvatica 'Pendula'
F. sylvatica 'Purpureo-pendula'
Fraxinus excelsior 'Pendula'
Ginkgo biloba pendula
Gleditsia triacanthos 'Bujotii'
Juniperus virginiana pendula
Larix decidua pendula
Malus 'Oekonomierat Echtermeyer'
M. 'Red Jade'
Morus alba 'Chaparral'
M. alba 'Pendula'
Picea breweriana
P. pungens 'Pendens'
Pinus strobus 'Pendula'
Prunus serotina pendula
P. subhirtella pendula
P. subhirtella 'Wayside Pendula'
P. subhirtella 'Yae-shidare-higan'
P. yedoensis 'Perpendens'
Pseudotsuga menziesii 'Pendula'
Pyrus salicifolia 'Pendula'
Salix alba 'Tristis'
S. babylonica

S. blanda
S. elegantissima
Sophora japonica 'Pendula'
Sorbus aucuparia 'Pendula'
S. folgneri 'Pendula'
Taxodium distichum 'Pendens'

Tilia cordata 'Pyramidalis'
T. petiolaris
Tsuga canadensis pendula
Ulmus americana 'Pendula'
U. glabra 'Camperdownii'

⇥≫ TREES PYRAMIDAL IN OUTLINE

Abies species
Alnus rubra
Betula species
Carpinus caroliniana 'Pyramidalis'
Cedrus species
Cornus nuttallii
Corylus colurna
Cryptomeria japonica
Cupressocyparis leylandii
Cupressus arizonica
C. sempervirens
Fagus species
Fraxinus americana
Ilex aquifolium
I. opaca and varieties
I. pedunculosa
Juniperus species
Lagunaria patersonii
Larix species
Liquidambar formosana
L. styraciflua
Magnolia acuminata
M. grandiflora
M. hypoleuca
M. kobus
M. loebneri
M. salicifolia
Metasequoia glyptostroboides
Metrosideros excelsus
Nyssa sylvatica
Ostrya virginiana

Oxydendrum arboreum
Picea species
Pinus cembra
P. koraiensis
P. muricata
P. nigra 'Pyramidalis'
P. peuce
P. resinosa
P. sylvestris 'Watereri'
Populus berolinensis
Pseudolarix kaempferi
Pseudotsuga menziesii
Quercus cerris
Q. palustris
Sciadopitys verticillata
Sequoia sempervirens
Sequoiadendron giganteum
Stewartia koreana
Taxodium distichum
Taxus cuspidata
Thuja species
Thujopsis dolabrata
Tilia cordata
T. platyphyllos
T. tomentosa
Tsuga canadensis 'Bradshaw'
T. canadensis 'Fremdii'
T. canadensis 'Pomfret'
T. canadensis taxifolia
T. diversifolia
T. heterophylla

⇉ TREES WITH HORIZONTAL BRANCHING

Abies species
Albizia julibrissin
Araucaria heterophylla
Cedrus species
Cercis canadensis
Chamaecyparis lawsoniana 'Nidiformis'
Cornus controversa
C. florida
C. kousa
Crataegus species
Gleditsia triacanthos 'Halka'
Metasequoia glyptostroboides

Nyssa sylvatica
Picea species
Pinus densiflora
P. sylvestris
Podocarpus macrophyllus
Pseudolarix species
Quercus alba
Q. palustris
Q. virginiana
Styrax japonica
Taxodium distichum

⇉ TREES THAT ARE ROUNDED AND SOMETIMES GLOBE-SHAPED

Acer japonicum
A. monspessulanum
A. palmatum
A. platanoides 'Almira'
A. platanoides 'Globosum'
A. platanoides 'Lorbergii'
A. platanoides 'Summershade'
Carpinus betulus 'Globosa'
C. betulus 'Incisa'
Castanea crenata
Catalpa bignonioides 'Nana'
Celtis bungeana
Cornus mas
Crataegus monogyna inermis

C. 'Toba'
Fraxinus species
Magnolia soulangiana
Malus arnoldiana
M. brevipes
M. floribunda
M. sargentii
Quercus alba
Robinia pseudoacacia 'Umbraculifera'
Tsuga canadensis 'Globosa'
T. canadensis pendula
T. diversifolia
U. glabra 'Camperdownii'

⇉ EVERGREEN TREES FOR THE DEEP SOUTH

Acacia species
A. pruinosa
Araucaria species
Arbutus menziesii

A. unedo
Bauhinia blakeana
Brachychiton populneum
Callitris robusta

Camellia species
Castanopsis chrysophylla
Castanospermum australe
Casuarina equisetifolia
C. stricta
Cedrus deodara
Ceratonia siliqua
Cinnamomum camphora
Cornus capitata
Corynocarpus laevigata
Crinodendron patagua
Cunninghamia lanceolata
Cupressus arizonica 'Bonita'
C. macrocarpa
C. sempervirens
Ensete ventricosum
Eriobotrya japonica
Eugenia paniculata
Ficus macrophylla
Fraxinus uhdei
Gordonia lasianthus
Grevillea robusta
Harpephyllum caffrum
Hymenosporum flavum
Ilex aquifolium
I. cassine
I. chinensis
I. latifolia
I. vomitoria
Juniperus deppeana pachyphlaea
J. drupacea
J. excelsa
J. lucayana
Keteleeria fortunei

Lagunaria patersonii
Leptospermum laevigatum
Leucadendron argenteum
Ligustrum lucidum
Macadamia ternifolia
Magnolia grandiflora
Maytenus boaria
Melaleuca leucadendron
Metrosideros excelsus
Myrica californica
Olea europaea
Phoenix dactylifera
Photinia serrulata
Pinus coulteri
P. halepensis
P. pinaster
P. pinea
P. radiata
P. torreyana
Pittosporum eugenioides
P. rhombifolium
Prunus lusitanica
Quercus agrifolia
Q. chrysolepis
Q. ilex
Q. suber
Q. virginiana
Quillaja saponaria
Schinus terebinthifolius
Sequoia sempervirens
Sophora tetraptera
Spathodea campanulata
Umbellularia californica
Vaccinium arboreum

⇶ SPECIMEN TREES WITH ORNAMENTAL FLOWERS

Acacia species
Acer platanoides
A. rubrum
Aesculus species
Albizia julibrissin
Amelanchier species

Aralia elata
Arbutus menziesii
A. unedo
Bauhinia variegata
Brachychiton acerifolium
Camellia japonica

Cassia fistula
Castanopsis chrysophylla
Castonospermum australe
Catalpa bignonioides
C. speciosa
Cedrela sinensis
Ceratonia siliqua
Cercis species
Chionanthus virginicus
Cladrastis lutea
Clethra delavayi
Cornus species
Crataegus species
Davidia involucrata
Delonix regia
Eriobotrya japonica
Eugenia paniculata
Evodia daniellii
Franklinia alatamaha
Fraxinus mariesii
F. ornus
Gordonia lasianthus
Grevillea robusta
Halesia species
Jacaranda species
Kalopanax pictus
Koelreuteria paniculata
Laburnum species
Lagerstroemia indica

Lagunaria patersonii
Leptospermum laevigatum
Liriodendron tulipifera
Lithocarpus densiflorum
Magnolia species
Malus species
Melaleuca leucadendron
Melia azedarach
Oxydendrum arboreum
Parkinsonia aculeata
Paulownia tomentosa
Poncirus trifoliata
Prunus species
Pterostyrax hispida
Pyrus species
Rhododendron maximum
Robina species
Sambucus coerulea
Sophora japonica
Sorbus species
Spathodea campanulata
Stewartia species
Styrax species
Symplocos paniculata
Syringa reticulata
Tecoma stans
Tilia species
Viburnum species

→≫ SPECIMEN TREES WITH ORNAMENTAL FRUIT

Acer ginnala
A. rubrum
A. spicatum
A. tataricum
Ailanthus altissima erythrocarpa
Arbutus species
Broussonetia papyrifera
Cedrus species
Cornus species
Crataegus species
Eriobotrya japonica
Eugenia paniculata

Euonymus species
Evodia daniellii
Hippophae rhamnoides
Ilex species
Juniperus species
Kalopanax pictus
Larix decidua
Liquidambar styraciflua
Magnolia species
Malus species
Melia azedarach
Myrica species

Oxydendrum arboreum
Phellodendron amurense
Photinia species
Prunus pensylvanica
P. serotina
Pseudolarix kaempferi
Pseudotsuga menziesii
Pterocarya fraxinifolia
Rhamnus davurica

Sambucus coerulea
Sapium sebiferum
Schinus molle
S. terebinthifolius
Sorbus species
Symplocos paniculata
Taxus species
Viburnum species

→» TREES UNUSUALLY SUSCEPTIBLE TO PESTS OR DISEASES

Some groups of trees are unusually susceptible to certain insect pests or diseases that frequently mar their beauty unless checked. These trees should never be planted where it is known in advance that they will receive no annual care. Usually (although not always) a single spraying at the proper time will suffice to control the pest and keep the foliage in good condition throughout the growing season, but this is frequently an annual necessity. These facts should be kept in mind especially in highway plantings where maintenance is always reduced to a minimum. The trees in this list are not the only ones troubled with insects or disease, but they are the groups in which destructive pests are most commonly encountered. Many individual tree species are seriously pest-ridden, and when such is the case, notes have been made to this effect in the various discussions pertaining to each tree, pages 103–461.

Aesculus species	*leaf rust*
Amelanchier species	*red spider, scale*
Betula species	*birch leaf miner*
Castanea, some species	*chestnut blight—no cure*
Crataegus species	*fire blight, borers, scale, lace bug, leaf miner*
Euonymus species	*scale*
Fraxinus species	*scale, leaf-eating insects*
Ilex aquifolium and *I. opaca*	*leaf disease, leaf miner*
Larix species	*larch case bearer*
Malus species	*borer, scale, leaf-eating insects*
Prunus species	*borer, scale, leaf-eating insects*
Salix species	*several diseases, leaf-eating insects*
Sorbus species	*fire blight, borers, scale, red spider*
Syringa species	*borers, scale, mildew*
Tilia species	*leaf-eating insects, borers*
Ulmus species	*phloem necrosis, Dutch elm disease, many kinds of leaf-eating insects*

→≫ TREES USUALLY PEST-FREE

In our experience these trees have usually been free of insects or disease. Occasionally they may be sprayed as a precautionary measure, but they can go several years without it. It must be admitted, however, that in certain areas where vicious pests such as the gypsy moth or Japanese beetle are prevalent, hardly anything is immune to injury. The magnolias listed here are another such example; if scale is prevalent on trees of *Magnolia soulangiana* close by and is not controlled, undoubtedly the magnolias listed here will eventually be infested. There are not many trees in the same class with the ginkgo, which seldom is attacked by any pest, but if trees are sought that are likely to be pest-free under reasonably good growing conditions, the following might be considered:

Ailanthus altissima
Brachychiton acerifolium
Calocedrus decurrens
Carpinus species
Cedrus species
Celtis australis
Cercidiphyllum japonicum
Chamaecyparis species
Cornus mas
C. officinalis
Corylus colurna
Cotinus americanus
Elaeagnus angustifolia
Eucommia ulmoides
Ficus species
Franklinia alatamaha
Ginkgo biloba
Gleditsia triacanthos
Grevillea robusta
Gymnocladus dioicus
Juniperus species
Kalopanax pictus

Koelreuteria paniculata
Laburnum species
Ligustrum lucidum
Liquidambar styraciflua
Magnolia acuminata
M. kobus borealis
M. salicifolia
M. stellata
Myrica species
Ostrya species
Parrotia persica
Phellodendron species
Pistacia chinensis
Podocarpus species
Populus alba
Rhamnus davurica
Sciadopitys verticillata
Sophora japonica
Stewartia species
Styrax species
Taxus species
Viburnum species

→≫ TREES DIFFICULT TO TRANSPLANT

Generally speaking, the smaller the tree, the easier it is to transplant. Fortunately, the professional arborists of this country have learned a very great deal about transplanting trees. With the power equipment now available, almost any tree that can be transported can be transplanted, but of course, the bigger the tree, the more difficult the operation and the larger (and heavier) the ball of earth required about the roots. Transplanting can be done now by the professional arborist at almost any time of year, but it is easiest when the tree is dormant and not in full leaf.

The experienced arborist is a reliable authority who has the equipment and the knowledge required for the successful transplanting of large trees. From his varied experience he knows in advance the chances of tree survival—the reason he can guarantee a certain tree to live if properly cared for after the transplanting operation. The moving of large trees is definitely a job for such experts.

Some trees have proved more difficult to move than others. This does not mean that large trees of these species cannot be moved by the expert. They can, especially if they have been satisfactorily root-pruned sufficiently far in advance. When purchased in smaller sizes, such trees often come with a ball of earth around their roots and should be moved just before they commence to grow in the spring. Transplanting trees and shrubs is done at different times throughout North America, but because the following trees are known to be difficult to move, this should be done only when conditions are optimum, in most areas just prior to spring growth.

Arbutus menziesii
Carpinus species
Carya species
Crataegus species
Gymnocladus dioicus
Ilex vomitoria
Juglans species
Kalopanax pictus
Lagerstroemia indica
Liquidambar styraciflua

Magnolia species
Nyssa sylvatica
Ostrya species
Pyrus species
Quercus alba
Q. coccinea
Stewartia species
Xanthoceras sorbifolium
Ziziphus jujuba

→» SUBSTITUTES FOR THE AMERICAN ELM

No tree has the same wide-arching habit as the American elm, but here are some that can be offered as excellent large shade trees that might be used as substitutes where it is inadvisable to plant large numbers of elms.

Acer platanoides
A. pseudoplatanus
A. saccharum
Celtis jessoensis
C. laevigata
Cercidiphyllum japonicum

Cladrastis lutea
Eucommia ulmoides
Fagus grandifolia
F. sylvatica
Fraxinus species
Ginkgo biloba

Gleditsia triacanthos inermis 'Moraine'
Kalopanax pictus
Liquidambar styraciflua
Magnolia acuminata
M. cordata
Phellodendron amurense
Platanus acerifolia
P. orientalis
Populus alba
Prunus sargentii
Quercus acutissima

Q. agrifolia
Q. bicolor
Q. macrocarpa
Q. palustris
Q. phellos
Q. rubra
Q. virginiana
Sophora japonica
Tilia species
Zelkova carpinifolia
Z. serrata

→» A SUGGESTED LIST OF TREES THAT HAVE COLOR INTEREST AT LEAST TWO SEASONS OF THE YEAR

All evergreen trees certainly would be in this group as well as the following deciduous trees:

Acer circinatum
A. davidii
A. ginnala
A. japonicum
A. japonicum 'Aureum'
A. maximowiczianum
A. negundo aureo-variegatum
A. negundo 'Variegatum'
A. palmatum
A. palmatum 'Atropurpureum'
A. palmatum 'Sanguineum'
A. palmatum 'Versicolor'
A. palmatum 'Yezo-Nishiki'
A. pensylvanicum
A. platanoides
A. rubrum
A. saccharum nigrum 'Slavin's Upright'
A. spicatum
A. tataricum
Alnus incana 'Aurea'
A. incana 'Coccinea'
Amelanchier species
Betula species
Broussonetia papyrifera
Carpinus species

Carya glabra
C. ovata
Catalpa bignonioides 'Aurea'
Celtis bungeana
Cercidiphyllum japonicum
Cercis species
Chionanthus virginicus
Cladrastis lutea
Cornus species
Crataegus species
Elaeagnus angustifolia
Evodia daniellii
Fagus species
Franklinia alatamaha
Ginkgo biloba
Gleditsia triacanthos 'Sunburst'
Ilex species
Jacaranda species
Kalopanax pictus
Lagerstroemia indica
Larix decidua
Liquidambar formosana
L. styraciflua
Liriodendron tulipifera
Magnolia heptapeta

The white-flowered shadblow serviceberry (Amelanchier canadensis) *blooms in late April.*

M. hypoleuca
M. kobus borealis
M. loebneri
M. macrophylla
M. salicifolia
M. stellata
Malus species
Melia azedarach
Myrica species
Nyssa sylvatica
Oxydendrum arboreum
Parrotia persica
Phellodendron amurense
Photinia serrulata
Populus alba
P. tremuloides
Prunus blireiana
P. campanulata
P. lusitanica

P. maximowiczii
P. nipponica
P. pensylvanica
P. sargentii
P. serotina
P. subhirtella
P. yedoensis
Pseudolarix kaempferi
Quercus alba
Q. coccinea
Q. imbricaria
Q. palustris
Q. phellos
Q. rubra
Q. velutina
Rhamnus davurica
Salix species
Sambucus coerulea
Sassafras albidum

Sorbus species
Spathodea campanulata
Stewartia species
Syringa reticulata

Tilia species
Ulmus parvifolia
Viburnum species

➜≫

SOME OF THE BEST SMALL SHADE TREES FOR SMALL PROPERTIES

Most of the following trees listed are comparatively small at their mature height, but the hemlocks and pines can be restrained easily by correct pruning and certainly should be included in this valued group of ornamentals.

Acer buergerianum
A. campestre
A. capillipes
A. carpinifolium
A. davidii
A. ginnala
A. japonicum
A. lobelii
A. mandshuricum
A. palmatum
A. palmatum 'Atropurpureum'
A. triflorum
A. tschonoskii
Albizia julibrissin 'E. H. Wilson'
Carpinus betulus 'Globosa'
C. caroliniana
C. japonica
Cercis canadensis
Cornus florida
C. kousa
Crataegus crus-galli
C. laevigata 'Paulii'
C. phaenopyrum
Elaeagnus angustifolia
Franklinia alatamaha
Fraxinus holotricha
F. mariesii
F. ornus
Halesia carolina
Ilex aquifolium
I. opaca

Koelreuteria paniculata
Magnolia dawsoniana
M. heptapeta
M. nitida
M. salicifolia
M. sargentiana robusta
M. sieboldii
M. soulangiana
M. stellata
M. veitchii
M. watsonii
Malus species and varieties
Oxydendrum arboreum
Pinus bungeana
P. strobus
Pistacia chinensis
Prunus armeniaca
P. 'Hally Jolivette'
P. nipponica
P. padus 'Spaethii'
P. serrulata 'Fugenzo'
P. serrulata 'Kwanzan'
P. subhirtella autumnalis
Styrax japonica
S. obassia
Syringa reticulata
Tsuga canadensis
T. caroliniana
Viburnum prunifolium
V. rufidulum
V. sieboldii

→≫ STATE TREES

The following trees have been selected by acts of the state legislatures as the various "official" trees of each state, unless noted as "unofficial." In this case a popular vote has been taken by some interested statewide organization, but no official act of the legislature has yet been passed. It is interesting to note that the sugar maple has been popular enough to be selected by five different states, the tulip tree by four, and the cottonwood *(Populus deltoides)* by three states. This list easily represents a cross section of the native trees valued across the continent.

ALABAMA—Southern pine—a compromise bill was passed to include under this general heading three native and valued pines, namely, slash pine *(P. caribaea)*, longleaf pine *(P. palustris)*, and loblolly pine *(P. taeda)*

ALASKA—Sitka spruce *(Picea sitchensis)* 1962

ARIZONA—Arizona cypress *(Cupressus arizonica)*

ARKANSAS—"Pine"

CALIFORNIA—Redwood *(Sequoia sempervirens)*

COLORADO—Colorado blue spruce *(Picea pungens glauca)*

CONNECTICUT—White oak *(Quercus alba)*

DELAWARE—American holly *(Ilex opaca)*

FLORIDA—Cabbage palmetto *(Sabal palmetto)* 1953

GEORGIA—Live oak *(Quercus virginiana)*

HAWAII—Kuki or Candlenut *(Aleurites moluccana)* 1959

IDAHO—Western white pine *(Pinus monticola)*

ILLINOIS—"Native Oak"

INDIANA—Tulip tree, Tulip or yellow poplar *(Liriodendron tulipifera)*

IOWA—"Oak" *(Quercus* species) 1958

KANSAS—Cottonwood *(Populus deltoides* or *balsamifera)*

KENTUCKY—Tulip tree, Tulip or yellow poplar *(Liriodendron tulipifera)*—unofficial

LOUISIANA—Southern magnolia *(Magnolia grandiflora)*

MAINE—White pine *(Pinus strobus)*

MARYLAND—White oak *(Quercus alba)*

MASSACHUSETTS—American elm *(Ulmus americana)*

MICHIGAN—"Apple"

MINNESOTA—White pine *(Pinus strobus)*

MISSISSIPPI—Southern magnolia *(Magnolia grandiflora)*

MISSOURI—Flowering dogwood *(Cornus florida)* 1955

MONTANA—Western yellow pine *(Pinus ponderosa)*

NEBRASKA—American elm *(Ulmus americana)*

NEVADA—Trembling aspen *(Populus tremuloides)*

NEW HAMPSHIRE—Canoe birch *(Betula papyrifera)*

NEW JERSEY—Red oak *(Quercus rubra)*

NEW MEXICO—Piñon or Nut pine *(Pinus edulis)*

NEW YORK—Sugar maple *(Acer saccharum)*—unofficial

NORTH CAROLINA—Tulip tree, Tulip or yellow poplar *(Liriodendron tulipifera)*—
   unofficial
NORTH DAKOTA—Green ash *(Fraxinus pennsylvanica lanceolata)*
OHIO—Ohio buckeye *(Aesculus glabra)* 1953
OKLAHOMA—Redbud *(Cercis canadensis)*
OREGON—Douglas-fir *(Pseudotsuga menziesii)*
PENNSYLVANIA—Canada hemlock *(Tsuga canadensis)*
RHODE ISLAND—Sugar maple *(Acer saccharum)*
SOUTH CAROLINA—Cabbage palmetto *(Sabal palmetto)*
SOUTH DAKOTA—Cottonwood *(Populus deltoides* or *balsamifera)*
TENNESSEE—Tulip tree, Tulip or yellow poplar *(Liriodendron tulipifera)*
TEXAS—Pecan *(Carya illinoinensis)*
UTAH—Colorado blue spruce *(Picea pungens glauca)*
VERMONT—Sugar maple *(Acer saccharum)*
VIRGINIA—Flowering dogwood *(Cornus florida)*
WASHINGTON—Western hemlock *(Tsuga heterophylla)* 1947
WEST VIRGINIA—Sugar maple *(Acer saccharum)*
WISCONSIN—Sugar maple *(Acer saccharum)* 1955
WYOMING—Cottonwood *(Populus deltoides* or *balsamifera)*

→≫ ARBOR DAY

Julius Sterling Morton (1832–1902), who had been Secretary of Agriculture under Grover Cleveland (1893–97), first conceived the idea of setting aside one day a year to plant trees. The first Arbor Day was in 1872, and after that day various committees tried to get legislation passed to continue the idea. By 1915 enthusiasm began to decline, but by 1939 a National Arbor Day committee was formed that tried to get every state to set aside one day a year when everyone would plant trees. There is a movement on in many states to celebrate Arbor Day on the last Friday in April, where feasible. At present, Arbor Day is observed in the following states on the following dates:

STATE	FIRST ENACTED	NOW OBSERVED
Alabama	1887	Last week in February
Alaska	1966	Third Monday in May
Arizona	1890	Friday after February 1 (Friday after April 1 in five counties)
Arkansas	1906	Third Monday in March

STATE	FIRST ENACTED	NOW OBSERVED
California	1886	March 7–14
Colorado	1885	Third Friday in April
*Connecticut	1886	Last Friday in April
*Delaware	1901	Last Friday in April
Florida	1886	Third Friday in January
Georgia	1887	Third Friday in February
Hawaii	1905	First Friday in November
*Idaho	1886	Last Friday in April
*Illinois	1887	Last Friday in April
Indiana	1884	Second Friday in April
*Iowa	1887	Last Friday in April
Kansas	1875	Last Friday in March
Kentucky	1886	First Friday in April
Louisiana	1888	Third Friday in January
Maine	1887	Third week in May
Maryland	1884	First Wednesday in April
*Massachusetts	1886	Last Friday in April
Michigan	1885	Third week in April
*Minnesota	1876	Last Friday in April
Mississippi	1890	Second Friday in February
Missouri	1886	Friday after first Tuesday in April
*Montana	1888	Last Friday in April
Nebraska	1872	April 22—Legal Holiday

STATE	FIRST ENACTED	NOW OBSERVED
*Nevada	1887	Last Friday in April
*New Hampshire	1886	Last Friday in April
*New Jersey	1884	Last Friday in April
New Mexico	1890	Second Friday in March
*New York	1889	Last Friday in April
North Carolina	1893	First Friday after March 15
*North Dakota	1882	Last Friday in April
*Ohio	1882	Last Friday in April
Oklahoma	1898	Friday after second Monday in February
*Oregon	1889	Last Friday in April
*Pennsylvania	1885	Last Friday in April
*Rhode Island	1887	Last Friday in April
South Carolina	1898	First Friday in December
*South Dakota	1884	Last Friday in April
Tennessee	1875	First Friday in March
Texas	1890	Third Friday in January
*Utah	1925	Last Friday in April
Vermont	1885	First Friday in May
Virginia	1892	Second Friday in March
Washington	1894	Second Wednesday in April
West Virginia	1883	Second Friday in April
*Wisconsin	1892	Last Friday in April

STATE	FIRST ENACTED	NOW OBSERVED
Wyoming	1888	Last Monday in April
District of Columbia	1920	Third Friday in April
Guam	—	Last Friday in October
Puerto Rico	—	Friday after Thanksgiving

---

*States that have passed legislation designating the last Friday in April as Arbor Day.

SIX

Street and Highway Planting

→≫≫

Planting along our streets and highways has become a highly specialized science. There are certain general principles relating to the use of trees that it might be well for everyone to understand, particularly those who drive the highways of the country, so that they can better appreciate the problems involved. Many things must be taken into consideration in planting trees along any highway, and the better the landscape engineer understands these and properly evaluates them, the more permanent will be the planting he creates. It has been justly said that some of the splendid old trees in the South, such as the live oak, when properly planted, will outlast anything along or in the highway that man can build, including the roadbeds and the bridges. Hence, it is most important to select the right trees and place them properly for permanent growth.

Generally speaking, it is advisable to use primarily trees that are native in the same vicinity in order that the highway as a whole merges with the surrounding open country. For this reason, definitely shaped trees like blue spruce and fir, especially when the color of the foliage is conspicuous, should not be used along highways where high speeds are common since they can easily divert the attention of the driver. Also, highly "ornamental" flowering or fruiting trees have been found to be a hazard because of their distracting beauty and falling fruit. Vandals also stop their cars at inappropriate and even dangerous places on the highway in order to break off flowering or fruiting branches. This also creates serious damage to the trees, often permanently marring their beauty.

In the open country, trees should not be regularly spaced but rather should be planted irregularly 75 to 300 feet apart so that if one tree dies or must be removed, it does not spoil the continuity of the planting. Regularly spaced highway trees are the most costly to maintain. Such planting is often done along slower-driven parkways, but a few missing trees can easily spoil the regular symmetry of any such planting. Hence, except on carefully policed parkways, the use of conspicuous ornamentals on high-speed highways in the open country is not advisable.

Trees might well be informally grouped, placed well back of the right of way so that a future widening of the highway would not necessitate their removal. They should be used to frame pictures in the landscape, to augment what nature has already provided and, in some cases, to hide objectionable views or objects. They are used to define the highways, for they are often planted on the outside of the curves in the road to warn the motorist of an approaching turn. They can be so placed as to give the impression of "funnel" planting—converging lines on either side of the road to give the psychological impression of approaching narrowness, especially when the road narrows or speed should be reduced for some permanent obstruction or hazard.

Trees should certainly not be planted under existing utility wires or where they will create hazards for the regular plowing of snow. They can be used to soften the harsh lines of bridges or other construction objects. A single variety of tree should not be planted along mile after mile of highway, for this lends monotony to the landscape and especially to the driver who is looking at it.

Selection of the varieties of trees used should be done carefully. Sturdy-wooded, long-lived trees that have a low maintenance cost should be selected. Disease-resistant and insect-free trees particularly should be chosen to reduce the ever-present maintenance costs. It is mere folly to plant a highway with disease-susceptible trees, knowing in advance that funds are not available for their annual care. Most of the *Prunus* species, for instance, should be omitted; because they are so susceptible to attacks from the tent caterpillar and other leaf-eating insects, they can be most unsightly unless properly cared for annually.

⇥⟫ *STREET PLANTING*

While the planting of our major highways is done chiefly by highly trained state and federal experts and is out of the hands of the average citizen, tree planting along the streets of the towns and cities is another matter. Frequently this type of planting can be undertaken within the boundaries of one's own property. There are a few generalities about this type of planting that need to be kept in mind.

Attempting to grow trees in the heart of our largest cities is one thing; growing them in the suburban areas of such cities or in the thousands of towns and villages across the country is another. Very few trees will thrive under the exceedingly tough growing conditions of the city (see the list of such trees on pages 51–52), while others might be tried in areas where more soil space is available and where traffic hazards, soot, and smoke are not so severe.

In the case of some of the major office buildings so frequently erected, trees are very much wanted as an ornamental feature, but they must resist terrific odds in order to survive. Paved walks are all about them, and in some places heating pipes are installed near their roots to be turned on in the winter to keep the snow melted on the sidewalks above. About all that can be said of such planting is that only the most resistant varieties should be selected, and the amount of open ground about their roots should be as much as will be allowed by the architects.

The minimum amount of open ground necessary for a tree to grow is 8 feet square, though the larger the better. Often a space 12 feet square is provided. In many European cities and in this country as well, widely woven iron grating is placed over this soil to allow water to seep through to the roots while at the same time providing for foot traffic over it without pounding it down to such an extent that it bakes almost as hard as concrete when it is dried out. Such a condition is not conducive to the free passage of air or rainwater to the roots, without which the tree will frequently sicken and die.

Much attention should be given to the matter of tree planting before a street is finally laid out by town engineers. In the horse and buggy days, trees were planted along the street with tree trunks often abutting the curb. This may have been all right then, but today, with automotive transportation what it is, much more room must be given drivers on these streets. If this is not done, accidents (often the result of skidding) are serious, not only to the traffic but to the trees themselves. Many trees will fail to recover from a serious trunk injury in which the bark has been stripped from the trunk for a longitudinal distance of 6 feet and halfway around the trunk.

The best method of planting along suburban streets is to set aside a strip of ground between the sidewalk and the property line on which trees are planted. This strip should be a minimum of 7 to 8 feet square—better still, 12 feet if some of the larger-growing types of trees are to be used. This arrangement is ideal, for it does not encroach on private property yet affords plenty of space for the future development of the trees. It places the tree away from the service lines, pipes, and sewers that are frequently placed at the edge of the street paving, a decided advantage because when these are opened up and tree roots are in the way, they are usually mercilessly cut. This system is working remarkably well in the suburban developments of many large cities, especially in Denver, Colorado, and some areas around Cleveland, Ohio. The property owner can take care of the grass in this strip, and the town will be responsible for the care of the trees. This type of cooperation between the town and the private property owner is obviously an arrangement feasible only when the street and abutting properties have been laid out with this in mind, and certain town ordinances have been approved for the arrangement to work successfully.

In older suburban areas where such space is not available but where the houses are set back considerably from the property line along the street, there has been a move on to plant the trees on the edge of the private property. In other words, the sidewalk may or may not abut the street, but even if it does not and there is a small grass strip between the sidewalk and street, no trees would be planted in it. They would instead be planted on private property, particularly if the property line abutted the sidewalk. This method of tree planting obviously creates several complications. It would require special town ordinances governing the care and removal of such trees. It would also require the cooperation and enthusiasm of the original property owners. Once the system is agreed on and approved, it is seldom that purchasers of such property already planted with street trees seriously object.

This plan has many good points, especially from the standpoint of the health of the trees. They would be away from the street and its destructive traffic; their major roots would be away from the destructive ditch-digging operations frequently encountered; and property owners as a rule would take pride in their general good health. This plan is working in some areas, but it is obvious that it takes considerable cooperation between property owners and town officials. It can result in more beautiful trees and more permanent trees, which both groups should obviously desire.

In many cities and towns neither one of these methods of tree planting is possible, and the trees must be planted between the sidewalk and the curb. No tree should ever be planted closer to the curb than 3½ feet, and the farther away it is, the better for the tree and the passing traffic. The ideal width for this strip of grass between curb and sidewalk would be 12 feet, and the tree should not be centered in it but planted closer to the sidewalk than the street.

Street trees should not be planted opposite each other but should alternate, allowing for a greater development of the tops. Spacing should be at least 75 feet apart. Planting closer than this (except in the use of very small tree species) only creates more costly maintenance and sometimes may necessitate the removal of some trees that are crowding others. It is far better to plant fewer trees and take care of them properly, allowing them plenty of room for development, than to crowd them in order to make a "show" while they are young, at the same time greatly increasing their maintenance cost later.

One other point should be mentioned in connection with this—the size of the tree planted. It has been found by many whose responsibility it is to plant trees along our town and city streets that smaller trees are much better for general street planting—smaller in size at the start and smaller in permanent stature. Some are recommended on page 86. It takes quite an expenditure of money, labor, and equipment to remove a 100-foot American elm, as many tree superintendents are finding out. Trees with a mature height under 40 feet can be far less costly to remove.

Also, it is far easier to plant several trees 1 inch in diameter than one 4 inches in diameter. Smaller trees are more easily acclimated to new situations and, if properly root-pruned and top-pruned in the nursery, will grow better the first two years than larger trees. The cost of transplanting is also considerably less. Consequently, the tree superintendent can concentrate on a comparatively deeper hole and on comparatively more good soil, and better attention can be given to the water requirements of the new, smaller tree. With mounting labor and transportation costs these two points are going to prove very important in every street tree-planting program in the immediate future. However, smaller trees are more easily broken, and admittedly there are always places where larger trees must be planted.

The question of whether all the trees on one street should be of the same species is a troublesome one and best not discussed here. It should be repeated, however, that formal tree planting (all one species) can prove to be the most costly type along streets where some may be killed or removed for one reason or other, since replacement costs of larger and larger trees mount annually. Many New England towns that planted only elm trees now wish that they had used several types of shade trees, for a fast-working disease can take its toll and destroy a "one-type" planting quickly.

Some towns, such as Brookline, Massachusetts, have a policy whereby small streets are planted with one type of tree only. The governing shade-tree commissioners see to it that many different types are used throughout the city. It is not without reason to expect that the majority of property owners on one street might decide on the Sargent cherry, for instance, whereas on another street another majority would request the littleleaf European linden. An intelligent shade-tree commission, with certain standard policies and always ready with helpful suggestions in such cases, could easily mold a most interesting overall tree-planting program that would go a long way to make the town beautiful and interesting and the citizens of that town proud of their trees for that reason.

⇢⟫ SMALL STREET TREES

Here are a few suggestions of small trees that might be used along suburban streets—a glance at the list of Low Trees on pages 56–57 will undoubtedly bring to mind many others. Trees for narrow streets could be selected from the list of Columnar Trees on pages 64–65, where one will find many suggestions. The approximate mature heights of the trees below are given for convenience:

	HEIGHT		HEIGHT
Acer argutum	35'	*C. monogyna inermis*	20'
A. buergerianum	20'	*C. monogyna* 'Stricta'	20'
A. campestre	25'	*C. nitida*	30'
A. capillipes	30'	*C. phaenopyrum*	30'
A. carpinifolium	30'	*C. pinnatifida major*	20'
A. circinatum	25'	*C. pruinosa*	20'
A. ginnala	20'	*C. punctata*	30'
A. glabrum	24'	*C. succulenta*	15'
A. griseum	25'	*C. viridis*	35'
A. monspessulanum	25'	*Evodia daniellii*	25'
A. tataricum	30'	*Fraxinus holotricha*	35'
A. triflorum	24'	*F. mariesii*	24'
A. tschonoskii	20'	*F. velutina glabra*	20–45'
Carpinus betulus 'Globosa'	25'	*Halesia carolina*	30'
C. betulus horizontalis	25'	*Koelreuteria paniculata*	30'
C. caroliniana	35'	*Ligustrum lucidum*	30'
C. caroliniana 'Pyramidalis'	36'	*Maytenus boaria*	35'
C. japonica	45'	*Prunus serrulata* and varieties	20'
C. orientalis	25'	*Pterostyrax hispida*	45'
Chionanthus virginicus	30'	*Quercus engleriana*	30'
Cornus florida	40'	*Q. libani*	30'
C. kousa	20'	*Robinia* 'Idaho'	25'
C. mas	24'	*Styrax japonica*	30'
Crataegus arnoldiana	30'	*S. obassia*	30'
C. coccinioides	20'	*Symplocos paniculata*	35'
C. crus-galli	35'	*Syringa reticulata*	30'
C. laevigata	15'	*Viburnum prunifolium*	15'
C. lavallei	20'	*V. rufidulum*	30'
C. mollis	30'	*V. sieboldii*	30'
C. monogyna	30'		

⇛ STREET TREES FOR MEDIUM-WIDTH STREETS

	HEIGHT		HEIGHT
Acer maximowiczianum	45'	*Ligustrum lucidum*	30'
A. platanoides	90'	*Liquidambar styraciflua*	125'
Celtis bungeana	45'	*Maytenus boaria*	35'
Crataegus crus-galli	36'	*Melia azedarach*	45'
Fraxinus ornus	60'	*Ostrya virginiana*	60'
F. velutina	20–45'	*Oxydendrum arboreum*	75'
Halesia monticola	90'	*Pittosporum undulatum*	50'

	HEIGHT		HEIGHT
Prunus caroliniana	20–40'	*Sassafras albidum*	60'
Quercus coccinea	75'	*Schinus molle*	40'
Q. ilex	60'	*Sophora japonica*	75'
Q. imbricaria	75'	*Tilia cordata*	90'
Q. laurifolia	60'	*T. euchlora*	60'
Q. phellos	50'	*T. platyphyllos*	120'
Q. suber	60'	*T. tomentosa*	90'
Robinia pseudoacacia 'Ihermis'	75'	*Washingtonia robusta*	90'

⇥≫ STREET TREES FOR WIDE STREETS

	HEIGHT		HEIGHT
Acer macrophyllum	90'	*Magnolia grandiflora*	90'
A. pseudoplatanus	90'	*Phellodendron amurense*	30'
A. saccharum	120'	*Pinus strobus*	100–150'
Brachychiton acerifolium	60'	*Pittosporum rhombifolium*	80'
Casuarina equisetifolia	70'	*Platanus acerifolia*	100'
Cedrus species	120–150'	*P. orientalis*	90'
Celtis jessoensis	70'	*P. racemosa*	120'
C. laevigata	90'	*Prunus sargentii*	75'
Cercidiphyllum japonicum	60–100'	*Quercus agrifolia*	90'
Cinnamomum camphora	40'	*Q. cerris*	100'
Cupressus macrocarpa	45'	*Q. macrocarpa*	80'
Eucalyptus species	20–200'	*Q. palustris*	75'
Fraxinus americana	120'	*Q. phellos*	50'
F. pennsylvanica lanceolata	60'	*Q. rubra*	75'
F. velutina	20–45'	*Q. virginiana*	60'
Ginkgo biloba	120'	*Roystonea regia*	70'
Gleditsia triacanthos	135'	*Tilia petiolaris*	75'
G. triacanthos inermis 'Moraine'	135'	*T. tomentosa*	90'
Grevillea robusta	150'	*Ulmus carpinifolia* 'Christine	
Kalopanax pictus	90'	Buisman'	90'
Lagunaria patersonii	50'	*Zelkova carpinifolia*	75'
Liriodendron tulipifera	150'	*Z. serrata*	90'

SEVEN

Dwarf Trees

→»

Dwarf trees can be placed in four general categories. First are those that occur naturally. If a thousand seedlings are lined out in the nursery row, a few may differ from the others in habit, color, form, and speed of growth, among them one or two that are slow growing or "dwarfs." These are the natural dwarfs. If seeds of these are planted, they might revert to the normal species in growth, but if they are asexually propagated by cutting or grafts, they will maintain their unusual slow-growth habit. Some species are more prone to produce such "sports," as they are known, than others. The Lawson cypress, Norway spruce, and Hinoki false cypress are good examples.

Then there are the dwarf fruit trees, which are dwarfed by grafting scions of normal varieties on root stocks of dwarf varieties.

Next there are espaliers—plants that are severely pruned to restrain vegetative growth and so dwarfed manually. Maintenance of espaliers is a continual undertaking.

Finally there is the group of plants that are kept dwarfed by the age-old Oriental practice of Bonsai. Thus, by finding dwarf trees in nature or training normal trees to grow in desired patterns, gardeners have dwarf trees for use in their modern gardens.

→» DWARF FRUIT TREES

In Europe, especially in England, much emphasis has been placed on growing smaller fruit trees as a result of gardens being crowded into smaller areas. The objective is to have a regular type of fruit, even a variety of fruit such as the 'McIntosh' apple, for instance, borne on a tree of much smaller habit than the standard 'McIntosh' tree. This is done by using special understock that has a retarding effect on the vegetative growth of the 'McIntosh' apple. Much work with dwarfing understocks was originally done at the East Malling Research Station, East Malling, Kent, England, which is why we hear so much about the 'Malling' understocks today. A series of such understocks was selected for apples and given numbers I to XVIII. 'Malling No. IX' is used a great deal now for some varieties of apples, resulting in very early bearing—often only two years after grafting—and low trees. Those under 10 feet tall are easily pruned and sprayed by a man on the ground. Such plants are desirable especially on small properties.

These are not the only dwarfing understocks for apples by any means. Much experimenting has been done at many of the state and federal experiment stations, to find new and better dwarfing understocks for other fruits as well as apples. A clonal understock is best (that is, one that is asexually propagated) so that all the understocks have the same genetic constitution and will not vary. A tree grafted on such an understock will produce results that can be predicted in advance.

Sometimes, as in the case of some pear varieties, "double working" is necessary; that is, one variety is grafted or budded on a certain understock, and after a year's growth another variety is budded or grafted on the first. The second variety may form a poor union with the understock itself, but the intermediate piece makes a strong union and the second variety makes a correspondingly strong union on the intermediate piece. The resulting tree is a strong, well-knit unit, dwarfed by the understock.

It is readily seen that the work with dwarfing understocks is long and arduous, taking years before final success or failure of the operation can be properly judged. It also takes an advanced technique in the art of propagation. Certain types of dwarf fruit trees are already available, but experimentation on dwarfing has by no means stopped. In fact, quite the reverse is true. It will not be long before dwarfing understocks will be sought for some of our overvigorous standard trees. Many is the time when a small, slow-growing tree is desired in cramped surroundings, and such trees are at present hard to find commercially.

⇶ *ESPALIERS*

The patient, time-consuming work necessary in growing espaliers against a wall or trellis is not as yet very popular in America. There are some who are growing fruit trees in this fashion, chiefly pears, apples, and peaches. One must have a thorough knowledge of pruning, when it is best done, and how to train and bend young stems so that they can finally be maintained in geometric patterns against the wall or on a wired support. Since this is an artificial way of coaxing growth, one must keep at it each year in order to keep the tree restrained and to enable it to produce flowers and bear the proper number of fruits.

Pruning small trees in espalier fashion is an art. No words can be substituted for experience in this respect, but a few general principles can be briefly mentioned. In the first place, the original side branches should come from well down on the trunk, possibly a foot from the ground level. The manner in which these are carefully selected and trained so that the tree will be well balanced is most important. These are actually the main shoots; side shoots originating from these leaders must be continually cut or pinched back practically to the fruit spurs during the months of July, August, and September, a painstaking process that must be undertaken at least once a month to keep the plant well restrained.

The leaders must be cut back also, preferably during the winter, the amount depending on the additional training needed. If the tree is a young one and has more area of trellis to cover, this leader pruning will not be as severe as it would be if the tree had reached its desired size. In such a case the leaders would be cut back to a single bud. Usually espaliers are not over 8 feet high.

There are several geometric patterns into which espaliers can be fashioned. Branches must be loosely tied to some trellis support so that the weight of the fruits will not break them. Fan espaliers also are popular, but in all types it is essential that the lateral branches coming from the sides of the main leaders continually be pruned or pinched back during the growing season.

When it is desired to force a horizontal branch into a vertical position, the horizontal is tied solidly at the point where the turn is wanted. Then, in order to get the branch to make a right-angle turn without breaking, it may be necessary to tie it up first only a third of the way, let it grow for several weeks or even months, then pull it a little more toward the vertical, and finally the last gap can be closed after a period of time. The fruit spurs are carefully chosen, some of them removed so that no one branch will be overloaded. The manner in which the fruit spurs are selected and others are removed develops into the intricate technique that makes for success or failure with espaliers.

The discouraging part to me has always been the realization that, after all, these plants are fruit trees and in order to obtain maximum fruit production from them they must be sprayed properly and on schedule, a time-consuming task for all except the most ardent enthusiasts. It nevertheless does make an interesting hobby for those who have the time and patience to pursue it.

Growing dwarf fruit trees either as dwarfs or as espaliers is a fruit-growing problem, one on which considerable information has been published. Space will not permit discussing it further here. Suffice it to say that considerable interest will be given dwarfing understocks in the immediate future, particularly for certain ornamental plants. It is a fascinating study, chiefly for the expert plant propagator, and one who has the time and patience to wait years for proper results to become apparent.

⇥⟫⟫ *"BONSAI," THE ART OF TRAINING DWARF TREES*

Ancient customs have been handed down by the Japanese regarding the training of the interesting dwarf trees so characteristic of their gardens and homes. There are several reasons for their existence. In the first place, Japanese and Chinese gardens are usually small, for space is at a premium. This is particularly true in Japan, where the art of making gardens on a very small scale is centuries old. Then, too, the Orientals' well-known appreciation of the aesthetic value of living plants has been a prime factor in their cultivation. It often takes fifty to one hundred years to grow a worthy specimen dwarf tree, yet it is possible by twisting the trunk and restraining the growth of tops and roots to give a comparatively young plant the appearance of great age. This treatment requires a thorough knowledge of horticulture as well as painstaking patience, but many Japanese are fascinated with "Bonsai" and practice it as a pastime.

⇥⟫⟫ TRAINING

Most woody plants can be dwarfed if given the proper training. If the branches and roots of growing plants are vigorously restrained from developing rapidly, the individuals soon become dwarfed and this is the principle underlying all training. Then, too, great care is given to the training of the trunk, the spread of the branches and their shape, and the spread of the roots since each can be so trained as to give the impression of great age. Many methods have been devised through the centuries for attaining these ends. Maples, bamboos, cherries, pines, hollies, oaks, azaleas, junipers, and many other plants have been used. They are grown in comparatively small containers, kept potbound throughout their existence, and carefully and judiciously pruned to maintain the desired type of growth.

Whenever possible, the Japanese start with plants that have already been

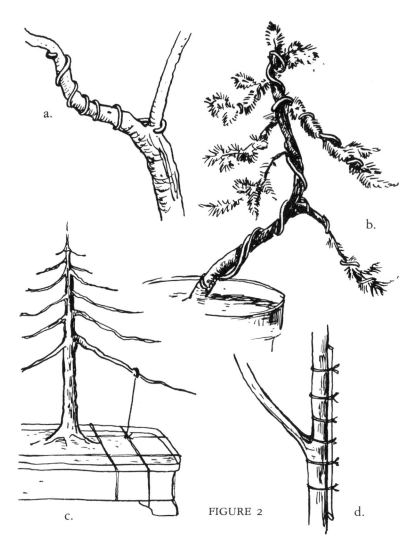

FIGURE 2

Training bonsai. (a and b) The branches are wound with bent copper wire and thus held in place. (c) A lower branch is tied down to its proper place. (d) A branch is pulled upright by tying it to a stake.

dwarfed by nature. These are searched for in the high mountains, in regions often unfamiliar to the ordinary traveler. Such plants are frequently found growing in high, rocky crevices, just barely existing for lack of sufficient nourishment. If these are dug immediately and removed, they may very well succumb at once, for the delicate balance between the size of the root system and its surroundings is easily upset. The plant hunter may wait several years before venturing to remove such plants from their rocky dwelling. At first he will root-prune a small portion of the plant and leave it in place for a year; then he will return and root-prune another small portion, repeating this process until it is safe to move the plant. In this way splendid specimens are obtained that have already been trained with the assistance of Mother Nature herself.

If dwarf plants are to be trained from the seedling stage, the smallest and weakest seedlings are selected. Conifers are considerably easier to train because they do not form adventitious buds as readily as do the broad-leaved plants. The seedling is placed in a very small pot. If there is a tap root, it is pruned considerably, and if a central leader is present, it, too, is cut back. In order to obtain the desired effect, only certain branches are allowed to develop. Sometimes a copper wire is bent around the branch to hold it in a certain position. Later, after a training period of months or years, it is removed when the branch holds its desired shape.

To give the correct appearance of wind-contorted shape, the main stem is often twisted around an upright, and after a formative period the upright is removed. This twisting in itself is a dwarfing process since frequently it breaks a large number of the conducting vessels in the stem. Branches are twisted in like manner. They may all be trained on one side of the plant or arranged to droop on one side of the pot or trained in any one of a dozen different ways. The Japanese gardener usually has a model in mind when he trains his plant, some wind-twisted tree that he is trying to reproduce in miniature form, and it is surprising for the uninitiated to observe how accurate these reproductions can be.

Often in nature one observes old, gnarled trees whose larger roots are exposed, especially when growing in rocky places where there is still soil. This effect is reproduced by the Bonsai artist by growing his seedling in charcoal and moss for a period sufficient to induce long roots. When the plant is removed to its permanent container, a part of these roots is left to develop above the soil level, eventually aiding in giving the plant the appearance of great age.

⇛ PRUNING, REPOTTING, AND WATERING

Not all branches are entirely removed. Some of these century-old plants have numerous picturesque stubs, certain gardeners believing that these add to the beauty of the plant. Any diseased tissue on such stubs is carefully scraped, disinfected, and painted. Sometimes, in order to gain the appearance of old age rapidly, taller plants that have been growing normally are used. The basal branches are cut back to give a stubby appearance, the top is entirely cut off, the plant is dug up, and after a substantial root-prune, it is

This bonsai-trained Japanese white pine (Pinus parviflora) *is over seventy-five years old.*

placed in a small pot. Then certain of the adventitious buds are allowed to develop, or else scions are grafted at the desired places.

Grafting is also resorted to when certain shoots die; if a very important branch has died, it may take many years for a new one to grow to sufficient size from an adventitious bud. The Japanese are particularly adept at this type of grafting and take great pains in training an individual branch by pinching the buds back here or twisting the branch there, forcing the latter to grow in the desired fashion. The pruning and pinching operations are done during the active growing period since the development of branches from adventitious buds is then more frequent.

Dwarf trees are repotted every four or five years for two reasons: it is necessary to remove some of the newly developed fibrous roots so that the tree will remain dwarfed; and it is necessary to mix a small amount of fertilizer with the soil. Since these trees are forced to grow in very small containers, there is insufficient room for enough soil to allow new root development unless the plant is artificially stimulated with nutrients.

It is also advisable to keep a fresh layer of green moss on the surface of the soil. This not only adds the impression of age but keeps the soil from drying out. The containers are usually provided with a hole in the base for proper drainage. Because of their small root system and the small containers in which they are grown, these dwarf trees cannot lose much water through transpiration and still survive. Consequently, they must be grown in a shaded location. The shade house in which the Arnold Arboretum maintains its collection was designed and erected especially for the purpose. Constructed of redwood, the top and sides of the house are covered with strips 1½ inches wide with similar spaces left between each strip. This supplies plenty of shade and at the same time keeps the atmosphere considerably cooler and reasonably moist. In the hot summer days there is some danger of the soil becoming too dry, and at such times the plants need special attention. Spraying the foliage with water once or twice a day during the hottest spells of summer is advisable in order to keep the plant in good condition.

Dwarf trees cannot be considered primarily indoor plants. They may be displayed indoors for short periods but must be grown in the open a greater part of the time.

⇢≫ WINTER PROTECTION OF BONSAI

Although many of these trees are hardy, they cannot survive our northern winters because of their shallow root system unless given some winter protection. A Japanese maple, for instance, growing normally in the ground may survive a winter during which the temperature goes to 20 degrees below zero, although the top of the plant may be killed to the ground. However, in these small pots the roots of the dwarf trees would be subjected to temperatures almost as low as those of the surrounding atmosphere, and consequently the whole plant would be killed. During the winter in the North, they are best put in cold frames or pits that are well protected with glass and over which boards and mats are placed during the most severe weather. In our cold storage house where these plants are displayed in winter, the temperature is maintained above freezing although occasionally the outside temperature may drop to zero. Another danger from freezing temperatures is that with the expansion of freezing soil the containers may break. Although these are seldom ornate because the Japanese believe that the plant itself should be the point of interest, their simplicity alone is beautiful and makes them important adjuncts to any such collection and thus worthy of full protection.

EIGHT

Pruning Ornamental Trees

→≫

A little knowledge of what to prune and how to do it goes a long way in assisting plants to grow into well-balanced specimens and assets in any garden. Conversely, the indiscriminate hacking of shrubs and trees at given heights is the quickest means by which otherwise beautiful plantings are rendered unsightly.

→≫ WHEN TO PRUNE

As far as the growth of the plant is concerned, pruning can be done almost any time except in the early summer; if done then, the new growth may not have sufficient time to mature before winter and killing may result. However, to maximize flowering, such ornamental shrubs divide into two groups: those that bloom in the early spring such as daphne, forsythia, and lilac, which should be pruned after they flower to obtain the full benefit of their flower in the current year; and those that bloom on the current year's wood, such as hydrangea and rose of Sharon, which can be pruned in the late winter or early spring and still be expected to bloom the same year. Trees are usually pruned in the late winter and early spring (with the exception of those that "bleed" profusely such as birch, maple, and yellowwood, which should be pruned in summer) for at that time of year, before the leaves appear, it is much easier to see which branches should be removed; it also gives the tree the entire spring and summer to form new growth. However, they can be pruned anytime, except the "bleeders" as noted above.

⇶ WHAT TO PRUNE

Young trees should be pruned early.

Timely corrective pruning saves trouble later. If the tree is one that normally has a single trunk, see that only one straight trunk develops and cut out any others that try to grow. Occasionally several branches grow out from the trunk at the same place, and these will always make weak crotches. All but one should be removed. Unless most of these are removed at once, the plant will be a bush (and a poor one at that) and never a fine tree. Sometimes young shrubs should be "headed back" a bit to force them to grow more branches from the base. A forsythia with just one leader, for instance, would never become an interesting shrub. In other words, know how the tree or shrub will develop at maturity and help it early in life by selecting the proper leaders and removing the others if necessary.

Dead, broken, or diseased branches.

Broken roots and one-third of the branches at transplanting time.

Some roots are always cut when a plant is dug. A good general rule is to remove about one-third of the total linear branch length when the plant is moved by thinning out weak or damaged branches and correcting structural defects. This compensates for the loss of roots that have been cut in the transplanting operation and always results in more vigorous plants at the end of the first year. This is hard for the home owner to do since the new plant looks smaller than the original specimen purchased from the nursery, but it is always better for the plant in the end. When plants are to be moved from their native place in the woods, it is advisable to root-prune (merely forcing a spade in the ground in a wide circle about the plant) one year in advance, to force the production of many roots close to the base so the transplanting operation will be easier. Nursery-grown plants are usually root-pruned periodically.

Structural defects.

Never allow two equally vigorous leaders to develop on exactly opposite sides of the same trunk. This will always be a "weak" crotch, susceptible to splitting as the tree grows older. It may spoil the symmetry of the entire tree when this happens.

Suckers from the bases of grafted or budded plants.

Many plants used in gardens, such as roses, crab apples, lilacs, and fruit trees, are either grafted or budded on another kind of understock. Usually this is never more than a foot or so from the ground. Hence all suckers developing *below* this point should be removed as soon as they are observed because if allowed to develop, they will not only spoil the symmetry of the plant and sap the strength of the variety wanted but will develop into an entirely different and usually undesirable plant. Frequently, when two kinds of blossoms or leaves are seen on one plant, this is the reason. Cut out understock suckers as soon as they develop.

Hedges, screens, and windbreaks.

The objective is to increase their density, for if a twig is cut back a few inches, it frequently sends out more than one new shoot to take the place of the one removed. This growth habit of plants can be utilized to force them to grow denser.

Certain limbs for utility purposes.

The lower limbs of street trees or limbs that interfere with a certain view, walk, window, or wire sometimes must be removed.

Girdling root.

Close observation of the base of poor growing trees often discloses a girdling root, that is, a root partly on the surface of the soil or just beneath which is growing in such a way as to choke or constrict the trunk of the tree or a larger root. Such girdling roots can do real harm and usually should be cut as near as possible to the trunk of the tree or at least at the point where they are doing the damage.

Older branches for shrub rejuvenation.

Thin out the older branches over a period of a few years or cut the shrub to within a few inches of the ground in late winter or early spring. The obvious exception to this would be weak-growing shrubs or those that have been budded or grafted. Never cut any shrub off at a horizontal line several feet above the ground. This is an artificial practice, outmoded for many years, and always results in unsightly specimens. Thin out here and there, cut one branch back hard and another not nearly as much, and thin out from the base, simultaneously. In this way an old plant can be reduced in size, still look natural, and produce new growth at different places from the ground on up to the top.

These, then, are the reasons for pruning. Be certain the reason for pruning is understood before it is done because it is always a dwarfing process, and some plants never need any. Study the situation and have a good reason for all pruning.

→>> HOW TO PRUNE

Make all cuts clean with sharp tools.

Never leave any long stubs.

A short stub may never heal over and this may prove to be a source of infection. Make all cuts back to a quarter of an inch above a bud or branch or the collar (a short, enlarged part at the base of the branch where wound-healing chemicals abound).

The removal of a large limb should be done in three cuts. First, an undercut is made, sawing one-third or one-half through the limb, about a foot from the trunk of the tree. Then the upper cut is started 1 to 2 inches beyond the first cut away from the trunk on the top of the branch and sawed down until the limb falls. As the two cuts near each other and the limb begins to sag, its weight will break the wood of the center and the wood will jump clear without stripping and tearing the bark down the tree trunk. Finally, the short stump is removed at the collar.

In the past it was suggested that all cuts over 4 inches in diameter should be painted with a tree paint, preferably one with a bituminous base, but recent tests made by the U.S. Department of the Interior have shown that no painting of any cuts is necessary if they are cleanly made.

Disinfect tools after each cut on a diseased plant.

A satisfactory disinfectant to have in a suitable can for this purpose is alcohol.

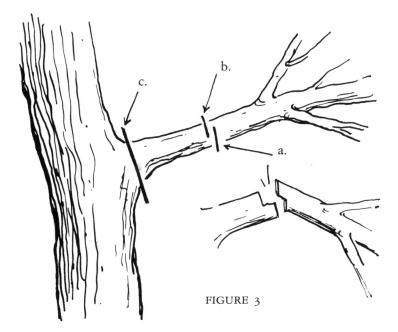

FIGURE 3

To remove a branch without stripping the bark from the tree: (a) cut halfway through the underside of the branch about a foot or so from the trunk; (b) make a second cut on the upper side of the branch about an inch or so closer to the trunk. The branch will now break away without stripping the bark. (c) After the branch has come down, carefully remove the stub.

Shear hedges wider at base than the top.

Both evergreen and deciduous hedges should be sheared in such a way that they are wider at the base than the top, thus allowing the important lower branches plenty of room, light, and air. If the hedge is pruned narrower at the base than the top, the lower branches often will die from lack of light. Once these lower branches die on an evergreen hedge, it is practically impossible to force any new ones to grow in the same place. Deciduous hedges, on the other hand, are mostly vigorous growing plants, and when they become open at the base, the entire hedge can be cut to within a few inches of the ground in the early spring and will quickly start a new vigorous growth from the ground, thus forming a new hedge in a few years' time.

Pruning need not be difficult. It is important, however, that one understand exactly why the contemplated pruning is necessary and can visualize the probable results. Even yews and rhododendrons can be heavily pruned and old plants rejuvenated by the expert gardener who has previously studied what to do and when to do it. In the case of pruning yews and rhododendrons heavily, always make the pruning cut *above* a few buds or branches. Never make the cut below the lowest buds or branches.

NINE

General List
of Recommended
Trees

→⟩⟩⟩

The following trees have been selected because of their superior landscape qualities. It is not intended that this be a record of botanical descriptions. Far from it! Rather, it is a description of the chief characteristics of these trees with special reference to their landscape usefulness. Both Latin and common names are given, height, coldest zone of hardiness according to the map on the inside covers of this book, origin or habitat, and the approximate time of introduction to cultivation. Information is given also concerning flowers, fruits, foliage, autumn color, and winter-twig characteristics but only when these are ornamentally significant. If no information is given in any one of these categories, it means that the tree in question is not valued for that particular reason in the garden.

The trees have necessarily been chosen somewhat arbitrarily but only after careful consideration has been given to those in the secondary list. Most of the hardiest trees listed here are grown in the Arnold Arboretum, where they have been under observation for years. The more tender types are among the best for the warmer areas of the United States. Both amateur and professional gardeners might do well to confine their interest to the trees in the recommended list, especially when time and space are limiting factors. All are grown in the United States and Canada, most of them available from commercial sources on record at the Arnold Arboretum. When time, money, and space are not limiting factors, trees might be selected from the secondary list for further trial.

Occasionally reference is made to the Horticultural Colour Chart of the Royal Horticultural Society. This and the Color Fan of the American Horticultural Society are the best color charts available for comparing the colors of plants, the latter being the easier to use in the field.

If an *x* appears in front of the specific name, for example, *x Amelanchier grandiflora,* it designates this tree as a hybrid, and seed sown from it may not yield seedlings like the parent tree. All offspring propagated from it by seed are clones, and to obtain young trees like the parent, propagation must be by asexual means, such as by way of cuttings or grafting.

An asterisk (*) in front of the description of habit, flowers, fruits, foliage, autumn color, or twigs means that the tree is grown particularly for this landscape characteristic. If no asterisk appears, these characteristics may still be present but not meritorious.

⇶ ABIES

Firs of one species or another are native over a wide part of North America, especially in the higher altitudes. Some such as the balsam fir *(A. balsamea)* and its southern counterpart, the Fraser fir *(A. fraseri)*, do not make good ornamentals in temperate regions because they require the cool, moist atmosphere of the mountains. The white fir *(A. concolor)* grows well in many places other than its native Rocky Mountains and is frequently seen to do well under city conditions, but only where soot and gases are not too prevalent.

All firs are generally stiff in habit, pyramidal in shape, and have regular whorls of rigid, horizontal branches. Because of this, they stand out markedly in any landscape and as a consequence should be used with discretion. Their needles usually remain on the trees four to five years before falling off. The cones of all firs are borne in an erect position and at maturity are 2 to 5 inches long but quickly fall apart, unlike those of the spruce, hemlock, and Douglas-fir *(Pseudotsuga)*, which are pendant and do not fall apart when mature. They are ornamental but do not appear every year and even then are not conspicuous for a very long time. Firs are seldom troubled with serious insect infestation or disease. Their biggest fault is that if their lower branches die or are removed, no new ones will grow back in the same place. Consequently, to be kept symmetrical, all the branches must be kept in a vigorous growing condition. Additionally, topping such trees permanently mars the form because of the single straight trunk and definitely pyramidal habit.

One marked characteristic of firs is that the needles, when they fall from the twig, leave it smooth to the touch, with no rough leaf bases, as in the case of hemlock and spruce. When other means of differentiating between the genera fail, this is certainly bound to work.

The firs are most popular as Christmas trees and are often grown commercially for this purpose. It used to be that they could be placed in a bucket of gravel filled with water to persuade them to hold their needles much longer than normal; now various sprays are used to accomplish the same purpose.

It is important to recognize that firs demand a cool, moist climate in which to grow. I have seen several community projects in eastern Massachusetts attempt to use the balsam fir as a living Christmas tree, only to see such trees eventually die after receiving the best of care. If only someone had informed the leaders of such projects at the start that the white fir or the Douglas-fir would have been greatly superior for the purpose, it would have saved much disappointment and time.

Firs, therefore, are trees of limited usefulness in landscape plantings because of climate requirements as well as their decidedly stiff pyramidal form. Hemlocks, in comparison, are soft, graceful trees with many uses, are amenable to pruning, and can be sheared in hedge form or allowed to grow in their own graceful fashion. Not so the firs, hence their landscape uses are greatly restricted.

It is not unusual, then, that only a dozen have been selected for recommendation, for it should be admitted that some of these may have ornamental value in a few small areas in the United States where temperature and high atmospheric moisture combine to provide ideal growing conditions.

Also, there is always the possibility that a new form or hybrid may arise with ornamental value. For instance, a hybrid *(A. cilicica x nordmanniana)* has been growing in the Arnold Arboretum since 1923 that might have considerable merit in certain landscape projects. It is perfectly hardy here, is 30 feet tall but only 9 feet in diameter, extremely dense, and clothed with branches from top to bottom. It originated in the Hunnewell Arboretum years ago and now looks like the peculiarly narrow firs one sees at very high altitudes in the Rocky Mountains. Such a clone might well be named and propagated.

⇶ SIMPLE FOLIAGE KEYS TO THE FIRS

The firs are perhaps the most difficult of the narrow-leaved evergreens to tell apart because their needles, as well as the color of the twigs and the amount of pubescence, vary little in size and shape.

There are ten fir species native to this country in addition to fifteen exotic species and six varieties, all of which are either native or being grown commercially in the United States and included in the following key. As with the pines and spruces, many more firs are being grown in botanical gardens and arboretums in this country, but their cultivation is limited to such an extent that they are not available at this time to the plant-buying public in sufficient quantity to warrant their inclusion in this key.

The habitats are given for all species appearing in the key because such information is often helpful in identifying these plants in the field.

The simple foliage keys to the evergreens *(Abies, Picea, Pinus, Tsuga—* see each genus) should materially aid the gardening enthusiast or woodsman in his associations with this valued group of plants. The keys cover practically all the pines, hemlocks, spruces, and firs native to large areas of this country or grown in quantity in our commercial nurseries. Actually, 105 evergreen trees are included in these keys, of which forty-one species are native to this country. This is the majority of the evergreen conifers in these groups that one would normally find in the woods, parks, and gardens of the United States and Canada. In using the key, merely go to the first number. If the statement there applies to the specimen, go to the next higher number until the tree is identified. If the statement there does not apply, proceed to the following group headed by the same number and proceed as above. It is hoped that these keys may stimulate an interest in the names and relationships of these conifers. They were planned to be used with living plants. Use them and learn to know your evergreens!

Leaves single; a circular scar remains when detaches; without persistent prominent leaf bases on the twigs . . . . *Abies, Pseudotsuga*

    1. End bud sharply pointed, long, and narrow, with many scales, not resinous; fruit a pendulous cone, needles spreading radially on all sides of twig. Douglas-fir . . . . *Pseudotsuga menziesii*
                                                                (taxifolia)
        (British Columbia to western Texas) Zone 6

    1. End bud not long and narrow and sharply pointed, mostly resinous; fruit upright; needles of most species (except *A. pinsapo* and *A. koreana*) not spreading radially on all sides of twig (See Fig. 4) . . . . *Abies* species
        alba—Silver fir   *cephalonica*—Greek fir
        amabilis—Cascade fir   *chensiensis*—Shensi fir
        balsamea—Balsam fir   *cilicica*—Cilician fir

(a) The twig of a fir, showing the smooth twig surface that reveals itself when the leaves have fallen. (b) The twig of a spruce, showing the small leaf bases (making a rough twig surface) that remain after the leaves have fallen. (c) The terminal bud of a fir. (d) The terminal bud of Pseudotsuga menziesii, *showing its many scales and long, pointed character, distinctly different from the buds of any other fir.*

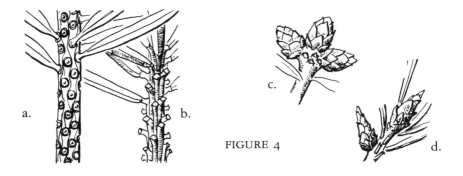

a.   b.   c.

FIGURE 4   d.

concolor—White fir
concolor violacea
firma—Momi fir
fraseri—Southern balsam fir
grandis—Giant fir
holophylla—Needle fir
homolepis—Nikko fir
koreana—Korean fir
lasiocarpa—Rocky Mountain fir
lasiocarpa arizonica
magnifica—Red fir

mariesii—Maries fir
nordmanniana—Nordmann fir
pinsapo—Spanish fir
procera (formerly *A.*
   nobilis)—Noble fir
religiosa—Sacred fir
sachalinensis—Sakhalin fir
sibirica—Siberian fir
spectabilis—Himalayan fir
veitchii—Veitch fir
venusta—Bristlecone fir

2. Needles mostly ¾ inch or less in length
   3. Needles spreading radially on all sides of twig
      4. Needles intensely white beneath, usually blunt and rounded at the tip .... *A. koreana* (Korea) Zone 4
      4. Needles greenish to greenish white beneath, usually pointed at the tip .... *A. pinsapo* (Spain) Zone 6

(a) Abies koreana, *with its radially spreading needles. (b)* A. alba, *with its distinctly two-ranked needles. (c)* A. nordmanniana, *its needles radiating from the sides and upper surface of the twig.*

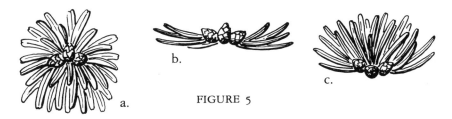

FIGURE 5

3. Needles not radially distributed; apparently more or less two-ranked, that is, with needles appearing on the two sides of the twig and frequently on the upper surface as well (see Fig. 5)
   4. Needles lustrous green above, white or whitish beneath; stomate lines present on undersurface only
      5. Needles, especially on two-year-old twigs, directed toward tip of branch (see Fig. 7b) ..... *A. mariesii* (Japan) Zone 5
      5. Needles, especially on two-year-old twigs, more or less at right angles to the twigs (see Fig. 7a)
         .... *A. balsamea* (Labrador to West Virginia and Iowa) Zone 3
         .... *A. fraseri*

(Allegheny Mountains, West Virginia, and Tennessee) Zone 4

(These two are closely related and difficult to tell apart without cones or without a lens. The undersurface of the needles of *A. fraseri* has 8 to 12 lines of stomates in each white band, while that of *A. balsamea* has only 4 to 8 lines in each white band.)

4. Needles gray-green above and below, due to the fact that stomate lines (seen with a lens) are on both upper and lower needle surfaces

    5. One-year-old twigs ash gray

        6. Bark on trunk gray . . . . *A. lasiocarpa*

        (Alaska to New Mexico) Zone 3

        6. Bark on trunk creamy white and corky

        . . . . *A. lasiocarpa arizonica*

    5. One-year-old twigs rusty brown—foliage bluish green . . . . *A. procera (A. nobilis)*

    (Washington to California) Zone 5

(a) The tip of the needle of Abies holophylla; *(b) the tip of the needle of a young* A. firma; *(c) the tip of the needle of* A. cephalonica; *(d, e, f) the rounded and slightly notched needles commonly found on most firs. When any one of these types makes up the majority of needles on a specimen, the needles are considered to be blunt, as far as this key is concerned.*

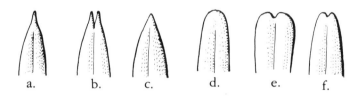

    a.   b.   c.   d.   e.   f.

FIGURE 6

2. Needles more than ¾ inch in length

    3. Needles green and lustrous above; no lines of stomates on upper surface of needles (when observed with a lens)

        4. Needles definitely pointed at tip

            5. Majority of needles, especially on two-year-old twigs, at right angles to the twigs (see Fig. 7a)

                6. Branchlets glabrous; vigorous shoots have needles with only one point

                    7. Twigs deeply grooved (see Fig. 7a)

                    . . . . *A. homolepis*

                  (Japan) Zone 4

7. Twigs not deeply grooved
   8. White lines clearly visible on the lower surface of the needles; needles frequently produced on all sides of twig . . . . *A. cephalonica* (Greece) Zone 5
   8. White lines only faintly visible on the lower surface of the needles; needles often curved and pointing directly upward, not appearing radially arranged . . . . *A. holophylla* (Manchuria, Korea) Zone 5
6. Branchlets slightly pubescent; vigorous young shoots may have needles with two sharp points (see Fig. 6b) . . . . *A. firma* (Japan) Zone 6
5. Majority of needles not at right angles to twig (see Fig. 7b)
   6. Needles less than 1½ inches long
      7. One-year-old twigs glabrous
         . . . . *A. holophylla* (Manchuria, Korea) Zone 5
      7. One-year-old twigs pubescent
         . . . . *A. religiosa* (Mexico) Zones 9–10
   6. Needles 1½ to 2¼ inches long . . . *A. venusta* (California) Zone 8
4. Majority of needles blunt and rounded at tip or slightly notched at the tip (see Figs. 6d, e, f)
   5. Needles, especially on two-year-old twigs, mostly at right angles to the twigs
      6. Branchlets glabrous

(a) Needles mostly at right angles to the twig, as in Abies homolepis, *also showing longitudinal lines or grooves in the twig. (b) Needles mostly directed toward the tip of the twig, as in* A. nordmanniana.

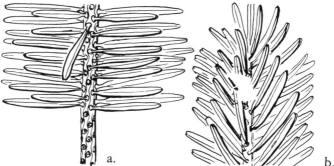

FIGURE 7   a.   b.

7. Foliage intensely white beneath; twigs deeply grooved (see Fig. 7a)
.... *A. homolepis*
(Japan) Zone 4

7. Foliage green beneath; twigs not deeply grooved................ *A. chensiensis*
(central China) Zone 6

6. Branchlets pubescent

7. Branchlets slightly pubescent; one-year-old twigs often have faint grooves; needles on vigorous shoots pointed and frequently up to 1½ inches long......... *A. firma*
(Japan) Zone 6

7. Branchlets densely pubescent; needles rarely more than 1 inch in length
.... *A. balsamea*
(Labrador to West Virginia and Iowa) Zone 3

.... *A. fraseri*
(Allegheny Mountains, West Virginia, and Tennessee) Zone 4
(These two are closely related and difficult to tell apart without cones or a lens. The undersurface of the needles of *A. fraseri* has 8 to 12 lines of stomates in each white band, while that of *A. balsamea* has only 4 to 8 lines in each white band.)

5. Majority of needles not at right angles but pointing toward the tips of the twigs (see Fig. 7b)

6. Lower side of one-year-old twigs olive green
.... *A. grandis*
(Vancouver to California and Montana) Zone 6

6. One-year-old twigs not olive green

7. Foliage grayish white beneath; needles 1/24 to 1/16 inch in width
(Note: This is a difficult measurement to make, but the point is that the needles of the following two firs are narrower than those of most other species.)

8. Needles dark green
.... *A. sachalinensis*
(Japan, Kurile Islands) Zone 2

8. Needles light green..... *A. sibirica*
(northern Russia to Kamchatka, Turkestan, and Manchuria) Zone 2
(These two are difficult to tell apart without a lens. The undersurface

of the needles of *A. sachalinensis* has 7 or 8 lines of stomates in each white band while that of *A. sibirica* has only 4 or 5 lines in each white band.)

7. Foliage of one-year-old shoots intensely white beneath; needles ¹/₁₂ inch or more in width

    8. Winter buds resinous

        9. Needles mostly more than 1 inch long (1 to 2¼ inches); twigs usually grooved.
        . . . . *A. spectabilis* (Himalayas) Zone 7

        9. Needles mostly less than 1 inch long; twigs not grooved

            10. Branchlets gray pubescent . . . . *A. amabilis* (British Columbia to Oregon) Zone 5

            10. Branchlets brown pubescent . . . . . *A. veitchii* (Japan) Zone 3

    8. Winter buds not resinous

        9. Leaves closely arranged in two ranks like teeth in a comb (see Fig. 5b) . . . . *A. alba* (mountains of central and southern Europe) Zone 4

        9. Leaves not in two closely arranged ranks

            10. Needles of one-year-old twigs very white beneath, the upper ones directed forward and closely appressed to the twigs
            . . . . . *A. nordmanniana* (Caucasus Mountains and Asia Minor) Zone 5

            10. Needles of one-year-old twigs merely greenish white beneath, more or less spreading and with a V-shaped depression above, not closely appressed to the twigs
            . . . . *A. cilicica*

(Asia Minor, Syria)
Zone 5
(These two are difficult
to tell apart without the
cones. The Nordmann
fir is by far the more
common of the two in
this country.)

3. Foliage dull grayish or bluish green above and below because of
   stomate lines on both upper and lower surfaces of the needles
   (these can be seen with a lens)
   4. Needles flat in cross section (as in *Picea omorika*)
      5. One-year-old twigs glabrous
         6. Foliage bluish green . . . . *A. concolor*
            (Colorado to California and New Mexico)
            Zone 4
         6. Foliage a bluish white . . . . . *A. concolor violacea*
      5. One-year-old twigs pubescent
         6. Twigs ashy gray—bark on trunk gray
            . . . . *A. lasiocarpa*
            (Alaska to New Mexico) Zone 3
         6. Twigs rusty brown
            7. Foliage bluish green
               . . . . *A. procera (A. nobilis)*
               (Washington to California) Zone 5
   4. Needles, at least some of them, quadrangular in cross sec-
      tion, similar to the cross section of those of *Picea glauca*
      . . . . *A. magnifica*
      (Oregon to California) Zone 5

Abies concolor   120′   Zone 4   White fir

* HABIT: stiffly pyramidal, rather narrow, horizontal branching
* FOLIAGE: evergreen, bluish green needles often 2″ long
  HABITAT: western and southwestern United States
  VARIETIES:
      conica—dwarf, pyramidal, slow-growing, needles under 1½″ long
      violacea—bluish white needles

One of the best of the firs for planting in northern gardens and thoroughly reliable
as far north as Boston, it is noted for withstanding heat and drought better than most
of the other firs. It also has the longest needles and makes an excellent color contrast
when planted in front of such evergreens as white pine or hemlock. Under good
conditions it should grow 1½ feet a year, which is fairly rapid for most evergreens.
Because of its habit of growth and even though the branching is horizontal, it forms
a softer looking tree than does the blue spruce, another frequently used conifer in
landscape planting. No serious insect pests or diseases.

Abies homolepis   90'   Zone 4   Nikko fir

* HABIT: stiffly pyramidal, horizontal branching
* FOLIAGE: dense, evergreen needles
  HABITAT: Japan
  INTRODUCED: 1861

Another one of the best firs for ornamental planting, this is easily distinguished from other firs because of the horizontal decurrent lines along the one-year-old twigs. It is the common fir of the mountains of central Japan and has been considered one of the best Japanese firs for planting in the northern United States. It is noted for its wide-spreading, regularly spaced branches and vigorous, dark green growth. A fine ornamental where it can be given plenty of room to grow naturally. No serious insect pests or diseases.

Abies koreana   50'   Zone 5   Korean fir

* HABIT: stiffly pyramidal, horizontal branching
* FOLIAGE: dense, evergreen needles, dark green above and whitish beneath
  HABITAT: Korea
  INTRODUCED: 1918

This tree grows very well but few specimens in this country have reached their mature height. It grows more slowly than some of the others and might be the only one considered for small gardens because of this fact. It is stiff and formal, but the whitish undersurface of the needles shows to good advantage.

Abies magnifica   200'   Zone 5   Red fir

* HABIT: stiffly pyramidal, horizontal branching
* FOLIAGE: dense, evergreen needles
  HABITAT: Oregon, California
  VARIETY:
      glauca—whitish needles

This fir does not do well where there is a great deal of soft-coal smoke in the atmosphere. Where it is hardy, especially on the West Coast, and the soil is rich, it grows into a fine specimen.

Abies pinsapo   75'   Zone 6   Spanish fir

* HABIT: stiffly pyramidal, horizontal branching
* FOLIAGE: dense, evergreen needles
  HABITAT: Spain
  INTRODUCED: 1837

VARIETIES:

    'Argentea'—silvery white foliage more pronounced than the easily available variety 'Glauca.' This is a beautiful fir under perfect growing conditions.

    'Glauca'—more easily obtained from commercial sources than 'Argentea,' but coloring of foliage not as pronounced. Both make good ornamentals but probably do better in Zone 7.

Abies procera   240'   Zone 5   Noble fir

* HABIT: stiffly pyramidal, horizontal branching
* FOLIAGE: evergreen needles
  HABITAT: Washington to California
  VARIETY:
    'Glauca'—slow-growing with glaucous foliage

A noble West Coast fir that can grow in the eastern United States, it is best used near its native habitat. (Formerly named *A. nobilis.*) The spruce bud worm, woolly aphis, and several cankers are pests of this species. Spray with malathion.

Abies spectabilis   150'   Zone 7   Himalayan fir

* HABIT: broadly pyramidal, wide-spreading branches
* FOLIAGE: needles 1–2" long
  HABITAT: Himalayan Mountains
  INTRODUCED: 1822

A fine fir of value only in the South.

Abies veitchii   75'   Zone 3   Veitch fir

* HABIT: stiffly pyramidal, horizontal branching
* FOLIAGE: dense, evergreen needles, dark green above, whitish below
  HABITAT: central Japan
  INTRODUCED: 1876

A very fine fir, hardier than most, of special interest because of the striking white undersurface of the needles. Woolly aphis, spruce bud worm, and several cankers can infest this species. Malathion is a good spray for this.

⇶ *ACACIA*

In California, about 1933, more than ninety species and varieties of acacia were in use for ornamental planting. A bad freeze occurred in 1937 and many were killed outright. Most are brittle-wooded trees, of short life and shallow roots. They cannot be used everywhere, but intelligently placed they add a delicate beauty to the subtropical garden. Only one or two of these should be used as street trees because of their brittle wood.

Mimosas can be heavily infested, especially in the Midwest, by the mimosa web worm, which can attack honey locusts in other areas as well. The small gray worms pull several leaves together to make their nests and often skeletonize the entire tree. A spray of malathion or methoxychlor should be applied as soon as the insects are first seen to prevent their spread.

Acacia baileyana   30'   Zone 10   Cootamundra wattle

* FLOWERS: feathery, light yellow, ⅛" in diameter on racemes 3" long
      TIME: January to March
  HABIT: spreading
* FOLIAGE: evergreen, fine textured, steel blue leaflets running spirally around the twig
  HABITAT: New South Wales

This short-lived tree needs good soil, and given that, is a very attractive small tree of very fine texture and color. It grows very fast and is used sometimes as a street tree in southern California.

Acacia dealbata   50'   Zone 9   Silver wattle

* FLOWERS: fragrant, profuse, small, clear yellow flowers in small, ball-like clusters
      TIME: March–April
  HABIT: vigorous in growth, more or less spreading
* FOLIAGE: very graceful, evergreen, finely divided, slightly blue to grayish in color
  HABITAT: Australia

This is the species best known to most gardeners in this country and in England, for it is perhaps the hardiest of some four hundred or more kinds. The small balls of flowers are only about ¼ inch in diameter and are conspicuous only because of the many stamens in the flowers. It is very rapid in growth and handsome indeed, doing well in good soil. It might be the first to be considered of this large group of exotic trees by the enterprising gardener who lives in the warmer parts of the South. It is used considerably as a street tree, but like most members of this genus, it is short-lived.

Acacia decurrens mollis   50'   Zone 10   Black wattle

* FLOWERS: small, light yellow
      TIME: June–July
  HABIT: slender but attractive spreading branches
* FOLIAGE: fine textured, yellowish when young, dull green at maturity
  HABITAT: Australia

This species does not require much water and grows quickly but is less popular than the silver wattle; it should be used more.

Acacia pendula   25'   Zone 10   Weeping boree acacia

  FLOWERS: inconspicuous, yellow
* HABIT: pendulous branches
* FOLIAGE: fine textured, bluish gray
  HABITAT: Queensland, New South Wales

Valued chiefly for its pendulous habit and not especially for its flowers.

Acacia pruinosa   60'   Zone 10   Bronze acacia, Frosty acacia

* FLOWERS: fragrant, cream and yellow
      TIME: June–September
  HABIT: spreading
  FOLIAGE: evergreen, light green, new fernlike foliage in copper shades
  HABITAT: Australia

This is being planted in southern California and is noted as a dense, spreading but graceful and beautiful tree.

→≫ ACER

Those interested in finding shade trees that have proved excellent over a long period of years will find some of the best among the maples. Then, too, if you are interested in something new, a shade tree that is neat and compact yet unusual and not much used, you will also find much to choose from among these fine trees. Varied in habit, in rate of growth, in size, and in leaf character, the maples should always be considered when one is selecting shade trees for street, highway, or garden plantings. Some may have their defects, some may not have bright-colored flowers or brilliant fruits, but all recommended here have some particular characteristic that makes them out-standing trees for producing shade.

Maples are dense in habit with the exception of one or two recom-mended solely for growth in wooded areas. Few have conspicuous flowers, but the red and Norway maples are two notable exceptions. The fruits of all maples are winged keys, samaras (a small nut with wings, attached usually in pairs), not too conspicuous, yet they are produced in quantity and are color-ful in some species such as *A. ginnala.* Some grow to be mighty giants over 100 feet tall while others remain neat and compact at about 20 feet in height. Some are comparatively low and squat like the Japanese maple, others are tall and columnar like *A. saccharum* 'Temple's Upright,' and still others are widely rounded like the serviceable Norway maple.

Our needs for shade trees change with the times. Fifty years and more ago, the silver maple was widely planted as an ornamental tree; now, with the recurrence of windstorms and with knowledge of other more recently introduced trees, the weak-wooded silver maples are definitely going out of fashion.

Smaller houses and smaller gardens require the planting of smaller trees, so there is an increasing interest in many of the maples that were overlooked years ago, either because they were not sufficiently well known or because the mature heights of some precluded their use on small properties.

Most commercial growers are thoroughly familiar with some of these maples, but very few know all in the recommended list. It should be particu-larly pointed out that more than thirty in the following list have mature heights of 30 feet or less, an excellent group for study because of modern planting demands. There will always be a demand for large trees, but the demand for smaller ones is definitely on the increase.

New clones or cultivars are continually being offered, but they should be carefully assessed since some are not necessarily any better than older standard varieties. Trees with variegated foliage are none too popular, and correctly so. Trees with definitely narrow or rounded forms have important uses on small properties and in congested areas, and among the maples are some of the best columnar trees available.

A few maples are valued for their interesting winter bark *(A. griseum, A. capillipes,* and so forth), but even the light gray bark of *A. rubrum* has merit. In fact, there are species among the maples for planting anywhere in cold *(A. ginnala),* hot *(A. barbatum floridanum),* dry *(A. negundo),* or wet *(A. rubrum)* climates.

Many maples display outstanding autumn color, the American and Asiat-ics turning brilliant red or yellow. Most of the European types, however, do not have any autumn color *(A. pseudoplatanus, A. campestre,* and so forth), while some of the *A. palmatum* varieties have excellent red foliage through-out the entire summer. All in all, this group consists of some of the best of our shade trees, diversified enough for some to be hardy almost anywhere in the United States under any but the most extreme growing conditions.

All maples apparently seem to grow in any good soil; some, such as the box-elder, will thrive in the poor, dry soils of the Great Plains area of the Midwest. During the growing season most have normally green leaves but some have variegated leaves, some have yellow leaves, and some have red or purplish red leaves.

During rainy seasons, anthracnose can be serious in *A. saccharum, A. negundo,* and *A. saccharinum,* as can some other diseases. Spraying with ferbam or thiram is recommended. Cut off the infected branches as soon as they appear. Oozing canker sores should be cut out and burned, and resulting wounds should be covered with tree paint. It is anthracnose that causes a scorched appearance on the leaves.

Cottony maple scale and terrapin scale often infest the branches of sugar and Norway maples. Spray with malathion for control when the insects are young or spray with dormant oil in the proper season. Norway maple aphid can be a nuisance on Norway maples when the small aphids drop "honey dew" from the branches, noticed usually on cars parked underneath the branches. Here again, spraying with malathion is suggested. You may also use it to control several kinds of borers. Methoxychlor can also be used to control these pests. Sometimes galls appear on sugar, silver, and red maples, in which case spray with captafol or malathion. Other insects can be controlled by spraying with methoxychlor, malathion, or carbaryl.

In order to assist in their general identification, the following groupings of maples are suggested, but it must be stressed that leaves of all trees vary and identifying trees by the lobing of their leaves alone is not always accurate:

LEAVES NOT LOBED
  A. carpinifolium
  A. davidii
  A. tataricum

LEAVES 3 LOBED
  A. barbatum
  A. buergerianum
  A. capillipes
  A. ginnala
  A. glabrum
  A. monspessulanum
  A. nigrum
  A. pensylvanicum
  A. spicatum

LEAVES 5 LOBED, WITH MILKY SAP
    AT PETIOLE BASE WHEN BROKEN
  A. campestre
  A. lobellii

  A. macrophyllum
  A. platanoides

LEAVES 5 LOBED AND NO MILKY SAP
    AT PETIOLE BASE WHEN BROKEN
  A. argutum
  A. diabolicum
  A. opalus
  A. palmatum
  A. pseudoplatanus
  A. rubrum
  A. saccharum
  A. tschonoskii

LEAVES 7 (OR MORE) LOBED
  A. circinatum
  A. japonicum
  A. palmatum (sometimes) and
    several of its varieties

LEAVES COMPOUND
  A. griseum
  A. mandshuricum

A. maximowiczianum
A. negundo
A. triflorum

Acer argutum   24′   Zone 5

HABIT: branches erect, rather narrow
FOLIAGE: leaves 5 lobed, dense
HABITAT: Japan
INTRODUCED: 1879

A graceful tree and good for the small property. Since much emphasis is being placed on planting small properties, such trees as this certainly should be considered where small shade trees are wanted.

Acer barbatum floridanum   50′   Zone 9   Florida maple

* BARK: very pale gray
FOLIAGE: dense
HABIT: rounded
HABITAT: southeastern United States

Planted in some parts of northern Florida as a shade tree.

Acer buergerianum   20′   Zone 6   Trident maple

* HABIT: rounded
FOLIAGE: leaves 3 lobed
HABITAT: Japan
INTRODUCED: 1892

Proving popular as a shade tree in surveys of shade trees made for the central United States. Diseases and insects are not serious problems.

Acer campestre   25′   Zones 5–6   Hedge maple

* HABIT: rounded
FOLIAGE: dense
AUTUMN COLOR: yellowish
HABITAT: Europe, western Asia
INTRODUCED: early colonial times
VARIETIES:
     'Postelense'—leaves golden yellow when young, gradually turning green
     'Queen Elizabeth'—a new clone from J. Frank Schmidt of Boring, Oregon, now being recommended for street tree use; more upright than the species

This maple is commonly used in Europe in clipped hedges because of its dense growth. It does not have the vivid autumn coloration of native species, but as a clipped hedge or screen it is ideal. From Long Island southward it makes a dependable screen plant requiring little attention. It is one of the few maples (along with the Norway) that shows a milky white sap at the base of the leaf petioles when they are pulled off the twig. It is practically free of insect pests and diseases.

Acer capillipes   30'   Zone 5

HABIT: slightly open
* BARK: branches striped white
FOLIAGE: leaves 3 lobed, red when unfolding, turning green later
AUTUMN COLOR: red
HABITAT: Japan
INTRODUCED: 1892

Similar to *A. pensylvanicum* and *A. rufinerve* in regard to the white striping of the bark on the branches, this small tree might have possibilities as an ornamental, doing better in the full sun than *A. pensylvanicum*.

Acer cappadocicum 'Rubrum'   60'   Zones 5–6   Coliseum maple

FRUIT: winged keys or samaras
HABIT: upright, vigorous growth
* BARK: bloodred shoots in winter
FOLIAGE: leaves 5–7 lobed, petiole when broken shows a milky sap, young leaves
        appear bloodred at first
AUTUMN COLOR: bloodred
HABITAT: Caucasus Mountains
INTRODUCED: 1838

This variety is chiefly of value for its bright red winter twigs.

Acer carpinifolium   30'   Zone 5   Hornbeam maple

* HABIT: vase-shaped with many stems from the base
FOLIAGE: dense, bright green leaves (not lobed), similar in size and shape to that
        of the hornbeam
AUTUMN COLOR: brownish yellow
HABITAT: Japan
INTRODUCED: 1881

An interesting, clean-growing, small shade tree that has performed well in Washington, D.C., as well as in the Arnold Arboretum. It should be added to the limited group of small shade trees for small properties and may have merit as a street tree because of its size.

Acer circinatum　　25′　　Zone 5　　Vine maple

* FLOWERS:　white and purple, in small drooping clusters
　　　TIME:　late April
　FRUIT:　red, winged keys or samaras
　　　EFFECTIVE:　summer
* HABIT:　wide-spreading, with several branches from the base
* FOLIAGE:　dense
* AUTUMN COLOR:　red to orange
　HABITAT:　British Columbia to California

A native maple of the West Coast adapted for use in gardens because of its small, compact size and its ability to grow in partially shaded situations, especially under evergreens. It is somewhat similar in habit to *A. palmatum* except that its stems twist and turn in a most interesting manner, thus giving rise to its name. The wood is very tough; the Indians, according to legend, used it to make fishhooks. It is one of the most ornamental maples when in flower.

Acer davidii　　45′　　Zone 6　　David maple

　HABIT:　rounded
* BARK:　branches striped white in winter

Acer davidii *is valued for its striped bark, conspicuous in the winter.*

FOLIAGE: leaves large, sometimes 8″ long, red as they first unfold, later turning a
    glossy green
AUTUMN COLOR: yellow and purple
HABITAT: China
INTRODUCED: 1902

Not completely hardy as far north as Boston but worthy of a trial farther south,
especially for its interesting bark in winter.

Acer diabolicum purpurascens   30′   Zone 5   Red devil maple

FLOWERS: purplish
* FRUIT: purple when young
* FOLIAGE: leaves reddish when unfolding
AUTUMN COLOR: purplish
HABITAT: Japan
INTRODUCED: 1878

This variety is a better ornamental than the species, which should not be used.

Acer ginnala   20′   Zone 2   Amur maple

* FRUIT: winged keys or samaras, usually red and conspicuous
        EFFECTIVE: summer
* HABIT: upright but rounded, dense branching
FOLIAGE: dense, fine textured
* AUTUMN COLOR: scarlet
HABITAT: central and northern China, Manchuria, Japan
INTRODUCED: about 1860
VARIETIES:
    'Durand Dwarf'—a fine shrubby, dwarf type. A five-year-old plant is only 3′
        tall but nearly 5′ across.
    'Flame'—introduced by the Soil Conservation Service; is extremely hardy and
        resistant to droughts. It is used for its form (better than that of the species)
        and its excellent brilliant red autumn color.
    'Red Fruit'—a clone with profuse red fruits
    semenowii—graceful leaves, deeper cut than those of the species, turning red-
        purple in the fall

A dense shrub or small tree with comparatively small leaves about 3 inches long and
extremely hardy. The fruits turn bright red in the summer while the leaves are still
green, making an interesting color combination. The scarlet autumn color of the
foliage is as brilliant as any of the maples. A good tree for specimen or for screening
purposes, requiring practically no care.
    One of the very few maples with fragrant flowers. Diseases and insect pests are
not a problem.

Acer glabrum   24′   Zone 5   Rocky Mountain maple

HABIT: upright, branching almost fastigiate
FOLIAGE: leaves large, 3–5 lobed
* AUTUMN COLOR: bright yellow
HABITAT: Montana to New Mexico

Used in the Rocky Mountain area and on the West Coast as a small shade tree.

Acer griseum   25′   Zone 5   Paperbark maple

HABIT: rounded, rather open
* BARK: exfoliating in paper-thin strips
FOLIAGE: rather open, compound leaf, 3 leaflets
HABITAT: western China
INTRODUCED: 1901

Very difficult to propagate in quantity because the embryos in the seeds do not develop. Otherwise, it could easily be one of the most popular maples. The bark is cinnamon brown and exfoliates in paper-thin strips similar to that of certain birches. This bark characteristic is easily noticeable from some distance away, making the tree of outstanding interest throughout the entire year. It is hoped that a reliable method can be found for propagating this plant on a large scale for it certainly merits wide use. Diseases and insect pests are not a problem.

Acer japonicum   25′   Zone 5   Fullmoon maple

* HABIT: rounded but broad in outline
* FOLIAGE: leaves 7–11 lobed, usually green
* AUTUMN COLOR: bright red
HABITAT: Japan
INTRODUCED: 1864
VARIETIES:
    'Aconitifolium'—leaves deeply divided
    'Aureum'—leaves yellow
    'Itayo'—leaves larger than the species. Autumn color is a good yellow.
    'Junshitoe'—leaves only 2–3″ across, autumn color a good yellow
    'Vitifolium'—the autumn color is an excellent rich purple to yellow, to crimson. The leaves are up to 6″ long.

Popularly classed as a "Japanese" maple, this is actually a different species from the more popular *A. palmatum.* They are similar in many ways, but the varieties listed above usually have more leaf lobes than most of the *A. palmatum* varieties.

Acer lobelii   60'   Zone 7   Lobel maple

HABIT: ascending branches
FOLIAGE: leaves 5 lobed
HABITAT: southern Italy
INTRODUCED: 1838

Similar to the Norway maple but for use in the South. The young bark is prominently striped.

Acer macrophyllum   90'   Zone 6   Bigleaf maple

FLOWERS: fragrant, small, yellow, in pendulous clusters 4–6" long
    TIME: May
FRUIT: winged keys or samaras, in pendulous clusters 4–6" long
    EFFECTIVE: early fall
HABIT: rounded head
FOLIAGE: dense, coarse, leaves the largest of all maples, 6–12" in diameter
* AUTUMN COLOR: a good yellow
HABITAT: West Coast from Alaska to California

A very popular tree on the West Coast, where it thrives. Its unusually large leaves make it an excellent shade tree, and they turn a bright yellow to orange in fall. Unfortunately it does not seem to do well in eastern North America. There is a narrow upright form of this growing in the University of Washington Arboretum at Seattle. It has been called 'Seattle Sentinal' but is not being propagated commercially at present in any great number.

Acer mandshuricum   30'   Zone 4   Manchurian maple

HABIT: rounded head
FOLIAGE: rather open, leaves compound, petioles red
* AUTUMN COLOR: red to scarlet early in the season
HABITAT: Manchuria, Korea
INTRODUCED: 1904

A close relative of the box-elder, this small tree also grows rapidly, has wide-spreading branches, and the red petioles afford a pleasing color contrast with the dark green color of the leaves. A good small shade tree. Free of insects and diseases.

Acer maximowiczianum (formerly *A. nikoense)*   45'   Zone 5
                                                         Nikko maple

* HABIT: round-topped, but generally vase-shaped
FOLIAGE: leaves compound, 3 leaflets, rather open

Possessing an attractive vase shape, the Nikko maple (Acer maximowiczianum) *is a good choice for the small property.*

* AUTUMN COLOR: brilliant red or purple
HABITAT: Japan, central China
INTRODUCED: 1881

This is not a fast-growing maple, but it is beautiful at most seasons and so is of interest for planting on smaller properties. One of the very few maples with an interesting vase-shaped habit.

Acer monspessulanum   24–30'   Zone 5   Montpelier maple

HABIT: rounded head
FOLIAGE: leaves 3 lobed
HABITAT: southern Europe, northern Africa
INTRODUCED: 1739

Popular as a street tree in Oregon and Washington, this somewhat resembles *A. campestre.*

Acer negundo   60′   Zone 2   Box-elder

HABIT: wide-spreading, rather open
FOLIAGE: open, leaves compound, 3–5 leaflets
HABITAT: eastern and central North America
VARIETIES:
>   'Auratum'—yellow leaflets. A good, colorful variety if grown in the right place.
>   'Aureo-marginatum'—leaf margins yellowish
>   'Flamingo'—best grown in partial shade. The leaves first appear light pink, later maturing to green with white or pink variegations. An unusually colored tree, of value only as an accent.
>   'Variegatum' *(Silverleaf box-elder)*—leaves with broad white margins, one of the most conspicuous of the variegated leaved trees

A very rapid-growing maple, recommended only for certain areas of the Midwest where drought and cold make it impossible to grow many other better ornamental trees. In the East the box-elder is considered a weed for it quickly seeds itself everywhere. It is very weak-wooded and splits easily in storms. It has no autumn color. The only excuse for using it at all in the East, where much better trees are available, is that it can be used for a very quick (and temporary!) deciduous screen. It will also withstand dry situations where nothing else but sumacs, Siberian elm, and the tree of heaven will grow.

In the West it is used considerably in shelterbelts, especially as a temporary, quick-growing screen to protect slower-growing but longer-lived trees while becoming established. The only reason for mentioning the variegated forms is to suggest something a little more colorful and unusual for those areas of drought and cold where few ornamental trees will withstand the cold winters or the terrifically hot, dry summers. For places other than the Great Plains areas and the southwest United States, the box-elder might well be omitted from any serious consideration.

Acer nigrum = *Acer saccharum nigrum*

Acer opalus   45′   Zone 5   Italian maple

* FLOWERS: small, yellow
        EFFECTIVE: April
HABIT: rounded
FOLIAGE: leaves 5 lobed
HABITAT: southern Europe
INTRODUCED: 1752

A beautiful tree in flower during early spring, especially valued for this reason.

Acer palmatum   20′   Zone 5   Japanese maple

* HABIT: rounded, often moundlike
* FOLIAGE: dense, green to red, leaves 5–9 lobed, up to 4″ in width

* AUTUMN COLOR: scarlet
HABITAT: Korea, Japan
INTRODUCED: 1820
VARIETIES:

1. Leaves usually with 5 main lobes—leaves small

'Atropurpureum' *(Bloodleaf Japanese maple)*—one of the hardiest and best of the 5 lobed group, with leaves a dark red throughout the entire growing season. Many other varieties or seedlings will produce red foliage early in the spring, but it will turn disappointingly green by early summer. This variety is one of the best and hardiest, and like many of the others on this list, it has been growing in America for the past eighty years.

'Atropurpureum Lozito'—about 15' tall with very dark, purplish red leaves; should be grown in full sun to bring out the best color

'Atropurpureum Oshiu Beni'—about 15' tall, light red foliage, and fine fall color in full sun

'Atropurpureum Wayside'—a very hardy maple, originating in Holland, with red-purple leaves. Slow-growing, it makes a fine specimen.

'Burgundy Lace'—an interesting cut-leaved form with reddish foliage

'Chishio'—only about 6' tall, growing into a small tree as wide as it is tall, with green foliage in summer, colored red in the fall

'Linearilobum'—leaves divided into extremely narrow lobes, slightly toothed. The foliage first appears reddish but turns green by early summer.

'Nomura-Nishiki'—dark red leaves with brown and lighter-colored variegations

'Sango Kaku' *(Coralbark maple)*—coral-red bark on twigs in winter and yellow autumn foliage, about 10' tall. Prune in summer for bright red twigs in winter.

'Sanguineum' *(Scarlet Japanese maple)*—similar to 'Atropurpureum' but a lighter red color. One of the most hardy. Leaves reddish above but green underneath; bark on young wood red. An old-fashioned favorite, still one of the very best, making an excellent specimen for its brilliantly colored foliage.

'Scolopendrifolium'—leaves cut to center, leaflets narrow, green

'Shindeshojo'—red and orange autumn color. In the summer the leaves are green, often with a few spots of white.

'Ukon'—young foliage is yellow, green in summer, and yellow and red in the fall

'Versicolor'—leaves green with white, pink, and light green variegation. Not as hardy as some of the others.

'Yezo-Nishiki'—a comparatively recent introduction with bloodred leaves and vermilion variegations

2. Leaves with 7 main lobes, large

'Elegans'—better for ornamental purposes than the above; leaves 5″ long, serrate, and when first open have a rose-colored margin

'Osakazuki'—large leaves, yellowish to light green but turning a brilliant red in the fall; one of the best for fall coloring

'Reticulatum'—a "multicolored" variety, leaves having green veins, with the leaf spaces between the veins yellow, white, and pale green

'Rubrum'—leaves large, deep red when young but turning nearly green by early summer; not one of the better ornamentals for this reason

3. Leaves dissected with 7, 9, or 11 lobes

'Dissectum' *(Threadleaf Japanese maple)*—This and the following varieties are often considered the most beautiful of all of the maples because of their delicate, lacy foliage. This particular variety has bloodred leaves, delicately cut, and what is even more important, gracefully pendant branches. A truly excellent specimen plant, it is a shame to use it for anything but a specimen since no other woody ornamental is like it in its grace and beauty. In the past this has also been termed the variety *multifidum* and *palmatifidum*.

'Dissectum Crimson Queen'—outstanding for its deep red foliage, is said to be a deeper red than any other fern-leaved Japanese maple. Mature height of 6–8'.

'Dissectum Garnet'—this is a red-colored fern-leaved Japanese maple that can grow up to 12' tall. It is usually grown top-grafted on a 2–3' stem.

'Dissectum Viridi'—extremely graceful and delicate in outline, with a spreading, rounded form, and gray leaves throughout the season

'Flavescens'—yellowish foliage

'Ornatum' *(Spiderleaf Japanese maple)*—similar to *A. palmatum* 'Dissectum' except that the foliage is colored a more brilliant red

This is a variable species of shrubs or small trees, very popular in Japan and grown to a considerable extent in this country as well. A Japanese nursery firm listed over twenty-five varieties a few years ago as the "best" of a large number. More recently an American nursery has listed seventy varieties. There are over eighty varieties being grown in the arboretums and nurseries in the United States today. It is impossible to make a selection of the best in this large, diversified group, but those listed above certainly are among the best. The leaves have 5–9 lobes, those of some varieties more deeply cut than others, with colors ranging from green to dark red. The nomenclature in the commercial nurseries both here and in Japan is pretty much confused. Some specimens have the desirable trait of holding their deep red color all summer long; others that have bright red young leaves early in the spring disappointingly turn green in the summer. Some make inadequate specimens as they grow older because of poor understock on which named varieties are grafted. Then, too, many nurseries adopt the questionable practice of growing these from seed and "selecting" the best seedling forms, often giving them accredited varietal names for clones that should be only asexually propagated. This only adds to the confusion, of course, since many of the seedling forms do not have all the traits of the varieties after which they are named.

Most of these trees are hardy south of a line from Boston to southern New York, Cleveland, central Illinois, most of Missouri to southeastern Kansas, and on the West Coast. Some varieties—such as 'Atropurpureum,' 'Burgundy Lace,' 'Elegans,' and 'Ornatum'—are hardier than others, and these are the ones to be tried first in the colder parts of their range. Other varieties may be more desirable for the South, but regardless of where they are grown, the first prerequisites for good growth are rich soil with the correct exposure.

Rich, well-drained soil with plenty of organic matter is the optimal medium for best growth. Apparently Japanese maples grow in either slightly acid or slightly alkaline soils because there are some fine specimens in both, but they cannot be expected to grow well on dry, poor, gravelly soils.

The Japanese maples have a tendency to leaf out early in the spring, and if the area is susceptible to late spring frosts, there can be injury to the young growing shoots; such injured branches should be pruned off in the spring after growth has started. Sometimes this dieback seriously weakens the plants. Although the completely green- or red-leaved varieties do best in full sun, some of the variegated types will grow better if placed in partial shade, especially in the South where summer sun can be very hot. Because the leaves of variegated varieties lack their full complement of chlorophyll, they are more difficult to grow than their green-leaved relatives, and usually such plants, regardless of whether they are Japanese maples or any others, are more susceptible to "sunburn" in the summer.

Ideally suited as specimens in the garden, the Japanese maples are especially excellent as focal points at the end of a path or vista. Also, they can be used as colored features (that is, the red-leaved varieties) to bring color relief into an otherwise green picture. Although there are some that will grow 20′ tall ('Atropurpureum' is one) many, such as 'Dissectum' and its related varieties, will seldom grow over 12 feet tall, and because of their slow growth (the branches tend to be pendulous) they will take many, many years before they are over 8 feet in height.

Acer pensylvanicum   36′   Zone 3   Striped maple, Moosewood

HABIT: open, indefinite
* BARK: striped white
FOLIAGE: open, leaves large, coarse
* AUTUMN COLOR: yellow
HABITAT: eastern North America
VARIETY:
> **'Erythrocladum'**—a rare but most unusual type with twigs in winter colored a brilliant red, almost as brilliant as some of the red-stemmed dogwoods. Originated about 1904.

A tree that does best in partially shaded woods, it is of value chiefly for the striped bark on its trunk and branches in the wintertime. Its open habit of growth and large, coarse leaves prevent it from having much appeal as a lawn specimen. But on the edge of woodlands or in naturalized plantings, it can add a touch of brightness to what might otherwise be a uniformly colored planting. Because it is native it should take preference over species that are somewhat similar such as *A. davidii, capillipes, crataegifolium,* and *rufinerve.*

Acer platanoides   90′   Zone 3   Norway maple

* FLOWERS: small, yellow, appearing in conspicuous clusters before the leaves
    TIME: late April
* HABIT: rounded
FOLIAGE: very dense, leaves lobed and bright green

* AUTUMN COLOR: bright yellow
  HABITAT: Europe, Caucasus
  INTRODUCED: early colonial times
  VARIETIES:

> 'Almira'—small, globe-shaped
>
> 'Cleveland'—oval, upright in habit
>
> 'Crimson King'—the first of three red-leaved clones made available in the United States. Some growers claim that both 'Fassen's Black' and 'Goldsworth Purple' are not only inferior in growth but do not keep their red leaf color in the late summer as well as 'Crimson King.' Others fail to see much difference. It may be that these three respond differently in different soils. If one is to be selected, the older 'Crimson King' might well be the one, for certainly all do not differ sufficiently to warrant their being grown. The much older variety 'Schwedleri' need not be grown any longer since it does not retain its reddish leaf color throughout the summer, and 'Crimson King' does.
>
> 'Crimson Sentry' *(Plant Patent #3258)*—dark purple foliage during the spring and summer, slow-growing, upright in habit, narrow, and columnar. Originated by Princeton Nurseries, Princeton, New Jersey.
>
> 'Deborah'—new growth is brilliant red. A new variety from the Holmlund Nursery, Gresham, Oregon.
>
> 'Drummondii'—an unstable variety; the leaf edges are white but can revert to green
>
> 'Emerald Green'—fast-growing, dense, dark green foliage
>
> 'Emerald Lustre'—originated in the Bailey Nurseries, St. Paul, Minnesota. It is very hardy and survives in cold areas where other Norway maple varieties such as 'Crimson King' do not.
>
> 'Erectum' *(ascendens)*—has larger leaves than 'Columnare' and short, stubby, lateral branching. A twenty-year-old plant in the Arnold Arboretum was 30' tall, and had a total branch spread of only 6'. The mature shape is supposed to be conical rather than columnar.
>
> 'Globosum'—an excellent low-growing, rounded tree for plantings under electric wires. It should be grafted high at about 6' on *A. platanoides* understock. 'Almira' is similar.
>
> 'Jade Glen'—yellow autumn color with dense-growing branches producing heavy shade
>
> 'Lorbergii'—leaves palmately divided to base of leaf but tips ascending from plane of leaf. A dense, rounded, very slow-growing tree without a central leader, superior to *palmatifidum* as an ornamental.
>
> 'Summershade' *(Plant Patent #1748, 1958)*—reported as being "rapid growing, heat resistant, and upright in habit, maintaining a single leader. The foliage is more leathery than other varieties."
>
> 'Undulatum'—leaves stiffly held in a horizontal plane, upright branching. The plant in the Arnold Arboretum is 30' tall and 16' wide.

Although a native of Europe, the Norway maple has become one of the most commonly planted street and shade trees in the eastern United States. Its widely rounded habit and dense foliage make it capable of giving dense shade, so much, in fact, that it is very difficult to grow anything underneath it. The feeding roots are very close to the surface, making the cultivation of other plants near it additionally difficult.

In the spring its yellow flowers appear before the leaves, making the tree a mass of yellow visible from a mile away. In the fall the leaves turn a clear yellow; in fact, it is one of the best of all shade trees for its yellow autumn coloration.

Because it has been grown for so long, over ninety varieties have been named. The columnar forms are widely used in the planting of narrow streets. Schwedler's maple, with its purplish red leaves in the spring and early summer, has been a widely used favorite, but its popularity is on the wane because 'Crimson King' holds its deep reddish color all summer long. It is one of the few maples, along with the Hedge maple, to show a milky white sap at the base of the leaf petiole when it is pulled from the twig.

Finally, it can be considered a quick screen because it grows more rapidly than other maples, although not as fast as the Siberian elm or Lombardy poplar. It has more ornamental and lasting qualities than either. As for diseases, it is susceptible to verticillium wilt, anthracnose, and leaf scorch.

Acer pseudoplatanus   90'   Zone 5   Sycamore maple

FRUIT: winged keys or samaras, in clusters 5" long
    EFFECTIVE: summer
HABIT: wide-spreading
FOLIAGE: dense, leaves large, lobed, often coarse
HABITAT: Europe, western Asia
INTRODUCED: early colonial times
VARIETIES:

> **'Brilliantissimum'**—an excellent variety with the young foliage pale pink, later changing to pale yellow-green, finally changing to green. Does not show off well in bright sun, but with partial shade it is excellent. Much used in Europe where cloudy conditions often prevail.
>
> **'Erectum'**—young trees are narrow and columnar, but as they mature, tend to grow into a narrowly pyramidal form
>
> **'Erythrocarpum'** *(Fruit sycamore maple)*—leaves smaller and lustrous, fruits bright red—scarlet
>
> **'Purpureum'** *(Purpleleaf sycamore maple)*—leaves purple on the underside. Several varieties are somewhat similar, including 'Spaethii' and 'Atropurpureum.' Especially susceptible to attacks from aphids, which can be controlled by spraying with malathion. This species is also susceptible to cankers.
>
> **'Worleei'** *(Yellow sycamore maple)*—leaves deep yellow, almost orange-yellow when young; petiole red. Considered by some a superior form.

A common old-world tree widely cultivated for centuries, it has earned a place for itself in North America. It has no autumn color and so cannot compete with American and Asiatic species in this respect. However, it is one of the best of all trees for withstanding the salt-laden blasts of wind in seashore gardens, where it is highly respected for this peculiar characteristic. Its 5-inch-long clusters of fruit are interesting and conspicuous for a greater part of the summer. This is especially true in the red-fruited variety 'Erythrocarpum.' *Acer heldreichii* is similar to the sycamore maple with slightly deeper-lobed leaves but is not superior to it from specimens growing in the Arnold Arboretum. There is often much dead wood and cankers, requiring considerable maintenance.

Acer rubrum   120'   Zone 3   Red maple, Swamp maple

* FLOWERS: very small but profuse, red
        TIME: early April
* FRUIT: bright red winged keys or samaras
        EFFECTIVE: late spring
    HABIT: rounded head but sometimes pyramidal or even elliptical when young
    FOLIAGE: dense
* AUTUMN COLOR: brilliant red
    HABITAT: eastern and central North America
    VARIETIES:

> 'Armstrong'—upright in growth, faster growing than either upright sugar or Norway maples. Often poor fall color.
>
> 'Autumn Flame'—rounded in habit, early fall color
>
> 'Bowhall'—upright in habit, often wider in growth than 'Armstrong'
>
> 'Columnare' *(Columnar red maple)*—densely upright in habit, not as narrow as *A. saccharum* 'Monumentale' or *A. platanoides* 'Columnare,' but an excellent, fast-growing upright type, sometimes densely pyramidal in outline at maturity. The sixty-year-old plant in the Arnold Arboretum is 75' tall and 36' wide.
>
> 'October Glory' *(Plant Patent #2116)*—clean, lustrous foliage turns a brilliant red in the fall, retaining its leaves much longer than do other red maples. An excellent variety, originated by Princeton Nurseries, Princeton, New Jersey.
>
> 'Phipps Farm'—yellow, orange, and brilliant red in autumn; holds color until most of the other red maples have dropped their leaves. Originated in 1977 in the woods of Weston Nurseries, Hopkinton, Massachusetts.

Over forty valid clone names have been given to plants of this species.

The red maple is commonly seen in low and swampy areas, especially evident in the early spring since its myriads of small, red flowers, each inconspicuous in its own right, are produced in such large numbers and bloom so early that they are noticeable for some distance. In many areas the bloom of the red maple is one of the first visible evidences of spring, just as the brilliant fall coloration is one of the first signs of approaching autumn. One reason the red maple colors before most other trees in the fall is that it is native in swamps or low spots where the frosts of fall are felt first. A fast-growing tree, somewhat weak-wooded, it is superior to the silver maple as a lawn tree, but in areas where snowstorms or ice storms are common it can be expected to break up more easily than sugar maples and most oaks. The red maple is especially susceptible to verticillium wilt and anthracnose as well as many other insect and disease problems. Drought conditions will often bring about leaf scorch. Leaf hoppers can be troublesome but can be controlled by spraying with malathion.

Acer saccharinum 'Silver Queen' 100′ Zone 3

HABIT: rounded, pyramidal
FOLIAGE: leaves bright green above and whitish underneath

'Silver Queen' is a hybrid, completely seedless, and fast growing, but having the silver maple *(A. saccharinum)* as one of its parents, it must be remembered that the wood is weak and splits easily in wind- or snowstorms. Valued only for its rapid growth; otherwise better and stronger maples should be used.

Acer saccharum 120′ Zone 3 Sugar maple

HABIT: oval; mature specimens have rounded head
FOLIAGE: dense, leaves lobed
* AUTUMN COLOR: yellow to orange and red
HABITAT: eastern North America
VARIETIES:

'Bonfire'—in neutral to alkaline soils sugar maples produce poor autumn color, but this clone was selected for its brilliant autumn foliage in slightly alkaline soils in Minnesota. Princeton Nurseries has noted it for its vigorous, rapid growth as well. Originated at Princeton Nurseries, Princeton, New Jersey.

conicum—of dense, conical habit. Many trees in the wild have this general shape.

'Globosum'—dwarf with a round head, useful when grafted high on *A. saccharum* understock for planting underneath utility wires

'Goldspire' *(Plant Patent #2917)*—vigorous and narrow in habit, resistant to leaf scorch, with bright yellow autumn color. Originated by Princeton Nurseries.

'Green Mountain' *(Plant Patent #2339)*—upright oval crown, hybrid between the black and sugar maples, exceptionally rapid in growth. Does well in dry or southern climates since it is scorch resistant and heat tolerant. Originated by Princeton Nurseries.

'Monumentale'—first introduced by F. L. Temple of Cambridge, Massachusetts, about 1887 and for many years grown and distributed as the sentry maple *A. saccharum 'Temple's Upright.'* A fifteen-year-old tree in the Arnold Arboretum is 50′ tall and 12′ wide. It does not have a central leader.

'Newton's Sentry'—originated in Newtonville, Massachusetts, prior to 1871. Characterized by a main central leader.

nigrum 'Slavin's Upright'—distinctly upright habit with dense foliage. Leaves turn red to yellow in autumn. Selected from seedlings in northern New York in 1903. B. H. Slavin, formerly superintendent of parks, Rochester, New York, stated that this was faster growing than the upright *A. saccharum* varieties. The original tree in Rochester was measured a few years ago and was 50′ tall and 25′ across, decidedly columnar in habit.

'Northwood'—a selection of the University of Minnesota, it can withstand

Acer saccharum
'Monumentale'

rugged winters that other sugar maples can't. The autumn color is a mixture
of red, yellow, and orange.

'Red Sunset'—not as hardy as 'Northwood' and *A. rubrum* 'October Glory'
but outstanding nevertheless.

Widely grown throughout the eastern part of North America, the sugar maple is one
of the best and most common of our native shade trees. One of the largest, among
the measured trees at least, is in West Virginia near Morgantown. It is 110 feet tall,
has a spread of 75 feet and a trunk circumference of 17½ feet at breast height, proving
that they do grow into stately specimens! But even while young they make excellent
shade trees requiring very little attention. The sap from these trees, when boiled
down sufficiently, yields maple syrup. Every country lad in New England is familiar
with the general process of tapping the trees in early spring and then collecting and
boiling the sap to make maple syrup. Most nursery trees are grown from seed, and
mature trees show considerable variation in general outline, some rounded, others
densely pyramidal or even oval. The sugar maple in its fiery red-and-yellow fall garb
is perhaps one of America's most colorful sights. It is sturdier and breaks up much
less in snow, ice, and windstorms than does the more brittle Norway maple. How-

ever, it and its varieties are slower growing than both the Norway and red maple. Sugar maple is susceptible to several types of insects and diseases. One that can be serious is anthracnose, and zineb seems to be good as a spray for its control. Pear thrips was prevalent recently, but as yet there seems to be no insecticide for its control. At the present time pear thrips is becoming extremely serious, and it is hoped that some material can be found to combat it. Sometimes, especially during drought periods, several problems seem to strike at once, causing what has been called a "maple decline" that is hard to control by spraying. Verticillium wilt also takes its toll on occasion.

Acer spicatum   25′   Zone 2   Mountain maple

* FRUIT: bright red winged keys or samaras
    EFFECTIVE: summer
FOLIAGE: rather open and coarse
* AUTUMN COLOR: orange and scarlet
HABITAT: Labrador to Saskatchewan, south to Georgia and Iowa

Another extremely hardy maple, found over a wide area of North America, no better than other shrubby maples suggested here but of value for its hardiness and ability to grow in partial shade. Recommended for planting in wooded areas only. Diseases and insect problems are not serious.

The Tatarian maple (Acer tataricum) *possesses dense, fine, bright green foliage throughout the spring and summer that turns an excellent red to yellow in autumn.*

Acer tataricum   30'   Zone 4   Tatarian maple

* FRUIT: red winged keys or samaras
        EFFECTIVE: summer
  HABIT: upright, elliptical
  FOLIAGE: dense, fine, bright green
* AUTUMN COLOR: red to yellow
  HABITAT: Europe, western Asia
  INTRODUCED: 1759

Another small tree for street planting, well shaped and in need of very little attention. It is perfectly hardy in New England and is grown readily from its profuse seed by commercial nurseries. Diseases and insect problems are not serious.

Acer triflorum   24'   Zone 5   Three-flower maple

  HABIT: round-topped
  FOLIAGE: leaves trifoliate
* AUTUMN COLOR: red
  HABITAT: Manchuria, Korea
  INTRODUCED: 1923

Interesting flaking bark, closely allied to *A. maximowiczianum.* Few diseases plague this species.

Acer tschonoskii   20'   Zone 5   Tschonoski maple

  HABIT: graceful, almost shrubby
  FOLIAGE: leaves usually 5 lobed, sometimes 7 lobed
* AUTUMN COLOR: bright yellow
  HABITAT: Japan
  INTRODUCED: 1892

A graceful, shrubby tree, reported as popular in shade tree surveys in the central United States.

Acmena smithii   10–25'   Zone 10   Lili-pili tree

  FLOWERS: small, white, terminal, in clusters 2–4″ in diameter
        TIME: May–July
* FRUIT: showy, edible, purplish berries
        EFFECTIVE: winter
* FOLIAGE: evergreen, bronze when young
  HABITAT: Australia
  INTRODUCED: 1790 (England)

Suitable for hedge, windbreak, or specimen plantings in either southern California or southern Florida. Is resistant to salt spray injury and does best in a partially shaded spot. (Formerly *Eugenia smithii.*)

⇶ *AESCULUS*

The horse-chestnuts and buckeyes as a group have been greatly overplanted in North America. *Aesculus hippocastanum* was brought over to this country by the earliest colonial settlers, and it has been planted ever since. It is definitely coarse in foliage texture, flower, and fruit, and is now considered a "dirty" tree in that it is always dropping something—twigs, flowers, fruits, and leaves. Its two weeks of bloom is the only time it is interesting, and even these flowers are large and coarse. In any event, none in this genus should be considered for the small property. If and when planted, it should be where they can be observed several hundred feet away, in large public areas, for example. They make poor street trees for the above-mentioned reasons. A leaf scorch often seriously disfigures *A. hippocastanum* but not *A. glabra* in late summer. Leaf blotch can also be a problem, causing curled, yellow leaves. When they fall, burn them and spray the tree with copper sulfate or ferbam. This also can be used for controlling leaf scorch.

x Aesculus carnea   75'   Zone 3   Red horse-chestnut

* FLOWERS: pink to red flowers, in upright clusters 10" tall
       TIME: mid-May
HABIT: rounded head, pyramidal when young
FOLIAGE: coarse but more resistant to rust than *A. hippocastanum,* palmately compound with 5 leaflets
HYBRID ORIGIN: *A. hippocastanum x A. pavia*
ORIGINATED: 1858
VARIETIES:
  'Briotii' *(Ruby horse-chestnut)*—slightly larger flowers of a bright scarlet color. The clusters are 10" tall, fairly dense, and symmetrical, and the flowers open completely.
  'Oneil's Red'—flowers double, red; is difficult to find in nurseries
  'Plantierensis' *(Damask horse-chestnut)*—originated before 1894; the 12" flower clusters of this variety are covered with light pink flowers with a red or yellow throat. These are lighter than either *A. carnea* or its variety 'Briotii,' and usually the leaves have 7 leaflets while those of the other two have 5-7 leaflets. One good characteristic is that the tree does not produce fruits.

Left to right, *the flower clusters of* Aesculus hippocastanum *'Baumannii,'* A. hippocastanum, *and* x A. carnea.

Originated in Europe over one hundred years ago, this species and its three varieties are the most ornamental of the *Aesculus* tribe, merely because of their brightly colored flowers. The flowers have a red throat when fully open, and although it is a hybrid the species is a tetraploid and comes remarkably true from seed. Like most horse-chestnuts it is very coarse in texture and has no autumn color.

Aesculus glabra   30'   Zone 3   Ohio buckeye

FLOWERS: small, greenish yellow, in upright panicles 6″ high
      TIME: mid-May
HABIT: rounded head
FOLIAGE: coarse, palmately compound, 5 leaflets
* AUTUMN COLOR: brilliant orange
HABITAT: central United States

Listed here because it is the only horse-chestnut with good autumn color. Its flowers are the least desirable of any, its foliage and fruits no better than those of *A. hippocastanum.* Seldom do we have space to plant a tree for autumn color alone, but this and its good form might be enough to recommend it for planting in situations where the taller horse-chestnuts would be out of place. Very susceptible to leaf blotch and several other diseases and insects.

Aesculus hippocastanum 'Baumannii' 75' Zone 3 Baumann
horse-chestnut

* FLOWERS: double white flowers, ¾" in diameter, in 12" upright spikes
    TIME: mid-May
HABIT: elliptical when young, massive and rounded at maturity
FOLIAGE: coarse, palmately compound, 5–7 leaflets
ORIGIN: as a sport about 1822 in Geneva, Switzerland
INTRODUCED: 1838

The common horse-chestnut, *A. hippocastanum,* has been widely used as a street tree and as a specimen in Europe (where it is native) and in America as well. It grows to be a stately tree and is covered with foot-long, upright panicles of conspicuous flowers. Often up to 100 feet in height, it is easily grown and propagated from seed. However, it has earned a bad reputation in most places. Its wood is rather weak, and its massive branches, broken off by winds, afford excellent spots for infection by rotting fungi, which eventually cause serious damage. Its large compound leaves are

The double-flowered Baumann horse-chestnut (A. hippocastanum *'Baumannii') bears no fruit, hence is one of the best of the horse-chestnuts for ornamental planting.*

coarse in texture, have no autumn color, and in most places are susceptible to a rust disease that seriously disfigures them the latter part of the summer. The fruits (nuts) are large and coarse, are profusely borne, have no ornamental or economic interest whatsoever (except to small boys who like to collect them), and result in a hazard on the street, walk or lawn, wherever they fall. There are many trees superior to the horse-chestnut, and these should be used in its place.

If a horse-chestnut must be used, the Baumann horse-chestnut should be selected, for it has double flowers and no fruits. Being double, the flowers naturally last longer than do the single flowers of the species. It is not superior to the species in other ways, but the absence of the fruit is quite a point in its favor.

Agonis flexuosa (syn. *Leptospermum flexuosum*)   25–35′   Zone 10
                                                              Peppermint tree

FLOWERS: small, white, in small heads ½″ wide
    TIME: June
* HABIT: pendulous branches
* FOLIAGE: evergreen, somewhat similar to that of *Eucalyptus*
HABITAT: Australia
INTRODUCED: 1886 (England)

Low-spreading tree, closely related to *Leptospermum.* It is handsome and should be better known.

Ailanthus altissima   60′   Zone 4   Tree of heaven

FLOWERS: small, yellow, in large pyramidal clusters
    TIME: late June
* FRUIT: female has red keys, somewhat similar to those of maples; sexes separate
    EFFECTIVE: August to November
HABIT: rounded but open, often giving very little shade
FOLIAGE: open, coarse
HABITAT: China
INTRODUCED: 1784
VARIETIES:

   erythrocarpa—fruits of pistillate plants are bright red
   'Pendulifolia'—while leaves of this species are usually 12–24″ long and rather
      stiffly held, the leaves of this variety are much longer (with usually more than
      the 25 leaflets of the species). Also, the leaves are not stiffly held but rather
      are drooping, giving some additional interest to this exotic tree.

No matter what city you go to, whether it be Boston, New York, Chicago, Washington, or any one of many other cities in this country or abroad, there is one interesting tree that is continually cropping up in the most unexpected places. It can grow between cement blocks; it seems to thrive on nothing but ashes; it will breathe in air laden with soot, gas, and smoke, yet produce an abundance of green foliage; it apparently likes the toughest and most trying growing conditions it can find. This is the tree of heaven, a native of northern China, which grows better under city conditions in this country than any other tree, native or exotic.

It was first brought to England by Peter Collinson in 1751 and reached the United States late in the same century. At one time it was highly recommended for city planting in this country (and still is in some places) so that it has become widely distributed here in America. It is easy to propagate, either by seeds or root cuttings, and because of its very vigorous growth has made itself at home in many out-of-the-way places. The large compound alternate leaves can be distinguished from those of the sumacs because the leaflets have a small point at the base of each near the petiole.

One of the unusual things about this tenacious tree is its fruiting habits. The sexes are separate; that is, the staminate, or pollen-bearing flowers, and the pistillate, or fruiting flowers, occur on separate trees. The flowers themselves are comparatively small, greenish yellow in color, and borne in large terminal clusters that are very conspicuous. Occasionally there are trees that have both male and female flowers on the same plant, but this is the exception rather than the rule. The staminate or male flowers, when fully open, give off a vile smell, and for this reason the male plant should not be propagated or used in any way.

The fruits produced by the pistillate or female plant are keys somewhat similar to the fruits of the maple except that the seed is in the center of the wing. These wings are slightly twisted at both ends, much like an airplane propeller. When the keys fall off the plant, they whirl around in the air; if there is any breeze at all, they are frequently carried quite a distance before they finally come to rest on the ground. Such seeds ensure the dissemination of the tree. They mature about the last of the summer, and if collected and dried will sprout readily when sown in a seed flat. The seeds do not require fertilization in order to mature, but if not fertilized they cannot germinate. This is another excellent reason for not using the male plant. The tree is actually becoming a pest in many places, and the fewer viable seeds produced, the less the plant will spread. Hence, only fruiting plants should be propagated vegetatively by root cuttings.

From an ornamental standpoint there are four things of importance about this tree. The first and that for which it is primarily used is, of course, its ability to withstand seemingly unfavorable conditions. It grows in wet or dry soil, with apparent disregard for slight changes in soil acidity and other conditions about which so many of our valued ornamental trees are very particular. It is not susceptible to any serious diseases or insect pests, a noble quality particularly for a tree in the city where care is often sadly neglected. Still another rugged characteristic has become apparent as a result of recent hurricanes: the tree of heaven can withstand submergence in salt water. I have seen it at Newport, Rhode Island, within about a hundred feet of the ocean in normal times when the hurricane tides covered their roots with seawater for days, yet they sent out normal leaves the following spring and altogether showed little effect of the trying ducking they received, a ducking that all too frequently proved disastrous for many other nearby plants.

In addition to its adaptability, a second important feature is that it has a well-rounded form when several years old. Furthermore, it can be used to create semitropical effects in gardens, for if the saplings are allowed to grow about 10 feet high and then are cut to the ground every so often, they sprout up vigorously from the base and produce an unbelievable luxuriance of foliage in one year. Finally, the fruits of the female tree are a bright reddish color in the late summer and lend considerable interest at that time of year—before most other trees bear colored fruits and before the foliage of other trees begins to take on vivid hues in the fall.

On the other hand, this tree should not be recommended for general landscape use. Because it grows so fast, often several feet a year, the wood is light and weak, readily splitting and breaking in heavy windstorms or when weighted down with snow and ice in the winter. Second, there is nothing particularly beautiful about the foliage. Large, compound leaves, like those of the tree of heaven, do not have "fine texture." The putrid odor of the male flowers makes it objectionable anywhere under any conditions. When both sexes are present, viable seeds are scattered and soon sprout everywhere, making the tree a pest all over the garden. In fact, it is said that there was once a city ordinance in Washington that prohibited the planting of the tree of heaven anywhere within the city limits.

Although this strange tree does have its uses, it is practically a weed at present. In the suburbs of large cities where good garden soil and intelligent care are available and one can grow many different kinds of trees, there is little room for *Ailanthus.* But in the crowded streets and alleys of the large cities, in unattractive backyards where nothing else will grow, on city dumps and fill-in areas, in a thousand and one places where "civilization" has encroached upon nature to the extent of nearly eliminating plants—there grows the tree of heaven. Its green leaves and brightly colored fruits, its vigorous growth and wide branches seem to be living proof that nature can find some tree to grow in even the poorest soil. Many a city dweller is unconsciously grateful to the little-known plant collector who brought this hardy tree from China.

Albizia julibrissin   36′   Zone 7   Silk tree

* FLOWER: prominent because of light pink stamens in rounded heads
   TIME: summer
* HABIT: flat-topped, spreading, often several trunks
* FOLIAGE: graceful, very fine, compound leaves
 HABITAT: Iran to central China
 INTRODUCED: 1745
 VARIETIES:
   'Charlotte'—one of two varieties found by the U.S. Department of Agriculture in 1949 to be resistant to the fungus wilt of mimosa
   'E. H. Wilson' *(rosea—Hardy silk tree)*—stamens deeper pink color, tree smaller than the species, hardier (Zone 5, up to Boston, Massachusetts), introduced by the Arnold Arboretum in 1918 when it was first brought over from Korea. Although the flower color does not differ much from that of the species, the tree itself is worthy of the varietal name if for nothing more than its increased hardiness and smaller size.
   'Tryon'—one of two varieties found by the U. S. Department of Agriculture in 1949 to be resistant to the fungus wilt of mimosa

It should be pointed out that, according to the fine points of the *International Rules of Botanical Nomenclature,* the generic name should be spelled *Albizia.* This is unfortu-

The graceful silk tree (Albizia julibrissin) *is flat-topped, possesses finely compound leaves, and blooms in July and August.*

nate since it was named in honor of an Italian naturalist by the name of Albizzi. This genus, popularly planted in the South for a century and a half as *Albizzia,* probably will be continued under that name and spelling, regardless.

This tree has exceedingly dainty foliage. The leaves are compound, almost like those of the sensitive plant, and in fact they do curl up on cool evenings. Being a legume, the seed is borne in small flat pods. The flowers are conspicuous, not because of petals (which are insignificant) but because of inch-long pink-colored stamens borne in ball-like clusters. The plant has the very desirable trait (variety 'E. H. Wilson,' at least) of opening its flowers consecutively throughout the summer months. In Boston they start to bloom about July 15 and are continuously in bloom until early September—a long flowering period that cannot be matched by any other northern ornamental tree. The leaves fall at the first frost without changing color.

It is fortunate, at least up to this time, that the serious fungus wilt of mimosa has not affected trees growing in New England. In the South this disease has proved one of the most destructive of all tree diseases. Since it is a soil fungus, the removal of infected trees has no effect on the spread of the disease, which enters through the tree roots.

The disease was first noticed in the United States in 1930 at Tryon, North Carolina. The U.S. Department of Agriculture has grown hundreds of plants, collected from Maryland to Louisiana, in an effort to find some that, when inoculated with the disease, appear to be resistant or immune. Two trees have been found, propagated, and distributed and have been named 'Charlotte' and 'Tryon.' These should be the ones to grow in the South.

Unfortunately, these varieties have not proved hardy in the Arnold Arboretum in Boston. Since this disease is a soil fungus, however, it apparently does not live over winter in northern soils.

This is a splendid ornamental tree and very much worth experimenting with in the North (variety 'E. H. Wilson' only). Although it can be grown in many soils, we have found that it does well on poor, dry, gravelly soils and so has an important use. The tree blooms early in life, sometimes when the seedlings are only two to three years old. Propagation is easily accomplished by seed or 3-inch root cuttings made in very early spring, using roots that are $1/3$ inch or more in diameter—smaller roots do not root nearly so well. It is important to protect the young plants carefully from the winter for the first two or three years since injury can be severe at this time. After the plants are larger and sturdier, they seem to be able to survive most winters as far north as Boston.

→≫ *ALNUS*

Most of the alders have little to recommend them for garden use. They have no special autumn color, no interesting fruits. It is true that the flower catkins are present all winter, but so are those of the birches. They are mostly short-lived trees, with several insects that thrive on them, especially the tent caterpillar. Carbaryl or Sevin is used in spraying. Aphids are best controlled with malathion.

However, alders are well adapted to growing in moist or wet soils and are recommended here solely for this purpose. Where better soils are available, other trees with more ornamental characteristics than the alders should be grown.

Alnus cordata   45'   Zone 5   Italian alder

HABIT: rounded head
FOLIAGE: dense, glossy, open
HABITAT: Italy, Corsica
INTRODUCED: 1820

This is considered one of the handsomest of the alders because of its glossy green foliage. Also, it does well in dry soils.

Alnus glutinosa   75'   Zone 3   European alder

HABIT: ovoid to oblong head
FOLIAGE: dark green leaves that fall off late in the season while still green

HABITAT: Europe to Siberia
INTRODUCED: colonial times
VARIETY:
   '**Laciniata**' *(Cutleaf European alder)*—leaves deeply lobed, fine texture

There is not much to recommend this for garden or street use except its adaptability to wet soil conditions. Where it is not needed for this specific purpose, better trees might well be substituted. However, Europeans think enough of this tree to have separated at least sixteen foliage forms, each varying only slightly from the others in leaf shape.

Alnus incana   60'   Zone 2   Speckled alder

HABIT: rounded head
FOLIAGE: dense, dark green leaves that fall off in the fall while still green
HABITAT: Europe, North America

Alnus incana *'Laciniata' is an interesting variety of the speckled alder and very popular in Europe.*

VARIETIES:

'**Aurea**' *(Yellowleaf speckled alder)*—young leaves and shoots yellowish; this
color is retained the better part of the summer

'**Coccinea**' *(Redstem alder)*—leaves yellowish, young twigs reddish

'**Laciniata**'—a very interesting cut-leaved variety

'**Pendula**' *(Weeping speckled alder)*—pendulous branches

'**Pinnata**' *(Featherleaf speckled alder)*—small but deeply lobed leaves

One of the hardiest of the alders, often shrubby, usually found growing in moist or
wet spots. It is suitable for planting in such situations where other trees will not grow;
however, in good soils, other more ornamental trees might be selected.

Alnus rhombifolia   75'   Zone 5   White alder

HABIT: rounded
* BARK: whitish brown to grayish brown
FOLIAGE: dense
HABITAT: British Columbia to California

Sometimes used in West Coast gardens for planting in wet spots or bordering streams.
Not needed in other parts of the country.

Alnus rubra   60'   Zone 4   Red alder

HABIT: pyramidal
FOLIAGE: dense, dark green
HABITAT: Pacific coast of North America
VARIETY:

'**Pinnatisecta**' *(Cutleaf red alder)*—leaves deeply lobed, making the foliage of
very fine texture.

A moisture-loving tree for planting on the West Coast, it is very susceptible to attacks
of the tent caterpillar.

→≫ *AMELANCHIER*

The genus *Amelanchier* contains about twenty-five species and botanical varieties, chiefly natives of North America, with very few natives of Europe and
Asia. Only twelve of this group are offered by American nurseries. They are
at their best in the early spring, before the leaves appear, for they always
produce billowy masses of small, white flowers in racemes. In warm weather
these flowers can fade and fall in a three-day period, which of course greatly

restricts their usefulness as flowering ornamentals. In the fall these plants are again outstanding because of their brilliantly conspicuous autumn colors of yellow and red. Sometimes in the early summer when their red fruits are attractive they also stand out, but usually these fruits (similar in size and shape to those of hawthorns) are quickly taken by the birds and do not remain on the plants long enough to be a predominant ornamental asset.

Unfortunately, serviceberries are susceptible to several pests that can become serious in certain areas. Lacewing fly, red spider, various scales, and fire blight all can attack, and because of this fact it is advisable not to use them in very large quantities, especially in areas where these pests are known to occur on other rosaceous plants. All the members of this genus are best used in naturalizing plantings. They are especially well suited for planting at the edge of woodlands, near ponds, or other such places.

So many are natives—one species or another being practically native from coast to coast—we must recognize the possibility of using them in certain kinds of plantings. However, because of the pests that attack them, one should use them with caution; that is the reason for recommending only three of the natives.

The common name shadblow has also been given to them because they were usually in bloom at the time shad used to run up New England rivers in the spring.

Amelanchier canadensis　　60'　　Zone 4　　Shadblow serviceberry, Downy serviceberry

* FLOWERS:　small, nodding, white racemes
　　　　TIME:　late April
　FRUIT:　maroon-purple, berrylike, edible
　　　EFFECTIVE:　early summer
　HABIT:　upright, often narrow
　FOLIAGE:　young foliage grayish, open
* AUTUMN COLOR:　yellow to red
　HABITAT:　eastern United States

The tallest of the *Amelanchiers,* this is admired by many because of the grayish foliage as it first unfurls in the spring.

x Amelanchier 'Cumulus' (Plant Patent #3092)　　40'　　Zone 4
Cumulus serviceberry

* FLOWERS:　masses of fleecy white flowers, much larger than most of the amelanchiers
　　　　TIME:　early May
　FRUIT:　red to black, berrylike
　　　EFFECTIVE:　early summer

HABIT: vigorous, upright
BARK: gray like that of beeches; good winter display
FOLIAGE: thick
* AUTUMN COLOR: orange to red
ORIGINATED: Princeton Nurseries, Princeton, New Jersey

Good as a street tree, with a single trunk. It does not sprout much from the base. Resistant to drought.

x *Amelanchier grandiflora*   25′   Zone 4   Apple serviceberry

* FLOWERS: pure white, 1¼″ in diameter
       TIME: early May
FRUIT: red to black, berrylike, edible
       EFFECTIVE: early summer
HABIT: wide-spreading branches
BARK: light gray
FOLIAGE: dense
* AUTUMN COLOR: yellow to orange
HYBRID ORIGIN: *A. canadensis x A. laevis*
ORIGINATED: 1870

This tree is of interest because it has larger flowers than any of the other serviceberries, and occasionally the flower buds and the petals are tinged pink at first; the petals quickly fade white, however. I have seen the variety named *rubescens,* and although the light pink color is very definitely there when the flowers first open, it lasts for such a short time—merely a day or two—that it seems wasted effort to propagate the plant, for in all other ways it is identical with the species. This apple serviceberry is considered by some the best of all the native species in this genus.

Amelanchier laevis   36′   Zone 4   Allegheny serviceberry

* FLOWERS: small, drooping, white racemes
       TIME: early May
FRUIT: red, berrylike
       EFFECTIVE: July
HABIT: spreading branches, often shrubby
* BARK: smooth, light gray
FOLIAGE: young leaves purplish
* AUTUMN COLOR: yellow to red
HABITAT: eastern North America

Not as tall as *A. canadensis* but the flowers are about the same size. Only mentioned because this species is native and widely distributed and makes just as good a small tree as the others. The winter bark of the trunk is especially distinctive.

Aralia elata   45'   Zone 3   Japanese angelica-tree

* FLOWERS: small, white flowers in large, pyramidal spikes, sometimes 18″ tall
    TIME: August
  FRUIT: small, black berries
    EFFECTIVE: early fall, but quickly eaten by birds
  HABIT: wide-spreading, often with several trunks, open
  FOLIAGE: compound, dark, glossy green leaves, up to 2½' long, very coarse, open
* AUTUMN COLOR: reddish orange
  HABITAT: northeastern Asia
  INTRODUCED: 1830

The devil's walking stick, as it is often called, is a peculiar, exotic-looking plant, decidedly out of place in most small gardens. It is a spindly-growing shrub or small tree, often suckering from the base, the main stems having sharp, triangular thorns and large compound leaves, sometimes 2½ feet long, that are usually clustered around the ends of the stems. The large, feathery spikes of small flowers are produced above the rather horizontal leaves, making them conspicuous from all sides, and are followed by small, black berries that quickly fall in the early autumn.

This is an unusual tree, conspicuous at all seasons and very difficult to use properly. It grows fairly well in almost any good soil. It is recommended in preference to *A. spinosa* merely because it is the hardiest member of this thorny genus. All do well under city conditions. No serious pests.

Araucaria araucana   90'   Zone 7   Monkey-puzzle tree

* HABIT: open, whorled branches; unique appearance but producing poor shade
* FOLIAGE: evergreen leaves sharply pointed and scalelike
  HABITAT: Chile
  INTRODUCED: 1795

Not a desirable specimen because of its weird, twisted branches, but nevertheless planted because it is the hardiest of this genus. The ropelike branches twist in various ways, forming an ungainly mass of foliage and giving rise to its common name.

Araucaria bidwillii   80–150'   Zone 10   Bunya-bunya

  FRUIT: heavy pineapplelike cones, up to 12″ long and 9″ wide, containing as many as 150 edible seeds
* HABIT: columnar but main branches sometimes drooping; branches produced in whorls
* FOLIAGE: evergreen, glossy, sharply pointed leaves, spirally arranged
  HABITAT: Australia
  INTRODUCED: 1843 (England)

*The monkey-puzzle tree
(Araucaria araucana) will
always make a conspicuous
and striking specimen.*

A rather unique-appearing tree, the branches are not clothed with foliage near the trunk but only from the middle to the ends. Has been used a good deal as an ornamental in warm countries.

Araucaria heterophylla (syn. *A. excelsa)*   100′   Zone 10
Norfolk Island pine

* HABIT: pyramidal, open, horizontal branches, producing poor shade
* FOLIAGE: evergreen leaves sharply pointed and scalelike, open
  HABITAT: Norfolk Island

Another picturesque member of this genus, used only to provide unusual effect in the warmest parts of the country. Widely grown in greenhouses, however, as a foliage pot plant.

Arbutus menziesii   75′   Zone 7   Pacific madrone

* FLOWERS: small (like those of *Vaccinium),* whitish, in pyramidal clusters 3–9″ tall
  and 6″ wide
  TIME: May

* FRUIT: red- to orange-colored berries
    EFFECTIVE: fall and winter
  HABIT: open, often with picturesque shape
* BARK: red to cinnamon; older bark peels off
* FOLIAGE: leaves evergreen, 2–6″ long, dark, glossy green
  HABITAT: British Columbia to California

An excellent broad-leaved evergreen tree, considered by some of the English garden-ers as one of the most beautiful of broad-leaved evergreens. It is certainly not used enough in its native country, one reason being that it is very difficult to transplant; seedlings not over 18 inches tall are about the safest to use and should be put in a permanent growing place. Second, it has the bad reputation of always dropping something—leaves, flowers, fruit, or bark—throughout the entire year. This can prove disconcerting, especially on a well-kept lawn.

However, if it is used in the flower border or shrub border, its untidy habits are not noticeable. Its beautiful spring flowers, conspicuous orange-colored fruits, cinna-mon-colored bark, and rich, broad, evergreen leaves make it an excellent specimen nevertheless. Unfortunately, like a great many other things, it does not do well in the East, but on the West Coast gardeners would do well to hunt situations where it could be grown and shown off to best advantage. Not the least of its attributes is its ability to grow in poor, dry soils.

Arbutus unedo   10–30′   Zone 8   Strawberry tree

* FLOWERS: small, white
  TIME: October to December

The bark at the base of an old strawberry tree (Arbutus unedo), *grown only in the warmer parts of the West Coast.*

* FRUIT: strawberrylike, brilliant orange-red berries, ¾" in diameter
     EFFECTIVE: October to December
  HABIT: with one or several trunks
* BARK: dark, cracking open on larger stems, showing the bright red inner bark
* FOLIAGE: lustrous, evergreen leaves, to 4" long
  HABITAT: southwestern Europe
  INTRODUCED: long in cultivation

An interesting, slow-growing shrub or tree with small flowers turning at once into strawberrylike red fruits that may remain on the tree for months. The dark brown bark cracks open to show the bright red inner bark of the larger stems. It should not be planted in alkaline soils.

Asimina triloba   35'   Zone 5   Pawpaw

FLOWERS: cup-shaped, purple, 2" in diameter
     TIME: late May
FRUIT: fleshy, yellow to brown pods, 2–3" long, edible
     EFFECTIVE: early fall
HABIT: erect
FOLIAGE: dense, coarse, drooping leaves, 6–12" long
* AUTUMN COLOR: yellow
HABITAT: eastern United States

This tree is rarely seen in cultivation. Its flowers are unique but not conspicuous. It likes good, rich soil. The most interesting ornamental characteristic is its drooping leaves, which, though large, are always moving in the slightest breeze. The large edible fruits were familiar to and hunted by the earliest American settlers. Pests are not serious problems.

Bauhinia blakeana 'Hong Kong'   20'   Zone 10   Hong Kong
                                                                      orchid tree

* FLOWERS: fragrant, orchidlike, rose-purple to crimson, 5½–6" in diameter
     TIME: October to March
FOLIAGE: evergreen
HABITAT: China

The most spectacular of subtropical trees, it is covered with flowers for a four-month period.

Bauhinia blakeana *'Hong Kong,' a variety of the orchid tree. Photograph courtesy of Monrovia Nursery Company.*

Bauhinia variegata   20′   Zone 10   Buddhist bauhinia

* FLOWERS: lavender to purple, like small orchids, flowers few together in leaf axils
        TIME: winter and spring
HABIT: umbrellalike form with round to flat head
FOLIAGE: 2-lobed or parted leaves
HABITAT: India, Burma

Widely planted in southern Florida and valued chiefly for its orchidlike flowers. It is partially without foliage in late winter. It is also frequently called mountain ebony or orchid tree.

⇶ *BETULA*

The birches have long been popular ornamental trees in America, chiefly in the northern United States and Canada. Several are native Americans, but many species have been introduced from Europe and Asia. In general, they are graceful trees, the most popular being those with white bark on the trunks and larger branches. Some of the others are very serviceable, either because they will grow well in wet soil or because they will exist as well as (or better than) any other tree in dry, poor soils.

Many of the exotic species and varieties, although interesting botanically, have little to offer as ornamentals when compared with those recommended.

In general, the birches are rather short-lived and are difficult to transplant, so that to ensure success they should be balled and burlapped and are best moved in the spring. Arborists know they are persistent "bleeders" and that pruning is best performed at almost any time of year except in the spring when the sap is running. Large branches seem to break readily under heavy coats of ice and snow, yet some, like the gray birch, have trunks that are extremely pliable. I have seen plants of this species 20 to 30 feet tall, covered with ice and bending down to and touching the ground, yet the additional weight had come so gradually that after the ice had melted, the trunks eventually returned to their normal upright position.

Most of the birches have bright yellow autumn color. The flowers are unisexual, with both male and female flowers on the same tree. The maturing of the catkins in the early spring and the pollen in the air are two of the first signs of plant activity. Those familiar with the woods know that "living" or "green" birch wood is one of the few woods that will burn, making this tree a welcome source of fuel when the woodsman is in a hurry to start his campfire.

Birches are susceptible to at least two serious insect pests that, if not properly controlled, can mar their effective use as ornamentals. The first is the bronze birch borer, a small, flat-headed grub about a half-inch to an inch long, which eats just under the bark and, if present in numbers, can kill the tree. *Betula pendula* is especially susceptible to this insect. I have seen mature trees in the Cleveland area that had to be removed because this insect had killed the tops of the specimens and done the damage before control measures were taken.

Betula papyrifera is supposed to be not nearly so susceptible to the inroads of this insect. The control, spraying with methoxychlor or malathion in late May and twice more at two-week intervals, is a chore that is sometimes overlooked. When this happens, especially if the tree is *B. pendula* growing in poor soil, attacks from the insect may soon follow.

The other insect that is most troublesome, in New England at least, is the birch leaf miner, a small insect that eats its way between the upper and lower epidermis of the leaf. If and when this happens, there is little that can be done. The leaf is marred for the rest of the season. Spraying with malathion is effective if done about the first of May, followed at ten-day intervals with two additional sprays. The second brood appears about July 1, when another spray (followed by still another on July 10) should be given.

With these hazards in mind, many a grower will not want to have a large number of birches. The list of seventeen here recommended is far too many for any one grower, but these are the better ones.

Of those recommended, *B. papyrifera, B. pendula, B. platyphylla,* and *B. populifolia* and their varieties have white bark. Those gardeners living in the northern United States and Canada have learned to appreciate the native canoe birch best of all. It does not have the graceful form or branching habits of *B. pendula* and its varieties, but when one has to consider the inroads of the bronze birch borer it may well be that the canoe birch is the safer of the two species to plant.

The gray birch is a much smaller tree and valued by landscapers because it grows in clumps, although it is not nearly as tall nor does it have as clear a white bark as the canoe birch. *Betula platyphylla* is the Asiatic counterpart of the canoe birch in America and the European birch in Europe. It might be the first to eliminate from this short list of recommended white-trunked trees.

The native American river birch *(B. nigra),* the sweet birch *(B. lenta),* and the Dahurian birch of northeastern Asia are the other birch species recommended that do not have white bark but nevertheless have ornamental values of their own. The river birch is valued chiefly as a tree for wet soils. The sweet birch is an excellent ornamental from the standpoint of foliage, general shape, and the vigor with which it grows. The Dahurian birch has an interesting bark formation, but if not deemed desirable, this might be another of these recommended species to omit.

Although usually associated with northern plantings, both *B. nigra* and *B. pendula* have been noted as doing well in California. The yellow birch *(B. lutea)* is native down the eastern coast into Florida.

This graceful, colorful group of trees has merit over a wide area, but they do have problems of growth that should be thoroughly studied and understood before they are grown or planted on a large scale.

Betula albo-sinensis   90'   Zone 5   Chinese paper birch

HABIT: rounded
* BARK: bright orange to orange-red, exfoliating
  FOLIAGE: open
* AUTUMN COLOR: yellow

HABITAT: central and western China
INTRODUCED: 1910

Not common in America but of special interest because of its bright orange-colored bark, especially noticeable in the winter.

Betula davurica　　60'　　Zone 4　　Dahurian birch

HABIT: wide-spreading branches
* BARK: curling, reddish brown, exfoliating
FOLIAGE: open
* AUTUMN COLOR: yellow
HABITAT: northeastern Asia
INTRODUCED: 1883

Somewhat similar to the river birch, but in the Arnold Arboretum this species grows remarkably well on a comparatively gravelly hillside. Hence it might have merit in situations where the river birch would not grow. The bark is especially interesting in that it peels or flakes off in regular pieces an inch or so square.

The canoe birch, Betula papyrifera.

Betula lenta   75′   Zone 3   Sweet birch

* HABIT: pyramidal and dense while young, round-topped at maturity
* BARK: cherrylike, reddish brown to black
  FOLIAGE: dense
* AUTUMN COLOR: golden yellow
  HABITAT: eastern United States

Common in the eastern part of the country, this makes an excellent specimen. Its shape, autumn color, and cherrylike bark are all in its favor. It is truly handsome, probably the best of all the birches for fall color. The young bark and twigs have an agreeable aromatic taste when chewed, giving rise to the common name.

Betula maximowicziana   100′   Zone 5   Monarch birch

  HABIT: fast growing, wide, upright
* BARK: orange, gray, exfoliating
* AUTUMN COLOR: yellow
  HABITAT: Japan
  INTRODUCED: 1988

This is a handsome, vigorously growing tree with large leaves.

Betula nigra   90′   Zone 4   River birch

* HABIT: pyramidal
* BARK: reddish brown, exfoliating
  FOLIAGE: open
* AUTUMN COLOR: yellow
  HABITAT: eastern United States
  VARIETY:
  > 'Heritage'—faster growing than the species discovered in St. Louis, Missouri, in 1968. Supposed to be highly resistant to the bronze birch borer. Great resistance to heat and cold, with colorful bark exfoliating in tan-colored sheets.

Commonly found native in lowlands and along stream banks where the soil is moist; often covered with water for several weeks during the course of the year. It is not long-lived in the North. The river birch is valued chiefly for its ability to grow in wet places and also for its beautiful, paper-thin, exfoliating, tan-colored bark in the wintertime.

Betula papyrifera   90′   Zone 2   Canoe birch

* HABIT: generally pyramidal
* BARK: white, peeling off in paper-thin sheets

FOLIAGE: open
* AUTUMN COLOR: yellow
HABITAT: north central and northeastern North America

The canoe, white, or paper birch is one of our best native ornamental trees, commonly found in the woods and mountains over a wide area of North America. Indian lore is rich in the legends surrounding the canoe birch, for it was this tree probably more than any other that supplied the coverings for wigwams and huts, as well as the materials from which canoes were made. It has good foliage and autumn color, and beautiful white bark. It should always be grown with a single trunk and planted in public places with discretion, for the bark-peeling propensities of the public frequently result in the permanent marring of these beautiful trunks. There is nothing more beautiful on the home grounds than one of these trees if it is allowed to grow unscarred. Summer and winter alike, its stately beauty and majestic habit will set it aside as one of our own most beautiful trees. It is superior to any of the other white-barked birches in that its trunk has considerably fewer black markings. This species is not seriously infested by the bronze birch borer that troubles the European species so much.

Betula pendula   60'   Zone 2   European birch

* HABIT: pyramidal; branches somewhat pendulous in older trees
* BARK: white, exfoliating
FOLIAGE: open
* AUTUMN COLOR: yellow
HABITAT: Europe, Asia Minor
INTRODUCED: colonial times
VARIETIES:

> 'Dalecarlica'—leaves deeply lobed, bark white, gracefully drooping side branches that always seem to be in motion in the slightest breeze
>
> 'Fastigiata' *(Pyramidal European birch)*—columnar in habit, dense and beautiful while young
>
> 'Gracilis' *(Cutleaf European birch)*—similar to the variety 'Tristis' but with lacinate leaves very finely dissected; a graceful specimen
>
> 'Purpurea' *(Purple European birch)*—leaves purplish green throughout most of the growing season. (Two new clones have been recently selected from this variety and named 'Purple Splendor' and 'Scarlet Glory.')
>
> 'Tristis' *(Slender European birch)*—very slender, pendulous branches with round regular head
>
> 'Youngii' *(Young's birch)*—gracefully pendulous branches; one of the best forms for the small garden

Formerly termed *B. alba* or *B. verrucosa,* this is a short-lived but exceedingly graceful tree. The species has slightly pendulous branches, but the varieties are markedly so. The variety 'Gracilis' is frequently found in catalogs under the name of *laciniata.* I have seen specimens of these varieties 20 feet tall that were simply perfect in every way. However, this species is most susceptible to the bronze birch borer, an insect that bores its way into the trunk high up in the tree, frequently killing the entire top. Since these are all grown with single trunks and are definitely pyramidal in shape, the tree can be ruined in one short growing season. I have seen a cemetery in Ohio where these trees were placed as the feature tree, beautiful specimens 15 to 20 feet tall that were completely ruined in a very few years by this pest. The entire planting, which had thrived for a dozen years, had to be removed and replaced with other kinds of trees.

The development of new sprays and possible repellents may eventually ensure longer lives for these trees, but they should be used on private properties only when the owner is fully aware of the quick destruction that can be caused by this pest if proper control measures are not taken. The leaf miner can also be a serious pest; because of this, in most cases, this species and its varieties should not be used.

Betula platyphylla japonica 'Whitespire'   60′   Zone 5

HABIT: triangular
BARK: white, peeling off in paper-thin sheets
FOLIAGE: leaves broadly ovate, triangular
AUTUMN COLOR: reddish
HABITAT: Japan

This variety is not susceptible to the bronze birch borer. Leaf miners can be a problem, but supposedly leaf hoppers are not.

Betula platyphylla szechuanica   60′   Zone 5   Manchurian birch

HABIT: open, wide-spreading branches
* BARK: white, peeling off in paper-thin sheets
FOLIAGE: thick, blue-green leaves, remaining on tree until late fall
* AUTUMN COLOR: yellow
HABITAT: western China
INTRODUCED: 1872

There are several forms of the Manchurian birch, but this one from the high mountains of extreme western China is perhaps the best. It approaches our canoe birch in size and form, but the twigs are a polished red-brown, and the thick, blue-green leaves remain on the tree longer in the fall. The species was formerly named *B. mandshurica.*

Betula populifolia   30′   Zones 3–4   Gray birch

* HABIT: usually with several trunks growing in clumps
* BARK: white with triangular black markings
FOLIAGE: open

A popular native, with several trunks at the base, the gray birch (Betula populifolia) *is not long-lived, and its trunks usually are not straight.*

* AUTUMN COLOR: yellow
HABITAT: northeastern North America

This certainly should not be confused with the taller, single-trunked birches. The gray birch is incorrectly named because its bark is white, with many triangular black markings. It is short-lived and grows with several trunks in clumps on poor, gravelly soil or even in very wet soil. The trunks are slender and pliable so that in heavy snowstorms or ice storms they are frequently bent to the ground. They have great recuperative powers from such storms, but their trunks are seldom straight, and once broken, disease and rot quickly take their toll. In New England this tree is frequently severely infested with the birch leaf miner, which quickly skeletonizes the leaf in the early summer unless promptly sprayed with methoxychlor or malathion as soon as the miners appear in the young foliage. If spraying will not be considered as an almost annual chore, one should consider selecting other trees not troubled with this pernicious pest. Fortunately, it is quite resistant to the bronze birch borer.

Brachychiton acerifolium   60'   Zone 10   Flame bottle tree

* FLOWERS: scarlet-red, in erect trusses
        TIME: July–August
  HABIT: fairly rounded, trunk bottle-shaped
  FOLIAGE: coarse, leaves lustrous, 10" in diameter, dense, drop prior to blooming
  HABITAT: Australia

This tree has a deep tap root and does best in deep soils. Used mainly in the South and in California. The trees of this genus are called "bottle trees" because the lower part of the trunk is usually swollen. These are not among the best ornamentals for subtropical areas and indeed are frequently considered a nuisance because they are always dropping something (like *Eucalyptus),* littering the ground beneath their branches. However, they seem to do well throughout lengthy dry periods.

Brachychiton discolor (syn. *Sterculia discolor)*   40'   Zone 9   Pink
                                                                          flame tree

* FLOWERS: large, bell-shaped, pink, in terminal spikes
        TIME: June, July
  FOLIAGE: maplelike leaves, 5–7 lobed, 4–6" wide
  HABITAT: Australia
  INTRODUCED: 1858 (England)

This has the largest flowers of this group of trees and is much faster growing than *B. acerifolium.* Popular in Florida.

Brachychiton populneum (syn. *Sterculia diversifolia)*   60'   Zone 9
                                                                    Bottle tree

  FLOWERS: small, bell-shaped, white
        TIME: May, June
* HABIT: bottle-shaped trunk
  FOLIAGE: evergreen leaves 3 lobed but give impression of poplar foliage
  HABITAT: Australia
  INTRODUCED: 1824 (England)

Especially noted for its bottle-shaped trunk and its ability for withstanding hot growing conditions, it is a messy tree but effective as a windbreak in drought areas. Used especially in California.

Broussonetia papyrifera   48'   Zone 6   Common paper-mulberry

  FLOWERS: female catkins are globular and interesting
        TIME: May

* FRUIT: round, orange to red, ¾″ in diameter
        EFFECTIVE: June and July
   HABIT: wide-spreading, broad, rounded head
* BARK: gray, trunk grows into irregular shapes
   FOLIAGE: dense, irregularly lobed
   HABITAT: China, Japan
   INTRODUCED: 1750

A neat tree with irregularly lobed leaves and interesting fruits. The common name comes from the fact that paper is made from the bark in China, the fibers being stuck together with rice paste. The bark has also been used to make cloth and the sap to make glue in Polynesia. In the South it is used as an ornamental and occasionally as a street tree. It does unusually well on poor, sterile, gravelly soil, where other trees will not survive, and seems to do equally well in areas where heat, smoke, and dust are prevalent. If the roots are disturbed, it has been noted to sucker freely. Not one of the best ornamental trees but a reliable one where growing conditions are difficult. Susceptible to various root rots and cankers.

Buxus sempervirens arborescens   20′   Zone 5   Tree box

   HABIT: dense, rounded
* FOLIAGE: evergreen, fine textured, dark, lustrous, green leaves, to 1¼″ long
   HABITAT: southern Europe, northern Africa, western Asia
   INTRODUCED: early colonial times

The common box in America and its many varieties are usually treated as shrubs. The arborescent variety is merely listed here to bring attention to the fact that it can grow into a small tree, although it does take many years to do so. It is only in certain parts of the South (Zone 6) where century-old specimens have reached sufficient size to be classed as trees rather than tall shrubs. Actually, this species is more ornamentally effective when grown as a shrub than as a tree with a single trunk.

Boxwoods have several disease and insect problems, among them the boxwood leaf miner, which produces orange maggots in blisterlike bumps on the underside of the leaves. Spraying with methoxychlor, diazinon, or malathion once in midsummer gives effective control. Boxwood psyllids cause terminal leaves to form cup-shaped bumps and can be controlled by spraying with malathion. Spider mites, which cause the leaves to turn brown, can be controlled by spraying with dicofol.

When the twigs show dying or dieback, the disease can be controlled by spraying with copper sulfate, ferbam, or thiram in late summer. Dead twigs should be cut out and burned.

Callitris preissii   15–70′   Zone 9   Sturdy cypress-pine

   HABIT: usually a shrub to a small tree
* FOLIAGE: evergreen, scalelike, dark, blackish green
   HABITAT: Australia

Common box (Buxus sempervirens arborescens), *reaching heights of 20 feet, is widely grown as an ornamental in the eastern and southern United States.*

This plant has been able to withstand drought in hot areas and has been planted in both California and Florida for use in windbreaks. In general appearance it reminds one of red cedar.

Calocedrus decurrens   135′   Zone 5   California incense-cedar

FRUIT: cones ¾″ long, at tips of branches
    EFFECTIVE: fall and winter
* HABIT: narrowly columnar
* FOLIAGE: evergreen, scalelike, lustrous branchlets with vertical or "edgewise" leaves
HABITAT: Oregon, northern California

An excellent tree for formal plantings, well clothed with branches to the base of the tree; it should be used considerably more than it is. The leaves are very aromatic when crushed and are borne in vertical planes (instead of horizontal like those of *Thuja plicata*). Practically no foliage pests attack the tree, but in the forests where it is native, mature tree trunks are often infested with dry rot of the heart wood. The wood has been used for pencil slats, cedar chests, the mothproof lining of closets, and door and window sashes, even for cigar boxes. It requires a moist, good soil, and provided this, develops into a splendid ornamental tree.

Camellia japonica   45'   Zone 7   Common camellia

* FLOWERS: conspicuous, large, single or double, white to red, 2–5″ in diameter
        TIME: October–April
  HABIT: upright while young, more rounded at maturity
* FOLIAGE: evergreen, dark, leathery, lustrous leaves, to 4″ long
  HABITAT: China, Japan
  INTRODUCED: 1797

This popular late-flowering camellia of the South is represented by several hundred varieties now being grown in this country. These range in color from pure white to a rich, deep red with all the variations in between. Flowers of some varieties are single, some are semidouble, and some are very double. It is popular for growing in shaded situations where other plants may not bloom well. It is interesting to note the large number of varieties that have occurred within one species. So often, as in roses for example, hybridization between several species has resulted in a large number of varieties, but here the large number of varieties has resulted chiefly from hybridization within a single species and also the raising of many bud sports.

Several scale insects of camellia can be controlled by spraying with malathion when young insects are at the crawling stage. Spraying with ferbam after infected blossoms have been raked up and burned proves helpful in controlling the devastating petal blight.

The flower forms of these camellias differ considerably, and some authors have divided the varieties into nine different groups or classes. Chief among these, however, are the single type with one row of no more than six petals with prominent yellow stamens in the center (var. 'Amabilis'); the semidouble type, variously named, with mature petals around the perimeter of the flower and many small petals or modified stamens in the center ('Adolphe Audusson'); and several ramifications of the double form with petals regularly placed in a very definite arrangement ('C. M. Hovey') or with no apparent petal arrangement but still very few stamens ('Debutante'); and others very definitely double but with a center of golden stamens when fully open ('Kumasaka'). The flowers of some varieties have the general form of roses while others are suggestive of peonies. The camellia specialist is particular about his selection of just the right flower type, but for the amateur they are all beautiful and the twenty-five suggested varieties include some of the best of all the flower types.

The camellia is widely grown from North Carolina to Florida along the Gulf Coast, and on the West Coast as far north as Seattle. Even when their large, waxy, brilliantly colored flowers are not evident, *C. japonica* makes a good evergreen shrub for its foliage alone. The varieties of this species, though they bloom at different times, come as a group after the varieties of *C. sasanqua,* which bloom from September to October. Most varieties can be grown in normally good soil of about 6.0 pH or slightly less in the full sun, though many withstand shade very well indeed. The following popular varieties now being grown in the South and on the West Coast have been selected to exemplify the wide range of color and type of flower in this most variable species. (The color notes are taken from *Camellias, Kinds and Culture* by H. H. Hume, 1951, and refer to the English Horticultural Colour Chart.) There are many, many varieties in the trade, and it is most difficult to select the best. Some that might be considered are as follows:

Red varieties:

'**Adolphe Audusson**'—flowers semidouble, 4″ in diameter, turkey red 721 to rose-madder 23

'**Arejishi**'—flowers double, 3–4″ in diameter and 1½″ high, turkey red 721, blooms early for this species

'**Aunt Jetty**'—flowers double, 4″ in diameter, 2″ high, turkey red 721. The parent plant of this variety in western Florida (Tallahassee) is about 132 years old. It is not injured apparently by cold weather.

'**C. M. Hovey**'—flowers double, 3¼–4″ in diameter and flat, carmine 21, slightly variegated. This was first raised over a century ago by Hovey & Co., of Cambridge, Massachusetts, in 1847, when camellia-growing in greenhouses was a popular industry in New England. This is a splendid type and might well be considered one of the best and most dependable.

'**Lady Vansittart**'—flowers semidouble, 4″ in diameter, 1¼″ high, carmine-rose 621. Sometimes the flowers are almost variegated, white with carmine stripes, but it is a comparative newcomer to the United States, having been introduced here in 1917.

'**Mathotiana**'—flowers double, 4″ wide and 2″ high; carmine 21/1 with a coloring along the edges of the petals. Flowers are shaped very much like those of a rose.

'**Professor C. S. Sargent**'—flowers double, 3–4″ in diameter, 2″ high, turkey red 721. It was named after Charles Sprague Sargent, the first director of the Arnold Arboretum, Boston, Massachusetts. This variety is an excellent one, grows vigorously, is among the hardiest, and is sometimes used as an understock on which other varieties are grafted.

Pink varieties:

'**Debutante**'—flowers double, 3″ in diameter and 1¾″ high, carmine to carmine-rose 621/1. This originated as a chance seedling in Magnolia Gardens on the Ashley River of South Carolina, a show garden where many excellent varieties of camellias are grown. It is free-flowering, tall, compact in habit, and the flowers are of a color, size, and shape desirable for use in corsages.

'**Frau Minna Seidel**'—flowers double, 2½″ in diameter, 1¼″ high, carmine-rose 621/3. This is one of the most commonly grown of all camellia varieties, often found under the name of 'Pink Perfection.' It is vigorous and compact in habit, a reliable sort, and one that might easily be the single selection for a small garden.

'**Lady Humes Blush**'—flowers double, 2¾″–3″ in diameter, 1¼″ high, white, blushed pink. This is a slow grower, and though long in this country, has not proved as popular as other varieties. It is a good color, however, and so is recommended in this small, selective group.

'**Magnoliaeflora**'—single flowers, 3½″ wide and 1½″ high, white but blushed a very delicate light pink

White varieties:

'**Alba Plena**'—flowers double, 4″ in diameter, often 3″ high, and pure white. This is one of the oldest varieties in the United States and is still very popular. It is vigorous and compact and has been known to endure short cold spells of 10°F.

'**Amabilis**'—flowers single, 3″ in diameter, white

'Imura'—flowers semidouble, 4¾" in diameter, white. This originated in the
Overlook Nurseries of Crichton, Alabama, from Japanese seed grown there
in 1925. It is very much like a water lily in the form of the flowers. Some
like this variety best of all for its general habit of growth, reliability, and
delicate floral beauty.

'Shira-giku'—flowers double, 3½" in diameter, 1¼" high, white. A widely
popular variety with flowers of long-lasting quality and desirable for corsages, the petals are slightly wavy and almost like porcelain in texture.

Variegated varieties:

'Daikagura'—flowers double, 4" in diameter and 2" high, carmine-rose 621
with blotches of white. This early flowering variety is one of the best in its
group and was introduced into this country from Japan. Unfortunately it
grows slowly and tends to be slightly open in habit.

'Donckelari'—flowers semidouble, 4" in diameter, 1½" high, turkey red 721,
with some flowers having white markings. Another hardy variety, it was
introduced from the Orient by that famous German naturalist Philip Franz
von Siebold, who spent several years in Japan beginning about 1823.

'Herme'—flowers double, 3½" in diameter and 1¾" high, and extremely
variegated red and white. This slightly fragrant variety is known under three
names: 'Herme,' 'Souv. de Henri Guichard,' and 'Jordan's Pride.' This
might be construed as an indication of its extreme popularity.

'Kumasaka'—flowers double, 4" in diameter, 1¼" high, carmine 21/1 or
variegated with white markings. Only moderately vigorous, it is compact and
upright in habit.

'Lady Clare'—flowers semidouble, 4¾" in diameter, 1¼" high, carmine-rose
621 with some variegation of darker colors in the petals. The flowers do not
remain in good condition as long as do those of some other varieties.

Carpinus betulus   60'   Zone 5   European hornbeam

FRUIT: small nutlets in leaflike bracts, borne in pendulous clusters
    EFFECTIVE: summer and fall
* HABIT: pyramidal when young but rounded at maturity
    FOLIAGE: leaves dense, 1½ × 3½" long
    AUTUMN COLOR: yellow
    HABITAT: Europe, Iran
    INTRODUCED: colonial times
    VARIETIES:

'Columnaris'—rated as excellent in Europe, this plant has undoubtedly been
mixed up in America, having erroneously been called 'Fastigiata.' The two
are decidedly different, 'Columnaris' being dense, narrowly columnar with
a central trunk, and almost egg-shaped, looking as if it has been sheared, with
all foliage at the perimeter of the branches. 'Fastigiata,' on the other hand,
has all upright branching, but an old tree at the Arnold Arboretum forty-nine
years old is 50' tall by 40' wide—almost vase-shaped now with no central
trunk since the branches are heavier with age and tend to spread more. Also,
the leaves are not all at the ends of the branches but are more distributed,
the entire habit being more open.

The European hornbeam (Carpinus betulus) *makes an excellent clipped hedge.*

'Fastigiata'—differs from 'Columnaris' as noted above

'Globosa'—A plant under this name has been growing in the Arnold Arboretum since 1888, when it was received from the Spaeth Nurseries in Germany. It is definitely rounded and globose in habit, and as such differs from both 'Fastigiata' and 'Columnaris.' Young plants, which may not have grown into proper shape, might be confused with small plants of 'Columnaris' since both apparently produce leaves at the ends of the branches, giving a sheared effect, but 'Globosa' does not have a central trunk while 'Columnaris' does. However, as they grow older, the 'Globosa' trees will be definitely rounded and the 'Columnaris' trees will be egg-shaped.

horizontalis—discovered growing wild in France and noted for its flat top

'Incisa'—leaves narrow, coarsely toothed, and usually deeply cut or lobed

'Pendula'—with pendulous branches. I have never seen a plant of this, but it is said to be very graceful indeed.

This species is used a great deal in Europe, especially in making hedges and pleached allées, for it withstands shearing very well. However, since it may be a little difficult to move as a large tree, it is best to use the smallest possible tree at the start. Several forms of this species are available and make for considerable variety in this fine foliage plant. Like many other plants native to Europe, it is not as striking in fall color as its American or Japanese relatives. No serious insect pests or diseases.

*Here is the European
hornbeam* (Carpinus
betulus) *in its natural form.*

Carpinus caroliniana   36′   Zone 2   American hornbeam

FRUIT: hard nutlets in leaflike bracts, borne in pendulous clusters 3½″ long
      EFFECTIVE: summer and fall
HABIT: several trunks, rounded and bushy
* BARK: gray
FOLIAGE: dense, 2½–4½″ long
* AUTUMN COLOR: orange to red
HABITAT: eastern North America
VARIETY:
      '**Pyramidalis**'—This was received by the Arnold Arboretum from B. H. Sla-
      vin, superintendent of parks, Rochester, New York, in 1919. He had found
      the original a year before. At forty-three years of age, the plant was 40′ tall
      with a spread of 33′. The habit is definitely V-shaped, with a somewhat
      rounded top.

This native is often called blue beech or ironwood and is commonly found in the
woods of eastern North America. Small boys know it because the wood is tough to
chop with an axe; the term "ironwood" seems appropriate. Unfortunately it is not

too easily transplanted but makes an excellent small tree for the small garden. It often grows with several trunks that are not completely rounded in cross section but more like the outline of the wrist with the fist clenched tightly. The delicately shaped leaves, splendid autumn color, and interesting pendulous clusters of fruits make it of considerable interest throughout its growing season, and its "muscled" trunk and gray bark, as well as its habit of growth, will make it a focal point during its leafless period as well. Botanists draw attention to minute distinguishing characteristics between a northern form (called var. *virginiana*) and a southern form, but for ornamental purposes one is just as good as the other. It will not withstand clipping as well as *C. betulus*. No serious insect pests or diseases.

Carpinus japonica   45'   Zone 4   Japanese hornbeam

FRUIT: hard nutlets in leaflike bracts, borne in pendulous clusters 2–2½" long
     EFFECTIVE: summer and fall
* HABIT: flat-topped, but very definitely fan-shaped from the base
FOLIAGE: dense, leaves larger than other species, 2–4" long
* AUTUMN COLOR: red
HABITAT: Japan
INTRODUCED: 1879

Most of the hornbeams make excellent small trees but are rather slow-growing. Because they give good shade, they are well adapted to use on the small property. This species has the coarsest texture of the four mentioned but a very interesting and distinctive habit of growth. No serious insect pests or diseases.

Carpinus orientalis   25'   Zone 5   Oriental hornbeam

FRUIT: small nutlets in leaflike bracts, borne in pendulous clusters
     EFFECTIVE: summer and fall
HABIT: several upright branches from the base
FOLIAGE: leaves only 1–2" long
AUTUMN COLOR: red
HABITAT: southeastern Europe, Asia Minor
INTRODUCED: 1739

This tree should be mentioned even though it is rare in America at this time. One of the smaller slow-growing trees, it has comparatively small leaves and a most interesting habit of branching. A 25-foot tree in the Arnold Arboretum has a single main trunk at the base, but about 2 feet above the ground several equally strong branches originate at right angles from the trunk and then shortly turn up definitely vertical. In other words, the branching is apparently U-shaped when viewed from a few feet away. Although difficult to move like other *Carpinus* species, the slow growth, fine foliage texture, and unique branching might lend value to this tree on the small property. No serious insect pests or diseases.

→≫ *CARYA*

The hickories are a sturdy lot of tap-rooted native American trees that have the reputation of being hard to move once established. Although baseball bats and axe handles are made from their wood, the trees themselves split rather easily in heavy storms. The fruits are of course known to all those familiar with America's woods, and the bark of some species has much ornamental value. The golden brown autumn color is a foliage characteristic of no mean importance. Their rugged habit, interesting form, and comparative freedom from serious pests or diseases make them of considerable ornamental value in many locations.

Commercial growers who frequently transplant or root-prune their trees in the nursery row are the ones from whom these trees should be bought. Native plants dug in the woods frequently fail to live, for growing in one place for a long time with the roots undisturbed, the delicate feeding roots may be at quite some distance from the tree and severed in the digging operation. The tap root also will be very large. Grown in the nursery, where these roots are cut every few years, feeding roots will be close to the trunk and the tap root will not be too extraordinary in length. In other words, to succeed with hickories, plant them in their permanent position early in life.

Hickory wood makes excellent fuel; in fact, it is probably the best of our native woods for this purpose. A cord of hickory wood is said to produce as much heat as a ton of coal. The wood has many uses, including, as already noted, as baseball bats and shock-absorbing tool handles, and the sawdust of green hickory is used by the meat-packing industries for smoking meats.

There are several insects that infest *Carya* species. Bark beetle is one of the most destructive, girdling branches and tunneling under the bark. Often the tops of the trees are attacked first, but by the time this is noticed, it is usually too late to control the pest. Spraying in midsummer with methoxychlor is helpful. Leaf galls are often evident but do not do much damage. Spraying with methoxychlor or malathion can be a help. Anthracnose can be controlled by spraying with zineb.

Carya cordiformis   90'   Zone 4   Bitternut

HABIT: broad, rounded
FOLIAGE: dense, compound leaves, 5–9 leaflets
* AUTUMN COLOR: yellow
HABITAT: central and eastern United States

Not as popular as the other hickories, nor as long lived, this species is nevertheless a symmetrical specimen if the others are not available to use in its place. The nuts are bitter and of little economic value. This species would probably not be of sufficient ornamental value to actually buy, but if, in clearing out an area to be landscaped, a mature bitternut is found growing, it certainly should be left to add its dignified habit to the surroundings.

Carya glabra   120'   Zone 4   Pignut

* HABIT: narrow to round
  FOLIAGE: dense, compound leaves, 3–9 leaflets
* AUTUMN COLOR: yellow
  HABITAT: eastern United States

The pignut grows in dry, rocky soils, and can be used in places where the pecan will not do well. It matures into a tall and handsome tree but grows slowly and is not recommended as a street or avenue tree. A well-grown specimen, well placed, can be just as beautiful in the large garden as can an American elm. The nuts are small, difficult to crack, and have little economic value.

Carya illinoinensis (formerly *C. pecan*)   150'   Zone 5   Pecan

HABIT: massive branches, rounded
FOLIAGE: not too dense, compound leaves, 11–17 leaflets
* AUTUMN COLOR: yellow
HABITAT: south central United States

Carya illinoinensis, *the popular pecan, is a native of the southern United States.*

This is the fastest growing of the hickories and will eventually grow into a massive, large-branched tree of rounded habit. Old trees may be as much as 350 years old. It is found chiefly in rich, moist bottomlands adjacent to streams and rivers, never in dry soils. There are many clones, grown chiefly for their nuts. The variety 'Burlington' (actually a hybrid and not a true pecan) produces good nuts and is the best as a shade tree; it seems to be hardy as far north as Ithaca, New York. Over twenty varieties of pecan are listed in current nursery catalogs, some of southern origin, some of northern. Among the latter would be 'Green River,' 'Major,' 'Posey,' and 'Starking Hardy Giant' (Plant Patent #1361, 1955). It should be pointed out that although pecan trees may survive in the North (New York, New England, and so forth), the growing season in such areas is usually not long enough for the trees to produce properly matured fruits. In fact, the flower buds are frequently killed by late spring freezes. Hence, the pecan should normally be considered a tree for the South.

Carya ovata   120'   Zone 4   Shagbark hickory

* HABIT: narrow, upright, irregular
* BARK: flaking off in loose plates

Shagbark hickory (Carya ovata).

FOLIAGE: not too dense, compound leaves, 5–7 leaflets
* AUTUMN COLOR: golden brown
HABITAT: eastern United States

Next to the pecan, this is the most popular of the hickories for its nuts, and many varieties are available. As an ornamental tree it is the best of the hickories, with its picturesque narrow, upright, open branching habit and its loosely flaking bark all winter long.

This species is the most economically important in the genus for its nuts and a number of varieties originating in the South and West have been named. Such varieties would include 'Davis,' 'Fox,' 'Glover,' 'Goheen,' 'Kirtland,' 'Miller,' 'Neilson,' 'Whitney,' and 'Wilcox.'

Carya tomentosa   90'   Zone 4   Mockernut

HABIT: upright with round head
FOLIAGE: dense, compound leaves, 5–9 leaflets
* AUTUMN COLOR: yellow
HABITAT: eastern and central United States

Suggested only because it is native in at least a third of the United States and in the open makes a beautiful, symmetrical tree. It grows to be 250 to 300 years old, but like all hickories it is hard to transplant, and the smaller the original plant purchased, the easier it is to transplant. The leaves are fragrant when crushed, and the common name "mockernut" stems from the fact that the fruits contain so little meat, it is really not worthwhile to try to dig it out.

Casimiroa edulus   30–50'   Zone 10   White sapote

FRUIT: greenish yellow when ripe, about the size of an orange, and supposedly peachlike in flavor
* FOLIAGE: evergreen leaves composed of 3–5 leathery leaflets, 2–5″ long
HABITAT: Mexico

Needs a rich soil and is usually used in areas where avocados are grown. It has proved popular in California; a good tree for patios.

Cassia fistula   30'   Zone 10   Golden shower senna

* FLOWERS: golden yellow, in racemes 1' or more long
TIME: spring, before the leaves
HABIT: rounded but upright
FOLIAGE: coarse
HABITAT: India

The long racemes of golden yellow flowers in the spring make this tree a popular one for ornamental planting.

Castanea crenata   30'   Zone 6   Japanese chestnut

HABIT: large shrub to small tree
* FOLIAGE: dense, coarse, upper surface lustrous, offering good shade
* AUTUMN COLOR: yellow to bronze
HABITAT: Japan
INTRODUCED: 1876

This chestnut is classed as resistant to the chestnut bark disease, whereas *C. mollissima* is "very resistant." These two species (and their hybrids) are the only two *Castanea* species sufficiently resistant to the disease to be recommended for cultivation in the United States. The Japanese chestnut has probably been in America longer than the Chinese, for there is a tree at Cheshire, Connecticut, with a trunk 4 feet in diameter and a spread of about 65 feet. The nuts of the Japanese chestnut are not as tasty as those of the American and Chinese, but they are satisfactory when cooked.

Castanea mollissima   60'   Zone 4   Chinese chestnut

HABIT: dense, rounded head
* FOLIAGE: dense, coarse, lustrous, giving good shade
* AUTUMN COLOR: yellow to bronze
HABITAT: China, Korea
INTRODUCED: 1903

Since the advent of the chestnut bark disease over eighty years ago, this is the only chestnut (with suitable nuts for eating) apparently resistant to the disease. Now it is being given great impetus by the U.S. Department of Agriculture and various commercial concerns for planting both as an ornamental and as a nut-bearing tree to bring about once again the growing of chestnuts in America. Four varieties have been introduced for trial: 'Abundance,' 'Nanking,' 'Meiling,' and 'Kuling.' These were grown from seed introduced from China in 1936 and, at the age of ten years, produced an average of seventy-five to one hundred pounds of edible nuts per tree. Chinese chestnuts have proved self-sterile so that at least two different varieties are needed to cross-fertilize. One single tree, grown alone, will produce only a handful of nuts. The nuts chiefly seen on the market in this country are imported from Europe and are of the blight-susceptible European species *C. sativa.* There are places in the United States where this species, also known as Spanish chestnut, is being grown, but it is not recommended because of its susceptibility to this disease. Finally it should be noted that although the Chinese chestnut is hardy enough in Zone 4, our experience in Massachusetts and New Hampshire has been that the growing season is not always sufficiently long enough for the fruit to mature properly.

Young trees cannot compete successfully with vigorous weeds, and as a result, the Chinese chestnut initially should be grown under conditions of clean cultivation. The dense foliage and rounded habit are good qualifications for a shade tree.

The interesting bark of the Spanish chestnut (Castanea sativa).

Dr. Arthur H. Graves, formerly of the Connecticut Agricultural Experiment Station, New Haven, Connecticut, spent many years hybridizing chestnuts in an attempt to find new varieties with nuts and timber of good quality, yet sufficiently resistant to the chestnut blight to be worth growing. These varieties have been named as being almost entirely blight-resistant: 'Essate-Jap,' 'Sleeping Giant' (*C. crenata x C. dentata* and a good timber tree), and 'Kelsey,' a smaller Chinese chestnut seedling with delicious small nuts. Whether or not these will become commercially available in the years to come remains to be seen, but these three cultivars should be of great interest to all who wish to grow the chestnut, either for its timber or for its fruits.

A word might be said here of our native *C. dentata,* for sprouts are still coming up in the woods throughout the East and, in fact, there are trees mature enough to bear much fruit. Suffice it to say that with hundreds of people looking for a blight-resistant native tree, none has been found to date. One may appear somewhere, but the enthusiastic amateur would save the experts time if he would continue to watch his tree that is "bearing nuts" in the woods for another five years. If, after observing it this long, it still does not show any branches or twigs that have been killed by disease, then he can call in the experts to investigate. It may still be susceptible even at that!

To sum it up, *C. crenata* and *C. mollissima* are the best species to grow at present. Both have lustrous foliage and give good shade. *C. crenata* is less hardy. In New England it may be that nuts will not have sufficient time to mature properly, but if two varieties or clones are growing near each other, *C. mollissima* can produce edible fruits in many areas. The nuts of *C. crenata* are not as tasty as those of *C. mollissima;* hence, *C. mollissima* and its varieties are the ones to plant in the United States, at present.

As for insects and diseases, there is no cure for the chestnut blight. The two-lined chestnut borer is a serious hazard to weakened trees. There are also many leaf-eating caterpillars that plague *Castanea.* These can be controlled by spraying with methoxychlor or malathion. Sometimes certain weevils eat the nuts as the fruits develop; these are best killed by fumigating the nuts with carbon disulfide.

Castanopsis chrysophylla   105'   Zone 7   Giant evergreen
                                                                                chinquapin

* FLOWERS: soft, fluffy spikes of creamy white flowers
        TIME: summer
  FRUIT: prickly burrs
  HABIT: pyramidal
* FOLIAGE: evergreen leaves, 2–5" long, dark green and lustrous above
  HABITAT: Oregon to California

This broad-leaved evergreen is valued for the fact that it grows well in poor, dry soils. It should be much more widely cultivated than it is within its hardiness limits.

Castanospermum australe   60'   Zone 10   Moreton Bay chestnut

* FLOWERS: yellow and red, in large, loose racemes 6" long
        TIME: July
  FRUIT: pods 9" long and 2" wide with large, edible, chestnutlike seeds
        EFFECTIVE: fall
  HABIT: unusually wide-spreading, often wider than it is high
* FOLIAGE: evergreen, coarse, compound
  HABITAT: Australia

Of value for its evergreen foliage and conspicuous flowers.

Casuarina equisetifolia   70'   Zone 9   Horsetail beefwood

  FRUIT: cones, ½" in diameter
  HABIT: open top, offering poor shade
* FOLIAGE: leaves are minute scales, resembling pines in appearance
  HABITAT: Australia

A peculiar tree but widely planted in southern Florida because it grows in all types of soils, can be easily clipped into hedges, and withstands brackish soils and saltwater spray, making it a valuable plant for seacoast gardens. It has been used also as a windbreak. No serious pests.

Casuarina stricta   30'   Zone 10   Coast beefwood

HABIT: slender but unusually rapid in growth
* FOLIAGE: evergreen, in feathery, long, jointed sprays somewhat akin to the northern native plant known as "horsetail"
HABITAT: Australia

These peculiar small trees grow well in sandy seashore situations, but when cultivated where the prevailing winds are all in one direction, they grow one-sided very quickly. They will even withstand brackish situations.

Catalpa bignonioides   45'   Zone 4   Southern catalpa

* FLOWERS: 2" long, white with yellow and brown markings, in upright panicles 7" high
    TIME: mid-June
FRUIT: long, beanlike pods, 15" long
    EFFECTIVE: hanging on until late fall and winter; not especially ornamental
HABIT: broadly rounded
FOLIAGE: coarse, ovate leaves, 4" long
HABITAT: Georgia, Florida, Mississippi
VARIETIES:
    'Aurea' *(Golden catalpa)*—planted considerably in Europe for its rich yellow leaves, which seem to retain their color throughout the summer
    'Nana' *(Umbrella catalpa)*—dwarf form, frequently grafted high on understock of the species, forming an umbrellalike plant

Smaller in height and with leaves less coarse than those of the Western catalpa, this tree might be considered easier to work into plantings properly. It is famed for its overplanted variety 'Nana,' which is grafted at about 6 to 7 feet high on the species and then allowed to grow with long, pendulous branches touching the ground. In order to force dense growth, these are often cut back to a few buds in the winter, making a most unsightly, stubby-looking plant. Because of its regularity of growth, many people like to use them as focal points on a lawn, but they are far too conspicuous all year round. The enterprising gardener will study available plant materials and select a combination of plants that will give more interesting effects than this unnatural-looking variety.

Catalpa speciosa   90'   Zone 4   Northern catalpa

* FLOWERS: 2" in diameter, creamy white with yellowish and brown markings, ar-
        ranged in upright panicles 6" high
        TIME: mid-June
  FRUIT: long, beanlike pods, sometimes 18" long
        EFFECTIVE: late fall and winter; not particularly ornamental
  HABIT: loosely pyramidal
  FOLIAGE: coarse, heart-shaped, leaves often 12" long
  HABITAT: Indiana to northern Arkansas
  VARIETY:
        purpurea—the new growth is purple, fast growing, and resistant to heat and
        drought

This common midwestern tree is often called the "Indian bean" because of its long,
podlike fruit. The tree withstands hot summers and dry soil but is certainly not
adapted for planting in the small garden. Its habit is large; the leaves, flowers, and
fruit are large and coarse in every way. For these reasons, it is very difficult to work
into a planting scheme properly. It is commonly used over a wide area, and in park
plantings it is at its best. Its large, conspicuous flowers appear at a time when few other
trees have any blossoms at all. Catalpa midge, leaf spot, powdery mildew, verticillium
wilt, mealy bug, and twig blight are sometimes problems.

Catalpa flower clusters appear in mid-June.

Cedrela sinensis   70'   Zone 5   Chinese toon

* FLOWERS: greenish yellow to white, in pendulous clusters 12" long
      TIME: June
HABIT: rounded and dense
FOLIAGE: coarse, compound, similar to that of *Ailanthus*
HABITAT: China
INTRODUCED: 1862

A tree resembling *Ailanthus altissima* but less hardy, although it makes a better ornamental specimen. It has been used as a street tree in Philadelphia with good results. Its compound leaves are coarse and look like those of *Ailanthus* except that the glandular tooth at the base of each leaflet is missing. The flowers do not have the disagreeable odor of those of *Ailanthus.* However, it usually takes a tree fifteen to twenty years before it produces the first flowers; consequently it cannot be considered as a specimen to be planted for its flower alone. It is mentioned here merely as a possible substitute for the *Ailanthus,* if such a tree is really needed. Like the *Ailanthus,* it has no autumn color. No serious pests.

⇝ *CEDRUS*

Three exotic species of the true cedar are recommended here because they grow in different hardiness zones and they all make excellent specimens. Their picturesque habit of growth is not for a small garden since eventually they will grow over 100 feet tall and be well over 40 feet in diameter of branch spread, hence requiring a great deal of room. They make fine lawn specimens (there are handsome examples on both the East and West coasts), needing little attention if they have good soil. Except for color and cones, these species are somewhat difficult to distinguish from one another. *Cedrus deodara* can be differentiated from the other two by its pendulous branchlets and cones, which are rounded on top. The other two species are not pendulous but very stiff, and their cones are either flat or slightly concave on top. *Cedrus libani* has branchlets that are either glabrous or only slightly pubescent, with needles 1–1¼ inches long, while *C. atlantica* has pubescent branchlets and needles mostly less than an inch long. These characteristics are sometimes hard to see but help in distinguishing one species from the other. Diseases and insect pests are not serious.

Cedrus atlantica *'Glauca,' an excellent ornamental tree.*

Cedrus atlantica   120'   Zone 6   Atlas cedar

* FRUIT: cones, upright on upper side of branches, 3" long and 2" in diameter,
        requiring two years to mature
        EFFECTIVE: most of the time
* HABIT: widely pyramidal
* FOLIAGE: evergreen, silvery to light green needles, in bunches
    HABITAT: northern Africa
    INTRODUCED: before 1840
    VARIETIES:
        'Argentea' *(Silver Atlas cedar)*—foliage a definite silvery gray-blue color
        glauca (Blue Atlas cedar)—foliage definitely bluish
        glauca **'Pendula'**—drooping branchlets

As a young tree, this is rather difficult to distinguish from *C. libani,* but its twigs are
always more pubescent than those of the other species. As it matures, it also develops
the flat-topped habit of *C. libani,* but its silvery to light green foliage color is distinctive. Tip blight and root rot are problematic.

Cedrus brevifolia   to 75'   Zone 7

    HABIT: slow growing, irregular branching habit

FOLIAGE: evergreen needles, shorter than those of *C. libani*
HABITAT: Cyprus

In general, similar to *C. libani,* but the dark green needles are shorter, only ¼ inch to ½ inch long.

Cedrus deodara   150'   Zone 7   Deodar cedar

* FRUIT: cones, upright on upper side of branches, 4" long and 2½" in diameter, requiring two years to mature
  EFFECTIVE: most of the time
* HABIT: pyramidal; gracefully pendulous branches
* FOLIAGE: rather dense evergreen needles, often in bunches
  HABITAT: Himalayas
  INTRODUCED: 1831
  VARIETY:
  'Shalimar'—a hardier cultivar than the species, selected in 1972 by the Arnold Arboretum

A native of the Himalayas, Cedrus deodara *is a popular evergreen in Zone 7 areas.*

In India the wood of this tree is used for incense. The main branchlet is always arching to pendulous, giving a decidedly graceful aspect to the whole tree that few coniferous evergreens can match. When grown from seed, as it usually is, it varies considerably as to color of foliage and habit, several varieties being offered in the trade. It is distinguished from the others because of this pendulous habit and longer needles. No serious diseases or insect problems.

Cedrus libani   120'   Zone 5   Cedar of Lebanon

* FRUIT: cones, upright on upper side of branches, 4″ long and 2½″ in diameter, requiring two years to mature
  EFFECTIVE: most of the time
* HABIT: narrow, pyramidal while young, branches stiffly horizontal
* FOLIAGE: evergreen needles, often in bunches
  HABITAT: Asia Minor
  INTRODUCED: colonial times
  VARIETY:
      'Pendula'—has graceful, pendulous branchlets, sometimes spreading over the ground with ends upright

There is no mistaking the stiff, horizontal habit of the cedar of Lebanon (Cedrus libani).

The cone of the cedar of Lebanon, popular as an ornamental since biblical times.

Although *C. libani* has been grown widely throughout the South, it was not until the Arnold Arboretum sent a special expedition to Asia Minor in 1903 to collect seed at the highest altitudes where these trees are native that plants could be grown which were reliably hardy in the northeastern United States. Mature trees are very wide at the base, but trees thirty to forty years of age have about the same dimensions as *Abies concolor*, although they are not nearly as dense. The dark green foliage, stiff habit, and picturesque and rigidly upright cones, some of which are almost always on the tree since they take two years to mature, give this tree a popular interest. Frequent reference is made to it in the Bible, and Solomon's Temple was supposed to have been built from its massive timbers, another reason considerable attention is shown to it today. It does not produce much shade and certainly is very formal in habit, but apparently has great popular appeal in areas where the other two members of this genus are not hardy. Diseases and insect pests are not serious.

Ceiba pentandra   120'   Zone 10   Kapok, Silk-cotton tree

FLOWERS: mallowlike, greenish white to pinkish
   TIME: summer
FRUIT: cucumberlike
   EFFECTIVE: early fall
* HABIT: huge buttressed trunk, with wide-spreading branches at right angles to it
BARK: smooth, gray

FOLIAGE: deciduous, digitately compound leaves
HABITAT: tropics of both hemispheres

One of the most conspicuous trees in southern Florida because of its massive size, profuse flowers, and great trunk. The kapok of commerce comes from the silky, lustrous floss about the seeds. A large tree, it needs plenty of space in which to grow properly.

⇥⟫ CELTIS

The hackberries (especially *C. occidentalis*) are widely planted in the South as street trees. Some have merit because of their foliage and dense habit of growth. The native *C. occidentalis* is susceptible to attacks from either a small mite or a mildew fungus or both, deforming the buds and resulting in a bunch of twigs growing from one place, often called "witches' broom" disease. A goodly proportion of these small twigs die each year, giving the tree a most unsightly appearance. It is well whenever possible to use species not so troubled by this pest, especially since no effective control measures are known. The fruit is a round drupe, one of the ways of distinguishing these plants from elms, for their leaves are similar. In general they have nothing special to recommend their use where better and more attractive trees are available.

Celtis australis   75'   Zone 6   European hackberry

FRUIT: dark purple berry, ½″ in diameter
        EFFECTIVE: summer and fall
HABIT: spreading branches, round-topped head
FOLIAGE: elmlike
HABITAT: southern Europe
INTRODUCED: 1736

This tree is valued for highway planting in hot, arid sections of the Southwest, where little soil moisture is available.

Celtis bungeana   45'   Zone 5   Bunch hackberry

FRUIT: hard, black berry, ¼″ in diameter
        EFFECTIVE: summer and fall
* HABIT: broad, rounded head
* FOLIAGE: lustrous, dark green

HABITAT: China, Korea
INTRODUCED: 1868

In general this species performs the best of those in the Arnold Arboretum. For this reason it is mentioned here even though it is as yet unavailable from commercial sources. The leaves are lustrous, dark green, and 1¾–3 inches long. It is not apparently infested with the witches' broom disease so troublesome on *C. occidentalis.* The plant at the Arnold Arboretum is easily 45 feet tall.

Celtis jessoensis   70′   Zone 5   Jesso hackberry

FRUIT: hard, black berry, ¼″ in diameter
    EFFECTIVE: summer and fall
HABIT: more open in habit than *C. bungeana*
FOLIAGE: open
HABITAT: Korea, Japan
INTRODUCED: 1892

Not infested with witches' broom disease and possibly of value as a substitute for the American elm. It makes a better and more dense tree than does *C. laevigata.*

Celtis laevigata   90′   Zone 5   Sugar hackberry

FRUIT: hard, black berry ¼″ in diameter
    EFFECTIVE: summer and fall
HABIT: spreading branches, sometimes pendulous; rounded head
FOLIAGE: fine texture, open
HABITAT: south central and southeastern United States

Recommended because it is a widely found native tree, very resistant to the witches' broom disease so seriously infesting *C. occidentalis* and widely used as a street tree in the South where it is native.

Celtis sinensis   60′   Zone 6   Chinese hackberry

FRUIT: reddish yellow, ⅓″ in diameter, edible
FOLIAGE: leaves 1½–3″ long
HABITAT: China, Japan, Korea
INTRODUCED: 1793 (England)

Not well known or thoroughly tried in the United States, this tree may be hardy in Zone 5. It has been reported as free from the witches' broom disease and so is apparently worthy of further trial.

Ceratonia siliqua   50'   Zone 10   Carob

* FLOWERS: small, red, on lateral racemes; sexes separate
       TIME: spring
  FRUIT: pods, 1' long, edible
       EFFECTIVE: early fall
  HABIT: rounded
* FOLIAGE: dense, glossy, evergreen leaves, with slightly wavy edges
  HABITAT: eastern Mediterranean region
  INTRODUCED: 1854

This can be grown in dry soils and still be expected to do well, which is one of the reasons it is extensively cultivated in southern California. It is difficult to transplant and should always be moved with a ball of soil about the roots. Its neat, evergreen foliage makes it a fine shade tree for specimen and avenue planting as well. It has been termed "St. John's bread" because the seeds and sweet pulp of this tree were supposedly the "locusts and wild honey" St. John ate in the wilderness. Since it has been grown and cultivated for centuries, many varieties have appeared through the years. Some are more susceptible to cold than others. There is a clone in southern California that has been named 'Cal Poly,' valued because it is fruitless.

The Katsura tree (Cercidiphyllum japonicum) *makes a narrow tree when grown with a single trunk.*

Cercidiphyllum japonicum   60–100′   Zone 4   Katsura tree

FRUIT: small, dry capsules on pistillate trees—not effective ornamentally; sexes
  separate
* HABIT: rounded, often with several trunks, but narrow when grown with only one
* FOLIAGE: open, fine texture
* AUTUMN COLOR: yellow to scarlet
HABITAT: Japan
INTRODUCED: 1865
VARIETY:
  'Pendula'—branchlets are pendulous

A wide-spreading tree with foliage very much like that of *Cercis canadensis,* usually growing with several main stems or trunks. The flowers are insignificant, but the fruit remains on the tree most of the winter. The rounded leaves are nearly 4 inches long. Valued as a shade tree because of its wide-spreading habit but also valued because of the rather loose foliage that allows for a great amount of air circulation. It has been termed the largest deciduous tree of China. The variety named *sinense* is merely the Chinese form, practically indistinguishable from the species. It is an excellent specimen tree of particular value for its graceful leaves which remain unattacked by insect pests throughout the entire season. This species normally grows with several main trunks from the base, making a very wide tree that, as it grows older, is susceptible to serious breaking up at the base. However, when it is grown with a single trunk it makes a narrow, almost columnar tree.

Cercis canadensis   36′   Zone 4   Eastern redbud

* FLOWERS: small, pealike, purplish pink, in clusters
      TIME: mid-May
* HABIT: flat top, irregular
FOLIAGE: heart-shaped, fine texture, open
* AUTUMN COLOR: yellow
HABITAT: eastern United States
VARIETIES:
  'Alba'—flowers white
  'Flame'—double, pink flowers
  'Forest Pansy'—new leaves are shiny red-purple changing to purple-green.
    Flowers are lighter pink than those of other species.
  'Oklahoma'—soft pink foliage, matures to heart-shaped, rich green leaves
  'Pinkbud'—a tree discovered growing wild on an estate near Kansas City a few
    years prior to 1961, having pure, bright, true pink flowers
  'Royal'—profuse white flowers
  'Silver Cloud'—leaves blotched or speckled with creamy white. Should be
    grown in partial shade to bring out the best color in the leaves.
  'Wither's Pink Charm'—a new clone, the flowers of which are soft pink
    without the purplish cast common to the species

A common sight in the eastern United States, especially in the woods of Pennsylvania, Maryland, and Virginia, where it blooms early in the spring. It is often planted with the flowering dogwood, blooming at the same time. The white-flowered variety is almost as hardy as the species, while the double-flowered variety *(plena)* is neither as interesting nor as conspicuous in flower. The two new pink-flowered forms have value for those who object to the purplish pink color of the flowers of the species. Canker and verticillium wilt can be serious, causing large branches to die. Cut out and paint the wounds.

Cercis chinensis   40′   Zone 6   Chinese redbud

* FLOWERS: dense, pealike, rosy purple
    TIME: mid-May
HABIT: often shrublike
FOLIAGE: fine textured, dense, heart-shaped leaves
* AUTUMN COLOR: yellow
HABITAT: central China
INTRODUCED: before 1850

Even though this is a tree in its native habitat, it has proved more or less shrubby in this country and is better grown this way, especially in the North. Its profuse, pealike, rosy purple flowers are its chief interest to gardeners. This is actually the tallest of the redbuds; otherwise it is similar in most respects to *C. canadensis.*

Cercis racemosa   30′   Zone 7   Raceme redbud

* FLOWERS: pealike, rosy pink, in pendulous racemes 1½–4″ long
    TIME: mid-May
HABIT: flat top
FOLIAGE: rather coarse, open
* AUTUMN COLOR: yellow
HABITAT: China
INTRODUCED: 1907

This species, introduced by the Arnold Arboretum, is distinct in that it has pendulous clusters of flowers that appear on the naked branches (before the leaves) on wood one to several years old.

Cercis siliquastrum   30′   Zone 6   Judas tree

* FLOWERS: profuse, small, pealike, bright purplish rose
    TIME: mid-May
HABIT: flat top
FOLIAGE: heart-shaped, open

HABITAT: southern Europe, western Asia
INTRODUCED: colonial times

The flowers usually are produced on twigs two to four years old but sometimes as much as twenty to thirty years old—often one hundred flowers on a twig only 5 inches long. A white variety *(alba)* has been reported, but I do not know where it is available in America. In sunny Italy it makes a wonderful display in April or early May.

⇶ *CHAMAECYPARIS*

The *Chamaecyparis* species and varieties are a decidedly variable group of evergreens, but many of them are most serviceable garden plants. Of the three species native to North America *(C. lawsoniana, nootkatensis,* and *thyoides),* only the first two are grown to any extent as ornamentals, and these do best on the West Coast in areas where atmospheric moisture is high. In Europe these are even more popular, for 127 varieties of *C. lawsoniana* are supposedly listed by commercial growers. American nurseries list only twenty-eight varieties and only three of *C. nootkatensis.*

Of the two Japanese species *(C. obtusa* and *C. pisifera)* American nurseries list twenty-two varieties of the former and twenty-six of the latter, but the literature is full of many names—so many that it is impossible to mention them all here. The nomenclature of this group at present is decidedly confused, and when it comes to color forms and dwarf forms, proper identification of what may or may not be in this country is extremely difficult.

It should be stated at the outset that these five species are tree forms, and those who know the West Coast have seen many a stately specimen of the two species growing there. Many medium-to-dwarf forms have originated through the years, and the connoisseur of dwarf evergreens knows that many exquisite specimens can be obtained if time is spent hunting for them both in this country and abroad.

The Japanese species are more popular in the eastern United States because these are better able to withstand the drier atmosphere. *Chamaecyparis obtusa* and its varieties are probably better ornamentals, where hardy, than are the *C. pisifera* varieties. Color forms are many, but it should be remembered that in the northern parts of the country, these tend to turn brownish in the winter and hence are not serviceable at a time when they are most needed.

Chamaecyparis pisifera and its varieties do not grow old gracefully, for the older they are, the more open the branching at the base of the trees and frequently the more dead foliage to be observed. As small specimens of shrubby habit, they are excellent, which is why they have been so popular over the years and why so many nurseries have grown them. But many are tree types, and one should know this at purchase time and be prepared to restrain them if they are to be used in situations where they cannot be allowed to grow into tree forms. All the *Chamaecyparis* are evergreens and remarkably free from insect pests and diseases.

Chamaecyparis lawsoniana   120'   Zone 5   Lawson false cypress

* HABIT: slender to broadly pyramidal tree
* BARK: shredding
* FOLIAGE: evergreen, scalelike
  HABITAT: southwestern Oregon to northwestern California
  VARIETIES:
> 'Allumii' *(Scarab Lawson cypress)*—columnar form with steel blue foliage
> 'Argentea' *(Silver Lawson cypress)*—silvery white leaves
> 'Erecta'—a columnar, dense form with bright green foliage
> 'Fletcheri'—an excellent ornamental, raised about 1913 in Fletcher's Nursery

One of the many varieties of the Lawson cypress (Chamaecyparis lawsoniana), *'Fletcheri' is a dense-growing form, widely used on the West Coast.*

in England. Noted for its close, feathery, blue foliage and pyramidal form. Mature plants are 12-20′ tall. It is best when young.

'**Gracilis Pendula**' *(Fountain Lawson cypress)*—very graceful pendulous form
'**Nidiformis**'—horizontal branches radiating from a dense center
'**Pendula**' *(Weeping Lawson cypress)*—pendulous branchlets
'**Stewartii**'—the foliage is at first a good golden yellow, turning to green later in the season, but in some areas in California it is recorded as keeping its yellow color through the winter
'**Triomphe de Boskoop**'—steel blue leaves; a much advertised variety

Native over very small corners of two states; often called the Port Orford cedar, it has been widely distributed in Europe and New Zealand, particularly in areas that are continually moist since it does not like dry weather. In areas near its native habitat or where climate is mild and moisture is always present, the Lawson cypress and its varieties offer interesting variations for the winter garden. Recently a root rot has killed considerable stands of this species.

Chamaecyparis nootkatensis   120′   Zone 4   Nootka false cypress

* HABIT: narrowly pyramidal
* BARK: shredding
* FOLIAGE: evergreen, scalelike, dark green
  HABITAT: southwestern Alaska to Oregon
  VARIETIES:
  '**Glauca**'—fast growing, wide, upright; coarse-textured, layered foliage
  '**Lutea**' *(Golden Alaska cedar)*—new foliage is yellow-green, turning to light green. Upright growing, coarse textured.
  '**Pendula**' *(Weeping Alaska cedar)*—grows tall with graceful hanging branches and branchlets

One of three native *Chamaecyparis* species. It does not have a wide distribution in this country merely because it needs a moist climate in which to thrive. It is not used much even on the West Coast, where it is native, but is considered one of the finest where it can be grown. No serious pests.

Chamaecyparis obtusa   120′   Zone 4   Hinoki false cypress

* HABIT: broadly pyramidal
  BARK: shredding
* FOLIAGE: evergreen, scalelike, dark, glossy green leaves, usually dense
  HABITAT: Japan
  INTRODUCED: 1861
  VARIETIES:
  '**Aurea**'—foliage tips of the branches yellow
  '**Crippsii**' *(Cripps golden Hinoki cypress)*—with fernlike, golden yellow foliage, conical as it grows older
  '**Erecta**' *(Column Hinoki cypress)*—fastigiate, ascending branches

Chamaecyparis obtusa
'Nana.'

'Filicioides' *(Fernspray cypress)*—of dense habit with twisting, frondlike
  branches, it will eventually grow fairly tall
'Gracilis' *(Slender Hinoki cypress)*—compact, pyramidal, pendulous branchlets
'Gracilis Aurea' *(Golden Hinoki cypress)*—slow in growth, irregular, upright;
  golden foliage becomes bronze in winter
'Lycopodioides' *(Club moss cypress)*—contorted, thick, cordlike, blue-green
  foliage
'Magnifica' *(Great Hinoki cypress)*—vigorous, wide, pyramidal, with broad,
  fan-shaped foliage that is lustrous green
'Nana'—branch tips condensed and curled

A slow-growing ornamental in both shrub and tree forms, it is a beautiful specimen
when properly grown. It needs a moist climate, but some of the tree forms are doing
well in the Arnold Arboretum in Boston. The foliage is usually a dark, glossy green,
and it might well be considered one of the most attractive in this genus.

Chamaecyparis pisifera   150'   Zone 3   Sawara false cypress

* HABIT: narrowly pyramidal, horizontally branching but rather loose and open
      throughout

BARK: shredding
* FOLIAGE: evergreen, scalelike, often open
HABITAT: Japan
INTRODUCED: 1861
VARIETIES:

    '**Aurea**' *(Golden Sawara cypress)*—foliage golden yellow. This might be discarded as a shrub, but there are very few trees of satisfactory yellow foliage in the summer and it might be included for this purpose only. In the winter the foliage is a very poor color, and the tree should not be counted as an attractive specimen at this time.

    '**Boulevard**' *(Blue moss cypress)*—slow growing, soft, steel blue foliage, grows into an irregular cone shape.

    '**Filifera**' *(Thread Sawara cypress)*—branchlets threadlike

    '**Filifera Aurea**' *(Golden thread cypress)*—threadlike, golden yellow foliage; foliage closer to the trunk of the tree is lighter in color

    '**Gold Spangle**'—bright golden yellow the entire year. Growth is pyramidal as it grows older.

    '**Plumosa**' *(Plume Sawara cypress)*—foliage frondlike but slightly feathery

    '**Plumosa Aurea**'—soft, feathery, golden yellow foliage. It retains this good color throughout the summer and can be classed as one of the best in this respect.

    '**Squarrosa**' *(Moss Sawara cypress)*—foliage very feathery, frondlike, and not flat

Chamaecyparis pisifera *'Squarrosa,' with its smooth, soft, bluish-colored foliage.*

'Squarrosa Cyano-viridis'—extremely light blue foliage. A good clone and probably appearing in the trade under several names. One of the best for bluish foliage, especially while young.

A variable species with many popular varieties, prone to lose its lower branches rather early in life. Most of these must be gone over annually to remove the dead branches in order to keep the trees in good condition. It should always be kept in mind that this species is a tree even in this country. Too often these plants are used in foundation plantings and put in front of windows without thought of their later development. In a few years' time they have naturally grown all out of proportion to other plants in such a planting, often obliterating the view from the windows. They can be kept under control by persistent pruning. Their brownish red, shredding bark is another interesting feature of older plants. Relatively free from insect and disease problems.

Chamaecyparis thyoides 'Hopkinton'   60'   Zone 3

HABIT: narrow, upright; rapid growth
ORIGIN: selected from a lowland meadow in Hopkinton, Massachusetts

The swamp white cedar (Chamaecyparis thyoides) *grows mostly in wet soils on the eastern seaboard and should not be planted in dry soil areas, where it grows poorly.*

Chionanthus retusus, *with its white flowers in June, is just as ornamental as its native relative,* Chionanthus virginicus.

INTRODUCED: about 1800 from China, Korea, Japan

An adaptable variety doing well in wet areas, in sun or shade. No serious pests.

Chionanthus virginicus   30′   Zone 4   Fringetree

* FLOWERS: feathery, white, in loose panicles
        TIME: early June
 FRUIT: grapelike, dark blue, in clusters
    EFFECTIVE: fall
* AUTUMN COLOR: bright yellow
 HABITAT: New Jersey to Florida

The native fringetree is just as ornamental as, if not slightly more so than, its Oriental relative, *C. retusus.* Its fleecy white flowers are produced in utmost profusion. Usually the sexes are separate, with the staminate flowers being larger. This species is closely related to the lilacs and also must be watched for scale infestations; otherwise it is a splendid ornamental, especially as a specimen in the full sun. It is considered by some Europeans to be the most beautiful and striking of our native shrubs. Its only drawback is that it is one of the last plants to produce leaves in the spring. In fact, they appear so late many people think the plants are dead.

Chorisia speciosa 'Majestic Beauty'   50'   Zone 9

* FLOWERS: pink, 3" in diameter
        EFFECTIVE: fall or early winter, when it has no leaves
   FRUIT: pea-shaped, seeds covered with a silky floss

Chorisia speciosa *'Majestic Beauty.' Photograph courtesy of Monrovia Nursery Company.*

HABIT: bright green trunk studded with thorns
FOLIAGE: evergreen, except for a short time in the fall
HABITAT: Brazil

A selection by the Monrovia Nursery Company, Azusa, California.

Cinnamomum camphora   40′   Zone 9   Camphor tree

FRUIT: black berries about the size of a pea but not effective
HABIT: rounded head; a 50′ tree may be 100′ wide
* FOLIAGE: evergreen, very dense, glossy
HABITAT: China, Japan
INTRODUCED: early colonial times?

Used considerably in the South as a street tree, it is slow growing, with attractive foliage the entire year except in the early spring. Camphor is distilled from the twigs and leaves which, if crushed, give off a distinct camphor odor. The lower limbs need some pruning or they will ruin the general character of the tree. It is not a good tree for the small garden because of its competitive roots, its dense branching habit that gives off a deep shade, and the fact that its fallen leaves do not decompose readily. Camphor scale can infest this species and weaken and kill some of the twigs. Spraying with dormant oil or a summer application of malathion or diazinon can prove helpful in controlling it.

Citrus species   Zones 9–10   Lemon, Orange, Lime, Grapefruit, Tangerine, Kumquat, Satsuma, and so forth

The citrus species are always possibilities for planting on the small property as dual ornamental and economic trees. Some are more frost resistant than others. Like their northern counterparts, the apples, pears, and peaches, they should not be planted solely for ornament because if their fruits are not cared for by proper and persistent spraying, they may easily become unsightly and actually defeat the purpose for which they were planted.

Cladrastis lutea   50′   Zone 3   American yellowwood

* FLOWERS: pendulous clusters of fragrant, white flowers, similar in size and shape to those of wisteria
   TIME: early June
HABIT: rounded
* BARK: smooth, light gray
FOLIAGE: dense
* AUTUMN COLOR: orange to yellow
HABITAT: North Carolina, Kentucky, Tennessee

VARIETY:

'Rosea'—a light, pink-flowered clone at the Perkins Institute for the Blind, Watertown, Massachusetts, that might well be worth propagating

An excellent tree for its flowers and foliage, making a handsome specimen. It may not bloom consistently every year, sometimes only becoming covered with flowers every third year. Pruning, when necessary, should be done in early summer since if pruned in spring it tends to "bleed" profusely. An immense specimen tree with pale pink flowers is growing on the grounds of the Perkins Institute for the Blind, at Watertown, Massachusetts, and would seem to be sufficiently distinctive to be worthy of propagation. No serious insect pests or diseases.

Clethra arborea   25′   Zone 9   Lily-of-the-valley clethra

* FLOWERS: fragrant, small, white, in nodding panicles 6″ long
      TIME: August and often September
FOLIAGE: evergreen
HABITAT: Madeira
INTRODUCED: 1784 (England)

A very beautiful small tree for the warmer parts of the country. Especially noted for its summer flowers, it is not suited to areas where the atmosphere is too dry.

Clethra barbinervis   30′   Zone 5   Japanese clethra

FLOWERS: white, in horizontal racemes
      TIME: late July
HABIT: wide-spreading, irregular, often with several trunks
BARK: rather attractive, brown, shredding
FOLIAGE: open
HABITAT: Japan
INTRODUCED: 1870

This is the first of the clethras to bloom and is considered by some to be the most beautiful. The racemes are held horizontally, and the plant is larger in every way than *C. alnifolia,* but the flowers are not as fragrant. For some reason or other, *C. barbinervis* has not been susceptible to the severe attacks of red spider often occurring on *C. alnifolia.* No serious pests.

Clethra delavayi   40′   Zone 7   Delavay clethra

* FLOWERS: bell-shaped, white, ½″ wide, in horizontally borne racemes 4–6″ long
      TIME: July
HABIT: open

FOLIAGE: open, leaves, 2½–6" long
HABITAT: western China
INTRODUCED: 1913

Rare, but the most beautiful of the clethras.

Cocos nucifera   80'   Zone 10   Coconut

* HABIT: palm tree
FOLIAGE: graceful but coarse, leaves often 15' long
HABITAT: southern Florida as well as other tropical regions of the world

A tree typical to many parts of the tropics, with a long, crooked or leaning trunk. Grown in this country only in southern Florida. Planted as an ornamental here, it is grown quickly from seed and may even bear a few nuts in five years' time. L. H. Bailey stated that a tree in good soil may produce seventy-five nuts a year but that the average is only about one-third of this. In the landscape of the tropics there is nothing quite as distinctive as the coconut. Many of the insects that bother this species are held in check by spraying with malathion or diazinon.

Coconut palms (Cocos nucifera) *growing near salt water.*

⇛ *CORNUS*

The members of this genus are some of the best ornamental shrubs and small trees available in America. They are easily propagated and quickly grown, with approximately ninety species and varieties having been named over the years; more than sixty-five are grown in the Arnold Arboretum in Boston, Massachusetts, at the present time. Among these are seven tree species that are certainly outstanding.

People who have visited Valley Forge in Pennsylvania in the spring know that there are thousands of the flowering dogwood planted there among the rolling hills as a memorial to the men who fought and suffered there during the Revolutionary War. These trees are beautiful every season of the year but are most conspicuous when in flower. Many interesting varieties have also been planted.

There is a trend now to name many of the clones of *C. florida*. This is as it should be, if properly done. This same thing has been done with the American holly *(Ilex opaca)*, which is native over much the same area as *C. florida*. During the past thirty years approximately 270 clones of this evergreen tree have been named and propagated asexually. It has been found that a variety of *I. opaca* that is outstanding in Virginia may not grow at all well in Massachusetts, and the reverse may also be true. So, great care (and probably time) should be taken in naming new clones of the flowering dogwood to make certain that they are worth naming and not similar to or even inferior to varieties already available.

The promiscuous naming of miscellaneous varieties will lead to confusion. There is some evidence that this is already happening with certain varieties of *C. florida* which have been quickly named, widely distributed because they were "new," and then later found to be wanting of desirable ornamental qualities after trial under many conditions. It takes many years to grow and test properly a tree valued for its flowers and fruits, and none should be named without good trials under varying conditions. A personal experience might emphasize this.

A few years ago I "found" an unusually large flowering form of *C. kousa* growing on the Case Estates of the Arnold Arboretum. Pictures were taken of the flowers; samples were compared with specimens growing in the Arnold Arboretum twelve miles away. This new "find" had larger flower bracts than any of the others. Telling this one day to the superintendent who had lived on the Case Estates almost a generation before they were given to the Arnold Arboretum, he laughed and explained to me that it ought to be that way. The particular tree in question was growing right on top of an old cesspool I knew nothing about! We made many cuttings, but eventually its flowers proved to be no larger than the others when grown away from its spot over the cesspool.

There is a dogwood for almost any part of the United States except the hottest and driest. *C. florida,* native throughout the entire eastern United States from Florida to Maine, is widely planted and is steadily more cultivated on the West Coast as well, even into central California. The native western species *C. nuttallii* is not as rugged and needs special growing conditions but is beautiful when placed in the right spot. Unfortunately it will not grow in the East. The Cornelian cherry is an excellent, rugged, serviceable plant for use in many situations and in many ways, from a clipped hedge to specimen plantings. The other species, though not as widely used, have special assets that make them desirable specimen plants. All in all, then, these small flowering trees are a versatile lot, and some one of them is usable in most of the planting areas in America.

Cornus alternifolia   24′   Zone 3   Alternate-leaved dogwood

FLOWERS: small, white, in clusters, similar to those of viburnums
       TIME: May
FRUIT: bluish black berries on red fruit stalks
       EFFECTIVE: summer
AUTUMN COLOR: reddish
HABITAT: eastern North America

An interesting tree except in certain areas where a twig blight infests the branches; in such locations, the other alternate-leaved dogwood, *C. controversa,* might be substituted.

Cornus capitata   40′   Zone 8   Evergreen dogwood

* FLOWERS: pale yellow bracts, 4–6 in number, 1½–2″ long
       TIME: June, July
* FRUIT: strawberrylike, red, 1–1½″ in diameter
       EFFECTIVE: October, November
* HABIT: rounded head, similar to *C. florida* but somewhat bushy
* FOLIAGE: evergreen to semi-evergreen, leathery, lustrous, dark green leaves, bronze in winter
HABITAT: western China
INTRODUCED: before 1900?

A delicate dogwood, unfortunately little seen in this country because of its tenderness, but a handsome tree, nevertheless, in flower and fruit. It should be given good soil and a spot to grow where it will have protection from the winds in winter. The fruits are quickly eaten by the birds but are effective for as long as they last.

There is an interesting evergreen hybrid in existence, noted by Donald W.

Stryker of Langlois, Oregon. Apparently a *C. capitata x nuttallii* cross, this plant is 25 feet tall but less than 10 feet wide, with short, horizontal branches literally covered with yellowish masses of flower clusters, with measurements from bract tip to bract tip of about 4 inches. The fruits are rose-magenta in color.

Cornus controversa   60′   Zone 5   Giant dogwood

* FLOWERS: small, whitish, in flat clusters, 3–7″ in diameter
        TIME: late May
* FRUIT: bluish black berries, in flat clusters
        EFFECTIVE: August and early September
* HABIT: picturesque, horizontal branching in tiers
  FOLIAGE: dense, lustrous
  AUTUMN COLOR: red
  HABITAT: Japan, China
  INTRODUCED: before 1880
  VARIETY:
        'Variegata'—apparently originated in England prior to 1893 with a white to
        pale yellow leaf margin

Unlike most members of the *Cornus* genus, the leaves of this plant are alternate. It is not susceptible to the twig blight that so seriously injures our native alternate-leaved dogwood, *C. alternifolia*. This tree makes an excellent specimen because of its picturesque habit but is rarely seen in gardens. The flowers are small, somewhat similar to those of certain viburnums or the wild carrot, but nevertheless are profusely borne, and the black fruits are rather prominent. In areas where *C. alternifolia* is native and is not bothered with the twig blight, this species might be substituted.

Cornus florida   40′   Zone 4   Flowering dogwood

* FLOWERS: white bracts, cluster about 3–5″ in diameter, true flowers inconspicuous
        TIME: mid-May
* FRUIT: bright red berries in tight clusters
        EFFECTIVE: fall
* HABIT: definitely horizontal branching
* FOLIAGE: dense, lustrous
* AUTUMN COLOR: scarlet
  HABITAT: eastern United States
  VARIETIES:
        'Apple Blossom'—a selection made about 1962 from thirty-year-old plants on
        a Connecticut estate, with flowers the color of apple blossoms
        'Belmont Pink'—found and named by Henry Hicks of Hicks Nurseries, West-
        bury, New York, about 1930. It was introduced but apparently has since
        disappeared from commercial sources, with flower bracts reported to have
        been a blush pink.

'**Cherokee Chief**'—with flower bracts a "rich ruby red" and new growth reportedly reddish; this was patented (#1710) in 1958 by Ike Hawkersmith of Winchester, Tennessee

'**Cloud 9**'—blooms at an early age with an immense number of flowering bracts. More compact and slower growing than the species; opening bracts are a creamy yellow, later changing to white.

'**Fastigiata**'—the original tree has been growing in the Arnold Arboretum since 1910 and has been widely distributed. With upright, branching habit, of value on the small property where space is at a premium, it retains this fastigiate habit only while young. After fifteen to twenty years the tree gradually takes on the form of the horizontally branched species.

'**Gigantea**'—found and named by Paul Vossberg of the Westbury Rose Co., Westbury, New York, on the nearby Phipps Estate about 1932, with flower bracts 6″ from tip to tip

'**Hohman's Golden**'—foliage is variegated with yellow and green; the autumn color is a deep red with the yellowish areas a lighter red than the green areas

'**Magnifica**'—also found on the Phipps Estate about 1926; reported to have full, rounded bracts about 4″ from tip to tip

'**New Hampshire**'—a form selected by Heinrich Rohrbach of Heatherfells Nursery, Andover, Massachusetts, from a hardy, flower-producing tree in Atkinson, New Hampshire. Observation over a long period of time has shown these flower buds do not last in cold winters as do those of clones from southern sources.

'**Pendula**'—with stiffly pendulous branches, but a well-grown tree makes a very good ornamental. It was named in 1887 in Vienna from material apparently received from New Jersey.

'**Pluribracteata**'—originated in Orange County, North Carolina, before 1914 and is noted because it usually has 6 to 8 large flower bracts and many aborted smaller ones

'**President Kennedy**'—a selection from the woods of the Weston Nurseries, Hopkinton, Massachusetts; bracts overlapping, giving the whole tree a more lush appearance. Does not tend to canker from winter injury.

rubra—has been found originating at several places in the wild, hence is not a clone and will vary. It is not as hardy as the species, and the color of the bracts varies from a washed-out pink to a deep red. It is much better to purchase some of the newer, named clones that supposedly can be depended on for standard flower color, although even these may change slightly from year to year with climate or soil conditions.

'**Spring Song**'—a selection made about 1962 from thirty-year-old plants on a Connecticut estate, with flowers advertised as a "gorgeous rose-red"

'**Sweetwater Red**'—named and introduced by the Howell Nurseries of Knoxville, Tennessee, in 1961, a good red-flowering clone. It is reported to have reddish foliage and larger blooms.

'**Welchii**'—leaves are a combination of green, creamy white, and pink. It was selected by Mark Welch, an Ohio nurseryman, about 1920. It has proved a sparse bloomer, sometimes burning in full, hot sun; nevertheless, it is very pretty in a lightly shaded situation, coloring well in full sun. It sometimes will revert to the green-leaved species. The "Kingsville form" of this (Kingsville

Nurseries, Kingsville, Maryland) is supposed to have better color and be a better grower.

'White Cloud'—a seedling selection of Wayside Gardens, then of Mentor, Ohio, in 1948. Supposed to have unusually numerous creamy white flowers, especially when the plant is very young.

'Xanthocarpa'—yellow fruit

Over sixty clonal names have been given to plants of this species. This tree is the best ornamental of all the natives growing in the northern United States. It has special interest every season of the year—in spring with flowers; in summer with good foliage not marred by insect or disease; in fall with brilliant red berries and vivid autumn color; in winter because of its picturesque horizontal manner of branching. The red-flowered variety is striking when in bloom in front of some of the white-flowered types. Some trees have been noted in which the tip-to-tip diameter of the flower bracts is 6½ inches. Many towns have adopted this tree as the major plant in war memorial planting projects. The New Jersey Highway Commission and cooperating garden club organizations are featuring these trees along certain highways in New Jersey—highways that can easily be most prominent in the future if care is taken of the plants as they develop. Because this tree starts into growth easily with the first mild weather, it is impossible to grow it properly in the vicinity of London, England, where its premature attempts to flower are always nipped by late frosts. Fortunately it makes an ideal tree in smaller gardens over a wide area of North America and is finding favor even in the Sacramento Valley of California.

Unfortunately it is susceptible to borers and various diseases, among them petal and leaf spots; it was especially susceptible in 1977 to what is now called dogwood anthracnose. This appeared on both the East and West coasts, on *C. florida* and *C. nuttallii.* It especially strikes trees weakened from drought or winter injury. The U. S. Department of Agriculture Forest Service notes that leaf symptoms develop first in the lower crown and then progress up the tree, exhibiting tan spots with purple rims on the leaves. Annual elliptical, brown cankers often form at the base of dead branches. Spread of the disease is aided by cool, wet weather.

Dogwoods receiving good cultural care are better able to withstand the inroads of anthracnose. Water the plants during periods of drought and mulch to conserve moisture. Prune out infected branches, rake up and dispose of fallen leaves, and avoid using high-nitrogen fertilizers because these aid in forcing overvigorous growth that is easily susceptible to the inroads of disease. Fungicides should be used only to supplement good cultural care.

Spraying with methoxychlor or carbaryl three times at weekly intervals in the spring or summer has given partial control. Trees growing in full sun are more resistant than those growing in the shade. Avoid sprinkling the leaves from above; this also helps in the disease control.

Cornus kousa   21′   Zone 5   Japanese dogwood

* FLOWERS: inconspicuous, in small clusters surrounded by large, pointed bracts that are white to pinkish on occasion
        TIME: mid-June
* FRUIT: raspberrylike, red

The flower bracts of Cornus kousa, *pictured here, are pointed; those of* C. florida *are rounded and notched.*

EFFECTIVE: late summer
* HABIT: horizontal branching
* FOLIAGE: dense, lustrous
AUTUMN COLOR: scarlet
HABITAT: Japan, Korea
INTRODUCED: 1875
VARIETIES:

> *chinensis (Chinese dogwood)*—practically identical from an ornamental stand-point except that the flower bracts may be slightly longer than those of the species
> '**Elizabeth Lustgarten**'—side branches droop slightly
> '**Milky Way**'—a selection of *C. kousa chinensis* made a few years prior to 1960, noted for its profuse flower production
> '**Summer Stars**'—flower bracts remain on the tree up to six weeks after opening. Originated at Princeton Nurseries, Princeton, New Jersey.

Over twenty-one clonal names have been given to plants of this species. Widely grown in gardens now, this plant blooms about three weeks after *C. florida* and for that reason is valued greatly. Its flower bracts are pointed (not rounded and notched as the native species) and often show splotches of pink as they fade.

An interesting comment here is the fact that an overly enthusiastic plantsman actually named a plant *Cornus kousa rubra* (in 1952) when he first saw the pinkish tinge of the flower bracts of a certain plant. When the plant was moved, it showed pure white flower bracts several years in a row with no pink coloring whatsoever, thus proving that soil location may have something to do with the flower color production in this genus. Like the native dogwood, the flower clusters are borne on the upper side of the horizontal branches so that to be most effective the plant should be looked down on from above. E. H. Wilson said that the form he introduced from China (var. *chinensis*) was superior to the species, but I have been unable to see any marked difference between the species and the variety, as they are growing side by side in the Arnold Arboretum, except that the bracts of the species are 1½–2 inches long while those of the variety are 2–3½ inches long. These differences, however, are not always evident.

Cornus macrophylla   45′   Zone 6   Largeleaf dogwood

* FLOWERS: small, yellowish white, in clusters, 4–6″ in diameter
        TIME: July–August
* FRUIT: bluish black berries
        EFFECTIVE: fall
  HABIT: rounded
* FOLIAGE: handsome, large leaves
  HABITAT: China, Japan
  INTRODUCED: 1827

Sometimes confused with *C. controversa,* the leaves of this species are opposite (those of *C. controversa* are alternate), about 4–7 inches long, and as much as 3½ inches wide. It is excellent as a foliage plant, but its flowers and fruits are not superior to those of *C. controversa.* Its late bloom is an important factor when trees for summer display are needed. No serious insect pests or diseases.

Cornus mas   24′   Zone 4   Cornelian cherry

* FLOWERS: small, yellow, appearing before leaves
        TIME: early April
* FRUIT: edible, scarlet, ½–¾″ long
        EFFECTIVE: August–September
* HABIT: round, dense, shrublike
* FOLIAGE: lustrous green
* AUTUMN COLOR: red
  HABITAT: central and southern Europe, western Asia
  INTRODUCED: probably before 1800
  VARIETIES:
        'Alba'—white fruits
        'Aureo-elegantissima'—leaves with creamy white and red variegation. This is
        not a vigorous plant.

Cornus mas, *with its small, yellow flowers, is one of the first trees to bloom in the spring.*

flava—yellow fruits
'Variegata'—leaves with yellow or white margins

One of the earliest blooming of the spring-flowering trees and shrubs, with flowers before the leaves, this sturdy, vigorous plant is useful as a specimen, small tree or large shrub, or as a hedge. Its fruits, which have been used in making preserves, are not too conspicuous, for many are hidden by the foliage. The yellow-fruiting form is more conspicuous in early summer, but except for color need not be grown in preference to the species. This plant is unaffected at present by insect pests or diseases, an uncommon but valuable trait.

Cornus nuttallii   75'   Zone 7   Pacific dogwood

* FLOWERS: 4–6 flower bracts, white, 4–5″ in diameter (tip to tip), similar to a large clematis blossom
    TIME: April
* FRUIT: bright red to orange berries
    EFFECTIVE: summer and fall
* HABIT: pyramidal, often horizontal branching
    FOLIAGE: dense

* AUTUMN COLOR: scarlet and yellow
HABITAT: British Columbia to southern California
VARIETIES:

>'Eddiei'—discovered growing wild about 1918 by H. M. Eddie, a nurseryman of Vancouver, British Columbia. It resembles the species in every respect except that the leaves are variegated an attractive green and gold, which gives it a spotted or mottled effect. It tends to bloom twice, once in the spring and again in August.
>
>'Pilgrim'—a clone named about 1960 and selected for its sturdy growth by the Saratoga Horticultural Foundation, Saratoga, California

Many consider this the most handsome flowering tree native of North America. It is unfortunate that it does not grow well on the East Coast but seems to require the moist, moderate climate of the West Coast, where it frequently has a second blooming period in August and September. The bracts are normally white but may fade to a rose-pink color that is rather attractive. The "flowers" are larger than those of *C. florida* and often have six bracts instead of four. An excellent specimen for planting on the West Coast.

Unfortunately this is also susceptible to dogwood anthracnose, a serious and disfiguring disease. For further information, see the discussion under *C. florida.*

The Turkish filbert
(Corylus colurna) *provides good form and good foliage in dry situations.*

Corylus colurna   75'   Zone 4   Turkish filbert

FLOWERS: male catkins 2–3" long
   TIME: winter and spring
HABIT: regularly pyramidal
FOLIAGE: leaves 2½–6" long, dense
HABITAT: southeastern Europe, western Asia
INTRODUCED: early colonial times

A well-shaped ornamental tree, perfectly hardy, of interest because of its form and good foliage. The male catkins appear very early in the season, another reason it is grown for early spring display. It is also excellent for planting in dry situations, for in some areas of New England during the past dry summers it has remained vigorous and green when maples have dropped some of their leaves for lack of sufficient moisture. No serious insect pests or diseases.

Corynocarpus laevigata   30–40'   Zone 10   New Zealand laurel

* FRUIT: plumlike, orange colored, 1–1½" long
* FOLIAGE: evergreen, stout, leathery, dark, glossy green leaves, 3–8" long
HABITAT: New Zealand
INTRODUCED: 1823 (England)

A small evergreen tree with showy fruit related to the hollies, it has leaves that remind one of those of *Magnolia grandiflora* and seems to do best in light semishade, not full sun.

Cotinus americanus   30'   Zone 5   American smoke tree

FLOWERS: feathery, greenish masses of fine-textured growths, appearing like "smoke" from a distance; sexes separate
   TIME: mid-June
HABIT: upright, rather narrow
FOLIAGE: dense
* AUTUMN COLOR: scarlet to orange
HABITAT: southeastern United States

The fruiting panicles of this are not showy, but there is little to surpass it when autumn has touched its leaves a brilliant scarlet to orange. It should be grown only for its fall effect, and in cases where the smaller smoke tree *(C. coggygria)* will suffice, this American species can be omitted from further consideration. No serious pests.

Cotinus obovatus   30'   Zone 4   American smoke tree,
                                              Chittamwood

HABIT: spreading or rounded
FOLIAGE: ineffective
* AUTUMN COLOR: gorgeous red
HABITAT: southeastern United States
INTRODUCED: 1882

Its wood yields an orange-colored dye. The American female species does not have as many fruit as does the European species; the sexes are separate. Leaves turn red to orange in the fall. No serious pests.

→≫ CRATAEGUS

At one time there were 550 species and varieties of *Crataegus* growing in the Arnold Arboretum, a great proportion of them American natives. Hawthorns are widely distributed over North America and are a common sight in pastures or along old hedgerows or even in valleys where they have crowded out other plants. This great group was one of the particular interests of Charles Sprague Sargent, the first director of the Arnold Arboretum. As his studies progressed, and those of others as well, it became evident that this is a most difficult group to study, and the separation of species and varieties on the basis of minute characteristics is a thankless task, to say the least. Some make meritorious ornamental trees. Many, many others are practically identical, certainly from a landscape point of view, and it seems valueless to continue producing them commercially for this reason. It is at this point that I would like to recommend strongly that the plant-growing public become interested in only a *very* few of the best and completely discard the others from planting plans and nursery catalogs.

All are dense, twiggy trees or bushlike shrubs, with thorns often an inch or more long. They are members of the rose family and as such are susceptible to some of the same serious troubles—scale, lace bug, borers, leaf miner, and red spider. In fact, most of them are in the group of trees that require annual attention in order to remain attractive, reason enough for using them with discretion in areas where such care may not be forthcoming. Many are difficult to transplant unless properly root-pruned considerably in advance, and since all are extremely thorny, maintenance people always like to give them a wide berth, and you cannot blame them.

The *Crataegus* are valued for their picturesque shapes, for their dense and thorny habit of growth, some for their glossy foliage, and most for their clusters of small, white (sometimes pink) flowers in the early spring and their bright red fruits (small pomes, often borne in clusters and usually colored bright red or yellowish red, varying from ¼ to 1 inch in diameter) in the fall. Indeed, some have beautiful autumn color. Many have proved amenable to shearing, and because of their twiggy habit, dense foliage, and sharp thorns, make excellent hedges and barrier plants. The seed usually does not germinate until the second year it is in the ground.

Species and varieties doing well locally in the range of their habitat are naturally among the easiest to establish. Such plants, where they are used well and serve a purpose, should not be discarded but should be used.

Many of the species can be sheared and have been used in large clipped hedges. The cockspur thorn is one example and has been used widely for this purpose in the past. Here again, however, hawthorns cannot be recommended for this purpose in many areas because of serious pest problems.

Fire blight takes its toll on many an old plant, some years more heavily than others. Juniper rust and hawthorn blight are other often troublesome diseases. Lace bug, mites, leaf miners, woolly hawthorn aphid, cottony maple scale, Lecanium scale, scurfy scale, leaf skeletonizers, tent caterpillars, western tussock moth, Japanese beetle, various borers—these are only some of the pests listed as troublesome to hawthorns.

Then, too, many are difficult to transplant, and certainly they are difficult to handle and propagate in the nursery. All these things considered, one should think several times before using hawthorns on a large scale.

On the credit side, they will thrive in poor soils, they will grow almost equally well in alkaline and acid soils, they are dense in habit, and often picturesque because of their wide-spreading and horizontal branches. They provide color in the spring and fall, and some of them retain their fruit all winter. If the foliage goes unmarred in the summer, many species present a glossy foliage that has merit in its own right.

A close examination of the thirty-two listed will show that there are some with unusually good red or pink flowers; others are outstanding for their habits of growth; still others have yellow to orange fruits.

If these things are not considered, I would list only six—*C. crus-galli, laevigata* 'Paulii' (Paul's scarlet hawthorn), *lavallei, nitida, phaenopyrum,* and *succulenta.* So, for those who care little for the group, these are the best six, and for those who see merit in them the list of thirty-two is one from which selections can be made. It should be emphasized again that these trees require annual maintenance to look good, a very important reason that they should not be selected for certain types of planting.

Crataegus arnoldiana   30′   Zone 4   Arnold hawthorn

* FLOWERS: white, ¾″ in diameter
        TIME: early May
* FRUIT: bright crimson, ¾″ long
        EFFECTIVE: middle August to early September
  HABIT: rounded, thorny, dense branching
  FOLIAGE: dense
  HABITAT: New England

This hawthorn has the most conspicuous early fruits of the entire group, reason enough for suggesting it here. If early fruits are not desired, other species might be selected.

Crataegus coccinioides   21′   Zone 5   Kansas hawthorn

* FLOWERS: white, ¾″ in diameter, borne in 5–6 flowered clusters
        TIME: mid-May
* FRUIT: dark red, ¾″ in diameter
        EFFECTIVE: fall and winter
* HABIT: rounded head, thorny, dense branching
  FOLIAGE: red when first unfurls in spring
  AUTUMN COLOR: orange to scarlet
  HABITAT: Indiana to Kansas

A very good hawthorn for foliage as well as fruit.

Crataegus crus-galli   36′   Zone 4   Cockspur thorn

* FLOWERS: white, ½″ in diameter
        TIME: late May
* FRUIT: bright red, ⅜″ in diameter
        EFFECTIVE: during most of the winter
* HABIT: rounded head, sometimes flat, wide-spreading and horizontal branches, thorny, dense branching
* FOLIAGE: lustrous, dense
  AUTUMN COLOR: orange to scarlet
  HABITAT: northeastern North America

The variety *splendens* is supposed to have leaves that are very glossy and hence more ornamental than those of the species. This species is typical of many hawthorns and as a specimen is truly excellent for its definite horizontal branching habit of growth. Where the glossy-leaved variety can be obtained it certainly should be used. This hawthorn also withstands shearing as well as any, making fine hedges.

Crataegus laevigata (syn. *C. oxyacantha*)   15′   Zone 4   English hawthorn

* FLOWERS: white, ⅝″ in diameter, in 5–12 flowered panicles
      TIME: late May
* FRUIT: scarlet, ¼–⅝″ in diameter
      EFFECTIVE: fall
* HABIT: thorny, spreading, rounded head, dense branching
   FOLIAGE: leaves 3–5 lobed, dense
   HABITAT: Europe, northern Africa
   VARIETIES:
       aurea—fruits are bright yellow
       'Autumn Glory'—probably a hybrid of *C. laevigata*, originating in California before 1945 and at one time called 'Crimson Glory.' It was selected for its good growth of 15′ to 18′, its white flowers, and its "giant red fruits remaining on the tree well into the winter." It has not proved as hardy at the Arnold Arboretum in Boston, Massachusetts, as the species.
       'Crimson Cloud' *(Plant Patent #2679)*—good single, red flowers; resistant to the leaf blight that is a problem with *C. laevigata*
       'Paulii' *(Paul's scarlet hawthorn)*—flowers double, bright scarlet. One of the showiest of all the hawthorns. Originated by the Princeton Nurseries, Princeton, New Jersey
       'Plena'—flowers double, white, with few fruits

The double, white flowers of **Crataegus** laevigata *'Plena.'*

Crataegus laevigata *'Rosea,' a popular dense-growing tree.*

'Rosea'—flowers single, light rose
'Rosea-plena'—flowers double, light rose
'Rubra'—the best in fruit; fruits bright red, ⅜" in diameter, flowers single

This is the "May tree" so often referred to in English literature and is one of the few species of *Crataegus* to have pink- to red-flowered varieties—reason enough for its wide popularity on both sides of the Atlantic Ocean. The varieties are grown more than is the species itself, at least in North America. The absence of autumn color puts the species at least in a lower class than, say, *C. phaenopyrum,* which has brilliant fall color. However, there are no other hawthorns with more colorful flowers than some of the varieties of this English hawthorn.

x Crataegus lavallei   21'   Zone 4   Lavalle hawthorn

* FLOWERS: white, ¾" in diameter, in many-flowered clusters
        TIME: late May
* FRUIT: brick red to orange-red, ⅝" in diameter
        EFFECTIVE: fall and winter
  HABIT: thorny, spines 2" long, dense branching
  FOLIAGE: dense
* AUTUMN COLOR: bronze-red
  HYBRID ORIGIN: *C. crus-galli x C. pubescens*
  ORIGINATED: before 1880

This is of particular interest because its fruits remain on the tree throughout the winter, increasing its ornamental value.

Crataegus mollis   30'   Zone 4   Downy hawthorn

* FLOWERS: white, 1″ in diameter
    TIME: mid-May
* FRUIT: pear-shaped, red, often 1″ in diameter
    EFFECTIVE: late summer and early fall
* HABIT: thorny, rounded, dense branching
    FOLIAGE: dense, leaves larger than many other hawthorns
    HABITAT: southern Ontario to Virginia and Kansas

This is one of the larger fruiting hawthorns, but because the fruits are so large they might be considered even coarse in some situations.

Crataegus monogyna   30'   Zone 4   Single-seed hawthorn

* FLOWERS: white, ⅜″ in diameter
    TIME: late May
  FRUIT: red, ⅜″ in diameter
    EFFECTIVE: fall
* HABIT: rounded head, with slightly pendulous branches, more thorny than *C. laevigata*, dense branching
    FOLIAGE: leaves 3–7 lobed, dense
    HABITAT: Europe, northern Africa, western Asia
    VARIETIES:

        'Biflora' *(Glastonbury thorn)*—often blooming in mild seasons in midwinter in England and again in spring. (Sometimes termed *C. monogyna praecox.*)
        There is a legend concerning the origin of this plant, demonstrating why this thorn has been so highly regarded through the years. Joseph of Arimathea, so the legend goes, came to what is now England shortly after the Crucifixion to found a Christian religion. His teachings apparently were not taken well by the inhabitants so he prayed to God to produce a miracle in order that the people would have faith in his spoken words. And so, one day—which happened to be Christmas—when he was preaching in Glastonbury, he thrust his staff into the ground and it burst forth in flower. It grew into a full-sized tree, and every year after that it bore flowers on Christmas Day.
        Of course, in the rugged climate of New England, the blooming at Christmas does not occur, but during mild winters in Virginia or the Carolinas it might. The number of flowers produced would be small in comparison to those that appear later in May, but nevertheless, the winter performance of this interesting tree has kept this legend alive in England for centuries.
        inermis—thornless, excellent mushroom-shaped habit. This tree, although subject to the various pests of all hawthorns, might prove an excellent one nevertheless for use along narrow streets. Its bushlike top, especially if it is

grafted high on understock with a single main trunk, is dense, well shaped, and requires very little pruning. It is not a fast-growing tree.

pendula—with pendulous branchlets

pteridifolia—leaves deeply lobed and closely incised

'Semperflorens'—a low, shrubby form often flowering continuously until August

'Stricta'—with upright branches, rather narrow, but as it grows older it quickly grows out of the narrow habit. The tree in the Arnold Arboretum is 30′ tall and 8′ wide.

Somewhat similar to *C. laevigata* but more thorny, this tree is better for use in hedges. In England there are hundreds of miles of hedges of this one species alone, for it is easily grown and lends itself well to clipping. It is used much more in hedges than is *C. laevigata,* and the two species are frequently confused. There is an old saying in England that if the "haws" of the thorns and "hips" of the roses are borne in great profusion, then a hard winter is ahead.

Crataegus nitida   30′   Zone 4   Glossy hawthorn

* FLOWERS: white
    TIME: late May
* FRUIT: dull red, ⅜″ in diameter
    EFFECTIVE: all winter
* HABIT: thorny, rounded head, dense branching
* FOLIAGE: lustrous
* AUTUMN COLOR: orange to red
    HABITAT: Illinois to Arkansas

This is another hawthorn that holds its fruit all winter.

Crataegus phaenopyrum   30′   Zone 4   Washington hawthorn

* FLOWERS: white, ½″ in diameter, in many-flowered clusters
    TIME: mid-June
* FRUIT: bright red, about ¼″ in diameter
    EFFECTIVE: all winter
* HABIT: broadly columnar, thorny, dense branching, eventually developing a rounded head
* FOLIAGE: leaves 3–5 lobed, lustrous, dense
* AUTUMN COLOR: scarlet to orange
    HABITAT: southeastern United States
    VARIETY:
        'Fastigiata' *(Pyramidal Washington hawthorn)*—columnar in habit; flowers and fruits smaller than those of the species

If only one hawthorn was to be selected from the many native or exotic types available in North America today, the Washington hawthorn would be the first one to consider.

It is excellent—of interest every season of the year, something that cannot be said of the majority of trees grown in gardens and along highways today. Its upright, dense habit, profuse flowers, and brilliant autumn color, as well as its solid little red fruits that remain colorful all winter long, are its best assets. It has been used as a specimen and lawn tree as well as for highway plantings. The dense, twiggy growth shields headlight glare from approaching cars when planted on the middle strip of a two-lane highway throughout the growing season and is even sufficiently effective in the wintertime. This is one of the last species to bloom in the spring.

Crataegus pinnatifida major   18′   Zone 5   Large Chinese
hawthorn

* FLOWERS: white, about ¾″ in diameter, in clusters
        TIME: late May
* FRUIT: brilliant red, 1″ in diameter
        EFFECTIVE: fall
* HABIT: thorny, rounded head, dense branching
* FOLIAGE: lustrous, leaves 5–9 lobed
  HABITAT: northern China
  INTRODUCED: about 1880

The leaves are often divided down to the midrib, and its fruit is so large that it is cultivated and eaten by the Chinese. Charles Sprague Sargent, who studied the *Crataegus* thoroughly for years, once said that it was one of the handsomest species grown in America.

Crataegus pruinosa   21′   Zone 4   Frosted hawthorn

* FLOWERS: white, ¾″ in diameter, borne in loose clusters, with rose-colored anthers
        TIME: late May
* FRUIT: red to orange, ⅜″ in diameter
        EFFECTIVE: fall
* HABIT: thorny, rounded, dense branching
  FOLIAGE: dense, bluish green
  HABITAT: Ontario to Virginia and Illinois

The frosted hawthorn is a beautiful hawthorn, especially in fruit.

Crataegus punctata   30′   Zone 4   Dotted hawthorn

* FLOWERS: white, ¾″ in diameter, in many-flowered clusters
        TIME: late May
* FRUIT: dull red, with small dots, ¾″ in diameter
        EFFECTIVE: fall

* HABIT: thorny, dense branching
FOLIAGE: dense
HABITAT: eastern North America
VARIETY:
        '**Aurea**'—yellow fruit

The fruits are among the largest of the native American hawthorns, and the tree may grow to be twice as broad as it is high. Because it may eventually reach a width of 40 feet, it might best be used chiefly in park planting.

Crataegus succulenta   15'   Zone 3   Fleshy hawthorn

* FLOWERS: white, ¾" in diameter, in many clusters
      TIME: late May
* FRUIT: bright red, ⅜" in diameter
      EFFECTIVE: fall
HABIT: thorny, dense branching
FOLIAGE: dense
HABITAT: northeastern North America

This was considered by Sargent to be one of the six handsomest hawthorns in North America and is included here out of respect for his expert judgment.

x *Crataegus* 'Toba'   15'   Zone 3

* FLOWERS: fragrant, double, light to bright pink, fading to deep rose in color
      TIME: late May
* FRUIT: bright red, ½" in diameter
      EFFECTIVE: fall
FOLIAGE: dense, glossy green
ORIGIN: *C. succulenta* x *C. laevigata* 'Paulii,' Dominion Experiment Station, Morden, Manitoba, Canada
INTRODUCED: 1949

Its chief claim to fame is that it is hardier than *C. laevigata,* which it resembles in general habit. Resistant to leaf spot.

Crataegus viridis   36'   Zone 4   Green hawthorn

* FLOWERS: white, ¾" in diameter, borne in flat clusters 2" across
      TIME: late May
* FRUIT: bright red, ¼" in diameter
      EFFECTIVE: fall and winter
* HABIT: thorny, spreading, rounded, dense branching

FOLIAGE: dense
HABITAT: central and southeastern United States

The green hawthorn is particularly valued for planting throughout its native habitat.

Crataegus 'Winter King'   36'   Zone 4

FRUIT: red, ⅜" in diameter
    EFFECTIVE: all winter
BARK: silver colored
FOLIAGE: glossy green
INTRODUCED: 1955

An introduction of the Simpson Orchard Co., Vincennes, Indiana, the parentage of this clone is not known but it appears similar in general to *C. viridis*. It fruits heavily when young with persistent red fruits that are showy throughout the winter.

Crinodendron patagua   20–30'   Zone 10   White lilytree

* FLOWERS: delicately bell-shaped, white
    TIME: June and July
FRUIT: cream and red seed pods
* FOLIAGE: evergreen, similar to that of an evergreen oak
HABITAT: Chile
INTRODUCED: 1901

This has been used in the vicinity of Santa Barbara, California, and recommended for wider use in the southwestern part of that state.

Cryptomeria japonica   150'   Zones 5–6   Cryptomeria

* HABIT: pyramidal with spreading, whiplike branches
BARK: reddish, shredding off in strips
* FOLIAGE: evergreen, dagger-shaped needles
HABITAT: Japan
INTRODUCED: 1861
VARIETIES:
    'Compacta'—compact, conical; short leaves
    'Elegans' *(Plume cryptomeria)*—densely branched, bushy

The cryptomeria is hardy in America as far north as Boston. The foliage is somewhat similar to that of the *Sequoiadendron*, or the big tree of California; the bark is often used by Japanese peasants to shingle the roofs of their houses and is the timber tree of Japan. It is symmetrical while young, which gives it special interest. It is not very difficult to grow. The plants grown from seed vary, and several varieties are available, all having small cones about ¾ inch long when they reach maturity. These cones, like those of the other coniferous evergreens, are interesting but cannot be depended upon annually since some years very few if any are produced. The much-talked-of variety 'Lobbii' does not differ from the species, and the Chinese form *sinensis* is not as ornamental as the species. Occasional leaf blight and leaf spot.

Cunninghamia lanceolata   75'   Zone 7   Common China fir

HABIT: spreading branches, pendulous at the tips
* FOLIAGE: evergreen needles, 1–2½" long, somewhat similar to that of the more common *Araucaria*
HABITAT: southern and western China
INTRODUCED: 1804

Only of value in the warmer parts of the country, the China fir has the meritorious quality that few evergreens possess of sprouting from the stump and roots when cut down. In China this method of quickly reproducing itself by suckers from roots or stumps makes it a very important tree for reforestation purposes. The cones are 1–2 inches long but cannot be depended upon annually. No serious insect pests or diseases.

x Cupressocyparis leylandii   100'   Zone 6   Leyland cypress

* HABIT: columnar to pyramidal
* FOLIAGE: evergreen leaves, similar to those of *Chamaecyparis nootkatensis*
ORIGIN: *Cupressus macrocarpa x Chamaecyparis nootkatensis*
INTRODUCED: 1888
VARIETIES:
       'Castlewellan'—a beautiful form with yellow foliage
       'Naylor's Blue'—soft grayish green foliage, columnar in height, and fast growing
       'Stapehill'—sprays flattened, columnar form

A vigorous growing (3 feet per year when young), excellent evergreen with fine, feathery foliage, truly a magnificent evergreen. Increasingly popular in the southeastern United States. It will make a fine hedge. No serious insect pests or diseases.

Cupressus arizonica   35'   Zone 7   Arizona cypress

HABIT: rounded, tall
* FOLIAGE: aromatic, evergreen, scalelike
HABITAT: Arizona

Staminate and pistillate flowers separate but on the same plant. Seldom used in American gardens farther north than Zone 7.

Cupressus bakeri   30′   Zone 5   Modoc cypress

HABIT: rounded and bushy
* FOLIAGE: glaucous, evergreen, scalelike
HABITAT: Oregon

This little-known cypress is the hardiest and should be used considerably more in gardens. The MacNab cypress of California is very similar but not nearly as hardy.

Cupressus macrocarpa   75′   Zone 7   Monterey cypress

HABIT: pyramidal when young, broadly rounded when old
* FOLIAGE: evergreen, small, scalelike (similar to junipers)
HABITAT: California coast south of Monterey
VARIETY:
   'Golden Pillar'—golden yellow foliage; needs full sun

The Monterey cypress is the best cypress for seaside planting and probably best used solely for this purpose, especially as a windbreak against ocean breezes. As a specimen tree or clipped hedge it withstands salt-laden ocean winds better than most other evergreens. In Monterey it has been forced to grow in picturesque habit by the winds off the Pacific Ocean. It grows very rapidly.

The Monterey cypress (Cupressus macrocarpa) *is usually grown only in the southwestern part of the United States. This fine hedge was photographed in Scotland where the moist climate is to its liking.*

Monterey cypress (Cupressus macrocarpa) *sheared to depict "The Hunt" in Ireland.*

Cupressus sempervirens   75′   Zone 7   Italian cypress

* HABIT: with horizontal or erect branches
* FOLIAGE: dark, evergreen, scalelike
  HABITAT: southern Europe, western Asia
  INTRODUCED: probably in colonial times
  VARIETIES:

> 'Glauca'—dense, narrow, columnar form with bluish green, scalelike foliage
> 'Horizontalis' *(Spreading Italian cypress)*—with horizontal branches forming a very wide head
> 'Stricta' *(Pyramidal Italian cypress)*—columnar in form, this variety is often only a few feet in diameter but 20′ or more in height. It is the most rigidly erect of the columnar trees and the narrowest of them all. It is therefore used a great deal in the gardens of southern Europe for this characteristic.

Probably the most popular form of this species is the columnar, since there is no other evergreen that grows so tall yet remains so narrow in habit. For purely formal gardens where erect lines are to be emphasized, this tree has no peer. One interesting note on the durability of this wood is the fact that the doors of St. Peter's Cathedral in Rome were supposed to have been made of this wood and were eleven hundred years old when they were removed, still in sound condition.

Davidia involucrata   60'   Zone 6   Dove tree

* FLOWERS: many stamens forming a yellow ball 1″ in diameter, and 2 white bracts,
    the lower being the longer, as much as 7″ long
    TIME: mid-May
HABIT: broadly pyramidal, especially while young
FOLIAGE: dense, rather coarse
HABITAT: western China
INTRODUCED: 1904

This tree was introduced by Ernest H. Wilson and is probably the most widely
publicized of his introductions. The story of how he made a special trip to China to
obtain this plant amidst great difficulties, only to find on his return to England that
it had been introduced the previous year into France, was one of his major disappointments. Many trees have been distributed in this country—a few are flowering, but
many have been disappointingly devoid of flowers. Even in the Arnold Arboretum
the plants bloom only about once in several years, but in Newport, Rhode Island,
there is a magnificent specimen that blooms every year. Several plants are performing
well on the West Coast also. The flower consists of two creamy white bracts, the upper
rather small but the lower one pendulous and nearly 7 inches long. Between the two
bracts is the flower head, rounded, ball-like, and yellowish. It is beautiful in flower,
but for many gardeners who live in cold areas or want quick results, this tree may
not be worth waiting for and, in fact, the flower buds may not be produced even if
the rest of the tree is apparently hardy. The variety *vilmoriniana* is hardy in Zone 5.
No serious insect pests or diseases.

Delonix regia   40'   Zone 10   Royal poinciana, Flame tree

* FLOWERS: bright scarlet and yellow, 2–3″ in diameter
    TIME: summer
FRUIT: pods, 2′ long and 2″ wide
HABIT: wide-branching
FOLIAGE: dense, fine texture, fernlike
HABITAT: Madagascar

This is probably southern Florida's most popular ornamental flowering tree. The
deciduous, fernlike foliage, topped by the brilliant scarlet and yellow blossoms, is
enough reason it should be so. It grows rapidly in almost any soil and is one of the
sights that a northern visitor to southern Florida rarely forgets, if he is fortunate
enough to see a tree in bloom.

Diospyros kaki   40'   Zone 7   Kaki persimmon

FRUIT: fleshy, edible, orange to bright yellow, 1½–3″ in diameter
    EFFECTIVE: early fall
HABIT: rounded head

FOLIAGE: rather dense, leaves 2–7″ long
HABITAT: China, Korea
INTRODUCED: before 1870

This tree is cultivated only in the subtropical United States in climates similar to that where figs are grown. It has some merit as a shade tree but can be very difficult as a bearer of edible fruits if only one tree is grown. The species is chiefly dioecious, but individual plants have been known to have all three types of flowers on the same tree—perfect, staminate, and pistillate. On the other hand, an individual tree has been known to produce a crop of staminate flowers one year and not produce them again for many years, producing pistillate flowers in the interim.

The importance of all this is that, in general, this species will not develop fruit (a very few clones may) unless properly fertilized. In California the growers have capitalized on a few "seedless" varieties, that is, varieties that produce fruits without being pollinized, but the fruits have no seeds. On the other hand, many Florida growers like varieties requiring pollination because they believe it increases the yield. Horticulturists have found some trees fairly dependable pollinizers, and of course these are grown.

In Japan more than eight hundred varieties of this species have been grown and at least one-fourth of these have been termed good varieties. This is the large persimmon of commerce, but home owners who may wish to plant only one tree would do well to investigate carefully the available varieties before they make their selections. The best information on this score can always be obtained from the nearest state experiment station.

Diospyros virginiana   75′   Zone 4   Common persimmon

FRUIT: yellow to orange, 1½″ in diameter, edible after frost
HABIT: rounded head, often pendulous branches
* BARK: deeply cut into regular, small blocks
FOLIAGE: dense
AUTUMN COLOR: yellow
HABITAT: eastern and southeastern United States

The common persimmon is found over a wide area. Sexes are usually separate, and plants have been selected producing bigger fruits than others. As a specimen tree (aside from the fruits, which are not ornamental) the persimmon has little to offer over many other better kinds of trees. The persimmon borer—somewhat similar to the peach borer—burrows into the lower stems and roots. Spray in summer with methoxychlor.

Elaeagnus angustifolia   20′   Zone 2   Russian olive

* FLOWERS: fragrant, small, silvery outside, yellow inside
      TIME: early June
FRUIT: yellow-coated berries with silvery scales
      EFFECTIVE: early fall

HABIT: wide-spreading, rather open
BARK: brown, shredding off in long strips
* FOLIAGE: narrow, dull gray-green leaves, 1–3½" long
HABITAT: southern Europe to west and central Asia
INTRODUCED: early colonial times

The flowers and fruit of this plant are none too conspicuous, but the gray foliage is outstanding and the plant can be used for this one feature. Hardy and vigorous, it grows easily in many kinds of soils and its unique crooked trunk is attractive in its own right, for it is covered with a shredding, brown bark that is of considerable interest throughout the winter. The leaves and stems are covered with silvery scales. Verticillium wilt is a serious pest of this plant, especially in the Midwest. Spots, scales, and crown gall also infest it. It has not proved popular in the Midwest as a highway plant for this reason.

Ensete ventricosum (syn. *Musa ensete*)   25′   Zone 9   Abyssinian banana

FOLIAGE: leaves up to 18′ long, 3′ wide, bright green with a red midrib
HABITAT: Abyssinia

Abyssinian banana (Ensete ventricosum).

Banana (Ensente
ventricosum) *flowers
opening up to show the
young fruits developing.*

Popular in California for its long leaves, this should be planted where wind will not
fray the foliage. It is often planted close to wall surfaces for this reason.

Eriobotrya japonica   20'   Zone 7   Loquat

* FLOWERS: fragrant, white, ½" in diameter, in panicles 5–7" long
      TIME: fall
* FRUIT: orange-yellow, pear-shaped, 1½" long, edible
      EFFECTIVE: spring
  HABIT: dense
* FOLIAGE: leathery, evergreen leaves, 5–10" long
  HABITAT: central China
  INTRODUCED: 1784

The leathery leaves are very handsome, but in order to do well this shrubby tree
requires deep, well-drained soil and full sun. It is grown in certain areas especially
for its edible fruits, but its rich foliage alone makes it desirable as an ornamental.

⇶ *EUCALYPTUS*

There are some eighty species and varieties of *Eucalyptus* (over five hundred in Australia) being offered in the trade today, certainly far more than are needed. Mostly planted on the West Coast, some species have found the environment so satisfactory that they have become naturalized. The blue gum *(E. globulus)* has unfortunately earned a poor name for the entire group, with its vigorous growth, rank feeding, shallow roots, ease with which it is blown over, and a reputation of always dropping something—bark, leaves, or fruit. However, experience with many *Eucalyptus* species on the West Coast has shown that there are species that make good ornamental trees without all the drawbacks of *E. globulus,* and some are well suited for growing in western gardens. Usually free from pests.

Consequently, as a group, they need not be blacklisted. Care should be taken in selecting the right species for the right situations, but with some

The bark of the eucalyptus, or gum, is of ornamental interest throughout the year.

hunting among those firms that specialize in growing rare trees, some of the following can be found along with many others. All are native to Australia, Tasmania, or New Zealand.

Eucalyptus camaldulensis (syn. *E. rostrata)*   150'   Zone 9   Red gum

FLOWERS: white
    TIME: spring and summer
HABIT: spreading, rather open
BARK: gray
FOLIAGE: narrow leaves

A fast-growing tree, 30 feet wide at maturity. One of the most drought-resistant species of *Eucalyptus.*

Eucalyptus cinerea   50'   Zone 9   Silver dollar tree

FLOWERS: white
    TIME: spring
BARK: reddish brown
FOLIAGE: coin-shaped; young leaves blue-green

A fast-growing, small tree, its leaves are excellent for cut foliage.

Eucalyptus ficifolia   30–50'   Zone 10   Red flowering gum

FLOWERS: red to pink, in 6–7″ clusters
    TIME: July–August
HABIT: rounded head
FOLIAGE: dense, coarse, reddish leaves, up to 6″ long

This is a popular species because of the masses of flowers that cover the tree when in bloom; it is probably one of the best of the red-flowered species.

Eucalyptus globulus   200'   Zone 9   Blue gum

FOLIAGE: young leaves a glaucous white, maturing to a lustrous dark green, 6–12″
    long, about 1½″ wide

Especially valued as a young plant for its glaucous white foliage, this is one of the species widely planted in southern Europe and throughout southern California in windbreaks. It is too coarse and tall-growing for most types of ornamental garden plantings. There is a variety, *compacta,* offered that is much better to use.

Eucalyptus gunnii   40–75′   Zone 9   Cider gum

FLOWERS: white, in small umbels
    TIME: October to December
FOLIAGE: up to 4″ long

A variable species, but it is supposed to be one of the hardiest.

Eucalyptus nicholii   40′   Zone 9   Narrowleaf black peppermint

FOLIAGE: evergreen, willowlike

Especially valued for its foliage, which emits a peppermint scent when crushed.

Eucalyptus polyanthemos   70′   Zone 9   Red gum, Silver dollar
                                                               gum

FLOWERS: small, white, in terminal panicles
    TIME: September
FOLIAGE: orbicular to narrow, grayish blue leaves with light reddish margins and
    veins, up to 6″ long

Excellent for cut foliage.

Eucalyptus sideroxylon ‘Rosea’   40′   Zone 9   Red ironbark

FLOWERS: pink, in large masses
    TIME: December to June
BARK: brownish red
FOLIAGE: pointed, bluish green, turning bronze in winter, up to 4½″ long

A profuse bloomer.

Eucalyptus torquata   15–20′   Zone 10   Coral gum

FLOWERS: rosy coral buds opening to vivid red flowers
    TIME: midsummer

A small tree, usually with multiple trunks, bearing masses of flowers that are effective
for several weeks.

Eucalyptus viminalis   50–150'   Zone 9   White gum

FLOWERS: globe-shaped, white
      TIME: spring and summer
FOLIAGE: evergreen, 4–8" long

One of the tallest growing of the *Eucalyptus,* doing well in poor soil. The common name comes from the fact that the branches are creamy white; they are also slightly pendulous.

Eugenia paniculata (syn. *Syzygium paniculatum)*   40'   Zone 9
                                                     Brush-cherry eugenia

* FLOWERS: white, ½" in diameter, with conspicuous stamens in small, terminal clusters
      TIME: a good part of the year
* FRUIT: a rose-purple berry, ¾" in diameter
HABIT: rounded
FOLIAGE: evergreen, glossy, dense, tinged with red when young
HABITAT: Australia

Widely planted in California and Florida, this is probably the most popular *Eugenia,* of which there are many. The variety *australis* is bushier and is supposed to bloom throughout the year. It will not withstand salt spray and is susceptible to drought, but it responds well to shearing. A popular ornamental where hardy.

Eugenia uniflora   15–25'   Zone 10   Surinam-cherry

FLOWERS: fragrant, white, ½" in diameter
* FRUIT: 8-ribbed, edible, color changing from green to yellow to orange to scarlet
      EFFECTIVE: winter
HABIT: compact
FOLIAGE: evergreen, glossy
HABITAT: Brazil

A common Florida hedge plant that withstands shearing well. Especially useful as a high screen.

Euonymus bungeana semipersistens   18'   Zone 4   Midwinter
                                                          euonymus

* FRUIT: opening, yellowish to pinkish white capsules
      EFFECTIVE: fall and early winter
FOLIAGE: semi-evergreen, light green leaves, 1½–4" long, often rather open
HABITAT: China, Manchuria
INTRODUCED: 1902

VARIETY:
  pendula (Weeping euonymus)—branchlets droop gracefully

The variety *semipersistens* is superior to the species because the abundant fruits remain on the plant long after the leaves have fallen, thus prolonging its landscape effectiveness. A loose-growing, vigorous small tree with light green leaves, this plant will grow into a splendid specimen or deciduous screen in record time. It is one of the better large shrubs for quick growth. It should be asexually propagated since there are only one or two clones in this country that fruit well, one of which is growing in Highland Park, Rochester, New York. Seedlings of this tree have grown vigorously for eight years, but hardly a fruit has developed.

It should be remembered that most euonymus are susceptible to infestations of the euonymus scale, a serious pest, and unless this can be controlled by constant care and spraying with dormant oil in late spring or methoxychlor or malathion at just the right time (when the young are crawling), these plants should be passed over. There is nothing quite as disreputable looking as an uncared-for euonymus that is sick and dying from an infestation of scale.

Euonymus europaea 'Aldenhamensis'   21'   Zone 3   Aldenham spindle tree

* FRUIT: opening, brilliant pink capsules
      EFFECTIVE: fall
  FOLIAGE: dense, dark green leaves, 1½–3" long
  AUTUMN COLOR: reddish
  ORIGIN: chance seedling at Aldenham, England
  INTRODUCED: 1922
  VARIETIES:
      'Alba' *(White-fruited euonymus)*—fruit white
      intermedia—bright red fruits

The varieties 'Aldenhamensis' and *intermedia* are the most colorful fruiting varieties of the old-fashioned, popular spindle tree, *E. europaea,* and so should be given preference to the widely distributed European species. Of vigorous growth, all varieties retain their leaves late in the fall and so afford an excellent foliage background for the display of the colorful fruits. These varieties, like other euonymus, are susceptible to infestations of scale insects. Scale is a serious pest, and euonymus should probably not be grown because it is such a difficult problem to keep abreast of all the time.

Euonymus sanguinea   21'   Zone 5

* FRUIT: opening, red to orange capsules
      EFFECTIVE: fall
* FOLIAGE: dark green, reddish underneath, leaves 1½–4" long

AUTUMN COLOR: red
HABITAT: central China
INTRODUCED: 1900

One of the best deciduous euonymus from the standpoint of foliage, its leaves appear as early in the spring as those of *E. latifolia* and at first are reddish, later becoming dark green above and reddish below. This tree has grown exceptionally well in the Arnold Arboretum, with vigorous branching, dense foliage, and fruit that opens early and falls quickly, usually before the leaves drop. Because of this and the fact that the fruits are not borne profusely, this species should be used only for its good foliage. Susceptible to scale.

Evodia daniellii   25'   Zone 5   Korean evodia

* FLOWERS: small, white, in large, flat clusters
        TIME: early to mid-August
* FRUIT: red to glossy black berries
        EFFECTIVE: September–November
  HABIT: open, often shrublike
  FOLIAGE: loose, open
  HABITAT: northern China, Korea
  INTRODUCED: 1905

The Korean evodia is fast becoming of interest because of its late summer flowers that come at a time when few woody plants are in bloom. The flower clusters, nearly 6 inches across, are made up of many small, whitish flowers quite similar to the flowers of *Viburnum lentago.* This might be considered a "new" tree for the small garden, especially where late summer bloom and early fall fruits are desirable. As a street tree it is not satisfactory because its wood is comparatively weak and splits easily and it is apparently short-lived (fifteen to forty years). No serious pests.

➤➤➤ *FAGUS*

Among deciduous trees there is nothing quite as majestic or as graceful as the beech. About ten species are recognized in the temperate regions of the Northern Hemisphere, but since they are so similar, only two will be included—our native American beech and its European relative, *Fagus sylvatica.* Both are beautiful all seasons of the year, something that cannot be said of many other trees. They are large, with solid, round trunks and thin, firm, smooth, gray bark. The European beech is one of the few native European trees that seem to thrive in North America. The two species are amenable to shearing and can be pruned in several ways, as arbors, hedges, and in pleaching, growing vigorously and quickly with many wide-spreading branches that frequently sweep the ground.

The feeding roots of these trees are mostly fibrous and near the surface of the soil. Because of this and the deep shade their low-hanging branches create, it is difficult and often impossible to get grass or other plants to grow underneath them.

But, when these trees are grown properly, they make excellent specimens, and it is really not necessary for anything else to grow under them since their low-spreading branches (if not cut off) will completely cover the ground.

The European beech has slightly darker gray bark than the American beech, and its leaves are not as sharply toothed. There are many varieties of the European (pendulous, fastigiate, colored foliage, cut-leaved) but not of the American beech. The American beech frequently sprouts profusely from the base of the trunk, while the European does not.

Because they are fibrous rooted, beeches are easy to move. Their dense foliage and golden autumn color, together with their splendid habit and colorful bark, make them among the best of specimens for ornamental planting. They are not suited for street trees; they need so much space in which to grow properly that it is not practical to plant them along streets or highways where space is always at a premium. Where plenty of room is available, either singly or in groups, there are no better trees that can be planted for year-round beauty.

Fagus grandifolia   90'   Zone 3   American beech

* HABIT: densely pyramidal
* BARK: light gray
  FOLIAGE: dense
* AUTUMN COLOR: golden bronze
  HABITAT: eastern North America

A splendid native tree, grown over a wide part of this country. Its excellent form, outstanding foliage throughout the spring, summer, and fall months, and its beautiful light gray bark for winter beauty provide ornamental interest every season of the year. The fibrous roots make all beeches notorious surface feeders, which means that it is most difficult to grow anything properly underneath their branches. It does not withstand city conditions well but is hardier than the European beech. A grove of native beeches is always a beautiful sight, and as a single specimen there is not a tree that will surpass it in year-round beauty.

Fagus sylvatica   90'   Zone 4   European beech

* HABIT: densely pyramidal
* BARK: dark gray

* FOLIAGE: dense, glossy, dark green
* AUTUMN COLOR: bronze
  HABITAT: central and southern Europe
  INTRODUCED: early colonial times
  VARIETIES:

> **'Asplenifolia'** *(Fernleaf beech)*—this has fine-textured foliage with the leaves finely divided, similar to those of 'Laciniata' except that sometimes they are almost linear. The common name accurately describes its feathery foliage texture.

> **'Atropunicea'** *(Purple beech)*—beeches with purple leaves have originated at several places in Europe and possibly in this country also, accounting for the slight variation in foliage color, shape of leaves, and even habits of the several varieties. It is unfortunate that some nurseries grow purple beech from seed, selecting the best and giving them "suitable" names. It would be much better if they were propagated asexually so that only the best forms would be perpetuated. Since this variety does come partially true from seed, it is no wonder that several variations have sprung up, some brighter or deeper purple than others.

> **'Cuprea'** *(Copper beech)*—originated with George Loddegis in Great Britain about 1836. Has young foliage a lighter reddish bronze than that of 'Atropunicea,' giving rise to its common name.

> **'Dawyckii'** *(Dawyck beech)*—originating in Scotland nearly fifty years ago, it is definitely fastigiate in habit—one of the best trees with this general habit

> **'Fastigiata'**—another narrow columnar form

> **'Laciniata'** *(Cutleaf European beech)*—has narrow leaves often deeply cut to almost regularly lobed. It differs from the variety 'Asplenifolia' in having wide, more regularly shaped leaves. It grows into a wide-spreading, very beautiful specimen of fine texture.

> **'Pendula'** *(Weeping European beech)*—a very popular variety, of which there are many excellent specimens in this country and abroad, it has several variations, some more wide-spreading than others. Only the best of these forms should be propagated asexually. It should best be grown where its branches can sweep the ground.

> **'Purpureo-pendula'** *(Weeping Purple beech)*—pendulous branches and purple leaves

> **'Quercifolia'** *(Oakleaf beech)*—its oaklike foliage has narrow, irregularly toothed leaves

> **'Riversii'** *(Rivers' Purple beech)*—a purple-leaved form originating in the English nursery of Thomas Rivers before 1869 that has proved one of the most popular over the years. The young foliage is reddish but turns a deep purplish later and remains that color throughout the summer. The tree is densely compact and symmetrical—an excellent specimen.

> **'Rohanii'**—purple leaves very similar in shape to those of 'Laciniata'

> **'Roseo-marginata'** *(Rosepink European beech)*—purple leaves with an irregular, light pink border. This tree lacks its full complement of chlorophyll, hence is more difficult to grow than the others. In full sun, the delicately colored leaf margins may burn to brown, so it should be grown in a slightly shaded situation. At best it can be considered of interest only while small.

'**Rotundifolia**' *(Roundleaf beech)*—one of the best of all the varieties. The leaves are rounded, only ½–1¼″ in diameter, originating in Woking, England, about 1872. The tree in the Arnold Arboretum has been growing since 1903 and is now 50′ tall with a branch spread of 42′. The branches are horizontal but turned upward at the end, making a dense, beautifully branched, pyramidal tree. This particular tree has the peculiar trait of holding its leaf buds shut until nearly two weeks after those of all other *F. sylvatica* varieties are fully open. This variety should be grown a great deal more than it is.

'**Spaethiana**'—the most recent addition to this group of purple-leaved beeches that originated in the Spaeth Nurseries of Germany a few years ago. The Dutch nurseries offering this form claim that it keeps its deep purple color throughout the entire summer. The Arnold Arboretum has only one small plant so it is too soon for us to say whether it makes an ornamental superior to the variety 'Atropunicea' itself.

'**Tortuosa**'—the seventy-five-year-old tree in the Arnold Arboretum is 18′ tall and about 36′ in diameter with a flat top similar in general outline to that of *Tsuga canadensis pendula*. Because of its very slow growth and unique picturesque habit, there is not a great demand for this plant.

The English beech and its varieties should be at the top of everyone's list of desirable large shade trees. Sixty-seven clones of this European species have been named, with those mentioned here being the best of the group as ornamentals. The glossy green or purple leaves, the excellent gray trunk in winter, the massive branching, the dense habit, and the interesting variations of foliage and habit of the different clones make this species and its varieties the most conspicuously graceful group of ornamental trees we have. It takes time to grow a beautiful beech, but the result is well worth waiting for.

The beech blight aphid feeds on the bark of the European species and the woolly beech aphid feeds on the leaves. It is seldom that either seriously attacks *F. grandifolia*. Spraying with malathion gives effective control. Other insects often feed on the foliage and can be controlled by spraying with methoxychlor. The woolly beech scale often covers large areas of the bark on the trunk and branches and starts trouble with nectaria canker. Sprays of dormant oil can control it but often injure the thin bark of the beech; for that reason you might be better off using lime sulfur spray instead.

Ficus carica   30′   Zone 6   Common fig

FRUIT: pear-shaped, greenish to brownish violet figs
HABIT: wide-spreading and rounded, often shrubby
* FOLIAGE: evergreen or deciduous, coarse
HABITAT: western Asia
INTRODUCED: colonial times

Contrary to popular belief, figs are grown as far north as Long Island, New York, where they are wrapped carefully and covered for winter protection. Farther south they are completely hardy and are grown on both coasts. They give a dense shade, and their leaves are very large and coarse. If grown for their fruit as well as their ornamental qualities, there are several good varieties available. This tree, if grown in too rich a soil, may not produce much fruit. An application of superphosphate or a root pruning (or both) is in order to assist fruit bud formation.

Ficus macrophylla   75′   Zone 10   Moreton Bay fig

* HABIT: dense, rounded, at least twice as broad as tall
* FOLIAGE: dense, coarse, but handsome and glossy, evergreen leaves, up to 10″ long
         and 4″ broad
  HABITAT: Australia
  INTRODUCED: before 1877

The famous Moreton Bay fig tree in Santa Barbara, California, is probably the largest of its kind in America. It was planted in 1877 and has a spread (branches) of 145 feet, and one of the exposed roots, 120 feet from the trunk, is 4 inches in diameter. It is estimated that ninety-five hundred people could stand in its shade at noon. This is one tree that grows twice as wide as it is tall, and it makes a wonderful evergreen shade tree where space is available. There are at least nine other species of fig trees now being grown in southern California nurseries. Mostly evergreen, they are adaptable only to gardens in the warmest areas.

Firmiana simplex   40′   Zone 9   Chinese parasol tree

FRUIT: borne at the edges of peculiar, leaflike, open pods, about 5″ long
HABIT: upright
BARK: green
FOLIAGE: deciduous, similar to leaves of sycamore, coarse, often 1′ in diameter
HABITAT: China, Japan

An interesting fast-growing tree for the South.

Franklinia alatamaha   30′   Zone 5   Franklinia

* FLOWERS: white, yellow stamens in center, 3″ in diameter
       TIME: September–October
  HABIT: upright
  FOLIAGE: loose, open leaves, up to 6″ long
* AUTUMN COLOR: brilliant orange to red
  HABITAT: Georgia, but not found wild since 1790

John Bartram, one of the early American plant collectors, first found this plant in Georgia in 1770 and later obtained a few plants for his garden in Philadelphia. For some strange reason no plants have ever been found wild since 1790. All plants now are direct descendants from those few trees Bartram first collected. North of New

York, this should not be grown as a tree but as a shrub in order to better combat winter cold. As a tree it is pyramidal and rather open, but its large white flowers in late summer, followed by its brilliant orange to red autumn color (if it is growing in the full sun), make it an excellent tree for late summer interest. It grows in either acid or alkaline soils but seems to do better in the latter. Wilt has been reported as a serious problem.

→≫ *FRAXINUS*

There are at least sixty species of ash in the Northern Hemisphere, half of them native to North America, but only a few have proved of value in ornamental planting. The trees are vigorous, rapid-growing, with compound opposite leaves, most of which color a brilliant yellow to purple in the fall, and are usually fibrous-rooted, hence not too difficult to transplant. The wood is tough, usually straight-grained, and has been used considerably for this reason. This group of trees is often susceptible to attacks of the oyster scale and must be sprayed occasionally to keep this pest under control. Since there are many other trees that are not so susceptible to scale pests, trees in this group should be selected with discretion. Certainly they are too vigorous to be used on the small property, and they frequently become pests by seeding themselves all over the garden.

Fraxinus americana   120′   Zone 3   White ash

HABIT: erect but with rounded top
FOLIAGE: dense, compound leaves
* AUTUMN COLOR: deep purple or yellow
HABITAT: eastern United States
VARIETIES:
   'Autumn Purple'—pyramidal in outline, a male tree, hence seedless; reddish purple autumn color
   'Rosehill'—seedless; dark green foliage, bronze-red in fall, will grow in poor, alkaline soils

A common tree, often considered a weed because it is reproduced rapidly from seed and quickly reseeds itself over the entire area where a mature tree grows; nevertheless, it is a vigorous-growing specimen that provides much of the wood for baseball bats. Its quick growth, vigorous habit, and lack of special soil requirements enable it to be used in many a situation, especially in places where better ornamentals would not make such a quick showing. The wood is used especially for handles for tools and agricultural implements. Since it is commonly available all over the East, this species is probably used more in landscape planting than any other ash.

The native American, or white, ash (Fraxinus americana).

As for pests, ashes are susceptible to many: leaf spot, dieback, cankers, ash borer, lilac leaf miner, oyster shell scale, and several others.

At least twenty other varieties of *Fraxinus americana* have been noted.

Fraxinus excelsior   120'   Zone 3   European ash

HABIT: rounded head
FOLIAGE: open, compound leaves
HABITAT: Europe, Asia Minor
INTRODUCED: early colonial times
VARIETIES:
> 'Aurea'—with yellow branchlets, the older bark is noticeably yellowish, especially during the winter
>
> 'Nana'—an excellent low, globe-shaped tree for planting under electric utility wires
>
> 'Pendula' *(Weeping European ash)*—branches pendulous, making a small, rounded, moundlike tree not much better than the weeping catalpa monstrosity, although the texture of the foliage is much finer

This tree, which is used a great deal in Europe as an ornamental, has been planted to some extent in America. Its leaves do not have the attractive autumn coloration of *F. americana* but drop off the tree while still green.

Fraxinus holotricha   35'   Zone 5

HABIT: upright and narrow
FOLIAGE: 9–13 leaflets
HABITAT: East Balkan Peninsula

This tree is being used more and more as a fast, low-growing shade tree. The Siebenthaler Nursery of Dayton, Ohio, thought enough of this species to patent a seedling (#1768, 1959) and named it 'Moraine.' It is noted for bearing very few seeds, an admirable trait among the proliferous-fruiting ash species.

Fraxinus mariesii   24'   Zone 7   Maries' ash

* FLOWERS: flowers conspicuous and ornamental during June
* FRUIT: purplish during late summer
  HABIT: rounded and dainty
  FOLIAGE: compound leaves
  HABITAT: China

One of the ornamental "flowering ashes" noted for its numerous and conspicuous flowers and its colorful fruit in late summer. This may be of value as a small tree in the South, although it has not been tried extensively. Smaller and daintier than *F. ornus.*

Fraxinus oregona   80'   Zone 6   Oregon ash

HABIT: narrow, upright to broad
FOLIAGE: dense, compound leaves
HABITAT: British Columbia to California

One of the important deciduous trees of the West Coast; it is often used in landscape work within this region as a shade tree.

Fraxinus ornus   60'   Zone 5   Flowering ash

* FLOWERS: small, white, in dense panicles 3–5" long
  TIME: mid-May
  HABIT: rounded head
  FOLIAGE: dense, luxuriant; compound leaves

Very popular in Europe, flowering ash (Fraxinus ornus) *has only recently become of interest in the United States.*

HABITAT: southern Europe, western Asia
INTRODUCED: before 1700

Has luxuriant foliage and interesting ornamental flowers, differing from most other ashes (except *F. mariesii*) in that each flower has a corolla and calyx and they are profusely produced, making the tree quite conspicuous at flowering time. The flowers are borne in 3–5-inch terminal clusters in mid-May. This tree has long been popular in Europe and only recently has become of interest in America. It is sometimes called the "manna ash" because of a sweetish exudate called "manna" that is obtained from the sap. This is sometimes used medicinally as a mild laxative.

Fraxinus pennsylvanica lanceolata   60′   Zone 2   Green ash

HABIT: dense and rounded
FOLIAGE: dense
AUTUMN COLOR: yellow
HABITAT: central and eastern North America
VARIETIES:
   'Marshall's Seedless'—was originally obtained by the Marshall Nurseries of Arlington, Nebraska, from the Porter-Walton Co. of Salt Lake City, Utah, some years prior to 1959. It was purchased as a "male green ash," but as the Marshall Nursery began distributing it here and there, and because it was the first *seedless* ash to be given prominence, it became known as 'Marshall's

Seedless' and that name will probably stay with it. The foliage is an excellent, dark, glossy green, and the young trees have a definite uniform pyramidal shape. Being the first male ash to be asexually propagated, it deserves special attention, for such a tree has been needed in landscape work for many years.

'Summit'—a clone of *F. pennsylvanica lanceolata* named by the Summit Nurseries of Stillwater, Minnesota, where this symmetrical ash was first noted and selected for propagation in 1948 by Frank L. Seifert, proprietor of the Summit Nurseries. The leaves are glossy and the habit is definitely upright with a strong central leader. However, the plant is not a male but a female and hence produces seeds.

This is the most widely distributed ash in North America, growing naturally in over half the continent. It is a vigorous, well-shaped, dense tree, used in many places throughout its habitat. At least twenty-one varieties of this species have been named.

It should be pointed out that commercial growers would be much better off to grow seedless plants of clones with good form rather than trust seedlings. Nursery experience has shown that at least 15 to 20 percent of the green ash grown from seed are unsalable in the nursery row because of irregularities in growth, whereas budded stock is 100 percent reliable.

Fraxinus uhdei   30′   Zone 9   Shamel ash

HABIT: rounded
* FOLIAGE: evergreen, bright glossy green
HABITAT: Mexico

Finding favor in California as a street or ornamental shade tree, this is fast-growing and requires some pruning especially when young, to prevent it from growing too lanky. Seedlings vary, and for the better or more hardy forms the plant should be propagated asexually from individual plants of known performance.

Fraxinus velutina   20–45′   Zone 5   Velvet ash

HABIT: rounded head
FOLIAGE: more or less open
HABITAT: Arizona, New Mexico, Mexico
VARIETY:
   glabra (Modesto ash)—of rapid growth with attractive glossy foliage appearing late in spring. The autumn color is a good yellow.

This tree is of value chiefly in the dry, alkaline soils of the Southwest where it has been used a great deal as a street tree. Although it should have fertile soil, it grows fairly rapidly almost anywhere throughout its general habitat, even in severely alkaline soils.

Ginkgo biloba   120′   Zone 4   Ginkgo, Maidenhair tree

FLOWERS: inconspicuous; sexes separate
FRUIT: round, plumlike, 1″ in diameter; the kernel is eaten by the Chinese but the
    outside flesh has an obnoxious odor when ripe
* HABIT: picturesque, wide-spreading, open
* FOLIAGE: fan-shaped, open leaves
* AUTUMN COLOR: clear yellow
HABITAT: eastern China
INTRODUCED: about 1784
VARIETIES:
    fastigiata (Sentry ginkgo)—columnar habit
    pendula—pendulous branchlets

Almost twenty other clones have been named.

NOTE: Because of the increasing interest in male varieties during the past
decade, several have been named and offered for sale, such as 'Autumn Gold,'
'Fairmount,' 'Lakeview,' 'Mayfield,' 'Palo Alto,' 'Princeton Sentry,' and 'Santa Cruz.'
Whether they differ materially one from the other remains to be seen, but it is such
clones that should be carefully increased by asexual propagation methods to ensure
good form and nonfruiting trees.

Gingko biloba *'Autumn
Gold.' Photograph courtesy
of Monrovia Nursery
Company.*

The ginkgo, one of the two most ancient known species of trees now alive, has been growing on this earth for 150 million years, as geological records have proved—from the Jurassic period on, with various rocks mute evidence that it was at one time native to what is now North America.

Over the two centuries this tree has been grown by the white man in America, it has become quite common along highways and as a specimen in gardens. Its picturesque wide, fan-shaped branching habit, together with its small, fan-shaped leaves, has become familiar to many. It should be remembered, however, that the fruiting or pistillate trees (staminate flowers are on one tree and pistillate flowers on another) bear round, plumlike fruits, the flesh of which has an obnoxious odor when ripe. Trees in the Arnold Arboretum, grown from seed, were twenty years old and at least 25 feet high before they had their first flowers, a long wait to determine whether the plants will bear fruit! Nurseries would do well to propagate staminate or nonfruiting trees asexually. It has been stated that staminate trees are more upright in habit, fruiting trees more wide-spreading, often with slightly pendulous branchlets. I have not been able to observe this firsthand. This is an excellent tree for street planting or as a specimen tree on a large lawn, but it is not a tree for the small property.

There are clones of the *fastigiata* form that are definitely staminate, making them ideal for street planting. One of the most conspicuous (and oldest) of such plantings is along Roosevelt Boulevard (U.S. Route 1) in northeast Philadelphia, Pennsylvania.

The most important fact of value is that the ginkgo is not infested with any insect or disease, hence needs no spraying. Trees of low maintenance cost like this are few indeed.

Gleditsia triacanthos 135' Zone 4 Common honey-locust

FRUIT: brown pods, 12–18" long
  EFFECTIVE: fall
HABIT: broad and open
* FOLIAGE: very open, fine-textured leaves, singly and doubly compound, 7–12" long
HABITAT: central United States
VARIETIES:
  'Autumn Gold'—the young new leaves are golden yellow; best shown when grown in full sun
  'Bujotii'—pendulous branches
  'Columnaris'—columnar habit
  'Elegantissima' *(Bushy honey-locust)*—thornless, dense, shrubby. Of merit for street planting only when grafted high on understock of *G. triacanthos inermis.*
  'Halka' *(Plant Patent #3096)*—wide-spreading, horizontal branching with lacy foliage
  'Imperial' *(Plant Patent #1605, 1957)*—a cultivar of *G. triancanthos inermis* with a straight trunk
  inermis (Thornless honey-locust)—thornless. This was a long-neglected variety until the Dutch elm disease killed large numbers of elms and substitute trees

were sought. When the 'Moraine' honey-locust was patented in 1949 this proved a most successful alternative, not only because it was thornless but because it did not produce fruit. Since it was patented, other similar trees were also sought with the same characteristics. Since that time 'Beatrice' (1955), 'Maxwell' (1960), 'Park' (1958), 'Sieler' (1949), 'Stephens' (1940), and others have been named and put on the market. In addition to being thornless, these have few if any seeds.

'**Majestic**' *(Plant Patent #1534, 1956)*—a cultivar of *G. triacanthos inermis* with compact growth

'**Moraine**' *(Plant Patent #836, 1949)*—a cultivar of *G. triacanthos inermis,* one of the first and still one of the best of the thornless, fruitless cultivars of *G. triacanthos.* This is wide-spreading and fast-growing and has proved excellent under a wide range of growing conditions.

'**Nana**'—narrow, upright, slow-growing. The thirty-six-year-old tree in the Arnold Arboretum is 35' tall with a spread of 16'.

'**Rubylace**' *(Plant Patent #2038)*—slow-growing, thornless; new growth is a bright, shiny red that darkens to bronze as the leaves mature. An interesting contrast between the red branch tips and earlier matured bronze foliage until September. Originated by Princeton Nurseries, Princeton, New Jersey.

'**Shademaster**' *(Plant Patent #1515, 1956)*—a cultivar of *G. triacanthos inermis;* upright form, at first distributed under the name 'Princeton'

'**Skyline**' *(Plant Patent #1619, 1957)*—a cultivar of *G. triacanthos inermis* pyramidal in general habit

'**Sunburst**' *(Plant Patent #1313, 1954)*—a cultivar of *G. triacanthos inermis;* young leaves bright golden yellow when they first appear, turning green in the summer under some conditions

Forty-eight other clones of this species have been named. A splendid tree for withstanding city conditions, its only drawback is its large, stiff, much-branched thorns, sometimes as long as 4 inches. In playgrounds and along city streets this is enough to blacklist the tree, since these thorns are dropped or broken off on occasion and present a rather serious hazard. The thornless variety has been widely used as a substitute for the American elm (see under *inermis* above) because it can be grown in so many situations. The long, twisted pods of the species are interesting because they remain on the tree after the leaves fall, though in certain landscapes this can be a troublesome nuisance. It is not seriously troubled with borers, as are the *Robinia* species, and has no particularly interesting flowers or autumn color.

There are some trees that don't develop fruits, and these should be asexually propagated. The 'Moraine' locust, one of the first trees in this category to be widely advertised, was named and patented by the Siebenthaler Nursery of Dayton, Ohio, in 1949. It has proved widely popular and is still one of the best, if not the best, of these thornless, fruitless cultivars to grow under many conditions.

The honey-locust can be a long-lived tree. One in Dayton, Ohio, that was cut down a number of years ago, showed 327 annual rings. The foliage appears late in the spring and falls early. Unfortunately, the pod gall midge is causing some injury to the young foliage of honey-locusts. Spraying with malathion or methoxychlor proves helpful in its control.

Gordonia lasianthus   60'   Zone 8   Loblolly bay gordonia

* FLOWERS: fragrant, white, 2½" in diameter
       TIME: summer, for nearly two months
   HABIT: dense, narrow head
* FOLIAGE: evergreen, lustrous, leathery leaves, 6" long
   HABITAT: southeastern United States

This tree is used in the far South, especially for its good foliage.

Grevillea robusta   150'   Zone 10   Silk-oak grevillea

* FLOWERS: golden yellow to orange trusses
       TIME: April
   HABIT: upright
* FOLIAGE: evergreen, feathery, 6–8" long and as broad, silky white on the undersur-
       face
   HABITAT: Australia

Often grown in pots in the greenhouse as a decorative pot plant, this tree has considerable merit as an ornamental specimen and a street tree in southern California because it grows in poor, sandy soils as well as in deep rich soils.

Gymnocladus dioicus   90'   Zone 4   Kentucky coffee-tree

   HABIT: picturesque open, large branches
   FOLIAGE: open, coarse, singly and doubly compound leaves
   HABITAT: central United States

Although this tree has no conspicuous flowers, no autumn color, and rather ugly large pods for fruits, its picturesque large branches and stubby twigs offer considerable interest throughout the winter and are noticeable for a good six months of the year. It is not a good shade tree and is often considered a "dirty tree" because it drops its pods and large leaves occasionally, but it might be given consideration particularly for its value in the winter landscape. No serious pests.

Halesia carolina   30'   Zone 5   Carolina silverbell

* FLOWERS: bell-shaped, white, ½" long
       TIME: mid-May
   FRUIT: dry, 2- or 4-winged pods, 2" long
       EFFECTIVE: fall
   HABIT: rounded
   FOLIAGE: open

AUTUMN COLOR: yellow
HABITAT: West Virginia to Florida and Texas

The smaller of the silverbells, of garden value only when the delicate, pendulous, bell-like flowers are in evidence. These do not remain on the tree very long. No serious pests.

Halesia monticola   90'   Zone 5   Mountain silverbell

* FLOWERS: bell-shaped, white, 1″ long
       TIME: mid-May
FRUIT: dry, 2- or 4-winged pods, 2″ long
       EFFECTIVE: fall
HABIT: pyramidal to round topped
FOLIAGE: coarse, open
AUTUMN COLOR: yellow
HABITAT: Tennessee and North Carolina to Georgia
VARIETY:
       rosea (Pink mountain silverbell)—flowers pale pink

With larger flowers than the Carolina silverbell, this species and its variety are planted more frequently because they are more easily seen when in bloom. The pendant flowers appear all along the twigs of the previous year's growth, making the well-grown tree a uniquely beautiful sight when in bloom. At other times of year the tree is not meritorious but has no serious insect pests or diseases, an important point to consider where annual maintenance and careful supervision will not be provided. Because of its loose foliage and comparatively small flowers, it might best be used where it can be closely observed or else planted with an evergreen background of white pine or hemlock.

Harpephyllum caffrum   35'   Zone 10   Kafir plum

FRUIT: olivelike, dark red
       EFFECTIVE: summer
FOLIAGE: evergreen, leathery, glossy

A tree for only the warmest parts of the country, its glossy leaves, colorful fruit, fast growth, and well-groomed, tropical appearance make it a nice addition to many a small garden in southern California.

Hemiptelea davidii   20'   Zone 5   David hemiptelea

HABIT: rounded, often shrubby, thorny branches
FOLIAGE: dense; leaves ¾–2¼″ long
HABITAT: northern China, Manchuria, Korea
INTRODUCED: 1899

A small tree, rarely used, but that might have considerable merit. It is dense in habit, often shrubby, and producing very prominent thorns that may be 4–5 inches long. In northern China it is used as a hedge or screen and so might have use in this country for the same purpose.

Hippophae rhamnoides   30'   Zone 3   Common sea-buckthorn

FLOWERS: inconspicuous; sexes separate
    TIME: early April
* FRUIT: bright orange berries, ¼″ in diameter, borne in large clusters, profusely on
    pistillate plants
    EFFECTIVE: fall
HABIT: open, rounded, often with lower trunk devoid of branches, spiny twigs
FOLIAGE: willowlike leaves, grayish green on upper surface, silver-green beneath
HABITAT: Europe, Asia
INTRODUCED: colonial times

Grown chiefly for its profuse, bright orange or orange-yellow fleshy fruits and silvery gray foliage. However, the sexes are separate, pistillate flowers all on one tree and staminate flowers on another. Both must be present to ensure fruiting, preferably in a ratio of one staminate plant to every six pistillate plants. The fruit is very acid, not quickly eaten by birds, and remains on the plant a long time. The English think highly of this shrub or small tree, some even saying that it should be present in every garden, probably because it not only does well in seashore plantings but in inland areas as well. For some reason we have had much difficulty in getting it established in the Arnold Arboretum, but once established, it makes a splendid ornamental for fall display. No serious pests.

Hymenosporum flavum   50'   Zone 10   Sweetshade

FLOWERS: fragrant, yellow, 1½″ long, in terminal panicles
    TIME: early summer
HABIT: short branches, often a long bare trunk, pyramidal
* FOLIAGE: evergreen, coarse, dark green
HABITAT: Australia

Frequently selected as a street tree because of its rapid growth. It is closely related to the pittosporums and often planted in southern California, where it does not seem to be susceptible to serious insect or disease troubles, and so can be considered in the select group of low-maintenance street trees.

Idesia polycarpa   45'   Zone 6

FLOWERS: fragrant, without petals, insignificant but dioecious or polygamous
* FRUIT: orange-red berries, in large clusters

EFFECTIVE: fall until heavy frost
FOLIAGE: rather coarse leaves, 6″ long
HABITAT: Japan, China
INTRODUCED: 1864

An interesting tree, looking something like a small-leaved catalpa. Rare in America. Trees in Virginia show remarkable colored fruits in the fall.

⇶ ILEX

The hollies comprise a most valuable group of ornamental trees and shrubs, some evergreen and some deciduous. There are those that are native to Asia, many to South America, some to Europe, and, of course, some native to North America. The hollies most commonly thought of when the name is mentioned are the European holly *(I. aquifolium)* and our native American holly *(I. opaca),* both small trees and highly valued for their ornamental red berries. Both have been cultivated for so long that there are over two hundred varieties of each, truly a bewildering number.

Eight of the following species, like *I. aquifolium* and *I. opaca,* have evergreen foliage, which makes them more valuable as ornamentals than the two deciduous types. All the species recommended here have bright red or yellow berries and are far more attractive than some shrub types with black berries. The flowers of all species are small and inconspicuous.

Hollies belong to that group of plants with separate sexes, staminate flowers on one plant and pistillate flowers on another. Both must be present in the near vicinity to ensure the fertilization of the pistillate flowers. In some regions where hollies are native, windblown or even insect-carried pollen may be sufficient so that only the pistillate form of the species need be planted in the garden. Usually the safer method to ensure fruiting is to have both sexes in the same garden. Planting a small staminate plant in the same hole with the pistillate plant is another alternative, though pains must be taken, as these plants grow older, to prune the staminate plant to a minimum number of branches. Pollen from one species of holly may fertilize the flowers of another species, but it is essential for the two to be in bloom together. Most of these trees bloom in late May or early June, or at the same time as the locust and the yellowwood. Fortunately, some commercial nurseries are recognizing the importance of growing the holly sexes separately, and it is from these sources that plants should be obtained. There is no positive way to identify the different sexes until they flower.

Hollies are propagated by cuttings and seeds, but the seeds take two years to germinate, sometimes three. The shrubby species are, for the most part, rather rugged individuals and easy of culture; the tree types are a little more difficult because they are not the easiest plants to move and must have a ball of soil about the roots if the operation is to prove successful. A normally good garden soil is all they need to thrive. If grown in a dry, sandy soil, it might be advisable to mulch the plants with oak leaves or pine needles.

Eleven species are recommended here, and each one could easily make a splendid garden specimen within its limits of hardiness. Other species are being grown, but the few here mentioned are certainly among the best.

Several hundred insect pests and diseases have been reported on hollies. The most important is the holly leaf miner, a little insect that eats its way between the upper and lower epidermis of the leaf. The trick is to spray with malathion or diazinon in very early June (in the vicinity of Boston) *before* the insect gets into the leaf. Also, spraying with diazinon in early summer when the insect is flying around to lay eggs proves helpful.

The most important diseases are tar spot (little black dots on the leaves), which is controlled by spraying with thiram, and anthracnose, which forms dark brown spots on the leaf and is controlled by spraying with thiram or zineb.

Ilex aquifolium   70′   Zone 6   English holly

* FRUIT: bright red berries on female plants, ¼″ in diameter, on previous year's growth; sexes separate
  EFFECTIVE: fall and winter
* HABIT: pyramidal, dense branching
* FOLIAGE: dense, evergreen, lustrous
  HABITAT: southern Europe, northern Africa, western Asia
  INTRODUCED: early colonial times
  VARIETIES:
    angustifolia (Narrowleaf English holly)—small, narrow leaves
    argentea marginata (Silver-edge English holly)—leaf margin silver-colored. There are several of this general color, such as "Silvery,' 'Silver Beauty,' 'Silver King', and 'Silver Queen.'
    'Camelliaefolia'—a very popular variety with few spines on the leaf margins, large, bright red fruit, and foliage coloring bronze in the winter
    ferox (Hedgehog holly)—leaves with short spines on the upper convex end; a male, often referred to as 'Porcupine' or 'Green Porcupine'
    'Golden King'—male; leaves variegated with golden yellow
    'Golden Milkmaid'—female; leaves variegated with yellow
    'Hodgins'—leaves 2½–3¾″ long and dark green, with prominent spines

Because the English holly has been grown for centuries, hundreds of varieties have been named and over two hundred are being grown in the United States today. These vary according to leaf size, shape, and color, tree habit, and fruit characteristics. Some of the interesting foliage forms are male plants. There are several beautiful variegated

The English holly (Ilex aquifolium) *bears its fruit on the previous year's growth. There are over two hundred varieties being grown in Europe and the United States.*

forms being grown on the West Coast especially for their foliage and berries at Christmastime in commercial orchards, cultivated and maintained like any other orchard, and their branches clipped in the late fall and sold "by the pound." Cut in this way, the larger, more lustrous green leaves and the larger berries are superior in every way to those of the native American species, *I. opaca.* On the East Coast, English holly is grown in ornamental plantings but seems to grow far better in the moister climate of the West Coast.

It will eliminate future disappointments to remember that in order to bear fruit, the pistillate plant *must* have a pollen-bearing plant in the near vicinity.

Ilex cassine   36'   Zone 7   Dahoon

* FRUIT: red berries, ¼" in diameter, profusely borne in dense clusters on two-year-
old wood; sexes separate
    EFFECTIVE: fall and winter
  HABIT: rounded, dense branching
* FOLIAGE: evergreen, entire and spineless margins, dense, 1½–5" long

AUTUMN COLOR: purplish green
HABITAT: southeastern United States

This tree is a native in the South in wet soils and is valued for its heavy fruit production. The common name "dahoon" may have originated with the Indians. Fortunately it will also grow in normal soils without excessive moisture, especially when grafted on *I. opaca* understock.

Ilex chinensis (syn. *I. purpurea*)　　40'　　Zone 7　　Kashi holly

* FRUIT: red berries, ¼" in diameter; sexes separate
　　TIME: fall
　HABIT: pyramidal, dense branching
* FOLIAGE: dense, evergreen leaves, 2½–4" long
　HABITAT: China, Japan
　INTRODUCED: 1900

Not too much is known about this plant in cultivation as yet, but some splendid specimens are being grown in the South, even as far north as Glenn Dale, Maryland. In China it grows with *I. cornuta* and is greatly admired by the Chinese, especially at New Year's when large bunches of it are collected for decorations. The evergreen leaves are stripped off the branches, leaving the brilliant red berries. This plant should be exploited more in America in areas where it proves hardy.

Ilex ciliospinosa　　10–20'　　Zone 5

* FRUIT: red berries, ¼" in diameter; sexes separate
　　EFFECTIVE: fall
　HABIT: compact
* FOLIAGE: dense, evergreen, leathery leaves, 1–1½" long and ½" wide
　HABITAT: China

A good, dense variety that has proved popular.

Ilex decidua　　30'　　Zone 5　　Possum haw

* FRUIT: orange to scarlet berries, ¼" in diameter; sexes separate
　　EFFECTIVE: fall and winter
　HABIT: spreading branches
　BARK: light gray
　FOLIAGE: deciduous, lustrous
　HABITAT: southeastern United States

Common over a wide area, especially in swamps, its evergreen foliage and willowy growth are its chief assets.

Ilex latifolia   60'   Zone 7   Lusterleaf holly

* FRUIT: dull red berries, $1/3''$ in diameter, in crowded clusters; sexes separate
    EFFECTIVE: fall
HABIT: rounded
* FOLIAGE: evergreen, dark, lustrous leaves, 4–8" long
HABITAT: Japan
INTRODUCED: 1840

An attractive, dark-leaved evergreen requiring good soil and a shaded situation. Regarded by some as being the most handsome broad-leaved evergreen tree in its native land.

Ilex montana   36'   Zone 5   Mountain winterberry

* FRUIT: orange-red berries, $1/3''$ in diameter; sexes separate
    EFFECTIVE: fall and winter
HABIT: rather slender
FOLIAGE: open, deciduous leaves, 2–6" long
HABITAT: New York to South Carolina

Red-fruiting trees are mostly in demand as ornamentals, especially when they retain their fruit for a long time. This is the reason this native holly is on the desirable list. As a shrub it can be discarded in preference to *I. verticillata.*

Ilex opaca   45'   Zone 5   American holly

* FRUIT: bright red berries on female plants, ¼" in diameter, on current year's growth; sexes separate
    EFFECTIVE: fall and early winter
* HABIT: pyramidal, dense branching
* BARK: smooth, light gray
* FOLIAGE: evergreen, spiny leaves, not lustrous, mostly dense
HABITAT: eastern United States
VARIETIES:
    subintegra *(Wholeleaf American holly)*—leaves entire or nearly so and not with spiny margins
    'Wayside's Christmas Tree'—an excellent introduction of Wayside Gardens, profusely fruiting and of dense, pyramidal habit, keeping this form without much pruning
    xanthocarpa *(Yellowfruit American holly)*—yellow fruits

The native American holly is one of the most sought-after trees for Christmas decoration. It is native in wide areas along the eastern seaboard and is frequently transplanted to gardens from the wild. Large amounts of it are collected every year, and in some places it is grown merely for the production of fruiting branches that are reaped for the Christmas trade. Individual plants differ widely in leaf size, shape, and size and number of fruits.

This tree prefers good, well-drained soil. If planted in an orchard pattern there should be at least one staminate tree to every ten pistillate trees. On the small property it might be well to have a pistillate tree onto which is grafted a staminate branch or to have a small staminate plant near the larger pistillate plant.

Nearly one thousand varieties of *I. opaca* have been named, but of course there are many that are quite similar. Desirable characteristics in holly varieties would include annual bearing, large and bright-colored fruits, good foliage, and a good, dense habit.

Commercial growers sometimes have their own pet holly tree that they propagate because they are sure of its performance. A very few of the varieties that have acquired widespread distribution are 'Old Heavy Berry,' 'Merry Christmas,' 'St. Mary,' and 'Goldie,' which has yellow fruit. 'Croonenburg' is one of the few hollies that has both staminate and pistillate flowers on the same plant in a ratio of ten female flowers to one male. Introduced in 1934 is 'Miss Helen,' conical, densely branched, with abundant fruit. Introduced in 1947 is 'Jersey Knight,' one of the male hollies.

In Rhode Island I had the pleasure of inspecting several acres of native holly that were being carefully attended, some of which were even fertilized. All the trees were there as Nature had planted them, some of them with solid trunks 8 inches in diameter. There was tremendous variation among these trees. Size and disposition of the fruit varied as much as the luster, size, and shape of the individual leaves. Even the habit of the tree varied, some being dense, making excellent ornamental specimens, and others being very open.

This experience with variation proved to me once again that it is impossible to select any of the varieties now named and offered commercially as being "best." Some may do better on certain soils than others, some will do better in warmer (or drier) climates—it will take years of experimentation and comparison to select the superior clones. The New Jersey Experiment Station at New Brunswick has undertaken a testing of these many varieties. It should always be remembered that, from an ornamental standpoint, fruit characteristics are only a part of the picture and that a good habit and a good, dense foliage go just as far in making a worthy ornamental specimen.

Dr. Charles H. Connors of the New Jersey Experiment Station was instrumental in starting the Holly Arboretum at Rutgers University many years ago in which many holly varieties were grown and evaluated. His work was later taken up by Dr. Elwin R. Orton, Jr., who has amassed a great deal of information on many varieties and is responsible for having introduced some of the best varieties available today. His notes on habit and hardiness lend credence to some of these clones:

'Dan Fenton,' introduced in 1987, is hardy to −10°F, produces excellent crops of bright red fruits, and is highly vigorous.

'Hedgeholly' is an introduction of Paul Bosley of Mentor, Ohio, and has been observed to come through an extremely cold winter (−25°F). Dr. Orton has given away hundreds of these cuttings; he believes it to be the best of the varieties grown in his experiments.

'Jersey Delight,' a cross with 'Old Heavy Berry,' is narrowly conical in habit, with glossy leaves.

'Jersey Knight,' hardy in Zone 6 and sometimes Zone 5, was selected in the wild and introduced in 1965. Dr. Orton believes it is the best of all the staminate forms being grown today. Established plants are hardy in Zone 5 and readily develop into a dense, conical mass of branches, with glossy, dark green foliage and masses of flowers.

'Jersey Princess,' introduced by Dr. Orton in 1976, has the darkest green foliage of any he has selected. Winter hardiness is Zone 5.

The trials at Cook College at Rutgers have brought out that some of the very best varieties of *I. opaca* are now being grown and recommended as a result of years of work and selection at New Jersey Agricultural Experiment Station.

One of the larger northern outposts of American holly is at Fort Hancock, Sandy Hook, New Jersey. Here, in a hundred-acre tract protected from the grasping hands of individuals seeking Christmas decorations, these hollies are growing under government protection. Some have trunks nearly 20 inches in diameter, with the tallest about 55 feet. It is estimated that some are over 275 years old and may have been growing there in 1609 when Henrik Hudson first sailed on the great river now bearing his name. In many places along the Atlantic seaboard—Cape Cod, New Jersey, Delaware, and Virginia—native stands are fast being destroyed, but this one, now under government surveillance, it is hoped, will continue to be protected for all time.

Ilex pedunculosa   30′   Zone 5   Longstalk holly

* FRUIT: bright red, ¼″ in diameter, on slender stalks nearly 1″ long; sexes separate
      EFFECTIVE: early fall to early winter
* HABIT: densely pyramidal
* FOLIAGE: evergreen, lustrous leaves, 1–3″ long
  HABITAT: Japan
  INTRODUCED: 1892

This is one of the hardiest of the exotic evergreen hollies and should be better known, especially in northern gardens. The fruits are often as large as those of *I. aquifolium*.

Ilex pernyi   30′   Zone 6   Perny holly

* FRUIT: red berries, ¼″ in diameter, in clusters; sexes separate
      EFFECTIVE: late summer and early fall
* FOLIAGE: glossy, evergreen leaf, ½–1¼″ long, with a few spines on the margin
  HABIT: pyramidal, especially when young
  HABITAT: central and western China
  INTRODUCED: 1900

Somewhat similar to the shrubby Chinese holly *(I. cornuta)*, it has smaller leaves and when young is very definitely pyramidal in habit. Since there are not too many red-fruiting evergreens, this species is kept on the recommended list. The fruits are in conspicuous clusters and borne in the axis of the leaves.

Ilex vomitoria   24'   Zone 7   Yaupon

* FRUIT: bright red berries, ¼" in diameter; sexes separate
     EFFECTIVE: fall and winter
  HABIT: rather loose and open
* FOLIAGE: lustrous, evergreen leaves, about 1–1½" long
  HABITAT: southeastern United States

This is one of the most interesting of the evergreen hollies. Often a shrub, occasion-ally a tree, it flowers on the previous year's growth with fruiting twigs usually literally covered with fruits. In fact, this might be considered the holly that produces the most fruit. It stands shearing well and so can be used in hedge-making. Large specimens do not transplant easily if collected from the wild.

Jacaranda mimosifolia   50'   Zone 10   Sharpleaf jacaranda

* FLOWERS: blue, 2" long, borne in great profusion
     TIME: early summer
  HABIT: spreading branches
* FOLIAGE: fernlike, very delicate texture
  HABITAT: Brazil

This is one of the most popular ornamental trees of the subtropical United States and is used a great deal in both southern Florida and coastal southern California. Its abundant clusters of lavender-blue flowers in early summer, together with its delicate, fernlike foliage, endear it to many a home owner and make it a valued subject for park and highway planting as well. The tree is without foliage for a short time only, prior to the appearance of its flowers. When used as a street tree it might best be spaced 40 feet apart. Often mistaken for the smaller *J. acutifolia.*

⇥≫ *JUGLANS*

The walnuts are not particularly beautiful specimen trees. They have no interesting flowers and their fruits can be troublesome if the tree grows in a neatly kept lawn. Certainly the fruit could not be considered ornamental. These trees are all tap rooted, and the large ones are rather difficult to transplant and have no autumn color. There are two varieties with cut-leaved foliage that might be considered better than the species as specimens, but as yet both are extremely difficult to locate commercially. In any event, these trees cannot be considered as specimens for the small property and should be overlooked where other types of ornamental trees are available. As timber trees, or grown primarily for their fruit, they have their uses.

The *Juglans* species are troubled with many disfiguring disease and insect problems. Anthracnose causes irregular brown spots on the leaves. Two sprays of ferbam or thiram before the leaves are fully developed will help control the problem. Disfiguring twig dieback can be controlled with pruning. White trunk fungus and wood rots also should be cut out at once.

The walnut caterpillar can defoliate a tree. Fall webworm can be most unsightly unless sprayed with malathion. Gypsy moth and canker worms require similar control measures in late spring and early summer. Aphids can infest the tree. The walnut span roller and fruit tree leaf roller should be sprayed with malathion. Various beetles, worms, and scales can be trouble-some and should be sprayed with Sevin or carbaryl. Dormant oil sprays can prove helpful also but should be carefully applied after reading the label for instructions.

Juglans cordiformis   60'   Zone 4   Heartnut

FRUIT: nuts, 1–1½" long
HABIT: rounded, massive branches
FOLIAGE: coarse
HABITAT: Japan
INTRODUCED: 1863

The heartnut is suggested here as an ornamental in preference to the Manchurian walnut (*J. mandshurica*) merely because its nuts apparently have a higher economic value. All these trees are rounded in habit with massive branches and coarse, com-pound leaves, but the heartnut produces nuts that are heart-shaped and easily cracked, sometimes even split open with a penknife. It is not unusual for the kernels to come out whole. Some varieties such as 'Fodemaier' are available. If a combination shade-and nut-producing tree is not desired, but merely a shade tree, some other tree would undoubtedly give better all-around satisfaction.

Juglans hindsii   50'   Zone 8   Hinds black walnut

HABIT: rounded head
FOLIAGE: dense, coarse, compound leaves
HABITAT: central California

On the West Coast this tree is used considerably as a street tree and as understock for *J. regia* because it grows more vigorously.

Juglans nigra   150'   Zone 4   Eastern black walnut

FRUIT: large nuts, 1–2" in diameter
HABIT: rounded to upright

FOLIAGE: coarse, rather open
HABITAT: eastern United States
VARIETY:

> 'Laciniata'—leaflets finely cut, giving the foliage a truly fine texture. An excellent foliage form, superior to the species from an ornamental viewpoint.

This walnut is included only because of the many associations people have with it throughout its native range. It is too coarse for a street tree, and its falling nuts would make driving hazardous. Its flowers have no interesting ornamental value, and it has no autumn color. It has been proved definitely that its roots give off a material that is toxic to many other kinds of plants, hence it should not be grown near valued specimens. It should therefore be used as a specimen only where it has plenty of room to grow. Even then, unless the owner has certain sentimental reasons for growing it, there are many other trees that would give better ornamental value in the same space.

There are many commercial varieties of this available, selected because of the size or edible qualities of their fruits. Among the best of these would be 'Thomas' (especially for growing in the northern limits of Zone 4); 'Ohio,' from that state; and 'Snyder' from New York. The black walnut requires a rich, deep soil, slightly alkaline or neutral.

Juglans regia   90'   Zones 5–6   English walnut, Persian walnut

FRUIT: nuts, 1½–2" in diameter
HABIT: broad, rounded head
BARK: silver-gray
FOLIAGE: dense, coarse
HABITAT: southeastern Europe, China
INTRODUCED: early colonial times
VARIETIES:

> 'Carpathian'—a geographic form introduced from Poland by Paul Crath of Toronto, Canada, in 1926. It has withstood temperatures of −40°F in its native habitat. Some of these trees in Canada and the northern United States show promise.
>
> 'Laciniata'—a fine, cut-leaved variety of value for its ornamental foliage, superior to the species from an ornamental viewpoint

A variable species, widely grown commercially in California for its nuts, this tree has merit, where hardy, as an ornamental specimen, but as in the case of *J. nigra,* the cut-leaved variety makes the better ornamental tree. It is round-headed and very dense, and some clones are grown as far north as Boston, Massachusetts. However, it can only be depended on considerably farther south. Some of the varieties are 'Broadview,' 'Eureka,' 'Franquette,' 'Mayette,' and 'Payne.' On the West Coast north of central California, the English walnut is commonly propagated on *J. hindsii.* In California alone there are over 125,000 acres of bearing Persian walnuts.

→≫ *JUNIPERUS*

The junipers, like the yews, are unusual among the evergreens in that the sexes are usually separate, and only the pistillate or fruiting trees will bear the small, round, blue berries (smaller than a pea) so desirable as a display in the fall and winter. Both male and female plants should be grown in fairly close proximity to each other, and since the flowers are minute, the distinguishing of one sex from the other (except when in fruit) presents a real problem. If the nurseries would only propagate these sexes asexually and thus keep them straight, it would be splendid, but this is a much slower process usually (and more expensive) than growing these species from seed. Trees can be transplanted in fruit so that the sexes can be told apart if large plants are to be purchased in the fall. When young, most junipers are easily moved with a ball of earth, but the older they grow, the more difficult it becomes to transplant them.

The small, scalelike foliage of these plants varies considerably, even on

Juniperus chinensis
'Ames,' not one of the best
clones but sometimes used.

trees of the same species and even on the same tree, depending on the age, making identification among them extremely difficult at times. Four native species have been recommended here, chiefly because they are native in different parts of the country and each one has a locale where it grows to best advantage. Taken out of that area, they cannot be expected to do well. Four commonly grown exotic species have also been recommended because of their good adjustment in this country. The junipers prefer alkaline soils and are tall, narrow, and dense in habit. The fruit of some species require two years to mature, while others ripen in one year. Incidentally, this can be the means of differentiating the native *J. virginiana* from its western counterpart, *J. scopulorum.* There are a large number of shrubs but comparatively few trees in this genus.

When junipers are grown in the vicinity of certain plants such as the shadbush, hawthorn, native crab apples, and so forth, some plants will harbor the juniper rust. The fungus has two cycles in its life: one is spent on the deciduous plants where it spots and mars the foliage, and the other is spent on the juniper where it is manifest in peculiar fleshy, hornlike, red to orange growths on the foliage, especially in wet weather. This is the teliospore stage. On junipers this can be controlled by spraying with ferric dimethyl dithio-carbonate (one of the commercial compounds is called Fermate). It does seem difficult to have to remove one or the other hosts of this fungus where it is prevalent since both are such important ornamental plants. Spraying in this fashion will break the life cycle and remove the fungus as a threat, thus allowing both types of host plants to be grown side by side.

Twig blight *(Phomopsis)* is a bad disease in certain areas, especially on young nursery stock, killing the young shoots early in the spring during wet weather. It can be controlled by timely and persistent spraying of Bordeaux, applied as soon as the young shoots begin to appear in the spring and at ten-day intervals, for five applications.

Juniperus chinensis   60'   Zone 4   Chinese juniper

* FRUIT: sexes separate; female plants with fruits ⅜" in diameter but ripening the second year
    EFFECTIVE: fall and winter
    HABIT: pyramidal
* FOLIAGE: evergreen, pointed, scalelike
    HABITAT: China, Japan
    INTRODUCED: 1767
    VARIETIES:

> *columnaris (Blue columnar Chinese juniper)*—columnar; sharp-edged silvery green foliage. Introduced by Frank Meyer of the U.S. Department of Agriculture, Bureau of Plant Industry.
> 'Hetz's Columnaris'—this was introduced in the 1940s by the Fairview Nur-

The foliage of Juniperus
chinensis *'Mountbatten' is
a grayish green color. It was
first introduced in 1948 as
a seedling of the species.*

sery of Fairview, Pennsylvania, the parent having been selected from a batch
of upright seedlings. Neil R. Hetz wrote that it is similar to *J. chinensis*
'Keteleeri' but is denser and "has both needles and threadlike foliage, but
as the tree grows older the threadlike foliage seems to predominate, giving
a rich green appearance to the entire plant."

'**Keteleeri**'—a broadly pyramidal tree with a stiff trunk and loose foliage,
selected about 1905. It is still one of the best varieties of *J. chinensis.* At one
time it was listed as a variety of *J. virginiana,* but there is no question about
its being a Chinese juniper, for its large, light blue fruits are almost ½" in
diameter. The foliage is green. The cultivar 'Mountbatten' has foliage of a
grayer color (that is, it is more juvenile), but 'Keteleeri' is a better specimen
than 'Excelsior,' for the latter is more irregular in habit.

mas—a densely columnar form mostly with acicular leaves and usually with
staminate flowers. This seems to be one of the excellent columnar forms of
J. chinensis and might well be used more than it is.

'**Mountbatten**'—introduced in 1948 by the Sheridan Nurseries, Toronto,
Ontario, Canada, this is an excellent narrowly columnar tree and a seedling
of *J. chinensis.* It may sometimes be found incorrectly listed as *J. chinensis*

Juniperus chinensis
'Excelsior,' not one of the best clones but sometimes used.

'Sheridan.' The foliage is grayish green because the majority of the leaves are the grayish juvenile or acicular type, but the dense compact habit gives one the impression that the plant has been sheared. This is one of the best of the fruiting Chinese juniper cultivars.

'Obelisk'—introduced by the F. J. Grootendorst Nurseries of Boskoop, Holland, in 1946, this is a fruiting pyramidal tree with steel blue foliage. This plant resembles *J. chinensis mas* but is claimed to be more attractive because of truncated branching and its excellent blue color. It keeps this compact habit without trimming and grows comparatively slowly.

pyramidalis—a narrow, pyramidal, compact form with upright branches and crowded, upright branchlets. The leaves are usually acicular and ternate, under ⅜" long and glaucous.

It should be clearly noted that the plant commonly known in the trade as *J. excelsa stricta* is actually this variety of the Chinese juniper. *Juniperus excelsa* is a tender juniper, hardy only in Zone 7.

'Story'—very narrow, columnar tree type, selected by Professor T. J. Maney, Iowa State College, in 1935 and introduced in 1947

A variable species with many named varieties offered in the trade, ranging from ground covers to standard trees. The leaves are of two kinds (as in *J. virginiana*), scalelike and acicular or sharp-pointed, the latter often being predominant. The sexes are separate in all junipers, and the fruits on the pistillate plants take two years to develop, being slightly larger than the fruits of *J. virginiana*. The general aspect of these plants is a lighter green than our native red cedar, often with not quite as dense foliage. I would personally prefer the native species in my garden, but many admire this Chinese native so it is included here merely because it offers variations for planting in Zone 4, where only these two tree types prove reliably hardy.

Juniperus deppeana   60'   Zone 7   Alligator juniper

* FRUIT: reddish brown berries, ½" in diameter; sexes separate
        EFFECTIVE: fall
  HABIT: spreading
  BARK: very beautiful, checkered
  FOLIAGE: on young plants the pointed, scalelike leaves are silvery white
  HABITAT: Arizona, New Mexico, southwest Texas, Mexico

One of the most ornamental of the native tree junipers but not hardy north of the Middle Atlantic states.

Juniperus drupacea   60'   Zone 7   Syrian juniper

* FRUIT: brown to bluish berry, ripening the second year; sexes separate
        EFFECTIVE: fall and winter
* HABIT: columnar
* FOLIAGE: evergreen, dense, pointed, scalelike
  HABITAT: Greece, Asia Minor
  INTRODUCED: 1853

An interesting and handsome juniper (especially in limestone soils) for the southern part of the country.

Juniperus excelsa   60'   Zone 7   Greek juniper

* FRUIT: round berries, ⅜" in diameter; sexes separate
        EFFECTIVE: fall
* HABIT: narrow, pyramidal
* FOLIAGE: dense, evergreen, usually juvenile foliage or scalelike type
  HABITAT: Greece, western Asia
  INTRODUCED: 1836
  VARIETY:
        'Stricta' *(Spiny Greek juniper)*—columnar form with juvenile, glaucous foliage.
        Sometimes this name is given incorrectly to *J. chinensis pyramidalis* in north-

ern nurseries, but the true *J. excelsa stricta* is not hardy in the North. Where it can be grown, it is most desirable as a densely compact, pyramidal, slow-growing shrub or small tree.

Juniperus lucayana   50'   Zone 9   West Indies juniper

FRUIT: small, blue berries; sexes separate
    EFFECTIVE: fall
* HABIT: dense, pyramidal, upright, but graceful
* FOLIAGE: evergreen, small, pointed, scalelike
HABITAT: southern Georgia to Florida

This is a substitute for the native *J. virginiana* (and similar to it) in the warmer parts of the country where the northern species will not grow. It is considered one of the most beautiful of the junipers.

Juniperus rigida   30'   Zone 5   Needle juniper

* FRUIT: ¼" in diameter, ripening the second year; sexes separate
    EFFECTIVE: fall and winter
* HABIT: pyramidal, pendulous branchlets
* FOLIAGE: evergreen, loose and open, pointed, scalelike leaves
HABITAT: Japan, Korea, northern China
INTRODUCED: 1861

A very graceful, narrowly pyramidal tree with loose, open branches and foliage but with gracefully pendulous branchlets. It will not shear well nor form a good windbreak but is recommended solely for its appearance as a specimen. *Juniperus formosana*, considerably more difficult to find in America, is similar in every way and need not be planted in preference to *J. rigida.*

Juniperus scopulorum   36'   Zone 5   Western red-cedar, Rocky
                                                        Mountain juniper

* FRUIT: bright, bluish berries, ¼" in diameter, ripening the second year; sexes separate
    EFFECTIVE: fall and winter
* HABIT: narrowly upright, sometimes devoid of branches at the base as it matures
* FOLIAGE: dense, evergreen, pointed, scalelike leaves, color varying from green to light blue
HABITAT: Rocky Mountains from British Columbia to California
VARIETIES:
    argentea—narrow, pyramidal form with silvery white foliage

'Blue Heaven'—sometimes listed as 'Blue Haven' and originating in the Plumfield Nurseries of Fremont, Nebraska, bearing fine fruits annually

'Blue Moon'—delicate, fine, textured blue foliage

'Chandler Blue'—probably selected by the Chandler Nursery of Prairie Village, Kansas

'Cologreen'—Marshall's Nurseries of Omaha, Nebraska, claim this to be one
of the best. It originated with them and is excellent in the area west of the
Missouri River, an upright form with light green foliage.

columnaris—a columnar form, the height is two and a half to three times the
width

'Gray Gleam'—selected by Scott Wilmore of the Wilmore Nursery, Wheat-
bridge, Colorado, this was patented (#848) in 1944. It originated as a chance
seedling, is staminate, and the very gray color is even more pronounced in
winter than in summer.

'Kansas Silver'—a selection of the Kansas Landscape Nursery Co. of Salina,
Kansas, with silvery blue foliage and a definitely upward growth of the ends
of the twigs. It is claimed to be fast growing and pyramidal in habit.

'North Star'—a tree with bright green foliage, originating in the nurseries of
the Westover Farms Landscaping Co., St. Louis, Missouri, about 1945

'Pathfinder'—introduced by the Plumfield Nurseries of Fremont, Nebraska,
in the early 1920s; a showy pyramidal form of light greenish silver color

pendula—a highly drought-resistant form with pendulous secondary branchlets. John B. Clarke of San Jose, California, says it was obtained from the
Boyce Thompson Southwest Arboretum in Arizona about 1950.

'Platinum' (Plant Patent #1070)—a selection of the Willis Nursery Co., this
dense, pyramidal plant has brilliant silvery foliage all year round. It does
especially well in the Great Plains and the Southwest.

'Skyrocket'—probably the most narrow of all the junipers. Formerly listed as
a variety of S. virginiana. Silver-blue foliage.

'Sutherland'—selected by W. G. Sutherland of Boulder, Colorado, many years
ago; has better green foliage than most varieties and is very bushy in habit

viridifolia—a pyramidal form with bright green foliage

A variable species, grown especially in the Rocky Mountain area where it is hardy,
and eastward to Illinois, it seems to withstand drought conditions much better than
J. virginiana. In fact, in the East it does not seem to do at all as well as the native
J. virginiana. When grown from seed it varies considerably with green, bluish green,
and greenish blue forms, some purplish in the fall and winter. Several varieties have
been grown rather widely in the trade and many others (over forty) have been
introduced by various individuals, most of them being forms selected for the marked
color of their foliage.

It should be mentioned here that J. occidentalis, the Western juniper, is a high-
altitude species of Utah and Idaho, especially suited for arid hills of that area, growing
10–25 feet high, with deep green to gray-green foliage. It does not do well except
in such very restricted conditions.

Juniperus virginiana   90'   Zone 2   Eastern red-cedar

* FRUIT: female plants have bluish berries, ¼" in diameter, ripening the first season; sexes separate
  EFFECTIVE: fall and winter
* HABIT: densely pyramidal, often columnar
* BARK: shredding in long strips
  FOLIAGE: evergreen, scalelike, and acicular; varies greatly
  HABITAT: entire eastern half of the United States
  VARIETIES:

> 'Burkii' *(Burk red-cedar)*—narrowly pyramidal, steel blue foliage, slightly purplish in winter
>
> 'Canaertii'—originating in Belgium before 1868, this has long been popular because of its compact, pyramidal habit, its dark green foliage which it maintains well throughout the winter, and its profuse bluish fruits that are always an ornamental asset
>
> *crebra*—the narrow, pyramidal, sometimes columnar form native in the northern part of the United States; it is to this variety that most garden forms are closely related. The species or typical "southern form" is usually much broader in habit, with pendant branches.
>
> *cupressifolia*—at first this plant was named *J. scopulorum* 'Hillspire.' When proper identification was made, the name was changed to *J. virginiana cupressifolia* "green," for at the time there was also a *J. virginiana cupressifolia* "blue." Later still it was changed to 'Hillspire.' The original plant was grown from seed sent to the den Ouden Nursery in Boskoop, Holland, in the late 1920s by the D. Hill Nursery of Dundee, Illinois. When a few grafts were returned to the Hill Nursery under the name of *J. virginiana cupressifolia* "green," the name 'Hillspire' was added. It is said to be symmetrical in habit with bright green foliage and a good green winter color. It is a pistillate plant. Undoubtedly this plant is grown widely in nurseries merely under the name *J. virginiana cupressifolia,* but it could have been given the simple name *J. virginiana* 'Hillspire.'
>
> 'DeForest Green'—a pyramidal tree, similar to *J. virginiana* 'Canaertii,' but the few Kansas nurserymen growing it say it is a deeper green and faster-growing cultivar
>
> 'Elegantissima' *(Goldtip red-cedar)*—popular because its branchlets are tipped with golden yellow. It is a pyramidal tree, usually not over 20' tall at maturity, and turns a good bronze color in the fall.
>
> *filifera*—a broadly pyramidal tree with very slender, much divided branchlets and gray-green foliage
>
> *glauca (Silver red-cedar)*—one of the best colored forms of this species, it is a narrowly columnar tree 15–20' tall and has been recognized as a botanical variety since about 1850. The silvery blue color of the foliage is, of course, brightest in the spring, gradually turning a silvery green in the summer.
>
> 'Manhattan Blue'—an introduction of Robert Scott, Manhattan, Kansas, this is a compact, pyramidal tree with bluish green foliage, as opposed to the gray-green color of *J. virginiana glauca*
>
> *pendula (Weeping red-cedar)*—spreading branches and pendulous branchlets. A

well-grown specimen does have merit, although it is more open in habit than
most of the columnar forms. It has been known since 1855.

pyramidalis '**Dundee**'—although this plant was known for a long time as *J. virginiana pyramidiformis,* Rehder made this name a synonym for *J. virginiana pyramidalis.* The D. Hill Nursery selected an apparently staminate tree in 1920, now named 'Dundee,' which has a pyramidal habit and soft foliage that turns a purple-green in the winter. It is best that the old name *pyramidiformis* be dropped.

'**Schottii**'—comparatively small, this dense, green, narrowly pyramidal tree is not planted as much now as it once was, possibly because its foliage may be yellow-green at certain times of the year. Known earlier than 1875, its origin is clouded

venusta—another columnar form that originated in the United States before 1915; has light green to sometimes bluish green foliage

Native from Florida to Canada and westward to the Rocky Mountains, this is the hardiest and most popular of the tree junipers. Over forty varieties have been named, for the species varies considerably in form, in color of foliage, and in type of foliage. Like other junipers it is dioecious; that is, staminate and pistillate flowers are on separate plants. Consequently, if fruiting plants are desired, care should be taken in their selection. Even then these trees may fruit once in only two or three years. Some of the clonal varieties are pistillate. The red-cedar is usually dense and can be pruned easily. Two geographical forms are recognized and easily noticed, those of the South being broadly pyramidal in habit (the true species) and plants found mostly from Pennsylvania northward are much more narrow in habit and not as tall (var. *crebra).*

The red-cedar grows slowly—trees with trunks 16 to 24 inches in diameter may be 150 years old. It will grow in most soils but is noted particularly for the fact that it does well in poor, gravelly soils. The wood is, of course, highly prized for many purposes, chiefly because of its fragrance. The shredding red bark has considerable interest ornamentally. It is a splendid evergreen and available from most nurseries.

Kalopanax pictus   90'   Zone 4   Castor-aralia

* FLOWERS: very small, in ball-like clusters 1″ in diameter, several clusters making up
         a large umbel 6–8″ across
         TIME: late July
* FRUIT: small, black seeds, quickly eaten by the birds
         EFFECTIVE: early fall
* HABIT: rounded head, massive branches, open
* FOLIAGE: leaves similar in shape to those of the sweet gum, but larger
  AUTUMN COLOR: reddish
  HABITAT: China, Korea, Japan
  INTRODUCED: about 1865
  VARIETY:
         maximowiczii—leaves more deeply lobed

This tree should be grown much more than it is. Typically a tall, rounded tree, its large, maplelike leaves give it a somewhat tropical appearance, and a deep, rich soil with plenty of moisture seems to be the best for good growth. Some of the younger branches and vigorous shoots have sharp prickles, but most of these disappear at maturity. The small balls of flowers that appear in late summer are unique, and the small, black fruit are eaten quickly by birds. It is possibly not grown more than it is because the seeds take two years to germinate, and there are very few fruiting trees in this country even though the tree has been growing here for almost a century. Many a grower has given up in disgust the first year because no seedlings appear, but by waiting patiently he would find that they germinate nearly 90 percent the second spring. A good shade tree devoid of insect pests or diseases, it should be planted more widely.

Keteleeria fortunei   90′   Zone 7   Fortune keteleeria

FRUIT: cones, 3–7″ long, purplish when young
   EFFECTIVE: fall
* HABIT: pyramidal when young, flat-topped like *Cedrus libani* when mature
* FOLIAGE: evergreen needles
HABITAT: southeastern China
INTRODUCED: 1845

Akin to the firs, and somewhat of the same general appearance, this tree will withstand somewhat drier situations.

Koelreuteria bipinnata   60′   Zone 7   Chinese flamegold tree

* FLOWERS: small, yellow, in large, upright, pyramidal clusters
   EFFECTIVE: early summer
* FRUIT: light yellowish, in bladderlike pods
FOLIAGE: 2 pinnate leaves, 7–12 leaflets
HABITAT: China

More hardy than *K. elegans* and differing from *K. paniculata* in that the leaves are twice pinnate, each leaflet being 1¾–4″ long. Used a lot in California.

Koelreuteria paniculata   30′   Zone 5   Goldenrain tree

* FLOWERS: small, yellow, in large, upright, pyramidal clusters
   TIME: early summer
* FRUIT: bladderlike, light yellowish to brown pods
   EFFECTIVE: fall
HABIT: flat-topped
FOLIAGE: coarse, open, compound leaves
HABITAT: China, Korea, Japan
INTRODUCED: 1763

VARIETY:
    'Fastigiata'—narrow, columnar habit

This and the laburnum are the only trees with truly yellow blossoms that can be grown in the Arnold Arboretum. It is quickly and easily grown from seeds, and its large, conspicuous flower clusters in early summer, followed by its equally conspicuous fruits, make it prominent throughout the summer period when most other trees have few if any flowers or colored fruit. It is used a great deal in the Ohio Valley, even as a street tree. Because of its weak wood, this might be none too advisable. It has no autumn color, and unless desired specifically for its summer bloom, other trees with a longer life of ornamental usefulness might be used instead. This much must be said in its behalf, however—it does seem to grow well in a wide range of soils. Pests are not especially problematic.

Laburnum alpinum   30'   Zone 4   Scotch laburnum

* FLOWERS: pealike, yellow, in pendulous clusters up to 16" long
    TIME: late May
HABIT: stiffly upright to vase-shaped
FOLIAGE: open
HABITAT: southern Europe
INTRODUCED: probably in colonial times

The Scotch laburnum is much hardier and the flower clusters last much longer than those of the common laburnum *(L. anagyroides)*, which is really inferior to both this and its hybrid, *L. watereri.* The hybrid is probably the better garden specimen, but this Scotch laburnum is recommended because of its hardiness. Without autumn color and interesting fruit, its only claim to fame is the profusion of pendulous, golden yellow flower clusters for the two-week period its flowers are open.

    There are several varieties of this Scotch laburnum and many more of *L. anagyroides* in European botanical gardens. Since the period of ornamental interest in these small trees is less than two weeks, these varieties are not being grown commercially in America. Actually, they differ from the species only in minor ways. Twig blight and leaf spot can be serious problems.

x Laburnum watereri   30'   Zone 5   Waterer laburnum

* FLOWERS: pealike, yellow, in pendulous clusters
    TIME: late May
HABIT: stiffly upright
FOLIAGE: open
HYBRID ORIGIN: *L. anagyroides* x *L. alpinum*
ORIGINATED: before 1864

Often called *L. vossii,* this hybrid has proved justly popular in the trade and is a better plant than its hardier parent, *L. alpinum,* because it is denser in habit and the flowers are larger and a deeper yellow. *Laburnum vossii* is listed as a synonym by Rehder, but European nurseries have hybrids under both names that are apparently distinct.

Lagerstroemia indica   21'   Zone 7   Crape-myrtle

* FLOWERS: bright pink to red, up to 1½" in diameter
      TIME: August
  HABIT: upright to rounded, dense branching
* BARK: flaking off in irregular patches, displaying a lighter underbark
  FOLIAGE: dense, fine-textured, privetlike leaves
  HABITAT: China, tropical and subtropical countries
  INTRODUCED: 1747
  VARIETIES:
      'Catawba'—dark purple flowers, originated by the National Arboretum
      'Cherokee'—bright, rich red flowers, originated by the National Arboretum
      'Glendora'—ruffled, snowy white flowers

Popular throughout the South, crape-myrtle (Lagerstroemia indica) has colorful bark all year.

'**Peppermint Lace**' *(Plant Patent #3169)*—flowers a deep rose-pink edged in
   white, originated by Monrovia Nursery Co., Azusa, California
'Seminole'—clear pink flowers, originated by the National Arboretum

Hardy as far north as Baltimore, the crape-myrtle is grown widely throughout the
South, especially for its profuse summer bloom. Blooming on the current year's
wood, it is amenable to heavy winter pruning when necessary to force compact
growth. It blooms over a lengthy period, and the crinkled flowers, combined with
its vigorous, rounded habit, make it popular. It is difficult to transplant and should
have a ball of earth about the roots whenever it is moved. Several varieties of
crape-myrtle are available, with white, pink, red, lavender, or bluish flowers. Powdery mildew and leaf spot can be problems.

Lagunaria patersonii   50'   Zone 9   Paterson sugarplum tree

* FLOWERS: pale pink, somewhat similar to those of *Hibiscus*
        TIME: May–June
   HABIT: pyramidal
* FOLIAGE: evergreen, dark olive green
   HABITAT: Australia

This tree is especially useful in seaside plantings and also as a street tree, where it is
hardy because of its shapely and regularly spaced branches.

⇥≫ *LARIX*

Stiffly pyramidal in habit yet most graceful in leaf, the larches are among the
few deciduous conifers that shed their leaves in the fall and bear cones similar
to those of their evergreen relatives. They are easily transplanted and of
exceptional beauty in the spring when their small green needles first appear,
but they are not used very much because of several pests that can disfigure
them quickly. The larch case bearer is one of the most severe pests because
infestations of this insect can ruin the appearance of the tree for all the time
it is in leaf, unless controlled by spraying at the proper time. The small worms
hatch outside the leaves but eat their way inside when the needles are only
half grown. Once inside, no spray reaches them, and if applied too soon the
spray is not effective. We have found at the Arnold Arboretum that only
three or four days in time of spray application makes all the difference
between an effective kill of the pest and normal green foliage the rest of the
season, or an ineffective kill and brown, partly eaten foliage for the remainder of the spring, and summer. Dormant sprays with lime sulfur followed

with sprays of methoxychlor or malathion when the needles are growing proves to be helpful control. Woolly larch aphid is controlled with malathion. Rust can be controlled by spraying with ferbam or thiram. Regular spraying with lime sulfur or colloidal sulfur is helpful as a general control.

Their pyramidal habit, often pendulous branchlets, and the very loose and open texture of their foliage, giving a very light shade, as well as their fast growth and striking appearance in leafing out during the early spring, are their chief qualifications for planting.

Larix decidua   100′   Zone 2   European larch

* FRUIT: cones about 2″ long
     EFFECTIVE: several years
* HABIT: pyramidal and open when young, rather irregular head at maturity
FOLIAGE: deciduous, needlelike, open
AUTUMN COLOR: yellow
HABITAT: northern and central Europe
INTRODUCED: early colonial times
VARIETIES:
    pendula—pendulous branchlets, very ornamental and graceful
    polonica—the main branches of *L. decidua pendula* are horizontal, whereas those
      of this variety, as well as the branchlets, droop

Popularly used in Europe as one of the better larches, it has also done well in the northern United States, probably being planted more than any other. One of its best features is its cones, which remain on the tree several years, providing much ornamental interest. These, however, are not borne until the tree is about twenty years old.

x Larix eurolepis   80′   Zone 4   Dunkeld larch

FRUIT: cones
    EFFECTIVE: fall
HABIT: broadly pyramidal
FOLIAGE: deciduous, needlelike
AUTUMN COLOR: yellow
HYBRID ORIGIN: *L. kaempferi x decidua,* originating in England about 1900

A natural hybrid, seedlings vary considerably and not all have good form. It might best be asexually propagated. Vigorous in growth, with foliage denser than that of *L. kaempferi,* this is one larch that can grow well in well-drained soils.

Larix kaempferi (syn. *L. leptolepis*)   90′   Zone 4   Japanese larch

* HABIT: short, very open, pyramidal, horizontal habit
BARK: peeling off in long strips, showing red underneath

FOLIAGE: deciduous, needlelike, open
AUTUMN COLOR: yellow
HABITAT: Japan
INTRODUCED: 1861

This is the best ornamental among the larches and seems to grow faster than some of the others. While it is not immune to the various troubles that plague most of the larch species, it is less susceptible to canker disease than are the European and American larches.

Larix laricina   60'   Zone 1   Eastern larch, Tamarack

* HABIT: very open and pyramidal
FOLIAGE: deciduous, needlelike, open
AUTUMN COLOR: yellow
HABITAT: Alaska, Canada, northern United States

One of the hardiest of all trees in North America—habitually grows in moist or wet spots but can thrive also in good, normal soil.

Laurus nobilis   30'   Zone 6   Sweet bay, Laurel

FLOWERS: greenish white
    TIME: early June
FRUIT: dark green, finally black, berries
    EFFECTIVE: fall
* FOLIAGE: aromatic, dense, evergreen leaves, 4" long
HABITAT: Mediterranean region
INTRODUCED: colonial times

This is the famous laurel of ancient history and poetry, cultivated for centuries by the Greeks and Romans. Amenable to shearing, it is often kept closely clipped and grown in tubs, especially in formal plantings. The aromatic leaves are used as a seasoning, and the oil from the fruit is used in making perfume. It is a splendid small tree yielding dense shade.

Leptospermum laevigatum   25'   Zone 9   Australian tea tree

* FLOWERS: white
    TIME: March to May
HABIT: rather ungainly
* FOLIAGE: evergreen, light green, doing well under marked exposure
HABITAT: Australia

This tree will grow in almost pure sand and as it reaches maturity becomes irregular in habit and sometimes very picturesque. It will not grow well in heavy soils with poor drainage.

Leucadendron argenteum   30′   Zone 10   Silver leucadendron

HABIT: distinctive, rounded
FOLIAGE: dense leaves, 6″ long, covered with silvery hairs
HABITAT: South Africa

This tree probably is grown only in southern California but is a beautiful small tree, according to Maunsell Van Rensselaer, formerly of the Santa Barbara Botanic Garden, who recommended it highly. In fact, he considered it the most "spectacularly beautiful" tree in Santa Barbara, a city noted for its many attractive trees. Its soft, silvery appearance is unique among woody plants, although it is rather short-lived (twenty-five to thirty years reported to be its length of usefulness) and difficult to grow properly.

Ligustrum lucidum   30′   Zone 7   Glossy privet

FLOWERS: small, pyramidal, white clusters
     TIME: August
FRUIT: blue-black berries
     EFFECTIVE: September to February
HABIT: upright, branching, dense
* FOLIAGE: dense, glossy, mostly evergreen leaves, to 6″ long
HABITAT: China, Korea, Japan
INTRODUCED: 1794

This, as a shrub, is inferior to *L. japonicum* with which it is frequently confused. There are several varieties of both in the trade, but since it is the tallest growing privet it can be mentioned here as a very rapid-growing tree, free from insect pests or diseases.

Liquidambar formosana   120′   Zone 7   Formosa sweet-gum

FRUIT: bristly balls, 1″ in diameter
     EFFECTIVE: fall
HABIT: pyramidal, similar to *L. styraciflua*
FOLIAGE: leaves 3 lobed
* AUTUMN COLOR: red
HABITAT: China, Formosa
INTRODUCED: 1884

Sometimes used on the West Coast. The young leaves are lavender tinted.

Liquidambar styraciflua   125'   Zone 5   Sweet-gum

* FRUIT: round, horned balls, 1″ in diameter
    EFFECTIVE: fall
* HABIT: broadly pyramidal
    BARK: deeply furrowed, branches often with corky twigs
    FOLIAGE: star-shaped, dense
* AUTUMN COLOR: scarlet
    HABITAT: eastern United States
    VARIETIES:
        'Burgundy'—leaves turn a wine-red in the fall
        'Moraine'—faster growing than the species, with excellent dark green foliage
        'Palo Alto'—especially good autumn color

At least eighteen other varietal names have been given certain clones.

The sweet-gum is an excellent specimen tree; it is rather difficult to transplant when large, but once established it has few troubles. It is in frequent use along the parkways and highways of the eastern United States and even in southern California. If given plenty of room in which to develop, few other trees can approach it in symmetrical beauty. The peculiar, ball-shaped fruit remains on the tree for a time after the leaves have fallen. The variety 'Variegata' has leaves colored irregularly with yellow.

Sweet-gum webworm, bleeding necrosis, cottony cushion scale, sweet-gum scale, and iron chlorosis can infest this tree. Try sprays of malathion to control.

Liriodendron tulipifera   150'   Zone 4   Tulip tree, Tulip poplar,
                                                                Yellow poplar

* FLOWERS: greenish yellow marked with orange, tulip-shaped and about the same
        size
    TIME: mid-June
    FRUIT: pyramidal, dry pods, 2–3″ long
        EFFECTIVE: not particularly effective
    HABIT: broadly pyramidal, massive branches
    FOLIAGE: dense; leaves uniquely shaped, squarish
* AUTUMN COLOR: yellow
    HABITAT: eastern United States
    VARIETIES:
        'Aureo-marginatum'—leaves with yellow margins. Monrovia Nursery Co. of
        Azusa, California, has selected a clone of this and named it 'Majestic Beauty.'
        'Fastigiatum'—upright in habit, listed as 'Arnold' by the Saratoga Horticul-
        tural Foundation of Saratoga, California

At least twenty other clones have been named. A common native tree, often growing to tremendous size with many living specimens estimated to be two hundred years old, it should be given plenty of room to grow; otherwise its beauty is not appreciated. The tulip-shaped flowers appear after the leaves are fully developed and so are none too conspicuous from a distance, but they are nearly 2½ inches long, greenish yellow with an orange band, and give the tree its name. Rather easily transplanted, the species is appropriate only for the larger gardens and parks where at least 75 feet of space can eventually be allotted each tree. The fastigiate form, however, does have possibilities for use as a narrow street tree. These trees are not seriously affected with insect pests or diseases.

Lithocarpus densiflorum   75′   Zone 7   Tanbark oak

* FOLIAGE: long, leathery, evergreen leaves, 1½–4″
HABIT: open, low
HABITAT: southern Oregon, California

The tanbark oak survives well only in the area of its native habitat in rich, moist, well-drained soil.

Livistona australis   50′   Zone 10   Australian fan palm

* HABIT: palm with orbicular head
* FOLIAGE: dense, fanlike, 3–5′ in diameter
HABITAT: Australia

A beautiful palm and one of the hardiest, with fan-shaped, dark green leaves and a rounded crown.

Maackia amurensis   45′   Zone 4   Amur maackia

* FLOWERS: small, white, in panicles 4–8″ long
       TIME: late summer
HABITAT: Japan
INTRODUCED: 1892

Only of value for its late summer flowers. If these are not valued, better trees might be used that have interesting fruits and colorful autumn foliage. No special pests.

Macadamia ternifolia   35′   Zone 10   Queensland nut

FLOWERS: white, in racemes 1′ long
       TIME: spring
HABIT: erect, rounded head
* FOLIAGE: leathery, lustrous, spiny, evergreen leaves, in whorls of 3 or 4, up to 1′
       long
HABITAT: New South Wales

A slow-growing tree from the tropics, it requires a deep, rich soil in which to grow but makes a fine, dense evergreen specimen, even in situations where there is little rainfall. It sometimes grows with several trunks but is usually clothed with branches from the ground on up.

Maclura pomifera   60′   Zone 5   Osage-orange

FRUIT: large, orangelike, green, 3″ in diameter; sexes separate
    EFFECTIVE: fall
HABIT: open, irregular, rounded top; thorny
FOLIAGE: loosely open
AUTUMN COLOR: yellow
HABITAT: south central United States

The Osage-orange is recommended for use only in the Midwest, where it seems to withstand cold winters and summer drought better than most other trees. It is used chiefly as a windbreak or hedge plant (along fence rows) because of its unusually vigorous growth and stout thorns and its ability to withstand heavy clipping. When planted along a fence row, it quickly grows into an impenetrable thorny mass capable of confining stock throughout the year. Other plants outstrip it in ornamental qualifications for general landscape use in the East and far West. The sexes are separate so only the pistillate plants will bear the large fruits from which this species takes its common name. No serious pests.

⇢≫ *MAGNOLIA*

Like the cherries, this group of plants is valued for its flowers, many of them appearing in early spring before the leaves. Fourteen of the recommended species are natives of Asia, six are natives of North America, and seven are hybrids. The flowers are large and conspicuous, white, pink, or red to reddish purple, some nearly a foot in diameter, making these the largest in any group of hardy plants in our north temperate area. They have no conspicuous autumn color, and their peculiar fruits are noticeable only for a very short time when they split open, revealing the red seeds within. These quickly fall to the ground and shortly thereafter the pod itself withers and falls off. Some species produce more of these fruits than others. The seeds quickly lose their viability, which is the reason magnolia seeds should be sown as soon as they are ripe.

Since magnolias are difficult to transplant, they should be moved with a ball of soil about their thick, fleshy roots. They must be handled very carefully and transplanted preferably in the spring of the year in most areas.

The foliage of many magnolias can be considered coarse, yet it is sturdy and seldom attacked by leaf-eating insects. Unfortunately, some species (especially *M. soulangiana*) are susceptible to a soft scale attacking the young twigs; when this happens, it must be kept rigidly under control by spraying with dormant oil or dead branches begin to appear. Leaf spot can be controlled by spraying with ferbam or thiram.

Some of the native species (*M. tripetala, fraseri,* and *macrophylla*) have unusually large leaves, the last-mentioned sometimes 30 inches long, while others (*M. salicifolia*) seldom have leaves over 4 inches long. The very coarse texture is not desirable under many conditions, and when grown in an exposed situation, the wind can whip the leaves about until they are shredded and unsightly for a greater part of the growing season.

It must be admitted that magnolias are desirable trees and should be considered for many situations where conspicuously flowered types are desired. Some, such as *M. soulangiana,* do well under city conditions. Most are rather wide-spreading, with bark that is easily injured, and thus not adaptable as street trees.

There are twenty-five species of magnolia trees recommended here, with many varieties. This seems an unusually large number, yet they all have a place in certain types of planting. For instance, *M. acuminata, campbellii, grandiflora,* and *obovata* are all tall trees over 90 feet high at maturity. On the other hand, *M. cordata, salicifolia, sieboldii, soulangiana, stellata, watsonii,* and *wilsonii* are all under 30 feet high at maturity—well adapted for medium-sized gardens, and each one deserving of use in its own right.

Magnolia loebneri and *M. veitchii* are mentioned because of their rapid growth and early flower production; *M. macrophylla* merely because of its unusually large leaves; *M. virginiana* because of its summer flowers; *M. fraseri* because of its large flowers; and *M. heptapeta* because they have been widely used and are very beautiful. Sixteen of these species have white flowers, all the more reason for growing those with colored flowers. The group is highly valued, and one of these magnolias will be found in all but the driest and the coldest parts of the country. As flowering trees, none surpass them.

Magnolia acuminata   90'   Zone 4   Cucumber tree

FLOWERS: greenish yellow, rather inconspicuous, 3" long
    TIME: early June
FRUIT: pink to red, in peculiar cucumber-shaped shells
    EFFECTIVE: early fall
* HABIT: pyramidal, upright while young, massive with wide-reaching branches at maturity
FOLIAGE: dense, large leaves, 5–10" long
HABITAT: eastern United States

Found native in a wide area, this tree is best used for its foliage and habit. The flowers are cup-shaped and greenish yellow, but because of their color and since they appear after the leaves are fully developed, they are not at all conspicuous and should not even be considered from an ornamental viewpoint. The leaves are not too coarse; they have no autumn color and turn brown in the fall before dropping. Mature trees have wide-spreading branches that arch and may even touch the ground, but trees even forty years old are stiff, fairly narrow, and upright in habit. It is one of the fastest-growing magnolias and should be used only where it will have plenty of room to develop normally since it does not look good when confined by restrained pruning. This excellent tree grows very vigorously, which is one of the reasons it is frequently used as understock in grafting other magnolias.

Magnolia campbellii   150′   Zones 8–9   Campbell magnolia

* FLOWERS: fragrant, cup-shaped, shell pink, 8–10″ in diameter
   TIME: very early spring
HABIT: few branches, rather open
FOLIAGE: coarse leaves, 6–10″ long
HABITAT: Himalayas
VARIETY:
   mollicomota—rose-colored flowers, appearing before the leaves in the spring. Young plants will bloom in six to seven years, whereas it takes young plants of the species twelve to fourteen years to bloom.

This is a rare plant, hardy in only a small area of this continent, but a huge tree in its native habitat. It does not bloom while young and its flower buds are very tender. Certainly it is worthy of a trial where it is hardy. This plant has come through temperatures of 15°F above zero without injury. In fact, a report from a Seattle nursery stated that it survived temperatures of zero to 5°F below on eight successive nights and still showed no injury, even to the tips of the branches, by April of the following spring.

Magnolia cordata   30′   Zone 5   Yellow cucumber tree

FLOWERS: cup-shaped, yellow, 2″ long
   TIME: late May
FRUIT: peculiar cucumberlike pods, splitting open to disclose numerous bright red seeds
   EFFECTIVE: fall
* HABIT: upright but open
FOLIAGE: coarse leaves, 3–6″ long
HABITAT: Georgia

The flowers are certainly more conspicuous than those of *M. acuminata,* and the leaves are slightly smaller. Because it is smaller in all of its characteristics this might be the substitute for *M. acuminata* in the small garden, especially since it does not grow nearly as rapidly as does the cucumber tree.

Magnolia dawsoniana   36′   Zone 7   Dawson magnolia

* FLOWER: rosy purple, about 10″ in diameter
         TIME: March and April
   FRUIT: peculiar cucumberlike pods, splitting open to disclose numerous bright
         red seeds
   EFFECTIVE: fall
   HABIT: loose and open
   FOLIAGE: leaves 3½–6″ long and about half as wide
   HABITAT: western China
   INTRODUCED: 1908

Often confused with the Sargent magnolia, its flowers are borne horizontally and
more profusely.

Magnolia fraseri   45′   Zone 5   Fraser magnolia

* FLOWERS: fragrant, creamy white, 8–10″ in diameter, 6–9 petals
         TIME: late May
   FRUIT: peculiar cucumberlike pods, splitting open to disclose numerous bright
         red seeds
   EFFECTIVE: early fall
   HABIT: open head, wide-spreading branches
   FOLIAGE: coarse leaves, 12″ long
   HABITAT: southeastern United States

Another large-leaved magnolia. One of these, growing in the Arnold Arboretum, is
over 12 inches in trunk diameter. However, this species is not dependable in the
Boston climate. John Bartram discovered it growing in South Carolina in 1776. The
leaves are thinner and smaller than those of the larger leaved *M. macrophylla.* It should
be kept in mind, however, that large flowers and coarse foliage do not make a really
interesting landscape specimen except under unusual conditions.

Magnolia grandiflora   90′   Zone 7   Southern magnolia

* FLOWERS: fragrant, white, 8″ in diameter, usually 6 petals
         TIME: late May and part of the summer
* FRUIT: peculiar cucumberlike pods, splitting open to disclose numerous bright
         red seeds
   EFFECTIVE: early fall
* HABIT: pyramidal, usually dense
* FOLIAGE: evergreen leaves, 5–8″ long, dropping at end of second year
   HABITAT: southeastern United States
   VARIETIES:
         'Goliath'—a very popular variety in England, with large flowers up to 12″ in
               diameter and broad leaves, rounded and blunt at the end, glossy green; first
               distributed by the Caledonia Nursery on the isle of Guernsey, probably
               before 1910. It is superior to the species in flower.

Magnolia grandiflora
*'Little Gem.' Photograph
courtesy of Monrovia
Nursery Company.*

'Lanceolata' *(exoniensis—Exmouth magnolia)*—this has a narrow, pyramidal habit that is commendable, but it takes many years for a young plant to bloom. The leaves are narrower than those of the species, with rusty tomentum beneath. It originated from seed in England before 1800 and was widely distributed by the Veitch Nursery firm there.

'Little Gem'—a heavy bloomer with white flowers, blooming in early and late summer. It is compact, upright, and small. The foliage is evergreen but darker green than that of 'St. Mary.' Rusty brown on undersurface of the leaves. Originated at Steed's Nursery, Candor, North Carolina.

'Majestic Beauty' *(Plant Patent #2250)*—flowers are fragrant, cup-shaped, and white, blooming in the summer. It is tall, very large, and pyramidal. The foliage is evergreen and dark, glossy green in color.

'St. Mary'—originated before 1950 at the Glen St. Mary Nursery, Glen St. Mary, Florida. Blooms at an earlier age than most *M. grandiflora* seedlings but especially named for the deep and conspicuously brown undersurface of the leaves. Excellent fragrant white flowers.

'Samuel Sommer'—Patented (#2015) in 1961 by the Saratoga Horticultural Foundation of Saratoga, California, because of its rapid growth, strong ascending habit, and large (10–14″), creamy white flowers with 12 concave petals.

'**Symmes Select**'—an interesting variety selected for its dark green foliage and round rosettes of leaves surrounding the blossoms. Zone 8. Propagated by cuttings.

This magnificent, single-trunked tree is precariously hardy as far north as Philadelphia and Harrisburg, Pennsylvania. There are several varieties, over thirty having been named over the years, varying in leaf size, length of flowering, and the amount of brown tomentum on the undersurface of the leaves. This magnolia is widely planted throughout the South, and its evergreen leaves are dried and used in "artificial" florists' combinations throughout the entire country. Flowers on well-grown specimens may be as much as 12 inches in diameter—truly striking. The southern magnolia is a fine specimen tree but does not take kindly to crowding and should be given plenty of room in which to develop.

Magnolia heptapeta (syn. *M. denudata*)   45'   Zone 5   Yulan magnolia

* FLOWERS: fragrant, white, 6" in diameter before the leaves appear, 9 petals
      TIME: early May
* FRUIT: peculiar cucumberlike pods, splitting open to disclose numerous bright red seeds
      EFFECTIVE: fall
HABIT: rounded
FOLIAGE: dense leaves, 4–6" long
HABITAT: central China
INTRODUCED: 1789
VARIETY:
      '**Purpurascens**'—flowers rose-red outside, pink inside; from Japan

Many people have come to know this excellent tree under two other names, *M. conspicua* and *M. denudata*, both now superseded by the name *heptapeta*. It has been cultivated in the gardens of central China since the earliest times—a splendid tree that should not be crowded by other plants but given plenty of room in which to develop. This means it should be allowed a ground space of about 30 feet.

x Magnolia hybrid '**Timeless Beauty**'   25'   Zone 6

* FLOWERS: fragrant, creamy white, 10" in diameter
      TIME: summer
HABIT: dense, upright
* FOLIAGE: evergreen

Hybrid origin listed as "new" by Monrovia Nursery Co. in 1988. Plant patent applied for in 1987.

Magnolia hypoleuca (syn. *M. obovata*)   90'   Zone 5   Whiteleaf
Japanese magnolia

* FLOWERS: fragrant, white, 8" in diameter, 6–9 petals
       TIME: early June
* FRUIT: peculiar cucumberlike pods, splitting open to reveal numerous bright
       red seeds
       EFFECTIVE: early fall
   HABIT: pyramidal, open
   FOLIAGE: leaves 8–16" long, coarse in texture, blue-white beneath
   HABITAT: Japan
   INTRODUCED: 1865

The native umbrella magnolia *(M. tripetala)* is similar to this species, but the flowers
are inferior to it and have a disagreeable odor, while those of *M. hypoleuca* are
fragrant, making this Japanese plant the more desirable ornamental specimen. The
leaves of both *M. tripetala* and *M. hypoleuca* are mostly pointed at the base and so easily
distinguished from those of *M. macrophylla,* which are rounded or somewhat cordate
at the base. The flowers of both appear after the leaves are fully developed, but the
leaves add to, rather than detract from, the general effectiveness of the flowers.

x Magnolia loebneri 'Ballerina'   50'   Zone 4

* FLOWERS: fragrant, pure white, up to 30 petals
       TIME: spring
   HABIT: pyramidal, rapid growing
   FOLIAGE: dense; like that of *M. loebneri*

This variety has larger flowers than the species and more petals than either 'Merrill'
or 'Leonard Messel.' Softwood cuttings can be rooted in June.

x Magnolia loebneri **'Leonard Messel'**   36'   Zone 4

* FLOWERS: lilac-pink; buds deeper colored
       TIME: spring
   HABIT: pyramidal, rapid growing
   FOLIAGE: dense; like that of *M. loebneri*

Slightly slower growing than 'Merrill.'

x Magnolia loebneri **'Merrill'**   50'   Zone 4

* FLOWERS: fragrant, white, 8–15 petals
       TIME: late April
   FRUIT: peculiar cucumberlike pods, splitting open to reveal numerous bright
       red seeds

EFFECTIVE: early fall
HABIT: pyramidal, rapid-growing
FOLIAGE: dense; leaves slightly larger than those of *M. stellata*
HYBRID ORIGIN: *M. stellata x kobus* at Arnold Arboretum, Jamaica Plain, Massachu-
   setts
ORIGINATED: 1939

This is an excellent ornamental. Five years after the seed was planted it bloomed, and
M. kobus often takes twenty years to bloom from seed. The flowers of 'Merrill' have
15 petals but they are slightly larger than those of *M. stellata*. It is a vigorous tree,
growing to a height of 25 feet in seventeen years, whereas forty-year-old plants of
M. stellata are only 18 feet tall.

Magnolia macrophylla   50'   Zone 5   Bigleaf magnolia

* FLOWERS: fragrant, creamy white, 10–12" in diameter, 6 petals
      TIME: early July
* FRUIT: peculiar cucumberlike pods, splitting open to reveal numerous bright
      red seeds
      EFFECTIVE: early fall
HABIT: rounded head, open
FOLIAGE: very coarse leaves, often 20–30" long and 10" wide
HABITAT: southeastern United States

The leaves of this tree are the largest of any native tree in temperate North America.
It is precisely these large coarse leaves that prevent it from being used extensively
in American gardens, for if planted where winds whip them about, they quickly tear
and break to such an extent that the tree becomes unsightly. As a novelty, where
winds do not continuously mar the foliage, it may find a few enterprising gardeners
who will want to grow it, but there are many trees much easier to establish.

Magnolia nitida   30'   Zone 8   Shinyleaf magnolia

* FLOWERS: fragrant, creamy white, 2–3" in diameter, 9 petals
      TIME: late March or early April
FRUIT: peculiar cucumberlike pods, splitting open to reveal numerous bright
      red seeds
      EFFECTIVE: fall
HABIT: rounded, often shrubby, thinly clothed with foliage
* FOLIAGE: evergreen leaves, 2½–4½" long and 1–2" wide
HABITAT: China
INTRODUCED: about 1917

Of limited usefulness in the United States because of its lack of hardiness.

Magnolia rostrata   40–80'   Zone 9

FLOWERS: pale pink to white
    TIME: June and July
FRUIT: cucumberlike pods, 5–6" long, 1½" wide, splitting open to reveal numerous
    bright red seeds
    EFFECTIVE: fall
HABIT: silvery gray bark, purplish twigs
* FOLIAGE: leaves up to 20" long and 8½" wide
HABITAT: China
INTRODUCED: 1917

The flowers are disappointingly small for the large leaves, hence this might be used
only for its extremely large leaves and only in the warmest parts of the United States.

Magnolia salicifolia   30'   Zone 5   Anise magnolia

* FLOWERS: fragrant, white, 5" in diameter, 6 petals
    TIME: late April
* FRUIT: peculiar cucumberlike pods, splitting open to reveal numerous bright
    red seeds
    EFFECTIVE: early fall
* HABIT: closely pyramidal
* FOLIAGE: dense leaves, 2½–4½" long, fine textured for a magnolia; leaves and bark
    have lemon scent when bruised
HABITAT: Japan
INTRODUCED: 1892
VARIETY:
    'Else Frye'—fastigiate form with flowers half again as large as those of the
    species. Named by the University of Washington (Seattle, Washington) in
    1961.

This is a splendid tree for its flower and form; particularly nice specimens are being
grown in the Morton Arboretum, Lisle, Illinois, and Swarthmore College, Swarthmore, Pennsylvania. The leaves are very narrow for magnolias, not over 1½ inches
wide. It has the desirable trait of blooming when quite young, something that cannot
be said of *M. kobus* or its varieties. The flowers have a fragrance similar to that of
lemon-scented verbena. So many magnolias spread out into what is often an ungainly
rounded habit at maturity that this species is particularly desirable in its being so
closely pyramidal.

Magnolia sargentiana robusta   40'   Zone 7

* FLOWERS: mauve and pink, 8–12" in diameter
    TIME: March or April
FRUIT: peculiar cucumberlike pods, 7–8" long, splitting open to reveal scarlet seeds

EFFECTIVE: fall
HABIT: wide-spreading
FOLIAGE: leaves 5½–8″ long
HABITAT: western China
INTRODUCED: 1913

One of the most beautiful of all magnolias, better than the species because the flowers are larger, the leaves longer, and it will bloom earlier in life than the species—when about twelve years old. Also and most important, the flowers are borne all about the tree, while in the species they appear mostly at the top. This plant needs plenty of space to develop properly. It is not a tree for the small garden.

Magnolia sieboldii (syn. *M. parviflora*)   30′   Zone 6   Oyama
                                                                      magnolia

* FLOWERS: fragrant, cup-shaped, white with scarlet stamens, 4–5″ in diameter
      TIME: early June
FRUIT: peculiar cucumberlike pods, splitting open to reveal numerous bright red seeds
      EFFECTIVE: early fall
HABIT: rounded, open, rather weak in growth
FOLIAGE: rather fine texture, leaves 2–6″ long
HABITAT: Japan, Korea
INTRODUCED: about 1865

The beauty of this Japanese species, formerly called *M. parviflora,* is its habit of producing flowers over a period of many weeks, not all at once. The numerous crimson stamens clustered about the center of the flower contrast very well against the white background of the waxy petals. It does not have very good foliage when compared with some of the others, hence its flowers alone are its chief claim to fame.

x Magnolia soulangiana   25′   Zone 5   Saucer magnolia

* FLOWERS: large, cup-shaped, white to purple, 5–10″ in diameter, appearing before the leaves
      TIME: early May to late May
FRUIT: peculiar cucumberlike pods, splitting open to disclose numerous bright red seeds
      EFFECTIVE: early fall
HABIT: often shrublike with many main stems but easily trained to a single trunk
FOLIAGE: rather coarse leaves, 6–8″ long
HYBRID ORIGIN: *M. denudata* x *M. liliflora*
ORIGINATED: about 1820
VARIETIES:
    'Alba' *(syn. 'Superba,' 'Alba Superba')*—introduced in 1867 by Louis Van Houtte, Belgium. Flowers white, outside of petals colored very light purplish. The tree is very compact.

x Magnolia soulangiana *'Verbanica' is a late-blooming (mid-May) variety.*

'**Alexandrina**'—introduced in 1851, Paris, France. Flowers flushed rose-purple outside, inside of petals pure white. One of larger and earlier flowering varieties.

'**André LeRoy**'—introduced in 1900, Barbier, Orléans, France. Flowers are dark pink to purplish on the outside (color close to that of 'Verbanica'). The petals are white inside and the flowers decidedly cup-shaped.

'**Brozzoni**'—introduced in 1900, Barbier. When wide open, the flowers are 10″ across, making this one of the largest flowered varieties of the *M. soulangiana* group. The outside of the petal is tinged a pale purplish rose, but all in all it is considered one of the best of the white-flowered varieties.

'**Burgundy**'—introduced in 1930 by W. B. Clarke, San Jose, California. Flowers are the deep purple color of Burgundy wine; they appear earlier than those of most other varieties.

'**Grace McDade**'—introduced in 1945, by C. McDade, Semmes, Alabama. Flowers are white with pink at the base of the petals.

'**Lennei**'—introduced in 1852; originated in Florence, Italy. This has the darkest purplish magenta flowers of this group (not as dark as *M. liliflora nigra*). 'Rustica' has more red in the flowers.

'**Liliputin**'—originated in the Semmes Nurseries, Crichton, Alabama, a number of years ago, with smaller flowers and smaller habit than most *M. soulangiana* varieties. It is slow in growth. The variety sold under the name "Late Soulangiana" is similar in every way, although this one supposedly came from England.

'Lombardy Rose'—introduced before 1957 by C. McDade, Semmes, Alabama. The lower surface of the petals is dark rose, the upper surface white. This is a seedling of *M. soulangiana* 'Lennei,' with flowers continuing to bloom for several weeks.

'Rustica' *(syn. 'Rubra' or 'Rustica Rubra')*—introduced about 1893, Boskoop, Holland. Flowers are more rose-red than those of 'Lennei' but are somewhat similar, 5½" in diameter. The inside of the petals is white but the general effect is more red than 'Lennei.'

'San Jose'—originated about 1938, San Jose, California. Flowers are larger than many other varieties, fragrant, vigorous growing, and rosy purple. Blooms earlier than most other *M. soulangiana* varieties; said to be deeper colored than most, with the exception of 'Lennei.'

'Speciosa'—introduced before 1830 in France. The flowers are almost white, 6" in diameter, very close to 'Alba' but have just a trifle more color than 'Brozzoni.' It is important because it is the last of this group to bloom. Upright, tall, and fast growing.

'Verbanica'—flowers outside a clear rose-pink, inside white. This is one of the late bloomers, making a beautiful effect when most of the other varieties are dropping their petals. Slow growing.

This popular hybrid originated as a chance seedling in the garden of M. Soulange-Bodin at Fromont near Paris, over a hundred years ago. Unlike many other trees, it will bloom when it is still very small; plants merely 2–3 feet tall, often producing several flowers. Since it is a hybrid species, there are many clones, the flowers ranging from white to a deep reddish purple, depending on variety. According to some reports, the flowers on a single tree may vary in color somewhat from year to year. Normally, the saucer magnolia is as wide as it is high with several main trunks. It is susceptible to rather serious infestations of the magnolia scale so that the spraying of trunks and branches in the early spring with a dormant oil is a must. These plants are popular because of their conspicuous large flowers before the leaves appear, and thirteen varieties have been listed merely to show a range in the color and size of the flowers and the time of bloom since some bloom nearly a week earlier than others. These magnolias do not have autumn color and all are rather coarse in leaf texture, so one should consider them carefully before devoting an appreciable portion of a small garden to this species.

Magnolia sprengeri 60' Zone 7 Sprenger magnolia

* FLOWERS: fragrant, saucer-shaped, light pink inside, rose-colored outside, 8" in diameter

TIME: March, before the leaves

FRUIT: peculiar cucumberlike pods, splitting open to reveal numerous bright red seeds

EFFECTIVE: fall

HABIT: pyramidal

FOLIAGE: leaves 4½–7" long

HABITAT: China

INTRODUCED: 1901

A beautiful magnolia, somewhat resembling *M. campbellii,* with 12 sepals and petals in the flower, and long, rose-red stamens.

Magnolia stellata   20′   Zone 5   Star magnolia

* FLOWERS: fragrant, double, white, over 3″ in diameter, at least 12–15 petals
       TIME: mid-April
* FRUIT: peculiar cucumberlike pod, 2″ long, splitting open to disclose numerous bright red seeds
       EFFECTIVE: early fall
* HABIT: dense branching, mounded to shrublike
* FOLIAGE: fine-textured, dark green leaves, 1½–4″ long
* AUTUMN COLOR: bronze to yellow
  HABITAT: Japan
  INTRODUCED: 1862
  VARIETIES:

   'Galaxy'—fast-growing, single trunk, profuse light purplish pink flowers
   rosea (Pink star magnolia)—flower buds pink, flowers usually white. This is mostly disappointing in flower since by the time the flowers are fully open, they have faded completely white.
   'Royal Star'—large, white flowers with pink buds
   'Rubra' *(Red star magnolia)*—flowers purplish rose; imported from Japan about 1925. Another form of this was purportedly raised in Boskoop, Holland, by Messers Kluis, before 1948. The flower color was noted as being fuchsia purple 28/3 on the Royal Horticulture Colour Chart. It is said to have been a chance seedling in a batch of *M. stellata.* I have not yet seen this in flower, but J. H. Johnstone noted that the flower color is vastly superior to that of *M. stellata rosea.*
   'Waterlily'—originated at Greenbrier Farms, Inc., Norfolk, Virginia, prior to 1939. It is more upright, bushy, and twiggy than *M. stellata.* The flower buds are pink, the flowers eventually white and slightly larger, with narrower petals. It has always been assumed to be a cross of *M. stellata x soulangiana,* but it looks very much like *M. stellata.* Paul Vossberg wrote that one thousand seedlings of 'Waterlily' were grown on Long Island, New York, and not one showed any traces of *M. soulangiana* or its parents, *M. liliflora* and *M. denudata.*

The star magnolia is the hardiest and in many respects the most ornamental of the Asiatic magnolias. The flowers have 12–19 petals, are very fragrant, and sometimes nearly 4 inches in diameter. The long, narrow leaves are thick and dark green, turning an excellent bronze in the fall, especially when grown in direct sunshine. The plant is dense, either a shrub or small tree, and is best used as a specimen plant, for its branches face the ground well. In the North, near its northern limit of hardiness, it may tend to bloom too early if given a southern exposure, for late frosts frequently mar the blossoms. With a northern exposure, the flower opening is retarded somewhat, proving helpful during those seasons with late frosts.

x *Magnolia veitchii*   40'   Zone 7   Veitch magnolia

* FLOWERS: pink, 6" in diameter, with 9 petals
     TIME: April, before leaves
HABIT: coarse, open
FOLIAGE: coarse leaves, 6–12" long, 3–7" wide
HYBRID ORIGIN: *M. campbellii x M. denudata*
ORIGINATED: Veitch Nursery, England, 1907; first flowered in 1917

This is an interesting hybrid with very brittle branches. Apparently, it has considerable hybrid vigor; a three-year-old plant grew up to 30 feet in height in only eight years. It is well worth growing where it is hardy because it produces flowers even when the tree is very young.

Magnolia virginiana (syn. *M. glauca*)   60'   Zone 5   Sweet bay

* FLOWERS: very fragrant, white, 2–3" in diameter
     TIME: late May
* FRUIT: peculiar cucumberlike pods, splitting open to disclose numerous bright red seeds
     EFFECTIVE: early fall
HABIT: a tree in the South; shrublike in the North
* FOLIAGE: green above, white below, leaves 2½–4½" long
HABITAT: coastal area of eastern United States

The very fragrant, waxy white flowers appearing in June and early summer, the gray bark, and good foliage with leaves white on the undersurface make this an attractive species. In the deep South this plant is a tree and nearly evergreen, but in New England it is much more shrubby and deciduous. It can be grown well in wet and even almost swampy soils, although it does not require such situations to grow well. An excellent native plant.

x *Magnolia watsonii*   20'   Zone 5   Watson magnolia

* FLOWERS: fragrant, white, with pink or red stamens and pink sepals, about 5½" in diameter
     TIME: mid-June
HABIT: small, rounded, rather straggly
FOLIAGE: rather coarse leaves, 4–7" long
HYBRID ORIGIN: *M. obovata x M. sieboldii*
ORIGINATED: Japan, 1889

This tree is suitable for the small garden but has the habit of being rather open and unruly. It is valued only for its fragrant conspicuous flowers with dense clusters of pink or red stamens in the center of the flower. This, like *M. sieboldii,* has also been formerly incorrectly termed *M. parviflora* and is distinguished from *M. sieboldii* by its larger flowers and larger, more leathery leaves, as well as its more robust growth.

Magnolia wilsonii   24'   Zone 6   Wilson magnolia

* FLOWERS: fragrant, white, with conspicuous ring of crimson stamens, 6" in
       diameter
     TIME: May
  FRUIT: peculiar cucumberlike pods, splitting open to disclose numerous bright
       red seeds
     EFFECTIVE: early fall
  HABIT: often shrubby and rather open
  FOLIAGE: rather fine textured leaves, 2–4½" long
  HABITAT: western China
  INTRODUCED: 1908

Fragrant, cup-shaped flowers are the chief attraction of this rare magnolia. Although
introduced over fifty years ago, it is extremely difficult to find a nursery that offers
it. It is not superior to other magnolias, but in the warmer parts of the country it might
have merit for its flowers.

→≫ *MALUS*

The crab apples as a group are about our most ornamental flowering and
fruiting trees. They should be used a great deal in park and parkway plantings
as well as on private grounds. Only one word of caution is necessary: they
should not be neglected. All are susceptible to scale infestations and borers,
and some are susceptible to fire blight. They should not be planted in long
hedges or windbreaks, for it is much easier to care for them properly when
planted as individuals or in small groups. Actually, they require a minimum
amount of attention, but spraying, pruning, and borer control must be given
regularly to ensure good growth. Otherwise, they are among our best ornamental trees, which is why over fifty species and varieties are suggested in
the following pages. Because of their importance, it might be of interest to
discuss briefly a little bit of their past history and the specific reasons that we
now value them.

→≫ HISTORY

The first plant that was thought of as a crab apple was undoubtedly *Malus
pumila,* native of eastern Europe. The fruits of this tree are comparatively
small and sour-tasting and are of little economic value, though they may be
used in preserves or in making cider. Apples have been known as such since

the earliest of times. Cato (third century B.C.) knew seven apple varieties and Pliny (first century A.D.) knew thirty-six apple varieties. Various seedlings of *M. pumila* and *M. sylvestris* occurred with fruits larger than usual, and these of course were the earliest of apple varieties. Seedlings of *M. pumila* were used as understock onto which scions of the more valued seedlings were grafted. About 1600, the term "crab apple" included some of the native *Malus* species noted by Captain John Smith as growing in Virginia, probably *M. coronaria* and *M. angustifolia*. He found the fruit to be small and bitter tasting, but the trees very beautiful in the spring when in flower. Because of the association of the term "crab apple" with these trees bearing small apples, the name was naturally used later when the Siberian crab apple was introduced, again when hybrids of this and the common apple appeared, and still later (after 1850) when the Asiatic species of the genus *Malus* was introduced into Europe and North America. Generally speaking, all the crab apples have fruits smaller than those of the common apple, and consequently we have considered the crab apple as any member of the genus *Malus* that has fruits 2 inches or less in diameter.

Most of the botanical species and varieties of the genus *Malus* constitute the wild crab apples of the world. Three are native of Europe—*M. pumila, M. sylvestris,* and *M. florentina* (Italy). In North America nine species are native, most of them with green fruits, but others have become naturalized. Seventeen species are considered native to eastern Europe and Asia, most of these being the crab apples with the delightfully colored, small fruits we frequently associate with China and Japan. These species and their varieties, then, constitute the native crab apples of the world. When grown together and promiscuously hybridized, their numerous offspring present a most diverse group, including hundreds of clones of dubious origin. This is the picture we have today. To understand it a little better, let us take a quick glance at early books and nursery catalogs in England and America.

In England there may have been a few hybrids between the native *M. pumila* and the large cultivated apples prior to 1784. In that year, however, the seeds of the Siberian crab apple (supposedly *M. baccata)* were introduced to Kew Gardens, and shortly thereafter numerous hybrids between this and varieties of the common apple began to appear. It is not known when *M. spectabilis* was introduced into Europe, but Dr. Fothergill, a famous English physician, was growing it in his spacious garden in 1780. The Siberian crab apple undoubtedly was listed in English catalogs about 1800, for in 1802 William Forsyth listed this and the double blossom apple (probably *M. spectabilis)* as being the only two crab apples grown in England at that time. Seven years later, the Siberian crab apple was offered in France, together with several of its varieties. Prior to 1768 no crab apples were listed in treatises of English pomology, so it is safe to surmise that after this date a few hybrids of *M. pumila* and the cultivated apples may have been offered as crab apples, but that crosses of the cultivated apple and *M. baccata* did not begin to appear until shortly after 1800. By 1826 over thirty crab apples, including several American species, were listed in English nurseries.

In America we can presume that the Siberian crab apple was introduced shortly after 1784, since John Bartram offered it for sale at his nursery in Philadelphia in 1814. Only one crab apple was listed by the Prince Nursery of Flushing, New York, in its catalog of 1790 and that was the Virginia crab apple. By 1831 this same nursery offered the Siberian crab apple, "large" and "small," the amber crab apple, which undoubtedly was a yellow-fruiting *M. baccata,* and the double-flowering Chinese crab apple, *M. spectabilis.* The Siberian crab apple "large" may have been either *M. prunifolia* or x *M. robusta.* The appearance of these exotic crab apples undoubtedly was the signal for many amateur experiments in hybridization, in which large-fruiting apple varieties were crossed with the smaller-fruiting Siberian. By 1835 'Montreal Beauty' was being offered by the Prince Nursery, it having originated in Quebec sometime prior to 1833. At any rate this was the time when exotic crab apples were beginning to be grown, hybridized, and offered for sale by American nurseries. Though *M. baccata* and *M. prunifolia* were introduced into America early, the majority of the Asiatic species did not reach here until after 1850, and some not until after 1900.

It is probable that crab apples were not grown in large numbers by the eastern colonists, for the larger-fruiting apple varieties were perfectly hardy from Maine southward, and these were most important economically. A few crab apples were needed for jellies and conserves, and it is probable that in the older colonies, as people had more leisure, they became interested in planting crab apples here and there purely for ornament. Certainly this was not done to any great extent.

The colonists alone were not responsible for disseminating European apple varieties in North America. The Indians undoubtedly did a great deal of it from the time the European apple first arrived in this country. Apples were apparently carried by the Indians and early traders to all parts of the country, and frequent mention has been made in early literature of Indian settlements with apple and peach orchards. There was the eccentric missionary John Chapman, better known as "Johnny Appleseed," who roamed the frontiers of Ohio and Indiana planting seeds and seedlings in hundreds of different places. It may be that what we now consider to be x *M. soulardii (M. pumila* x *M. ioensis)* had as one of its parents a seedling planted by this somewhat eccentric person.

In the colder parts of Vermont and New Hampshire it became increasingly apparent that the apple varieties of those times were not completely winter-hardy but that the newly introduced Siberian crab apple was extremely so. With the westward movement of settlers and the desire to establish the apple everywhere, it became evident that many apple varieties could not survive the extremely cold midwest climate while the Siberian crab apple did. This knowledge brought about feverish activity in sowing the seed of apples—any apples—in order to find trees that would prove hardy. In 1845 Andrew Jackson Downing wrote that many individuals were experimenting with *M. baccata* because of its remarkable hardiness, and many crosses were being grown. However, he listed only *M. baccata* and *M. spectabilis* in his book published in 1845, though later, in another edition (1869), crab apples were of sufficient importance in this country that he listed thirty-seven varieties. Some of these may have been introduced from Europe, but several certainly originated in North America. Both 'Brier' and 'Gibb' originated in America sometime between 1860 and 1870 as the result of crossing the Siberian crab apple with common apple varieties of those times. It is of interest to note that of the thirty-seven varieties Downing listed, at least five are being grown today, namely, 'Hyslop,' 'Montreal Beauty,' 'Orange,' 'Soulard,' and 'Transcendent.'

By 1862 some of the Asiatic crab apples had reached America. *Malus floribunda, sieboldii, x micromalus,* and *halliana parkmanii* all were being grown in this country prior to 1865. In 1892 Professor Charles S. Sargent, director of the Arnold Arboretum, went to Japan and sent several Asiatic crab apples back from the Orient, including one that was named after him, *M. sargentii.* A few years later, E. H. Wilson, also of the Arnold Arboretum, sent several back from his various expeditions to China and Japan. Among these was *M. toringoides,* one of the handsomest of all in fruit, sent to this country in 1904. Hundreds of other varieties have been introduced since. They are now widely distributed over the United States and Canada. Because of the ease with which cross-fertilization takes place, new hybrids are continually appearing, and there is always the possibility of a new hybrid being decidedly worthwhile.

⇢≫ REASONS FOR GROWING CRAB APPLES

1. **Flowers.** Crab apples have many uses both ornamentally and economically. In the first place, they are planted for the beautiful flowers that usually appear in May before the lilacs bloom. The majority of the species and varieties have single flowers, but there are some with semidouble and double blossoms, comparing favorably with the double-flowering Oriental cherries, though the flower clusters are not as large. The colors range from pure white to dark purplish red, with many variations of pink and red between the extremes. Consequently, there is a wide range of color in the flowers, and within the limits noted, varieties can be selected for one particular color that may fit in with a planting scheme better than another. Not the least of the assets of the crab apples is their beauty in bud. Even though the flowers of many are

pure white, the buds may be pink or even red and white. As the flowers open, this color may gradually fade to white. In some varieties the color of the flower buds and the flowers is identical.

Most varieties have flowers that are very fragrant—another valued asset. *Malus baccata* and its varieties are exceptionally so, and this characteristic adds materially to the effectiveness of these plants when in bloom.

2. **Fruits.** The fruits range in size from that of a small pea to 2 inches in diameter, and the colors from pure red to pure yellow, with all intermediate shades and combinations. Many of the species native to this country have green fruits that are not of particular ornamental value. The fruits of some varieties begin to show color in early August, while almost all have colored fruits during the month of September. After that, the fruits of many varieties begin to drop, while those of a few varieties may remain all fall and even well into the winter. These bright-colored fruits are decidedly ornamental and make the crab apples bearing them doubly valuable since there are two seasons during which these plants are of ornamental interest. The Oriental flowering cherries cannot boast two seasons of effective beauty.

3. **Habit.** The crab apples in general are small trees, less than 20 feet tall. A few are standard trees while others are round and moundlike in habit, more like large shrubs. A few have very pendulous branches and are comparable to the weeping cherry so popular in American gardens. Others are supposed to be, but apparently as they grow older the weight of the fruits they bear forces the upright branches to a more horizontal position. Thus, with columnar, pendulous, moundlike, small- and tall-growing varieties available, there is a considerable variation of habit that can be utilized in planting.

4. **Foliage color.** The majority of the crab apples have leaves that are a normal green, but some have leaves that retain a reddish to bronze color throughout the entire growing season. These colors are not brilliant but nevertheless are sufficiently evident so that the plants can be used to splendid advantage. The color of the foliage is just red, bronze, or dark green enough to make these varieties stand out from surrounding plants, while at the same time blending pleasingly with them. There are other varieties that have conspicuously colored young foliage, but the color usually disappears after the leaves reach maturity.

Contrary to general belief, there are a few crab apples that do have autumn color. Whether they do depends largely on the climatic conditions of an area; when temperature, sunshine, exposure, and even soil conditions are just right during the early fall, autumn coloration on certain types of plants can be expected. One of the most important factors is a southwestern exposure, where the warm rays of the sun late in the afternoon will warm the leaves and a quick drop in temperature immediately after sunset (approximately to 45°F) may bring autumn coloration. Only a few varieties of the genus *Malus* have been known to color materially in the fall, but these should be noted and this characteristic might be used in planting.

5. **Wildlife preservation.** The fruits of crab apples are very attractive to many kinds of birds, and because of their ability to hold their fruits long into the winter, certain varieties are excellent as sources of food for wildlife. 'Bob White' is one example. It is a hybrid and came to the attention of Arnold Arboretum staff members because it held its fruits all winter. In the fall, when birds eat the fruits of other crab apples, none touch the hard fruits of this variety. However, in January and February, after the fruits of most other plants fall to the ground and after successively cold days freeze the fruits of 'Bob White' and they become somewhat softened, they are sought out especially by the pheasants. On a day in February, I once counted six pheasants eating the fruits from this tree at one time, and when one considers that this tree is only a few hundred feet from one of Boston's main automobile arteries, one can understand the value of this variety in offering food at a time when other natural food is practically unobtainable.

6. **Economic uses.** Crab apples replace apples in the colder portions of the Midwest and the provinces of Canada where winter temperatures are so low that the ordinary apple varieties do not prove hardy. One of the recently introduced economic varieties of crab apples has withstood temperatures of 59°F below zero. In the past many varieties have been bred solely for this purpose, and even now some new varieties are appearing from certain of the Canadian government experiment stations. Of course in such areas it is those crab apples with the largest fruits that are of value. A number of these are now being grown, but the demand for them is limited, of course, to certain very cold areas.

Even though ornamental crab apples are grown purely for their noneconomic qualities, some people do like to experiment with making jelly from the fruits. A number of years ago, fruits of fourteen different species of *Malus* were made into jellies by one of the staff members of the Arnold Arboretum. The fruits of *M. purpurea, glabrata, lancifolia,* and *coronaria* made good jelly with fair pectin content. Some were improved by the addition of a few fruits of *M. purpurea* for additional coloring. Fruits of *M. sargentii, floribunda, baccata, micromalus,* and *zumi* made rather poor jelly because the fruits were so small they did not yield much juice. Usually the larger the fruits, the easier (and the more practical) it is to obtain sufficient juice to make good jelly.

⇢≫ DISEASES AND INSECT PESTS

Crab apples are susceptible to the various troubles of the common apple, namely, fire blight, scale, and borers. The scale insects are kept in check by a dormant spray of some miscible oil applied anytime between the middle of February and early April. Lime sulfur can be used, but since crab apples are frequently growing in prominent places, it might be inadvisable because of the discoloring effect on the trees themselves and on adjacent shrubbery or buildings.

Apparently the Oriental crab apples are not severely infested with fire blight. Varieties that have been hybridized with the common apple (this refers particularly to certain "economic" crab apples bred for their large fruit) may suffer from this pernicious disease. 'Transcendent' is one variety that has been notably susceptible to the disease in southern Canada and has been discarded in many places for this reason. There is little that can be done in the matter of controlling fire blight except to cut out infested branches or trees, sterilizing the tools afterward, and burning the affected parts at once. Often an unusually heavy application of nitrogenous fertilizer will cause excessive vegetative growth, and fire blight may become pronounced. This can usually be alleviated somewhat by correspondingly heavy applications of phosphorus and potash fertilizers.

Several borers infest all apple and crab apple trees, especially the flat-headed and round-headed apple tree borers. About the only method of control is to examine the bases of young trees in the spring and fall for fresh borings and to eradicate the borers at once. This can be done by digging them out with a knife and killing them by forcing a wire up the hole, or by inserting a few drops of paradichlorobenzene in the hole and stopping it up at once.

Certain crab apples, notably *M. ioensis* 'Plena,' are susceptible to the cedar rust disease, serving as alternate hosts with the junipers. In the late summer the leaves become covered with disfiguring brown blotches. Spraying with colloidal sulfur has proved effective, using five to six applications seven to ten days apart, beginning before the first expected rains after the leaf buds have opened. Also a trade fungicide called Fermate has proved very effective in the control of this disease.

Fortunately, the Oriental crab apples do not appear to be susceptible to this disease, a very important fact that should be noted in making selections of varieties for planting. It is equally important to note that Oriental crab apples do not appear to be severely troubled with fire blight. At least this has proved the case in the Arnold Arboretum, where the collection is adjacent to a severely infested group of pear trees.

Apple scab has emerged as a serious disease on certain Oriental crab apples, especially in the Midwest, defoliating many trees. Some nurseries in this area have stopped growing some of the more susceptible varieties. At present apple scab is not a serious disease on Oriental crab apples in the northeastern United States. Dr. Lester P. Nichols, of the Department of Plant Pathology at Pennsylvania State University, has made preliminary studies in many collections of the eastern United States, and I have noted his findings as "resistant" or "susceptible" in the following text. Further studies may alter these, but the information is presented for what it is worth.

It is not necessary to spray the fruits of crab apples if they are meant only to be ornamental. If the fruits are to be used for any economic purpose, however, it may be necessary to follow the apple spray schedule recommended for each particular region by the state agricultural experiment stations.

We have made a careful survey of the 250 crab apple species and varieties in the Arnold Arboretum each year during the past twelve years in order to determine those trees that flower and fruit annually and those that do so only in alternate years. With so many crab apple varieties available now, it seems unwise to recommend alternate-bearing ones. Alternate-bearing varieties that have been found to be susceptible to apple scab have also been dropped from the following list. 'Aldenham,' 'Almey,' 'Crimson Brilliant,' 'Eleyi,' 'Hopa,' 'Strathmore,' and some other popular varieties are not recommended for further planting for this reason. New varieties such as 'Blanche Ames,' 'Red Jade,' 'Snowbank,' and 'Vanguard' have been added to the list of recommended varieties merely because their annual bearing habit is a valued ornamental characteristic.

Malus 'Adams'   24'   Zone 4

* FLOWERS: single, 1½" in diameter, carmine buds and flowers, fading to dull pink
        TIME: mid-May
* FRUIT: red, ⅝" in diameter
        EFFECTIVE: September and October
HABIT: rounded and dense
ORIGIN: Adams Nursery, Westfield, Massachusetts
INTRODUCED: before 1952

A good annual-bearing tree, resistant to apple scab.

Malus 'American Beauty' (Plant Patent #2821)   30'   Zone 4

* FLOWERS: large, double, red
        TIME: spring
FRUIT: sparse
HABIT: upright

A desirable crab apple because of its double, deep red flowers and its few fruits, where these can prove superfluous. However, it is extremely susceptible to scab.

x Malus arnoldiana   20'   Zone 4   Arnold crab apple

* FLOWERS: bud rose-red; flower fragrant, phlox pink outside, fading to white inside,
  2" in diameter
  TIME: early May
* FRUIT: yellow and red, ⅝" in diameter
  EFFECTIVE: September and October
* HABIT: mounded, dense branching
  FOLIAGE: dense, fine textured
  HYBRID ORIGIN: *M. floribunda x M. baccata*
  ORIGINATED: 1883

Originated as a chance seedling in the Arnold Arboretum and one of the best in flower, especially because of its deep red flower buds that contrast well with the light pink to white of the opening flowers. Some clones bear annually.

x Malus atrosanguinea   20'   Zone 4   Carmine crab apple

* FLOWERS: buds crimson; flower rose-madder, 1¼" in diameter
  TIME: mid-May
  FRUIT: dark red, ⅜" in diameter, not ornamental
  EFFECTIVE: late August to late October
* HABIT: mounded, almost shrublike, dense branching
  FOLIAGE: dense, glossy, dark green
  HYBRID ORIGIN: *M. halliana x M. sieboldii*
  ORIGINATED: before 1889

This hybrid is cultivated a great deal in Japan and was introduced into America from Japan by the Arnold Arboretum. When it is in full bloom, the flowers are a rich carmine, but they fade to a rather unsightly pink just before they fall. One of the smaller trees, it is good for contrast with some of the taller white-flowering varieties. The foliage of this species is about the best of any crab apple. It bears annually and is resistant to apple scab.

Malus baccata   50'   Zone 2   Siberian crab apple

* FLOWERS: very fragrant, white, 1–1½" in diameter
  TIME: early May
* FRUIT: red or yellow, ⅜" in diameter, varies considerably
  EFFECTIVE: late August to late October
  HABIT: vigorous, upright, narrow head, dense branching
  FOLIAGE: dense

HABITAT: northeastern Asia
INTRODUCED: before 1800
VARIETIES:

> *gracilis*—white flowers, 1⅜" in diameter, more dense than the species, with the tips of the branches slightly pendulous. The leaves are smaller, giving the entire tree a more refined appearance. Commercial growers will continue to offer the species because it grows readily from seed, but this and the following variety are really superior and should be used instead where possible.
> 'Jackii'—one of the best of the Siberian crab apples for its glossy red fruits, about ⅜" in diameter, but susceptible to fire blight
> *mandshurica*—flowers white, 1½" in diameter, appearing in late April, making this the first of the crab apples to bloom

Actually a standard tree, one of the hardiest of all the *Malus,* used considerably in hybridizing in an effort to obtain hardier apples of commercial sizes, especially for the prairie provinces of Canada. Many varieties of this widely distributed species have been described, some very meagerly indeed. The point to keep in mind is that since these are readily grown from seed by the commercial grower, the sizes of flowers and the sizes and colors of the fruits will vary considerably. If a particular type is wanted, make certain the plants have been asexually propagated from the desired specimen. It is one of the taller crab apples and so should not be used on small properties. On the other hand, in parks or other large areas, it has its place especially as a background tree for other crab apples since its flowers are white and profusely borne annually. It is resistant to apple scab.

Malus 'Barbara Ann'   25'   Zone 4

* FLOWERS: deep purplish pink, 2" in diameter with 12–15 petals
      TIME: mid-May
FRUIT: purplish, ½" in diameter
      EFFECTIVE: fall
FOLIAGE: purplish green
ORIGIN: Arnold Arboretum, 1957; seedling of 'Dorothea'

A good ornamental because of its double flowers but unfortunately susceptible to scab.

x *Malus* 'Baskatong'   30'   Zone 4

* FLOWERS: single, 1¼" in diameter, carmine buds and flowers, fading to a dull pink
      TIME: mid-May
FRUIT: red
      EFFECTIVE: early fall
HYBRID ORIGIN: second generation cross ('Simcoe' x 'Meach')
INTRODUCED: Central Experiment Farm, Ottawa, Canada, before 1950

One of the most ornamental of the rosybloom crab apples, this retains its reddish bronze foliage throughout the season and is resistant to apple scab.

Malus 'Beauty'   24'   Zone 3

* FLOWERS: single, white, 1¾" in diameter
          TIME: mid-May
* FRUIT: bright red, 1" in diameter, edible
          EFFECTIVE: early fall
* HABIT: fastigiate
   FOLIAGE: very resistant to fire blight
   ORIGIN: N. E. Hansen, Brookings, South Dakota, from seed imported from Russia, probably a clone of *M. robusta*

Bears flowers well only in alternate years but is resistant to apple scab.

Malus 'Blanche Ames'   24'   Zone 4

* FLOWERS: semidouble, pink and white, 1½" in diameter
          TIME: mid-May
   FRUIT: yellow, ¼" in diameter
          EFFECTIVE: October
   HABIT: rounded and dense
   ORIGIN: seeds from an open-pollinated *M. spectabilis* 'Riversii' in the Arnold Arboretum in 1939
   INTRODUCED: 1947 under the number 6639

This was named by Dr. Karl Sax of the Arnold Arboretum, Jamaica Plain, Massachusetts, in honor of Mrs. Oakes Ames, wife of the former supervisor of the Arnold Arboretum. It is recommended here because it has proved to be annual-bearing with fine crops of flowers during each of the past thirty-six years and apparently is resistant to apple scab.

x *Malus* 'Bob White'   20'   Zone 4

* FLOWERS: buds cherry color; flowers fragrant, fade to white, 1" in diameter
          TIME: early May
* FRUIT: yellow, ⅜" in diameter
          EFFECTIVE: all winter
   HABIT: rounded, dense branching
   FOLIAGE: dense, fine textured
   HYBRID ORIGIN: clone of *M. zumi*
   ORIGINATED: before 1876

Of interest because the fruits remain on the tree all winter and afford food for the birds at times when snow covers most of the available food, but they are borne in alternate years.

Malus 'Brandywine'   24'   Zone 4

* FLOWERS: double, deep rose-pink
      TIME: spring
  FOLIAGE: vigorous, large, dark green

Bothered moderately with scab, severely with rust.

Malus brevipes   15'   Zone 5   Nippon crab apple

* FLOWERS: fragrant, whitish, ¾″ in diameter; borne in alternate years
      TIME: early May
* FRUIT: red, ⅜″ in diameter
  EFFECTIVE: late August to mid-November
* HABIT: mounded, dense branching
  FOLIAGE: dense, fine textured
  ORIGIN: unknown, cultivated since 1883

Chiefly valued because it is small, dense, and rounded and because its fruits turn color in early August, thus making a conspicuous color combination with the green foliage considerably before the fruits of most crab apples color. It fruits well only in alternate years.

Malus 'Callaway'   15–25'   Zone 4

* FLOWERS: white
      TIME: spring
* FRUIT: large, reddish maroon, ¾–1¼″ in diameter
  EFFECTIVE: remaining on plant for some time
  ORIGIN: seedling selection by Callaway Gardens from *M. prunifolia* seedlings

One of the best for southern gardens.

Malus coronaria 'Nieuwlandiana'   20'   Zone 4

* FLOWERS: double, pink, 1¼–2¼″ in diameter, 13–27 petals
      TIME: late May to early June
  FRUIT: green, 1¾″ in diameter
  HABIT: wide, often shrubby
  ORIGIN: raised by B. H. Slavin, Rochester, New York, in 1931

This is similar to 'Charlottae,' but the flowers are larger and a deeper pink. It is very fragrant and bears flowers annually. 'Charlottae,' however, is an excellent annual-flowering crab apple also resistant to apple scab.

Malus 'Dolgo'   40′   Zone 3

* FLOWERS: fragrant, white, 1¾″ in diameter, blooming well in alternate years
   TIME: early May
* FRUIT: bright red, 1¼″ in diameter
   EFFECTIVE: August
 HABIT: rather open but vigorous
 FOLIAGE: dense
 ORIGINATED: grown from seed collected in Russia by Dr. Niels E. Hansen in 1897

Dr. Niels E. Hansen, formerly professor of horticulture at the South Dakota Agricultural Experiment Station, was interested in the production of hardier fruits for over half a century. This crab apple was one he introduced in 1917, especially for its early fruits that color and ripen in August, before the fruits of most other *Malus* species and varieties color. It is a vigorous grower, recommended as being particularly hardy and adaptable for growing in the prairie provinces of Canada, where many other crab apples fail. Its fruits make excellent jelly. It is scab resistant.

x Malus *'Dorothea.'*

Malus 'Donald Wyman'   30'   Zone 4

* FLOWERS: buds pink; flowers single, white
        TIME: spring
* FRUIT: glossy bright red, ⅜" in diameter, abundant
        EFFECTIVE: persistent into winter
   HABIT: spreading
   ORIGIN: seedling in Arnold Arboretum

An excellent form, one of the best as an ornamental.

x *Malus* 'Dorothea'   25'   Zone 4

* FLOWERS: buds rose-opal colored; semidouble (16 petals), crimson to Tyrian rose,
        1⅝–2" in diameter
        TIME: mid-May
* FRUIT: bright yellow, ½" in diameter
        EFFECTIVE: fall until early winter
   HABIT: rounded, dense branching
   FOLIAGE: dense, fine textured
   HYBRID ORIGIN: *M. halliana parkmanii x arnoldiana*
   ORIGINATED: found as a chance seedling in Arnold Arboretum, May 17, 1943

The yellow fruit of x Malus *'Dorothea.'*

This seedling was first noted in bloom when it was 5 feet high. The foliage resembles the Parkman crab apple somewhat, while the fruit resembles that of *M. arnoldiana*. It is one of the very few semidouble-flowered crab apples that also bear fruit, and particularly beautiful fruit. It is named after my older daughter, Dorothea, and is a valuable addition to the crab apple group. Another very important characteristic is that it bears flowers and fruits annually, something that unfortunately cannot be claimed for many crab apples. Also it blooms early in life; young plants grafted one year frequently bloom the next. Unfortunately it is severely susceptible to scab and fire blight.

Malus 'Edna Mullins'   20'   Zone 4

* FLOWERS: double, white
        TIME: May
  FRUIT: small, cherrylike, salmon-coral
        EFFECTIVE: red twigs in the winter
  HABIT: pendulous branches, gracefully growing
  ORIGIN: 1974, originated at Arnold Arboretum but grown and named by Weston
        Nurseries, Hopkinton, Massachusetts. Named for a receptionist there.

Relatively disease resistant.

x Malus 'Evelyn'   20'   Zone 3

* FLOWERS: single, pink, 1½" in diameter
        TIME: mid-May
  FRUIT: red, 1¼" in diameter
        EFFECTIVE: fall
* HABIT: erect
* FOLIAGE: purplish, turning bronze-green in the summer
  HYBRID ORIGIN: A. F. den Boer, Des Moines, Iowa, 1939 (probably *M. ioensis x purpurea*)

One of the few crab apples to have interesting autumn color (under certain conditions), that being purple, red, and orange. It is resistant to apple scab.

Malus 'Flame'   25'   Zone 2

* FLOWERS: pink buds; flowers fading white
        TIME: early May
* FRUIT: bright red, ¾" in diameter
        EFFECTIVE: late August to mid-November
  HABIT: rounded
  FOLIAGE: dense
  ORIGIN: about 1920 as a chance seedling at the University of Minnesota State Fruit
        Farm, Excelsior, Minnesota

'Flame' has proved a valuable ornamental in the colder areas of Minnesota and so has value in such areas where other crab apples may not prove hardy. It bears annually and is resistant to apple scab.

Malus floribunda   30′   Zone 4   Japanese flowering crab apple

* FLOWERS: buds deep pink to red; flowers fragrant, gradually fading to white, 1–1½″ in diameter
    TIME: early May
* FRUIT: yellow and red, ⅜″ in diameter
    EFFECTIVE: late August to mid-October
* HABIT: rounded and densely branched
    FOLIAGE: dense, fine textured
    HABITAT: Japan
    INTRODUCED: 1862

This standard flowering ornamental tree has performed very well indeed all over its hardiness range in America since it was introduced. It grows readily from seed, makes vigorous growth, and blooms while comparatively young. It is dense and rounded in habit, with branches facing the ground well on all sides. Other crab apples may surpass it in color, size of flower, or fruit, but none are more dependably beautiful year in and year out. It bears annually.

Malus 'Gorgeous'   30′   Zone 4

* FLOWERS: pink buds followed by single, white flowers, 1¼″ in diameter
    TIME: mid-May
* FRUIT: red, 1″ in diameter
    EFFECTIVE: fall
  HABIT: dense, rounded
  ORIGIN: seedling received from H. R. Wright, Auckland, New Zealand, 1925
  INTRODUCED: U.S. Department of Agriculture, Glenn Dale, Maryland (P. I. [Plant Introduction] 64833)

Another annual bearer, apparently resistant to apple scab.

Malus halliana parkmanii   15′   Zone 5   Parkman crab apple

* FLOWERS: double (15 petals), rose color, 1¼″ in diameter
    TIME: early May
  FRUIT: dull red, ¼″ in diameter
    EFFECTIVE: September to mid-November
* HABIT: upright, almost vase-shaped, dense branching
  FOLIAGE: fairly open, lustrous, leathery
  INTRODUCED: 1861 from Japan where it was cultivated—a garden plant of unknown origin

A very beautiful, double, pink crab apple, the least hardy of over 150 kinds growing in the Arnold Arboretum. The foliage is dark, glossy green, but the fruit is very small, dull in color, and hence not too noticeable. This is very definitely not a crab apple with two seasons of interest, but many who have come to like this old-fashioned variety will not want to part with it for one of the hardier varieties. It carries the names of the two men responsible for introducing it as well as some other interesting and valued Japanese plants. Dr. George R. Hall was a doctor who practiced medicine in the foreign settlement of Shanghai, China, in 1861, and he also traveled widely in Japan. He sent this Asiatic garden specimen to his good friend Francis Parkman of Boston, who grew it for the first time in America.

x *Malus* 'Henry F. DuPont'   20'   Zone 4

* FLOWERS: carmine buds; flowers single or semidouble, fading to dull pink, 1½" in
        diameter
        TIME: mid-May
* FRUIT: red, ½" in diameter
        EFFECTIVE: fall
* HABIT: low, rounded
        HYBRID ORIGIN: seedling of 'Henrietta Crosby' at the Arnold Arboretum, Jamaica
        Plain, Massachusetts, 1946

A fine, low-spreading type with better-colored flowers than some of the others, bearing annually. It is resistant to apple scab.

Malus hupehensis   24'   Zone 4   Tea crab apple

* FLOWERS: deep pink buds; flowers fragrant, gradually fading to white, 1½" in
        diameter
        TIME: early May
    FRUIT: greenish yellow to red, ⅜" in diameter
        EFFECTIVE: September and October
* HABIT: vase-shaped, decidedly picturesque
    FOLIAGE: loose and open
    HABITAT: China
    INTRODUCED: by the Arnold Arboretum, 1900

The tea crab apple is the most picturesque of all because it is vase-shaped in habit, with long-reaching, single branches growing from the trunk and spreading out like the ribs of a fan. In bud and flower it is beautiful, and its marked habit is clearly evident every season of the year. The flowers are produced on small spurs or short branches up and down the entire length of the long, straight branches (only in alternate years); the fruits are small and not especially colorful.

x *Malus hupehensis* 'Strawberry Parfait' (Plant Patent #4632)
30'   Zone 4

* FLOWERS: very fragrant, carmine-red, with deep pink edges
       TIME: spring
  HABIT: same as the species
  FOLIAGE: disease-free
  ORIGIN: male parent was *M. atrosanguinea*
  INTRODUCED: 1982

Malus ioensis 'Plena'   30'   Zone 2   Bechtel crab apple

* FLOWERS: buds and flowers fragrant, double (33 petals), pink, 2" in diameter
       TIME: late May
  FRUIT: green, 1⅛" in diameter, few produced
  HABIT: rounded head, open
  FOLIAGE: leaves rather large and coarse, susceptible to spots of juniper rust
  ORIGIN: discovered in a fence row by E. A. Bechtel of Staunton, Illinois, between
       1840 and 1850
  INTRODUCED: 1888

A very popular crab apple for the past seventy-five years, its place is now being taken by several of the exotic Oriental crab apples because all native species belong to the group often seriously infested with the unsightly brown spots of the cedar apple rust. This can be controlled by excessive spraying if red-cedars must be grown in the near vicinity of the crab apples, but the species native to the Orient are not susceptible. The Bechtel crab apple has only a few fruits and these are green; not at all ornamental, while several of the double-flowering Orientals (and their hybrids) have brightly colored red or yellow fruits.

It must be admitted that it is beautiful when in full bloom; its flowers look like small rambler roses and it blooms late, after most of the other crab apples have passed. All in all, however, I think that several of the newer varieties will take its place.

x *Malus* 'Katherine'   20'   Zone 4

* FLOWERS: double (20 petals), light pink fading to white, 2¼" in diameter
       TIME: mid-May
  FRUIT: dull red, ¼" in diameter
       EFFECTIVE: fall and early winter
  HABIT: loose and open
  FOLIAGE: dark green
  HYBRID ORIGIN: *M. halliana x M. baccata*
  ORIGINATED: as a seedling in Durand-Eastman Park, Rochester, New York, about
       1928

This seedling was first noted by B. H. Slavin of the Rochester park system, where the original plant still grows. I named it after Mr. Slavin's daughter-in-law, Katherine

x Malus *'Katherine,'*
another double-flowered crab
apple.

Clark Slavin, and the Arnold Arboretum introduced it in 1943. 'Katherine' has unusually large double flowers, followed by small red fruits. It is more open in its branching habits than many members of this genus. This tree is simply covered with flowers and fruits each year.

Malus 'Liset'   15–24′   Zone 4

* FLOWERS: single, rose-red to light crimson, 1½″ in diameter
     TIME: mid-May
* FRUIT: glossy, deep crimson, ½″ in diameter, persistent
     EFFECTIVE: fall
FOLIAGE: purplish green
ORIGIN: Netherlands

Slightly susceptible to fire blight. Rounded in habit.

x *Malus* 'Makamik'   40′   Zone 4

* FLOWERS: China rose color, 1⅝″ in diameter
    TIME: one of the latest of the rosybloom crab apples to flower, early May
* FRUIT: purplish red, 2¼″ in diameter
    EFFECTIVE: fall and throughout the winter
HABIT: rounded
FOLIAGE: dense
HYBRID ORIGIN: *M. pumila niedzwetzkyana* open pollinated
ORIGINATED: 1920; named 1930

This tree is one of the better annual-blooming rosybloom crab apples, so named by Isabella Preston of the Dominion Experimental Station, Ottawa, Canada, who was responsible for collecting the seed and naming twenty-two selected forms. This variety is an improvement over *M. pumila niedzwetzkyana,* for on this species the fruit is nearly 2¼ inches in diameter, so large that it should be sprayed at frequent intervals (like commercial apples) or the fruit will be disfigured by insects and disease. In any event, the fruit is so large that it is really out of the crab apple class—and at the same time is too small for a commercial apple. It is resistant to apple scab.

    The flowers of most of the rosybloom crab apples, like their parent, have the disconcerting habit of fading rapidly to a washed-out reddish color that is not particularly desirable, but when they are approaching full bloom, there certainly is nothing quite like them.

Malus 'Marshall Oyama'

* FLOWERS: single, pink buds followed by white flowers, 1⅝″ in diameter
    TIME: mid-May
* FRUIT: yellow and red, 1″ in diameter
    EFFECTIVE: fall
* HABIT: narrowly upright
ORIGIN: probably from Japan
INTRODUCED: Boyce Thompson Institute, Yonkers, New York, 1930

This is the most narrowly upright of the crab apples; to retain this habit, it should be pruned occasionally to prevent the development of too many side shoots. It bears annually and is resistant to apple scab.

Malus 'Mary Potter'   20′   Zone 4

* FLOWERS: single, open to white, 1″ in diameter
    TIME: mid-May
* FRUIT: red, ½″ in diameter
    EFFECTIVE: fall
ORIGIN: 1947, introduced by the Arnold Arboretum, a cross between *M. atrosanguinea* and *M. sargentii rosea*

Will come true from seed; moderately susceptible to several diseases.

x *Malus* 'Oekonomierat Echtermeyer'   15'   Zone 4

* FLOWERS: purplish red, 1½" in diameter
    TIME: early May
* FRUIT: reddish purple, 1" in diameter
    EFFECTIVE: September
* HABIT: semiweeping
  FOLIAGE: bronze-green
  HYBRID ORIGIN: *M. pumila niedzwetzkyana x M.* 'Exzellenz Thiel'
  ORIGINATED: Spaeth Nurseries, Germany, 1914

Interesting because of its graceful, semipendulous habit; it should be grafted or budded rather high on upright understock to be most effective. A plant now in the trade called 'Pink Weeper' is synonymous with this variety. It is unfortunate that it is susceptible to apple scab.

Malus 'Ormiston Roy'   24'   Zone 4

* FLOWERS: single, pale pink to pure white, 1½" in diameter
    TIME: mid-May
* FRUIT: yellow, ⅜" in diameter
    EFFECTIVE: fall and sometimes most of the winter
  ORIGIN: unknown; before 1933
  INTRODUCED: A. F. den Boer, Des Moines, Iowa

Bearing annually, this is especially noted for its profuse fruits, which may last until March, thus proving excellent winter bird food.

Malus 'Pink Perfection' (Plant Patent #2912)   24'   Zone 4

* FLOWERS: red bud, opening to a double, clear pink flower, 1¾" in diameter
    TIME: May
  FRUIT: yellow, ½" in diameter, sparse
  FOLIAGE: dense
  ORIGIN: cross between 'Katherine' and 'Almey.' Originated by the Princeton Nurseries, Princeton, New Jersey

This tree has a great future as a street tree.

x *Malus* 'Prince Georges'   25'   Zone 4

* FLOWERS: double (50 petals), light pink, 2" in diameter
    TIME: late May

HABIT: upright, dense
FOLIAGE: dense, rather coarse
HYBRID ORIGIN: *M. ioensis* 'Plena' x *M. angustifolia*
ORIGINATED: 1919

Seeds of this crab apple were collected in the Arnold Arboretum by the Division of Plant Exploration and Introduction of the U.S. Department of Agriculture in 1919, and in 1930 scions from one of the resulting seedlings were returned to the Arnold Arboretum. The flowers have more petals and the leaves are narrower than those of *M. ioensis* 'Plena.' Also, it apparently is not as much troubled with disease as the Bechtel crab apple, although the flowers are similar. It is named after the county in Maryland where it was first grown by the Department of Agriculture. It bears annually and is resistant to apple scab.

x *Malus purpurea* 'Lemoinei'   25'   Zone 4

* FLOWERS: single and semidouble, Tyrian rose, the deepest color of any of the varieties of this species, 1½" in diameter
   TIME: early May
* FRUIT: purplish red, ⅝" in diameter, bearing annually
   EFFECTIVE: late August to late October
HABIT: dense
* FOLIAGE: dark green to almost purplish green
HYBRID ORIGIN: *M. pumila niedzwetzkyana* x *M. atrosanguinea*
ORIGINATED: in the Lemoine's Nursery, France, 1922

At the time this is being written, Lemoine's crab apple has the darkest flowers of any of the *Malus* species. It is decidedly ornamental and is prominent anywhere. It is far superior to *M. purpurea* and *M. pumila niedzwetzkyana* because of the darker colored flowers and also because they do not fade nearly as much.

Recently it has been found to be resistant to apple scab, and examinations at the Arnold Arboretum have shown it to be annual-bearing. Since both the 'Aldenham' and the 'Eley' crab apples have proved susceptible to scab and both are alternate-bearing, they have been suggested for discard. This makes 'Lemoinei' about the best and most reliable of the purple-flowering crab apples.

Malus 'Red Baron'   24'   Zone 4

* FLOWERS: single, deep red
   TIME: mid-May
* FRUIT: glossy, dark red
   EFFECTIVE: fall
HABIT: narrow, columnar

This is severely susceptible to scab and slightly susceptible to fire blight, but it has been left on the list because of the deep red color of the flowers.

x *Malus* 'Red Jade'   20'   Zone 4

* FLOWERS: small, single, white
        TIME: mid-May
* FRUIT: bright red, ½" in diameter
        EFFECTIVE: fall and into winter
* HABIT: pendulous branches
  ORIGIN: hybrid
  INTRODUCED: 1953, by the Brooklyn Botanic Garden

An interesting pendulous-branched tree noted for its habit and profuse scarlet fruit that lasts well into the winter. It has proved alternate in its bearing.

x *Malus robusta*   40'   Zone 3   Cherry crab apple

* FLOWERS: fragrant, white, sometimes slightly pink, 1¾" in diameter
        TIME: early May
* FRUIT: red and yellow, ¾–1½" in diameter
        EFFECTIVE: September and October
  HABIT: oval-shaped, dense branching
  FOLIAGE: dense
  HYBRID ORIGIN: *M. baccata* x *M. prunifolia*
  ORIGINATED: about 1815
  VARIETIES:
      'Erecta'—only mentioned for its upright habit while young; as it matures the
          side branches are often weighted down with fruit and it loses its narrow,
          upright habit
      'Persicifolia' *(Peachleaf crab apple)*—excellent ornamental red fruit, ¾" in diam-
          eter, that remain colorful on the tree until the first of the year

Since this is a so-called hybrid species, every one of the progeny of this cross is a clone. In the Arnold Arboretum there were growing at one time nearly twenty clones of this cross, varying considerably in size of flowers and size and color of the fruit. One of the best was a white-flowering clone with fruit about an inch in diameter, deep red on the side exposed to the sun and yellow on the shaded portion. One should be very careful in buying plants offered under this name because of this considerable varia-tion. It bears every other year.

x *Malus* 'Rosseau'   40'   Zone 4

* FLOWERS: China rose color, 1¾" in diameter
        TIME: early May
* FRUIT: rosy red, about ½–1" in diameter
        EFFECTIVE: late August to mid-October
  HABIT: rounded
  FOLIAGE: dense

HYBRID ORIGIN: *M. pumila niedzwetzkyana* open pollinated
ORIGINATED: 1920, named 1930

An annual-bearing rosybloom crab apple (see *M.* 'Makamik'), valued because its fruits are a little more colorful than others of this group.

x *Malus scheideckeri*   20′   Zone 4   Scheidecker crab apple

* FLOWERS: double (10 petals), pale pink, 1½″ in diameter
      TIME: early May
FRUIT: yellow to orange, ⅝″ in diameter
      EFFECTIVE: September
HABIT: upright
FOLIAGE: dense
HYBRID ORIGIN: *M. floribunda x M. prunifolia*
ORIGINATED: before 1888 in the Scheidecker Nursery, Germany

An old-fashioned crab apple, it is resistant to apple scab and bears annually.

Malus 'Sentinel'   24′   Zone 4

* FLOWERS: single, pale pink
      TIME: mid-May
* FRUIT: small, red, ½″ in diameter
      EFFECTIVE: fall
HABIT: narrow, upright
ORIGIN: introduced by Simpson Orchard Co., Vincennes, Indiana. Named in 1978.

This has only slight susceptibility to fire blight and scab.

Malus sieboldii arborescens   30′   Zone 5   Tree toringo crab apple

* FLOWERS: pink buds; flowers fragrant, fading to white, ¾″ in diameter
      TIME: mid-May
* FRUIT: yellow to red, ½″ in diameter, bearing annually
      EFFECTIVE: late August to mid-November
* HABIT: mounded, dense branching
FOLIAGE: dense
HABITAT: Japan, Korea
INTRODUCED: 1892

Not particularly outstanding but mentioned here only because of its late bloom, for it is one of the last to flower. If time of bloom is not a factor in the selection of varieties, this one might well be overlooked.

x *Malus* 'Sissipuk'   40'   Zone 4

* FLOWERS: purplish red, 1⅛" in diameter
     TIME: mid-May
* FRUIT: purplish red, ¾" in diameter
     EFFECTIVE: fall and throughout the winter
HABIT: rounded
FOLIAGE: dense
HYBRID ORIGIN: *M. pumila niedzwetzkyana* open pollinated
ORIGINATED: 1920, named 1930

Another of the rosybloom crab apples (see under *M.* 'Makamik'). It is an annual bearer, and since the fruit remains all winter, it has considerable merit in the winter garden. It is the last of the selected rosybloom crab apples to bloom.

Malus 'Snowbank'   24'   Zone 4

* FLOWERS: buds pink; flowers single, white, 1¼" in diameter
     TIME: mid-May
FRUIT: yellow, ¼" in diameter
     EFFECTIVE: October
HABIT: dense, rounded
ORIGIN: a seedling or hybrid of *M. floribunda* selected by H. P. Kelsey, East Boxford, Massachusetts, prior to 1934
INTRODUCED: Kelsey-Highlands Nursery, East Boxford, Massachusetts, 1934

Although this is supposed to be considerably mixed up in American nurseries, possibly with other *M. floribunda* seedlings, the plant in the Arnold Arboretum has been a consistent annual bearer and is apparently resistant to apple scab—two important reasons that it should be grown.

Malus 'Snowcloud' (Plant Patent #2913)   30'   Zone 4

* FLOWERS: double, pure white, 2" in diameter
     TIME: May
FRUIT: sparse, yellow, ½" in diameter
HABIT: upright, rapid growth
FOLIAGE: dark green, disease-free
ORIGIN: cross between 'Katherine' and 'Almey.' Originated by Princeton Nurseries, Princeton, New Jersey

An excellent crab apple with better flowers than any other white-flowered double variety.

Malus spectabilis 'Riversii' 24' Zone 4 River's crab apple

* FLOWERS: double (9–12 petals), pink, 2″ in diameter, bearing in alternate years
  TIME: early May
FRUIT: green, 1¼″ in diameter, not effective
HABIT: open
FOLIAGE: open
ORIGINATED: in an English nursery before 1872 as a variety of *M. spectabilis* which
  has never been found in nature
INTRODUCED: before 1883

Malus spectabilis and its varieties are undoubtedly considerably mixed up in the trade. The species has never been found outside of cultivation. Considerably superior in flower are the two double-flowered varieties, *M. spectabilis* 'Riversii' and *M. spectabilis albi-plena*. The former has large, many-petaled flowers and is often termed *"roseo-plena"* in the trade. The latter has pure white, double flowers. Both are excellent in flower but have poor fruits. Some of the newer hybrids, such as 'Katherine' which has double flowers and brightly colored fruits, may supersede these two old-fashioned favorites.

Malus toringoides 25' Zone 5 Cutleaf crab apple

* FLOWERS: fragrant, white, ¾″ in diameter, bearing only in alternate years
  TIME: late May
* FRUIT: pear-shaped, ¾″ in diameter, yellow on shaded side, red on sunny side
  EFFECTIVE: late August to late November
* HABIT: upright, pyramidal, dense branching
FOLIAGE: dense
HABITAT: western China
INTRODUCED: 1904
VARIETY:
  macrocarpa—originating about 1933 in England, this has fruit up to 1″ in
    diameter; otherwise it is similar to the species

One of the last to bloom and one of the best in fruit, which remain on the plant in splendid condition until after the first hard freeze. E. H. Wilson used to consider this the best of all species in fruit, but it must be admitted that there are several superior to it for their colorful flowers.

x *Malus* 'Van Eseltine' 20' Zone 4

* FLOWERS: double (about 15 petals), pink, 1¾″ in diameter
  TIME: late May
FRUIT: yellow and red
  EFFECTIVE: early fall
* HABIT: narrowly upright

The cutleaf crab apple (Malus toringoides) *has pear-shaped fruit that are colorfully effective on the tree from late August to late November.*

ORIGIN: *M. arnoldiana x spectabilis*
INTRODUCED: 1938, New York Agricultural Experiment Station, Geneva, New
    York

Valued for its double, pink flowers and upright habit of growth. Severely susceptible
to scab and fire blight.

Malus 'Vanguard'   18'   Zone 4

* FLOWERS: single, bright rosy pink, 2" in diameter
    TIME: mid-May
* FRUIT: red, ¾" in diameter
    EFFECTIVE: September 1 to early winter
HABIT: dense, somewhat vase-shaped
ORIGIN: probably an open-pollinated seedling of 'Hopa'; selected by Professor
    L. E. Longley of the Minnesota Agricultural Experiment Station about 1940
INTRODUCED: 1963 by University of Minnesota, Agricultural Experiment Station,
    St. Paul, Minnesota, and first distributed as number 11AA

This variety has been recommended as an annual bearer, "highly resistant to cedar
apple rust and fire blight and moderately resistant to apple scab."

Malus 'White Angel'   24'   Zone 4

* FLOWERS: buds pink; flowers single, pure white, 1" in diameter
        TIME: mid-May
* FRUIT: glossy red, ½–¾" in diameter, abundant
        EFFECTIVE: fall
    HABIT: rounded

x *Malus zumi calocarpa*   25'   Zone 5   Redbud crab apple

* FLOWERS: pink buds, followed by fragrant, white flowers, 1" in diameter
        TIME: early May
* FRUIT: bright red, ½" in diameter
        EFFECTIVE: late August to February
    HABIT: pyramidal, dense branching
    FOLIAGE: dense
    HYBRID ORIGIN: *M. baccata mandshurica x M. sieboldii*
    HABITAT: Japan
    INTRODUCED: 1892

One of the best crab apples for ornamental fruit, some of which remain on the plant far into the winter. Bears only in alternate years.

Maytenus boaria   35'   Zone 9   Chile mayten tree

    HABIT: pendulous branchlets
* FOLIAGE: evergreen, dense, light green
    HABITAT: Chile

This evergreen makes a beautiful specimen and is highly recommended by many as a street and avenue tree as far north as San Francisco, California. It is also used in seashore plantings.

Melaleuca leucadendron   40'   Zone 10   Cajeput tree

* FLOWERS: creamy white, in spikes 6" long
        TIME: June to October
    HABIT: slender and upright
* BARK: thick, soft, gray, peeling off in thin strips
* FOLIAGE: evergreen, pale green
    HABITAT: Australia

Fast-growing, resistant to grass fires and the effects of saltwater spray, this tree has many uses in both southern Florida and California. Apparently it does not suffer from poor drainage. The flowers, with very long and exposed stamens, give the general effect of a bottle brush, characteristic of the other members of this genus. In places where the soil is moist, it may reseed itself vigorously and quickly become a weed.

Melia azedarach   45'   Zone 7   Chinaberry

* FLOWERS: fragrant, lilac-colored clusters, 5–8" long
    TIME: April to May
* FRUIT: yellow berries, ½" in diameter
    EFFECTIVE: fall and winter
* HABIT: rounded head, dense branching
FOLIAGE: dense
HABITAT: Himalayas
INTRODUCED: colonial times
VARIETY:
    umbraculiformis (Umbrella chinaberry)—branches more or less densely upright, tree with a flattened head

A common tree throughout the South and, in fact, naturalized throughout all tropical and subtropical countries, it grows rapidly from seed and blooms early in life, quickly yielding a dense shade. It seems to do very well in the hottest of summers as well as in dry soil. The fruit is very much sought after by the birds. However, it must be admitted that it is not a clean tree, that it continually drops fruit or leaves, and its seedlings quickly come up wherever it grows well. Where it can be used, it is always dependable for giving shade, but it is rather short-lived.

Metasequoia glyptostroboides   100'   Zone 5   Dawn redwood

FRUIT: small cones
* HABIT: upright, pyramidal, with single straight trunk
FOLIAGE: loose, open, deciduous needles
HABITAT: Szechuan, China
INTRODUCED: 1948

This metasequoia, known prior to 1945 only in Mesozoic paleobotanical records, was found in China and identified that year. Three years later the Arnold Arboretum received viable seeds of this interesting tree and distributed them in all parts of the world. It is as old as *Ginkgo biloba*, but aside from its interesting background may not prove to be as good an ornamental. The needles are deciduous—about the same size as those of a hemlock—and it can be propagated by softwood or hardwood cuttings.

It is thoroughly hardy in Zone 5 and is being tried in colder areas. However, it has a tendency to grow late in the summer, so if it is in an area with early frosts, the young growth may not have sufficient time to harden properly and will be killed by such dips in temperature. Growing best in soils suited to hemlocks, especially where there is plenty of moisture, one tree at Winterthur, Wilmington, Delaware, grew to 50 feet from seed in fifteen years, so it does grow rapidly. The habit or outline of the tree is definitely pyramidal, and if the lower branches are cut, this silhouette is spoiled. Definitely a specimen tree, it is planted chiefly for its fast growth and interesting history since it has been growing and reproducing itself for at least 50 million years.

Metrosideros excelsus (syn. *M. tomentosa*)   30'   Zone 10   New Zealand Christmas tree

* FLOWERS: terminal clusters, 2–4" across, reddish stamens giving a special beauty to the flowers
     TIME: June–July
HABIT: wide-spreading
* FOLIAGE: leathery, evergreen leaves, dark, lustrous green above, white underneath
HABITAT: New Zealand
INTRODUCED: 1840 (England)

It does well under salt spray conditions, making it most desirable for seaside planting in both Florida and California.

Morus alba   45'   Zone 4   White mulberry

FRUIT: similar in size and shape to blackberries, white, pinkish, or purplish, ½–1" long; sexes usually separate
     EFFECTIVE: early summer
* HABIT: round-topped, dense
FOLIAGE: often irregularly lobed, bright green
HABITAT: China
INTRODUCED: colonial times
VARIETIES:
     'Chaparral'—bright green leaves, pendulous branches, producing no fruit
     'Pendula' *(Weeping mulberry)*—slender, pendulous branches; frequently planted for its form
     tatarica (Russian mulberry)—supposed to be the hardiest form, with fruit less than ½" long

None of the mulberries should be considered good choices for a general ornamental planting, and all might well be placed in the discard list. The trees have no particular autumn color. The fruits are profusely borne and are very attractive to all kinds of birds. If grown by pavement or a paved road, the falling fruit causes a continual litter. There are one or two fruitless clones on the market, sold as such, that could be used if the fruiting characteristics prove objectionable. 'Kingan' is one, with leathery, lustrous leaves. It is drought-resistant and can be used near the seashore. Its hanging branches, however, become very troublesome if the tree is planted along streets; they require frequent maintenance to keep them trimmed back to reasonable proportions.

     The white mulberry varies considerably as far as its foliage is concerned and has been cultivated by the silkworm industry for centuries. It was brought to this country in colonial times in an attempt to establish the silk industry here, especially in the plantation areas of the southeastern United States. This never proved profitable, but every now and then great publicity is given to these "silkworm" trees and many gardeners are urged to grow them. The white mulberry and its varieties are included here merely because so many people are interested in them, not because they measure up to better ornamental trees. However, the mulberry does have its uses, especially in hot climates, for it grows well and fast in almost any soil—even gravel—and also does well in drought areas. With rapid growth, it does create quick shade.

Morus alba is infested with many insect and disease problems. When these appear, try spraying with malathion or, if diseased, streptomycin.

Myrica californica   30'   Zone 7   California bayberry

* FRUIT: small, purple berries; sexes separate
    EFFECTIVE: fall and winter
  HABIT: upright shrub or tree
* FOLIAGE: lustrous, evergreen, bronze-colored leaves, to 4" long
  HABITAT: Washington to California

Easily grown and valued especially on the West Coast for its berries and evergreen leaves.

Myrica cerifera   36'   Zone 6   Southern wax-myrtle

* FRUIT: small, gray berries; sexes separate
    EFFECTIVE: fall and winter
  HABIT: rather open, irregular in shape
* FOLIAGE: evergreen leaves, to 3" long
  HABITAT: New Jersey to Florida and Texas

This is the southern counterpart of the northern bayberry *(M. pensylvanica)* and is taller growing and more dense, tending to be evergreen in the South. A good ornamental, but probably not too dependable as a tree.

Nyssa sinensis   20–60'   Zone 7   Chinese sour gum

  FOLIAGE: deciduous leaves, 3½–7" long
* AUTUMN COLOR: yellow with some red
  HABITAT: central China
  INTRODUCED: 1902

Good as a lawn tree, best transplanted while young, and outstanding in autumn color.

Nyssa sylvatica   90′   Zone 4   Black tupelo, Black gum

FRUIT: small, blue berries; sexes separate
    EFFECTIVE: midsummer, but usually hidden by foliage
* HABIT: pyramidal with somewhat pendulous branches, dense branching
* FOLIAGE: dense, lustrous, leathery leaves
* AUTUMN COLOR: brilliant scarlet to orange
HABITAT: eastern United States

An excellent ornamental, native over the greater part of the eastern United States, especially in swampy places. It is one of those trees difficult to transplant so that small specimens, especially dug with a ball of soil about the roots, are the most likely to succeed after transplanting. The dense, lustrous, dark green foliage turns a gorgeous red color in the fall, and its pyramidal habit, somewhat similar to that of the pin oak, makes it a desirable ornamental specimen. The sexes are separate, the flowers are inconspicuous, but the fruits are small dark blue drupes about the size of small cherries. Strangely enough, specimens from this tree are sent to the Arnold Arboretum more frequently than any other for identification, especially when it is in fruit.

Olea europaea   25′   Zone 9   Common olive

FRUIT: purple olives
* HABIT: densely rounded in poor soil, open and asymmetrical in good soil
* FOLIAGE: distinctive, evergreen, gray-green, silvery beneath
HABITAT: Mediterranean region
INTRODUCED: colonial times?
VARIETY:
    'Majestic Beauty' *(Plant Patent #5649)*—grows to about 25′, Zone 8. A small evergreen tree. Foliage is lighter green, narrower, and longer than that of other olives, and it bears no fruit, a very important characteristic when used as a street tree.

Probably best used as a tree for dry soils since it tends to keep its excellent shape best in such soils. The fruit, not frequently borne in Florida for some reason, can become a nuisance, littering the ground. This economic tree, grown in orchards on a commercial scale, can also be raised on the home grounds and has been used considerably in California as a street tree.

Ostrya virginiana   60′   Zone 4   Hop hornbeam

FRUIT: bladderlike pods in pendulous clusters, 1½–2½″ long
    EFFECTIVE: summer and early fall
HABIT: pyramidal
FOLIAGE: rather dense

AUTUMN COLOR: yellow
HABITAT: eastern North America

The hop hornbeam is of interest because it is fairly free from serious insect pests and disease and is a nice medium-sized tree (usually under 40 feet) for ornamental use. The clusters of bladderlike fruits are evident throughout the summer. However, experience has shown that it grows slowly and is rather difficult to transplant.

Oxydendrum arboreum   75′   Zone 5   Sorrel tree, Sourwood

* FLOWERS: small, white, in slightly pendulous racemes
        TIME: mid-July
* FRUIT: dried capsules
        EFFECTIVE: far into the winter
* HABIT: pyramidal
* FOLIAGE: lustrous, leathery, dense
* AUTUMN COLOR: brilliant scarlet
  HABITAT: eastern and southeastern United States

This is one of the superior ornamental trees, especially while it is young and can be kept clothed with branches from top to bottom and is grown in a situation where it

The sorrel tree, or sourwood (Oxydendrum arboreum), *blooming in mid-July. It also makes a brilliant red display in autumn.*

is exposed to full sunshine. Its leaves are similar in size and shape to those of mountain-laurel; they are lustrous and effective throughout the growing season. The late summer flowers, brilliant autumn color, and graceful pyramidal habit give this tree additional interest every season of the year.

Leaf spot and twig blight are usually not serious pests.

Parkinsonia aculeata   30'   Zone 9   Jerusalem thorn

* FLOWERS: fragrant, yellow, in loose axillary racemes
  TIME: early spring
HABIT: open
BARK: green
FOLIAGE: thin, wiry, fine-textured leaves often 1' long
HABITAT: tropical America

Of little use as a shade tree because of its open habit and peculiar foliage, this tree nevertheless has been used considerably as an ornamental because of its attractive flowers. It also can be clipped and formed into an excellent hedge, especially effective because of its numerous, inch-long thorns. It is used also in California as a street tree, where it grows well in light sandy soil.

Parrotia persica   50'   Zone 5   Persian parrotia

* HABIT: wide-spreading, rounded, with several trunks
* BARK: mottled gray and white
  FOLIAGE: dense leaves, somewhat similar to those of the witch-hazels
* AUTUMN COLOR: brilliant scarlet to orange and yellow
  HABITAT: Iran, Iraq
  INTRODUCED: 1840

An excellent tree for foliage, it usually grows with several trunks from the base and has leaves somewhat similar to those of the witch-hazel but more lustrous. The flowers, appearing before the leaves, are insignificant, but the bark flakes off in patches and leaves a colorful trunk like that of the stewartias or *Pinus bungeana,* giving it special interest in winter. Also, the branches tend to be more or less horizontal and covered with leaves all in one plane. When allowed to grow with branches to the ground, older specimens can become very graceful indeed. This tree is apparently not infested with any serious insect pests or diseases and might well be grown considerably more than it is.

Paulownia tomentosa   45'   Zone 5   Royal paulownia, Empress
tree

* FLOWERS: large, pyramidal clusters (up to 10" high) of fragrant violet flowers
  TIME: mid-May

FRUIT: dried capsules, 1½" long
HABIT: open, rounded head
FOLIAGE: dense, coarse, very large leaves, sometimes 2–3' in diameter
HABITAT: China
INTRODUCED: 1834

This very rapid-growing tree is similar to the catalpa in habit, with very large leaves and fragrant, funnel-like, lilac-colored flowers, up to 2 inches long in large, conspicuous clusters. Its texture is coarse, but it does give dense shade. The picturesque and pubescent flower buds are present all winter long and as a result are frequently killed or severely injured by cold winters in the vicinity of Boston and New York. Otherwise, it is a striking tree, especially when in flower, for these appear before the leaves. In England several of these plants are grown close together and then heavily pruned each year, resulting in vigorous shoot growth of up to 12 feet in a season, with leaves up to 3 feet across. This method of forcing overvigorous growth has little merit except for producing an oddity. In Japan the wood was formerly used for making sandals, clogs, and lutes. It is not considered a "clean" tree, for leaves, fruit, and twigs always seem to be littering the ground beneath its branches. Usually not infested with serious pests.

Phellodendron amurense   30'   Zone 3   Amur cork tree

   FLOWERS: small, whitish, in panicles
       TIME: early June
* FRUIT: round, black berries, ½" in diameter, in clusters; sexes separate
      EFFECTIVE: fall
* HABIT: wide, open, massive branches
* BARK: deeply fissured, corklike
   FOLIAGE: loose, open, appears late
   AUTUMN COLOR: yellow, but leaves drop quickly
   HABITAT: northern China
   INTRODUCED: about 1856

There has been some misunderstanding about the *Phellodendron* species because C. S. Sargent stated back in 1905 that *P. sachalinense* was best under cultivation. This statement has since been copied by many authors. The fact of the matter is that of the five species growing in the Arnold Arboretum, *P. amurense* has been outstanding, and C. S. Sargent himself noted this in 1924. The other species are similar but *P. amurense* has the large branches of picturesque habit and corky bark that is of interest all winter. Like other species in this genus, the sexes are separate and only pistillate plants will bear the numerous clusters of black berries. The autumn color is only of passing interest since the leaves quickly drop once they have turned yellow. It is a vigorous-growing tree and easily and quickly grown from seed (seedlings are continually sprouting up all over the Arnold Arboretum, more so than any other plant); the roots are fibrous, making it easy to transplant. This wide-spreading tree produces only light shade and is of no particular beauty in flower, but of interest in winter because of the massive branches and unusual bark.

The Amur cork tree (Phellodendron amurense) *has deeply fissured, corklike bark.*

There is a slight difference in branching habit among the various species of *Phellodendron. P. lavallei* is taller and *P. sachalinense* is more regularly vase-shaped than the irregular branching habit of *P. amurense.*

There has been some interest in times past concerning the cork-producing qualities of *Phellodendron* species, but it is not nearly as thick as that of *Quercus suber* or even *Q. variabilis* (which is nearly ½ inch thick), and as a consequence probably has little economic value.

Usually not infested with serious pests.

Phoenix dactylifera   100′   Zone 10   Date palm

* FRUIT: in large clusters; sexes separate
  HABIT: tall, long, arching
* FOLIAGE: bluish green

This is the true date palm of North Africa, planted widely throughout the tropics and cultivated for over four thousand years. The segments of the fronds are 12–18 inches long and bluish green. Male and female blossoms are on different trees. The fruits are 1–3 inches long and borne in large clusters.

Phoenix reclinata   25'   Zone 10   Senegal date palm

* HABIT: tall trunk, rounded top
  FOLIAGE: featherlike, compound leaves, long and gracefully arching
  HABITAT: Africa

Next to the true date, the best palm tree from Africa for ornamental purposes is the
Senegal date palm. It is used in southern California as a street tree of some merit for
it is most graceful in habit and fairly rapid in growth, but the fruit is not edible. *Phoenix
rupicola* is considered even more graceful and refined than this species because the
trunk is devoid of leaf bases.

Photinia serrulata   36'   Zone 7   Chinese photinia

* FLOWERS: small, white, in flat heads 6" in diameter
       TIME: mid-May
* FRUIT: bright red berries
   EFFECTIVE: fall and early winter
* FOLIAGE: evergreen, dark, lustrous green leaves, to 8" long
  HABITAT: China
  INTRODUCED: 1804

This very vigorous tree may become too leggy unless occasionally restrained through
pruning. The new foliage is a brilliant reddish bronze, considered by some to be
sufficient reason to recommend it. If new growth is occasionally cut back, new shoots
will be forced so that the young foliage can be evident for a considerable part of the
growing season. However, its lustrous evergreen leaves are really its best display. The
tree requires well-drained soil and not too much moisture, especially during the
summer.

Phyllostachys bambusoides   70'   Zones 7–8   Japanese timber
                                                                    bamboo

HABIT: tall, upright
FOLIAGE: leaves 4–6½" long, 1¾" wide
HABITAT: Japan

The Japanese timber bamboo is not to be considered an ornamental tree, but a clump
of this vigorous bamboo in the right place can be most interesting. This real timber
bamboo is one of the tallest species growing in North America.

-≫ *PICEA*

Spruces are native in most of the mountainous regions of North America. Some of the species that have been introduced from Europe and Asia have proved better from an ornamental viewpoint than our natives. Practically none grow old gracefully; that is, as they mature they begin to lose their lower branches. As forest trees this may be an ideal trait, but for specimen trees in good plantings it is not. As young trees they look splendid, some retaining their needles for six to eight years, making their foliage very dense, and they are as symmetrical as any other evergreen, but the person who is planting for permanence should not be led astray by their youthful appearance. It should be pointed out that nearly half the spruces recommended here mature at heights of 100 feet or more, hence they certainly are not trees for the small property. When crowded into mass plantings or when planted in the shade, they quickly lose their lower branches. The red spruce *(P. rubens)*, black spruce *(P. mariana)*, and white spruce *(P. glauca)* are the three most widely distributed natives. The white spruce has been used in ornamental plantings considerably in the past, merely because it was readily available and easily grown from seed, but it does not mature into a fine ornamental as do some of the others, although several varieties of this species do have good habits. The red and black spruces do not mature into good ornamentals either.

The native Colorado spruce of the Rocky Mountains is very stiff in habit, while the Norway, Serbian, Oriental, and Brewer spruces are quite the opposite, having graceful, more or less pendulous branchlets that give them considerable merit in ornamental plantings. Like many other conifers, the spruces are definitely pyramidal in outline and for the most part, stiffer and more rigid in habit than the more soft-textured pines. They vary also in the color of their foliage, in soil requirements, and in hardiness.

Spruce gall aphid on Norway spruce and Cooley's gall aphid on blue and white spruce are common pests and can be controlled by spraying with dormant oil or malathion (or a combination of them) in early spring. Spruce bud worm, a serious pest, is controlled by spraying with malathion in early summer. Spruce mite is another serious pest and is controlled with malathion in summer, or pentac or dicofol.

Canker kills lower or inner branches and cannot be controlled with fungicides; diseased branches should be removed and burned during the winter.

Each of the species recommended has its peculiar qualifications for landscape plantings, but where other trees can be used, the spruces as a group might be overlooked. Several of the spruces are completely hardy in the coldest parts of the United States and Canada, but in slightly warmer areas pines or hemlocks should be given first consideration because of their softer foliage texture.

For assistance in identification, the keys on pages 329–34 will be of some help. It should prove advantageous in distinguishing spruces from other evergreens to note that the spruces have needles that are square in cross section (except four species) while the hemlocks and firs have needles that are flat. Also, the leaf bases of all spruces are tenacious and remain on the twigs long after the needles have dropped, making the twigs very rough to the touch. Spruce species frequently resemble one another very closely, making accurate identification difficult indeed. This is just one more reason that a comparatively small number of the species need be recommended for growing as ornamental specimens.

→≫ SIMPLE FOLIAGE KEY TO THE SPRUCES
Native or Available in North America

The key that follows is prepared solely for the determination of material which is fresh. It cannot be used with dead material. Such a key has its good points and its bad points—good because the obvious characteristics such as color of foliage and twigs are utilized, and it can be used in the field without the aid of a lens (in most cases); bad because the key is usable only for the period of a few days after the branches have been taken from the living tree.

The key is offered for the individual who is not a trained botanist, and it should not be used as a means of final identification, for standard texts and illustrations should be consulted. In using the key, merely go to the first number. If the statement there applies to the specimen, proceed to the next higher number until the tree is identified. If the statement there does not apply, go to the following group headed by the same number and proceed as above.

It is interesting to note that there are only seven species of spruce native to North America, and all are included in this key. There are about twenty-two species available in the trade, all of which are included in the key, as well as eight varieties in addition. There are about thirty varieties of *P. abies* offered by various nurseries, and the differences among these are frequently so slight, especially in the younger stages of plant development, that it is impossible to make a satisfactory key for them. Consequently, it has been possible to list only the dwarf varieties of *P. abies* as a group.

Needles borne singly, leaf bases persistent. . . . . *Picea* and *Tsuga*
    1. Needles without distinct petioles (See Fig. 13b, page 447). *Picea* species

abies—Norway spruce

abies vars.—some 30 varieties available in the trade

asperata—Dragon spruce

bicolor—Alcock spruce

breweriana—Brewer spruce

engelmannii—Engelmann spruce

glauca—White spruce

glauca albertiana—Alberta spruce

glauca conica—Dwarf Alberta spruce

glauca densata—Black Hills spruce

glehnii—Sakhalin spruce

jezoensis—Yeddo spruce

koyamai—Koyama spruce

mariana—Black spruce

obovata—Siberian spruce

omorika—Serbian spruce

orientalis—Oriental spruce

polita—Tigertail spruce

pungens—Colorado spruce

pungens 'Argentea'—Silver spruce

pungens 'Bakerii'—Baker's spruce

pungens glauca—Blue Colorado spruce

pungens 'Moerheimii'—Moerheim spruce

pungens 'Pendens'—Koster spruce

purpurea—Purple cone spruce

rubens—Red spruce

schrenkiana—Schrenk spruce

sitchensis—Sitka spruce

smithiana—Himalayan spruce

wilsonii—Wilson spruce

    2. Needles on current year's growth mostly at right angles to twig; also see Fig. 8. (Note: In no specimen are all needles exactly at right angles to the twig. Some needles always point toward the end of the twig, hence making an angle less than a right angle. However, the plants in the group with needles at right angles should have more than 50 percent of their needles at right angles to the twig. In case of reasonable doubt, certain plants can be located again under the second No. 2— "needles mostly at an angle considerably less than a right angle.")

        3. Needles ½ inch long or less

            4. Needles showing intense white lines when observed from the tip, looking toward the base of the branch; branchlets pubescent . . . . *P. mariana*
               (Labrador to Alaska; Wisconsin and Michigan) Zone 2

            4. Needles not showing intense white lines, plant a low, dense pyramid of tightly compact, light green foliage; branchlets glabrous. . . . . *P. glauca conica*

        3. Needles mostly more than ½ inch long

            4. Terminal bud lustrous, dark brown, prominent, about ¼ inch long; its tight-fitting scales remain snugly tight-fitting and blackish at base of branchlets for several years
             . . . . *P. polita*
             (Japan) Zone 5

            4. Terminal but not lustrous nor as prominent, light brown. The scales, if they remain at the base of the current year's branchlets, are curled and indistinct, not snugly tight-fitting.

               5. Foliage of one-year-old twigs definitely blue
                . . . . *P. pungens glauca*
                . . . . *P. pungens* 'Argentea'
                . . . . *P. pungens* 'Moerheimii'

The only way to tell these three apart is to determine the degree of blue color. *P. pungens glauca* is the least blue, *P. pungens* 'Argentea,' the typical "Koster spruce" of the trade, is next, and *P. pungens* 'Moerheimii' is the deepest blue. (Note: Visualize the blue of *P. pungens* 'Argentea' and the green of the Norway spruce. These are the two sharp color divisions. Plants with foliage a color between these two extremes come under the second No. 5—"Foliage bluish green to grayish green.")

The tip of a one-year-old shoot of Picea pungens, *showing a majority of the needles at nearly right angles to the twig.*

FIGURE 8

The end bud and base of one-year-old shoots of (a) Picea abies *and (b)* P. polita. *Notice the tight-fitting scales on the bud and shoot base of* P. polita *compared to those of* P. abies.

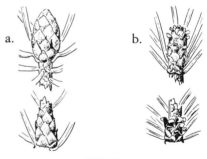

FIGURE 9

5. Foliage bluish green to grayish green
    6. Needles rigid, extremely sharp to the touch, one-year-old shoots strong and vigorous, often 6–10 inches long
        7. Needles frequently curved .. *P. asperata* (west China) Zone 5
        7. Majority of needles straight . *P. pungens* (Wyoming to New Mexico) Zone 2
    6. Needles not so rigid, extremely sharp to the touch, one-year-old shoots not so vigorous

       7. One-year-old twigs greenish gray
          . . . . *P. wilsonii*
          (central and west China) Zone 5
       7. One-year-old twigs yellowish to orange-
          brown . . . . *P. glauca*
          (Canada and northern United States)
          Zone 2–7
     5. Foliage uniformly green. Most of the needles of this
       species are not at right angles to the twigs except on
       very vigorous shoots . . . . *P. abies*
       (north and central Europe, naturalized in eastern
       United States) Zone 2
2. Needles on current year's growth mostly at an angle considerably less
  than a right angle with the twig; that is, needles pointing toward the
  tip of the twig
     3. Foliage of current year's shoots uniformly blue. (Note: Visualize
       the blue of *P. pungens* 'Argentea' and the green of the Norway
       spruce. These are the two sharp color divisions. Plants with
       foliage a color between these two extremes come under the
       second No. 3—"Foliage bluish to grayish.")
       4. One-year-old twigs densely pubescent, noticeable without
         a lens . . . . *P. engelmannii*
         (British Columbia to Arizona) Zone 2
       4. One-year-old twigs glabrous
         5. Plant with rigid, horizontal branches
          . . . . *P. pungens* 'Bakerii'
         5. Plant with pendulous branchlets
          . . . . *P. pungens* 'Pendens'
         (Not to be confused with the Silver spruce, *P. pungens*
         'Argentea,' which does not have pendulous branch-
         lets)
     3. Foliage of current year's growth bluish to grayish or whitish,
       especially when viewed from the tip of the branch, looking to-
       ward the base of the branch; green when viewed from above the
       branch
       4. Needles ¾ inch or less in length
         5. One-year-old twigs greenish gray . . . . . *P. purpurea*
          (west China) Zone 5
         5. One-year-old twigs yellowish to brown
          6. Needles flat in cross section
            7. Winter buds resinous
              8. Branchlets glabrous and horizontal,
              foliage intensely white when viewed
              from underneath the branch
                9. Needles pungent, ½–1 inch
                long . . . . *P. sitchensis*
                (Alaska to California)
                Zone 6

9. Needles not pungent, ½–¾
inch long . . . . *P. jezoensis*
(Manchuria and Japan)
Zone 4

8. Branchlets pubescent, usually mark-
edly pendulous; foliage not intensely
white when viewed from beneath
. . . . *P. breweriana*
(Oregon to northern California)
Zone 5

7. Winter buds not resinous; branchlets pubescent . . . . *P. omorika*
(southeastern Europe) Zone 4

*The tip of a one-year-old
shoot of* Picea
engelmannii, *showing a
majority of the needles at
less than right angles to
the twig.*

FIGURE 10

*Cross sections of needles
from (a)* Picea omorika
and (b) P. glauca.

FIGURE 11

6. Needles angular in cross section, usually 4-sided
7. Two- and three-year-old twigs black on
upper side of branch at least, giving a dark
appearance to the tree; needles sharp;
branchlets pubescent . . . . *P. mariana*
(Labrador to Alaska, Wisconsin to Michigan) Zone 2

7. Two-year-old twigs usually light brown;
branchlets glabrous, needles blunt
. . . . *P. glauca densata*
. . . . *P. glauca*
. . . . *P. glauca albertiana*

(Canada and northern United States) Zone 2.

    5. One-year-old twigs definitely a red-brown

        6. Cones 2¼–4¾ inches long . . . . *P. bicolor* (Japan) Zone 4

        6. Cones 2–3 inches long . . . . *P. glehnii* (Japan) Zone 3

        (Here is a case where differentiation between these two species without lens and without fruit is difficult; the differences are largely those of degree. The white markings on the upper surface of the needles of *P. bicolor* are more intense, whereas the pubescence of the branchlets and the dark green color of the branchlets of *P. glehnii* are more marked.)

  4. Needles more than ¾ inch long

    5. Needles flat in cross section

        6. Branchlets glabrous; foliage intensely white when observed from underneath branch . . . . *P. sitchensis* (Alaska to California) Zone 6

        6. Branchlets pubescent; usually markedly pendulous; foliage not intensely white when observed underneath branch . . . . *P. breweriana* (Oregon to northern California) Zone 5

    5. Needles angular in cross section, usually 4-sided

        6. Winter buds resinous . . . . *P. smithiana* (Himalayas) Zone 6

        6. Winter buds not resinous . . . . . *P. schrenkiana* (central Asia) Zone 5

3. Foliage uniformly green

  4. The majority of the needles ½ inch or less in length

    5. Needles flattened against branchlets; a markedly uniform, dark, glossy green above and below . . . . *P. orientalis* (Caucasus and Asia Minor) Zone 4

    5. Needles not flattened against branchlets except in some *P. abies* varieties that are dwarf shrubs and not trees; nor a marked uniform glossy green above and below, except sometimes in *P. rubens*

        6. Plants usually low, dense, dwarf shrubs . . . . *P. abies* varieties (Note: Some thirty dwarf varieties are offered in the trade.)

        6. Plants not low, dense, dwarf shrubs, but trees

            7. One-year-old twigs yellowish, foliage gray-green . . . . *P. glauca* (Canada and northern U.S.) Zone 2

7. One-year-old twigs reddish brown; foliage green

    8. Needles only slightly glossy, branchlets pubescent. . . . . *P. rubens* (Nova Scotia to North Carolina) Zone 2

    8. Needles not glossy, branchlets glabrous . . . . *P. koyamai* (Japan and Korea) Zone 4

4. The majority of the needles at least ½ inch and usually approaching ¾ inch in length

    5. Foliage dark green, branchlets usually orange

        6. Terminal bud lustrous, prominent, dark brown, about ¼ inch long; its tight-fitting scales remain snugly tight-fitting and blackish at base of branchlets for several years; foliage decidedly harsh to the touch . . . . *P. polita* (Japan) Zone 5

        6. Terminal bud not lustrous; the scales, if they remain at the base of the current year's branchlets, are curled and indistinct, not snugly tight-fitting; foliage not harsh to the touch

        . . . . *P. abies* (north and central Europe, escaped in United States) Zone 2

FIGURE 12

                                                          a.   b.

Side views of shoots from (a) Picea obovata *and (b)* P. glauca, *showing the difference in the way the needles are borne on the twig.*

5. Foliage grayish green, one-year-old twigs yellowish

    6. Needles usually rigidly upright on the upper side of the branchlets; needles dense, even on four-year-old branchlets; tree open in habit

        . . . . *P. glauca* (Canada and northern United States) Zone 2

    6. Needles usually appressed or held closely along the upper side of the branch, not upright; needles sparsely borne; tree dense and conical in habit . . . . *P. obovata* (northern Europe to Kamchatka and Manchuria) Zone 2

Picea abies   150′   Zone 2   Norway spruce

FRUIT: pendulous cones, 4–6″ long
    EFFECTIVE: fall and winter
* HABIT: pyramidal, pendulous branchlets, stiff while young but often graceful at maturity
* FOLIAGE: dense, evergreen, dark green needles, mostly less than 1″ long
HABITAT: northern and central Europe
INTRODUCED: colonial times
VARIETIES:
    'Columnaris' *(Columnar Norway spruce)*—narrow and columnar in habit
    nigra (Black Norway spruce)—very densely branched, pyramidal, needles dark green
    'Pyramidata' *(Pyramidal Norway spruce)*—a narrow, slender pyramid in habit

The Norway spruce has been considerably overplanted in North America, certainly in the eastern part of the country. It does not mature gracefully. As a young specimen, it grows vigorously and well—the obvious reason so many have been used. But once the top begins to become thin and open (after about thirty years) no amount of soil moisture or fertilizer can correct it.

Young plants are usually stiff and upright, but as they grow older, the branches grow wider and more horizontal or even pendulous, while the branchlets themselves actually become pendant, making a very graceful tree. The large, conspicuous cones, the largest of any spruce, are always an added interest in a fruiting year. Unfortunately, none of the coniferous trees can be counted on to produce profuse fruit every year, for they vary markedly, some years bearing practically none.

The Norway spruce has a natural inclination to throw "sports," and because of this tendency and the centuries during which it has been cultivated, many "sports" or varieties have arisen, which of course are maintained by asexual propagation. Some of these are very dwarf; others are trees with varying habits.

Picea asperata   75′   Zone 5   Dragon spruce

* HABIT: pyramidal
* FOLIAGE: dense, evergreen, stiff, light green to light bluish needles
HABITAT: western China
INTRODUCED: 1910

Somewhat similar to the Norway spruce in general appearance while young, this tree is finding a place for itself in seaside plantings where it does better than most spruces. The needles of this species remain on the tree approximately seven years, the main reason that the foliage is so dense. Aside from this, it probably is no better than some of the other recommended species.

Picea breweriana   120'   Zone 5   Brewer spruce

* HABIT: pyramidal, long, graceful, whiplike pendulous branches
* FOLIAGE: evergreen needles
  HABITAT: southern Oregon and northern California

Used in certain areas of the West Coast but rather rare in the East, where it does not thrive in cultivation. Of interest because of its long, pendulous branches. Apparently this tree needs the cool, moist atmosphere of the higher altitudes along the northern Pacific coast in order to do well, but where it can be grown it makes an excellent ornamental specimen.

Picea engelmannii   150'   Zone 2   Engelmann spruce

* HABIT: densely pyramidal
* FOLIAGE: dense, evergreen, bluish green needles
  HABITAT: southwestern Canada to Oregon
  VARIETIES:
>   'Argentea'—silvery gray leaves
>   *fendleri*—pendulous branches
>   'Glauca'—bluish to steel blue leaves

This tree is one of the better spruces for ornamental planting, particularly because of its light bluish needles and dense habit. Like many other spruces it does not grow old gracefully and eventually loses many of its lower branches. When this occurs depends on several factors, including soil and climate. There is a tree in the Arnold Arboretum 25 feet tall and still clothed with branches to the ground.

Picea glauca   90'   Zone 2   White spruce

HABIT: pyramidal
FOLIAGE: evergreen, light bluish green needles
HABITAT: Canada, northern United States
VARIETIES:
>   *coerulea*—of dense habit, with glaucous leaves
>   *conica*—the popular dwarf white spruce, a compact pyramidal plant found in southwestern Canada in 1904 and widely distributed by the Arnold Arboretum. Forty-year-old specimens are not much more than 10 feet tall even when grown in good soil.
>   *densata*—the Black Hills spruce, a slow-growing, compact tree, with bright to bluish green foliage

This native tree can endure heat and drought better than some others, but it is not as outstanding an ornamental as *P. engelmannii* and *P. omorika*. It is extremely hardy and hence must be left in this recommended list. In the eastern United States several other spruces will make better ornamentals.

Picea koyamai   60'   Zone 4   Koyama spruce

* HABIT: narrowly pyramidal
* FOLIAGE: evergreen, light green needles
  HABITAT: Japan
  INTRODUCED: 1914

This fine specimen lacks the "layered" branching appearance of some of the other spruces, making it a better ornamental.

Picea mariana 'Doumetii'   30'   Zone 2   Doumet black spruce

HABIT: densely pyramidal
FOLIAGE: evergreen, bluish green needles
HABITAT: Labrador to Alaska

This variety is much better than the species for use as an ornamental because it is denser and rounded and can be propagated by cuttings. A twenty-year-old tree in the Arnold Arboretum is 8 feet tall and 9 feet in branch spread.

Picea omorika   90'   Zone 4   Serbian spruce

* HABIT: dense, narrow, and pyramidal with short, ascending branches and often graceful, pendant branchlets
* FOLIAGE: dense, evergreen needles, whitish on the underside
  HABITAT: southeastern Europe
  INTRODUCED: about 1880
  VARIETY:
  'Pendula'—an excellent, graceful, branching variety with slightly drooping and twisted branches

One of the best spruces for landscape planting. It has done very well indeed in the Arnold Arboretum since it was first introduced there seventy years ago. Its dense habit and very beautiful glossy green needles, which show much of their whitish undersurfaces as they move in the wind, make it decidedly beautiful the entire year. Some of the trees have pendant branchlets that add materially to their beauty. The Serbian spruce can be termed almost columnar in habit, for old plants in the Arnold Arboretum 60 feet tall have a branch spread of no more than 15 feet at the base. This is one of the few spruces with needles flat in cross section like hemlock and not four-sided, as are the needles of most other spruces. If only one spruce is to be chosen for a planting, this should certainly be considered first.

Picea orientalis   150'   Zone 4   Oriental spruce

* HABIT: densely pyramidal, branchlets often pendulous, graceful
* FOLIAGE: dense, evergreen, glossy, dark green needles, smallest of the spruces

HABITAT: Asia Minor
INTRODUCED: 1837
VARIETIES:

'Aurea'—bronzy yellow leaves; a fine ornamental

'Gowdy'—listed as an extremely upright form of very narrow habit. The leaves are small and a rich green.

'Nana'—low, broadly pyramidal form

A most graceful and compact tree with very dark green foliage. It grows slowly and frequently has pendulous branches. This also can be considered one of the best of the spruces, but it is susceptible to the destructive action of the spruce bud worm more than some of the other species. Also, in New England at least, it may suffer browning of foliage in late winter more quickly than some of the others. If proper spraying is practiced and winters are not too cold and dry, this can easily grow into a splendid ornamental tree. Its needles are smaller than those of most spruces so that its fine texture adds materially to its other desirable qualities.

Picea pungens   100′   Zone 2   Colorado spruce

* HABIT: stiffly pyramidal
* FOLIAGE: dense, evergreen, stiff, green to bluish
  HABITAT: Rocky Mountains, Utah to New Mexico
  VARIETIES:

'Argentea' *(Silver Colorado spruce)*—foliage silvery white. It is this variety that is widely distributed in the trade as 'Koster blue spruce.' The true Koster blue spruce is *P. pungens* 'Pendens' with pendulous branches and a horizontal trunk (unless it is staked to force it to grow in a treelike manner).

'Bakerii' *(Baker's blue spruce)*—originated in a batch of seedlings of *P. pungens glauca* in Massachusetts. This variety, according to Roland E. Baker of Pomfret, Connecticut, is a deeper blue than that of 'Argentea' and possibly even a shade more colorful than the Moerheim spruce. Our specimen in the Arnold Arboretum is slow in growth, for at thirty-two years it is only 12′ tall and 6′ across. A Moerheim spruce the same age growing nearby is 50′ tall.

'Coerulea' *(Cerulean Colorado spruce)*—leaves bluish white

glauca (Blue Colorado spruce)—leaves bluish green

'Henry D. Fowler'—densely branched, wide, upright, with sharp, blue-green needles around the stem, growing less than 8″ each year. Selected in the 1960s.

hoopsi—fast-growing, upright, intense silvery blue needles; thought to be one of the bluest forms

hosteriana—one of the oldest varieties, with deep blue foliage

'Hunnewelliana'—a slow-growing, densely pyramidal tree found in a Massachusetts nursery. It is a dense pyramid of light blue foliage; a thirty-two-year-old tree in the Arnold Arboretum is 15′ tall and 8′ in branch spread.

'Moerheimii' *(Moerheim spruce)*—compact, dense-growing form with very blue foliage

*The Baker's spruce (*Picea pungens *'Bakerii') has deep blue foliage.*

'**Pendens**' *(Koster weeping blue spruce)*—foliage bluish white, pendulous branches, originally propagated by the Koster Nurseries of Boskoop, Holland. The main trunk of this tree tends to be prostrate and must be staked to grow in treelike fashion. Actually, this is the real Koster spruce, but it is found infrequently in the trade as such. Formerly this was called *P. pungens kosteriana.*

The Colorado blue spruce and its varieties make ideal plants from the standpoint of the commercial grower, and that is why so many plants are grown. They grow quickly from seed, vary considerably in color, and make dense, pyramidal young plants that are desirable in various types of planting. Nurserymen should propagate the varieties asexually (by grafts or cuttings) rather than always by seed and merely making selections from the seed bed on a color basis alone.

The important fact to remember is that these plants, like most other spruces, do not grow old gracefully. They lose their lower branches, often early in life. Fifteen- or twenty-foot specimens of blue spruce do have branches to the ground, but as they grow taller some of the lower branches die out and the trees quickly become unsightly. In other words, this is an ideal tree while young, retaining its needles for seven to eight years, making the foliage very dense. Plan on using it only while it is at its best and replacing it after twenty years with something else. This spruce requires more spraying (to control spruce gall aphids) than any other and in fact requires more than most other evergreens.

Because of its stiff growth habit and pronounced color, it always stands out prominently wherever it is used. Placing these trees properly in the landscape is really very difficult. All too often we see them brazenly spotted in the geometrical center of the lawn, destroying any possible beauty in that area for all time.

Picea sitchensis   140′   Zone 6   Sitka spruce

* HABIT: narrowly pyramidal
* FOLIAGE: evergreen needles
   HABITAT: Alaska to California
   VARIETY:

     'Speciosa'—of compact habit, slower growth, and more ascending branches

This tree is very ornamental but can be grown only in a cool, humid climate. It does not grow at all well in the eastern United States but is a prominent timber tree in the moist atmosphere of the northwest coastal area.

Picea smithiana   160′   Zone 5   Himalayan spruce

* HABIT: broadly pyramidal, branchlets pendulous
* FOLIAGE: evergreen needles
   HABITAT: Himalayas
   INTRODUCED: 1818

A handsome tree with wide-spreading branches and pendulous branchlets of considerably wider habit than many other spruces. Worthy of trial, but the young growth starts very early; hence it should not be planted where there is the possibility of late frosts in the spring.

Picea wilsonii   75′   Zone 5   Wilson spruce

* HABIT: pyramidal
* FOLIAGE: evergreen, light green needles
   HABITAT: China
   INTRODUCED: 1901

This has some merit for trial as a slow-growing conifer of dense, pyramidal habit.

⇛ *PINUS*

The pines constitute the most important group of lumber trees in the world, and as ornamentals they are equally at the top of any list of evergreens. North America has its full share of native species and varieties, but many others are widely grown about the northern temperate regions of the world. These, together with those imported from Europe and the Orient, give the American gardener a glorious collection from which to choose for ornamental planting.

American nurseries are offering at least seventy-seven species and varieties. Fifty-one are recommended here as having sufficient qualities to be worthy of consideration for ornamental planting. No doubt others now being hybridized and tested will be found to have ornamental value and will be added to future lists of recommended trees.

Pines are mostly trees but there are a few shrubs among them, growing in soils ranging from good to very poor, from the seashore to the highest timberline. The needles, produced in bundles of two, three, or five, will vary in length on almost every tree, but it is fairly well known that a few such as *P. banksiana, aristata,* and *parviflora* will have needles under 1½ inches in length, while others such as *P. canariensis, caribaea,* and *patula* will have needles nearly a foot in length; and *P. palustris,* known as the longleaf pine, may have needles more than a foot long.

The flowers are unisexual, but both types are borne on the same tree. The cones vary in shape and length, too, and it is these that botanists describe carefully as a final means of properly identifying one species from another. However, it may take a number of years before the small tree becomes large enough to produce fruit, hence nurseries and gardeners in general must rely as much as possible on vegetative characteristics for identification.

Pines have ornamental value for various reasons. Some, such as *P. banksiana* and *P. rigida,* are of merit only for planting in poor soils where better pines or deciduous plants will not grow. Others, such as *P. pinaster* and *P. halepensis,* are best used only for planting at the seashore where most evergreens have a difficult time, for these seem to withstand seashore conditions well. The Japanese black pine *(P. thunbergii)* can be noted as the best evergreen tree of any kind for planting in seashore gardens of the northeastern United States. Hurricanes and frequent drenchings with saltwater spray fail to retard its normal growth, and even after the worst storms, the foliage of this species is always a fine dark green.

Then there are *P. caribaea, patula,* and *pinea* of the Florida, California, or northwest coastal gardening areas. Certain species such as *P. resinosa* and *P. strobus* have produced varieties that are strictly shrubs and are of value only in shrub borders, foundation plantings, and rock gardens.

The best species for the small garden are *P. aristata, cembra, contorta, koraiensis,* and *peuce,* and possibly *nigra,* together with any of the shrubby varieties that appear to have merit for the specific situation. White pines *(P. strobus)* are of course widely used even on small properties, but it should be understood that they are not small trees by any stretch of the imagination, and when used in cramped situations, they must be heavily pruned to keep them restrained within limits. The silver Japanese white pine *(P. parviflora glauca)* is certainly a beautiful tree, but one specimen in the Arnold Arboretum is 60 feet tall and 60 feet wide. Pruning back a specimen tree such as this to keep it within a 20-foot area would be difficult indeed.

A word should be said about some of the new hybrid pines originated during the past thirty-five years at the Institute of Forest Genetics of the United States Forestry Service, Placerville, California. Originally known as the Eddy Arboretum, founded in 1925 by James E. Eddy, this fifty-five-acre tract is planted with sixteen thousand trees, including seventy-two species, thirty-five varieties, and ninety hybrids, comprising what is probably the most nearly complete collection of pines in the world. The thirty-year-old slow-growing species are about 20 feet tall, while faster-growing species of the same age are up to 80 feet.

Several of the ninety hybrids already produced show hybrid vigor, growing faster than either parent. Naturally this is of prime interest to foresters, but even at that, as more becomes known about these hybrids, as they are tested over a wide area of the country, as their sometimes greater resistance to insect pests and diseases becomes known, it may well be that certain ones will have outstanding ornamental characteristics other than rapid growth.

White pine aphids on the needles and pine bark aphids on the trunk and larger branches are common pests unless controlled by sprays of malathion. Pine needle scale, especially on Mugo pine, is controlled with sprays of malathion when crawlers are hatching in early summer. Larvae of the white pine weevil, a snout beetle, girdle and kill the leaders of white pine and Norway spruce. Spraying with methoxychlor just before the new growth (candles) begins in the spring kills the beetles, and cutting and burning the wilted leaders while the grubs are in them decreases later infestations. Trees in shade are infested more often than those in sun. Pales weevil, another snout beetle, gnaws the bark of seedlings and is a serious pest in nurseries and in new plantings near freshly cut slashes, in which the beetles breed. Small plantings and ornamental trees can be protected by spraying the trunk with methoxychlor. Pine web worms that web needles of red and white pine into masses of froth, pine sawflies that eat the needles, pine tube moths that live in cases among webbed needles, and pine spittlebugs that live in bubbles of froth after sucking the sap are all controlled by timely spraying with methoxychlor. European pine shoot moth is a serious pest of red and Scotch pine. It kills the buds and new shoots and causes crooked leaders. The young that hatch in midsummer can be killed by sprays of methoxychlor when the young start feeding. Two or more applications may be necessary. In the Northeast pitch pine and red pine are infected with matsucoccus scale, which is difficult to find until yellow needles attract attention. No complete control is known.

White pine blister rust develops cankers on the bark that swell and produce orange spores. Branches, twigs, and small trees are killed. It must live on currant and gooseberry for part of its life, and the elimination of these plants within 300 yards is advised. Most states in the infected area have quarantines on currants. Spraying with chlorothalonil (Bravo) has been helpful experimentally. Needle cast is caused by both fungi and by windburn. The fungus may be killed by spraying with ferbam (fermate) or thiram (arasan) when the needles are about half grown.

→≫ SIMPLE KEY TO THE PINES
Native or Available from Nurseries in North America

This simple key is offered chiefly for the benefit of the amateur who is frequently confronted with difficult keys that he finds unnecessarily complicated. All measures of leaf length should be considered as approximate only. On one individual tree needles may vary in length from 2 inches to as much as 8 inches, but in the key the length given would be 4 to 6 inches, meaning that mature needles—not the young ones that are elongating nor the ones on weak or on overvigorous branches—are mostly within the 4- to 6-inch length. If this is clearly understood by those using this key, it will undoubtedly prove helpful in the identification of most of our commonly grown pines.

The key is designed to be used chiefly with living material, hence the color of the foliage and the general habit of the tree sometimes play an important part. Occasionally, as in differentiating between *P. strobus* and *P. monticola,* the two species are so much alike that cone characteristics are used, but these are resorted to only when absolutely necessary, for many a tree that one would like to identify is not graced with cones at the time one wishes to identify it. Habitats are given because sometimes such information may prove helpful in assisting in plant identification.

There is no excuse for avoiding a simple key such as this one merely because of a lack of thorough botanical training. It is understandable, and if used with a full knowledge of its limitations, it can prove most helpful. In using the key, merely go to the first number. If the statement there applies to the specimen, go to the next higher number until the tree is identified. If the statement there does not apply, go to the following group headed by the same number and proceed as above. Identifications made by the use of any "short" key, and this one in particular, should not be considered final

The needles and cones of thirteen different pines: (1) P. strobus, *(2)* P. cembra, *(3)* P. flexilis, *(4)* P. parviflora, *(5)* P. bungeana, *(6)* P. rigida, *(7)* P. virginiana, *(8)* P. thunbergii, *(9)* P. sylvestris, *(10)* P. densiflora, *(11)* P. banksiana, *(12)* P. nigra, *(13)* P. resinosa.

but should be checked further against a complete description in some standard text and available illustration.

Needles in bundles of 2 to 5, rarely solitary, enclosed at the base by a deciduous or persistent sheath . . . . *Pinus*

1. Needles 5 in a sheath
   albicaulis—White bark pine   *parviflora glauca*
   aristata—Bristlecone pine   *peuce*—Balkan pine
   cembra—Swiss stone pine   *pumila*—Japanese stone pine
   flexilis—Limber pine   *strobus*—Eastern white pine
   koraiensis—Korean pine   *strobus* 'Fastigiata'
   lambertiana—Sugar pine   *strobus nana*
   monticola—Western white pine   *torreyana*—Torrey pine
   parviflora—Japanese white pine   *wallichiana*—Himalayan pine

   2. Needles usually less than 1½ inches long and smooth margin
      . . . . *P. aristata*
      (California to Colorado) Zone 5
   2. Needles usually 1½–2 inches long
      3. Bark of trunk brown to creamy white, needles rigid and stout,
         margin smooth . . . . *P. albicaulis*
         (British Columbia to California) Zone 3
      3. Bark of trunk blackish, needles more flexible

       4. Needles bluish green, often twisted, intensely white under-neath, leaf margin finely serrulate . . . . *P. parviflora* (Japan) Zone 5

       4. Needles intensely bluish green . . . . . *P. parviflora glauca*

       4. Needles light green, not twisted

           5. Mature twigs glabrous, needles smooth . . *P. flexilis* (Alberta to California) Zone 4

           5. Mature twigs pubescent; leaf margin finely serrulate . . . . *P. pumila* (Japan) Zone 3

2. Needles mostly 2½–4½ inches long; leaf margin serrulate

   3. Mature twigs glabrous

       4. Plant shrubby, not treelike . . . . *P. strobus nana*

       4. Branches upright, tree dense

           5. Needles stiff . . . . *P. peuce* (Balkan Mountains) Zone 4

           5. Needles soft and flexible . . . . . *P. strobus* 'Fastigiata'

       4. Branches horizontal, tree more open

           5. Cones usually 2–4¾ inches long; twigs glabrous or only slightly pubescent . . . . *P. strobus* (eastern United States and Canada) Zone 3

           5. Cones usually 4¾–10 inches long; twigs pubescent when young . . . . *P. monticola* (British Columbia to Idaho and California) Zone 5 (These two species are difficult to tell apart with the naked eye, except that the habit of *P. monticola* is more narrow and dense and the needles stiffer than are those of *P. strobus.*)

   3. Mature twigs pubescent

       4. Tree densely upright, pyramidal in habit . . . . . *P. cembra* (Alps of Europe) Zone 4

       4. Tree not as above, more open

           5. Needles lustrous, dark green . . . . *P. koraiensis* (Japan, Korea) Zone 3

           5. Needles dull green

               6. Terminal bud blunt, almost globular, cones 12 to 20 inches . . . . *P. lambertiana* (Oregon to California) Zone 5

               6. Terminal bud sharply pointed, definitely not globular, cones 4–10 inches . . . . . *P. monticola* (British Columbia to Idaho and California) Zone 5

2. Needles 4½–8 inches long . . . . *P. wallichiana* (Himalayas) Zone 5

2. Needles 8–12 inches long . . . . *P. torreyana* (southwestern California) Zone 9

1. Needles 3 to 4 in a sheath, only occasionally 5; leaf margin smooth Zone 9 . . . . *P. cembroides parrayana*

1. Needles 3 in a sheath

attenuata—Knob-cone pine   *ponderosa*—Ponderosa pine
bungeana—Lacebark pine   *radiata*—Monterey pine
canariensis—Canary pine   *rigida*—Pitch pine
coulteri—Coulter pine   *sabiniana*—Digger pine
jeffreyi—Jeffrey pine   *taeda*—Loblolly pine
palustris—Longleaf pine

2. Needles mostly 2–5 inches long
3. Leaf sheaths deciduous, bark of older twigs smooth, bark of trunk flaky with white or yellow patches . . . . *P. bungeana* (China) Zone 4
3. Leaf sheaths not deciduous, bark of older twigs very rough, bark of trunk dark brown to black
4. Foliage dark green, cones usually 2–4 inches long . . . . *P. rigida* (eastern United States and Canada) Zone 4
4. Foliage bright or bluish green; cones 3–7 inches long
5. Bark on upper part of trunk and branches smooth . . . . *P. attenuata* (Oregon to California) Zone 8
5. Bark on upper part of trunk and branches rough . . . . *P. radiata* (southern California) Zone 8
2. Needles mostly 5–10 inches long
3. Winter buds resinous
4. Twigs fragrant when broken; cones 3 to 6 inches; foliage dark green, branchlets orange-brown . . . . . . *P. ponderosa* (western United States) Zone 5
4. Twigs not fragrant when broken; cones 9 to 14 inches; foliage bluish green . . . . *P. coulteri* (California) Zone 8
3. Winter buds not resinous
4. Foliage bluish green
5. Needles stout, bark cinnamon red, cones 6–12 inches . . . . *P. jeffreyi* (Oregon and California) Zone 5
5. Needles slim, bark red-brown, cones 3–6 inches . . . . *P. taeda* (New Jersey to Florida and Texas) Zone 6
4. Foliage dark green; cones 5–12 inches . . . . *P. coulteri* (California) Zone 8
2. Needles 8–18 inches long
3. Foliage gray-bluish green
4. Needles slender, drooping . . . . *P. sabiniana* (California) Zone 6
4. Needles stiff, erect . . . . *P. coulteri* (California) Zone 8
3. Foliage green

4. Needles mostly 8–10 inches long, light green, lustrous
.... *P. canariensis*
(Canary Islands) Zone 10?
4. Needles mostly 12 inches long or more, dark green
.... *P. palustris*
(southeastern United States) Zone 7

1. Needles 3 and 2 in a sheath
caribaea—Slash pine
cembroides—Mexican pinyon pine
echinata—Shortleaf pine
ponderosa scopulorum—Rocky Mountain ponderosa pine
tabulaeformis—Chinese pine

2. Needles less than 2 inches long .... *P. cembroides*
(southern California and Arizona) Zone 9
2. Needles more than 2 inches long
3. One-year-old twigs greenish to purplish, covered with glaucous
bloom .... *P. echinata*
(eastern United States) Zone 5
3. One-year-old twigs yellow-brown to brownish
4. Terminal bud very resinous ..... *P. ponderosa scopulorum*
(Rocky Mountain region) Zone 4
4. Terminal bud not resinous or only slightly so
5. Needles 2–7 inches long; cones 1½–2 inches long
.... *P. tabulaeformis*
(China) Zone 5
5. Needles 8–12 inches long; cones 3–6½ inches long
.... *P. caribaea*
(southeastern United States, Bahamas, Honduras)
Zone 8

1. Needles 2 in a sheath

banksiana—Jack pine
densiflora—Japanese red pine
densiflora oculus-draconis
densiflora umbraculifera
echinata—Shortleaf pine
mugo—Swiss mountain pine
mugo compacta
mugo pumilio

nigra austriaca—Austrian pine
pinaster—Cluster pine
pungens—Table Mountain pine
resinosa—Red pine
sylvestris—Scotch pine
tabulaeformis—Chinese pine
thunbergii—Japanese black pine
virginiana—Virginia pine

2. Needles ¾–3 inches long
3. Foliage with each needle marked with a yellow band
.... *P. densiflora* 'Oculus-draconis'
3. Foliage bluish green, bark of upper trunk red
(Europe) Zone 2 .... *P. sylvestris* and vars.
3. Foliage green
4. Plant usually shrubby, with several branches from the base
5. Needles ¾–2 inches long, bark black
.... *P. mugo* and vars.
(central Europe) Zone 2

        5. Needles 3–5 inches bark red to reddish
          . . . . *P. densiflora* "Umbraculifera'
    4. Tree with a central leader
        5. Needles 1¼–3 inches long
            6. Branchlets usually with glaucous bloom, often greenish to purplish or yellowish
                7. Foliage bluish green, cones usually not persistent, bark of upper trunk red; leaves flexible . . . . *P. densiflora* (Japan) Zone 4
                7. Foliage bright green, cones persistent, bark of upper trunk black; leaves stiff
                  . . . . *P. virginiana* (eastern United States) Zone 4
            6. Branchlets without glaucous bloom, orange to yellow
                7. Vigorous shoots often with more than one whorl of branches on the current year's growth
                    8. Needles more than 1 inch long; cones not prickly and straight
                      . . . . *P. pungens* (southeastern United States) Zone 5
                    8. Needles often less than 1 inch long; cones prickly, curved. .*P. banksiana* (northeastern United States and eastern Canada) Zone 2
                7. Vigorous shoots with only one whorl, branches on the current year's growth
                    8. Winter buds white or whitish to light yellow. . . . .*P. thunbergii* (Japan) Zone 4
                    8. Winter buds dark brown
                    . . . . *P. tabulaeformis* (China) Zone 5
2. Needles 3–8 inches long
    3. Winter buds resinous
        4. Needles slender and flexible, not breaking when bent
        . . . . *P. resinosa* (northeastern United States and eastern Canada) Zone 2
        4. Needles stout and stiff, breaking when bent
        . . . . *P. nigra austriaca* (central Europe) Zone 4
    3. Winter buds not resinous (or slightly so in . . . *P. tabulaeformis)*
        4. Buds stout, up to 1 inch long; branchlets bright reddish brown . . . . *P. pinaster*

(Portugal to Greece) Zone 8
4. Buds less than ½ inch long
    5. Bark of upper trunk red . . . . *P. densiflora*
        (Japan) Zone 4
    5. Bark of upper trunk black
        6. One-year-old twigs with glaucous bloom, green
           to purplish . . . . *P. echinata*
           (eastern United States) Zone 5
        6. One-year-old twigs without glaucous bloom,
           yellow to brown
           7. Winter buds dark reddish brown
              . . . . *P. tabulaeformis*
              (China) Zone 5
           7. Winter buds light yellow to white or whit-
              ish . . . . *P. thunbergii*
              (Japan) Zone 4

Pinus aristata   8–45′   Zone 5   Bristlecone pine

* HABIT: dwarf and picturesque
FOLIAGE: evergreen; 5 needles in a bundle, bluish, usually less than 1½″ long
HABITAT: Arizona, Colorado, California

When planted in gardens in the eastern United States this tree is a dwarf, growing very slowly, a sixteen-year-old plant being only 4 feet tall. It does not conform to any particular growth habit but is picturesque with short, bluish green needles closely bunched together, on which there are white spots of resin. It is most interesting to note that old trees, dwarfed by age and drought in Arizona, have been estimated to be four thousand years old, hence are older than the giant sequoias of California.

Pinus banksiana   75′   Zone 2   Jack pine

HABIT: broad, open head, often shrubby
* FOLIAGE: open, evergreen, 2 needles in a bundle, mostly 1″ long
HABITAT: northern and northeastern North America

Not among the best ornamental pines, for the needles frequently are yellowish in the winter and remain on the tree only one or two years. Its only qualification for consideration here is the fact that it is one of our hardiest pines and will do well on dry, sandy banks, where most other evergreens (and deciduous plants as well) will fail. Because of its loose and open habit of growth it is not recommended for planting in good soil where better pines might be used.

Pinus bungeana   75′   Zone 4   Lacebark pine

* HABIT: often with several trunks, rounded to pyramidal
* BARK: exfoliating in irregular plates, exposing the light, creamy-colored inner bark
* FOLIAGE: dense, evergreen, bright green, 3 needles in a bundle, 3″ long

The mottled bark of the
lacebark pine (Pinus
bungeana).

HABITAT: northwestern China
INTRODUCED: 1846

A rather slow-growing, dark green foliage tree with excellent possibilities as a specimen plant because of its habit of growth and interesting bark. Very young plants will
show the characteristic exfoliating bark when the branches are only an inch in diameter. Also, this tree has the most desirable trait of holding its needles about five years,
longer than most pines. Consequently, this excellent specimen pine should be planted
considerably more than it is. Its picturesque habit of growth with several major trunks
is also one of its attractive qualities. It was named after Alexander von Bunge, a
Russian author from St. Petersburg who recorded much about the plants of northern
and northeastern Asia before he died in 1890.

Pinus canariensis   80'   Zone 8   Canary pine

HABIT: picturesque, rounded head, but often pyramidal, open
* FOLIAGE: evergreen, lustrous needles, 3 in a bundle, 9–12″ long

HABITAT: Canary Islands
INTRODUCED: about 1850?

This tree is of value only in California and the extreme southern states. It is very picturesque with its long needles and grows rapidly, especially in dry, rocky situations, where it does better than *P. radiata.*

Pinus caribaea   100′   Zone 9   Slash pine

HABIT: coarse, loose, and open
FOLIAGE: evergreen needles, 2 and 3 in a bundle, 8–12″ long
HABITAT: North Carolina to Florida

Although an excellent tree for lumber and for producing turpentine, this is used only occasionally in the southeastern states as an ornamental. The long needles and open branching give the tree a coarse appearance.

Pinus cembra   75′   Zone 2   Swiss stone pine

* HABIT: dense, tightly pyramidal, not round-topped until fully mature
* FOLIAGE: soft-textured evergreen needles, 5 in a bundle, 2½–4¼″ long
HABITAT: central Europe, northern Asia
INTRODUCED: before 1875
VARIETY:
   'Columnaris'—more narrow and columnar in habit than the species

A very slow-growing pine, frequently disappointing for this reason. Nevertheless, it makes a tightly molded pyramidal specimen while young, often well suited to formal planting. It retains its needles for about three years; they are the same shade of green as are those of *P. strobus.* It is of interest to note that this is proving hardy at Dropmore, Manitoba, Canada.

Pinus contorta   30′   Zone 7   Shore pine

HABIT: round-topped, dense head
FOLIAGE: evergreen needles, 2 in a bundle, 2″ long
HABITAT: Alaska to California
VARIETY:
   latifolia—a hardier (Zone 5) and taller-growing (75′) form, this is the most common tree in the northern Rocky Mountain area where it can be used if desired

This tree grows under many different soil and climatic conditions on the West Coast and has been widely recommended for use there. Apparently it is not being used much, but it adapts equally well to boggy soils and dry soils. It has rich, deep green foliage and makes a good garden tree.

Pinus coulteri   75'   Zone 7   Big cone pine, Coulter pine

HABIT: loose and open
* FOLIAGE: coarse, evergreen needles, 3 in a bundle, 6–8" long
HABITAT: California

This tree of loose habit and sparse foliage has been used in California plantings. It is not common in cultivation but is very striking in its somewhat gaunt branching. It takes its name from the cones that are sometimes 14 inches long.

Pinus densiflora   100'   Zone 4   Japanese red pine

* HABIT: horizontal branches, irregular head
* BARK: orange-red, even on the older branches
* FOLIAGE: bright bluish green needles, 2 in a bundle, 3–5" long
HABITAT: Japan
INTRODUCED: 1854
VARIETIES:
> 'Oculus-draconis' *(Dragon's eye pine)*—each leaf marked with two yellow lines making the general effect interesting and colorful
> 'Pendula'—with pendulous branches
> 'Umbraculifera' *(Tanyosho pine)*—low, umbrellalike

A picturesque tree, no better ornamentally than some of the other pines native to this country but of a distinct flat-topped habit. The specific name comes from the flowers that are borne in dense clusters, which of course are followed by numerous cones. The foliage turns a yellowish green to pale green in the winter and the needles are retained for only two years, but the bark is certainly interesting throughout the year.

Pinus flexilis   45–75'   Zone 2   Limber pine, Rocky Mountain
                                                                    white pine

* HABIT: narrow and pyramidal while young, broad and round-topped when mature, branches horizontal, often slightly pendulous, open to dense
* FOLIAGE: fine-textured, evergreen needles, 5 in a bundle, 1½–3" long
HABITAT: western North America
VARIETIES:
> *glauca*—bluish green foliage
> 'Pendula'—wide-spreading with weeping branches

A desirable ornamental pine, it is widely spread over the mountains of the West Coast area with a tendency to become flat-topped as it grows older, the foliage remaining on the tree about four years. It is slow in growth, for individual trees may be over two hundred years old before the trunk reaches a diameter of 9 inches. The largest tree in the Arnold Arboretum is only about 30 feet tall and was planted in 1884. Unless its habit is desirable, it is not as good and vigorous an ornamental as *P. strobus,* but as a perennial small specimen in the small garden, it certainly has its advantages.

Pinus halepensis   60'   Zone 9   Aleppo pine

HABIT: open, round-topped
* FOLIAGE: evergreen needles, 2 (rarely 3) in a bundle, 2½–6" long
HABITAT: Mediterranean region
INTRODUCED: early colonial times

Where better growing conditions are available, this pine should not be used—recommended only for seashore plantings.

Pinus jeffreyi   120'   Zone 5   Jeffrey pine

HABIT: pyramidal, often spreading or even pendant branches, open
* BARK: cinnamon red to brown
FOLIAGE: evergreen, pale bluish green needles, 3 in a bundle, 5–8" long
HABITAT: Oregon to California

Somewhat similar to *P. ponderosa* but its needles are bluish green. This tree is of value only as an ornamental on the West Coast.

Pinus koraiensis   90'   Zone 3   Korean pine

* HABIT: pyramidal, dense
* FOLIAGE: evergreen, 3–5 needles in a bundle, 2½–4" long
HABITAT: Japan, Korea
INTRODUCED: 1861

This is a slow-growing tree, and although it eventually grows very tall, it makes an excellent tree for small gardens because of its slow growth. It is truly handsome with dark green foliage all winter and should be planted a great deal more than it is.

Pinus lambertiana   180'   Zone 5   Sugar pine

* HABIT: narrowly columnar
* FOLIAGE: evergreen, 5 needles in a bundle, about 3–4½" long
HABITAT: Oregon to California

The tallest of the native American pines, this is not a tree for the small garden. It is of interest because it bears the largest cones of any of the pines, sometimes 20 inches or more in length. Although hardy in Boston, Massachusetts, it is probably only of ornamental use on the West Coast.

Pinus monticola   90′   Zone 5   Western white pine

* HABIT: narrowly symmetrical
* FOLIAGE: evergreen, 5 needles in a bundle, mostly 3–4½″ long
  HABITAT: British Columbia to California

Different from *P. strobus* in being more narrowly symmetrical, this makes a fine ornamental. In the East it is doubtful whether it will ever be used in preference to the more readily available *P. strobus*, but it should be kept in mind that it is hardy and might be used where a more narrow tree is desired. It makes a beautiful specimen.

Pinus muricata   45′   Zone 7   Bishop pine

* HABIT: regularly pyramidal
  FOLIAGE: evergreen needles, 2 in a bundle, about 4–6″ long
  HABITAT: California

A handsome tree, this is sometimes used as an ornamental but only in the area of California where it is native.

Pinus nigra   90′   Zone 4   Austrian pine

* HABIT: densely pyramidal, wide-spreading and round-topped, stiff
* FOLIAGE: evergreen, dark green needles, 2 in a bundle, 3½–6½″ long
  HABITAT: central and southern Europe, Asia Minor
  INTRODUCED: 1759
  VARIETIES:
>   *austriaca*—needles supposed to be slightly shorter than the species, mostly about 3–4″ long. Actually this is a geographic variety and there is practically no difference in ornamental characteristics between this and the species. Most of the Austrian pines in this country are grown from seed anyway so that a certain amount of variability is to be expected.
>   'Pyramidalis' *(Pyramidal Austrian pine)*—narrow pyramidal form with closely ascending branches

A fast-growing species, with very stiff needles, making a splendid specimen in several forms, with glossy, dark green foliage. It makes an excellent windbreak or screen and should grow well in limestone soils. Certainly it does well in acid soils. This is an excellent, stiffly formed tree, well adapted to specimen planting, and holds its needles for three years.

Pinus parviflora   90′   Zone 5   Japanese white pine

* HABIT: densely pyramidal, wide-spreading
* FOLIAGE: evergreen, bluish to dark green needles, 5 in a bundle, 1½–2½″ long

HABITAT: Japan
INTRODUCED: 1861
VARIETIES:

'Gimborn's Ideal'—slow-growing, upright when young, widening with age; green needles, bluish underneath

glauca (Silver Japanese white pine)—needles silvery blue in color; much better than the species because of this

The Japanese white pine is an excellent ornamental pine with short, often slightly twisted needles that remain on the tree two years, forming brushlike tufts at the end of the branchlets. One plant in the Arnold Arboretum is 60 feet tall and almost as broad. Consequently, it needs plenty of room for future expansion

Pinus patula   60′   Zone 9   Jelecote pine

* HABIT: loose and open
* FOLIAGE: gracefully hanging, evergreen needles, usually 3 in a bundle but sometimes 4 or 5, up to 9″ long
  HABITAT: Mexico

This pine is used only in southern California. Its lovely needles make it an outstanding specimen.

Pinus peuce   60′   Zone 4   Macedonian pine, Balkan pine

* HABIT: dense, narrowly pyramidal
* FOLIAGE: evergreen needles, 5 in a bundle, 3–6″ long
  HABITAT: Balkans
  INTRODUCED: 1863

Of slow growth, hence good for the smaller property. An eighty-year-old tree in the Arnold Arboretum is 45 feet tall and has a spread of 15 feet. The branches are produced in whorls, but the foliage is obviously more dense than that of *P. strobus.*

Pinus pinaster   90′   Zone 7   Cluster pine, Maritime pine

  HABIT: pyramidal, sometimes pendant branches
* FOLIAGE: evergreen, often twisted and glossy green needles, 2 in a bundle, 5–9″ long

This is often called the "Maritime pine" because it is well adapted to seaside planting. Because it is difficult to transplant, young seedlings should be used whenever possible. If sand dune areas at the seaside are to be planted, this pine certainly merits first consideration where it proves hardy.

The interesting bark of the Italian stone pine (Pinus pinea).

Pinus pinea   80′   Zone 9   Italian stone pine

HABIT: broad and flat-topped at maturity
* FOLIAGE: evergreen needles, 2 in a cluster, 8″ long
  HABITAT: Mediterranean region

This is a slow-growing, picturesque pine, often with umbrellalike branches. The seeds are large, nearly ½″ long, and are edible.

Pinus ponderosa   150′   Zone 5   Ponderosa pine

* HABIT: upright, open
* FOLIAGE: evergreen, 2 or 3 needles in a bundle, 5–11″ long
  HABITAT: western North America

A fast-growing tree making up large forests in western North America, it is used as an ornamental tree because of its rapid growth and its dark, yellowish green foliage. Older trees develop a characteristic platelike bark. It is definitely not the tree for the small place. The variety *scopulorum* is smaller in all its parts and is hardier and more columnar in habit.

Pinus radiata 60′ Zone 7 Monterey pine

HABIT: irregular, open
* FOLIAGE: evergreen, bright green needles, 3 in a bundle, 4–6″ long
HABITAT: southern California

This tree is especially valued for seaside planting.

Pinus resinosa 75′ Zone 2 Red pine, Norway pine

* HABIT: stout, spreading branches forming a broad, pyramidal head
BARK: reddish brown
* FOLIAGE: soft textured, evergreen, lustrous, dark green needles, 2 in a bundle,
    4–6″ long
HABITAT: north central and northeastern North America

This is a fine ornamental pine as well as a valued timber tree. I have seen splendid trees in the Finger Lakes parks of central New York that were two hundred years old and still in perfect condition. The long needles are flexible and thus differ from the stiff needles of the Austrian pine. The bark of the trunk and some of the larger branches is reddish—an interesting, desirable feature. In some sections of the country, the pine bud moth is a serious pest on the red pine, disfiguring its branching habit to a considerable extent, but this pest is easily controlled by spraying with methoxychlor just when the new growth begins.

Pinus rigida 75′ Zone 4 Pitch pine

HABIT: very open
* FOLIAGE: evergreen, 3 needles in a bundle, 2–4″ long
HABITAT: eastern North America
VARIETY:
    'Sherman Eddy' *('Little Giant')*—up to 15′ in height, upright, dense, slow-growing, 4–6″ a year. Distinctive and unusual.

The pitch pine is not an ornamental tree and is used only for planting on dry, rocky soil where little else will grow. Old mature trees are very picturesque with their open branching, and cones remain on the trees for several years, but the needles drop after the first year or two and the remainder turn brownish in the winter. If good soil is available, much more attractive trees could be selected.

Pinus strobus 100–150′ Zone 3 Eastern white pine

* HABIT: rounded or pyramidal, picturesque at maturity
* FOLIAGE: soft, flexible, evergreen needles, 5 in a bundle, 2½–5½″ long
HABITAT: eastern North America

VARIETIES:

'Fastigiata' *(Pyramidal white pine)*—narrowly upright and columnar in habit
glauca (Blue white pine)—foliage light bluish green
'Pendula' *(Weeping white pine)*—branches pendulous, a most graceful looking
  pine even though the branches are stiff and lack the pleasing flexibility of a
  Cedrus deodara or *Picea omorika*

The second tallest pine native in North America (the sugar pine, *P. lambertiana,* is
tallest)—a top-notch ornamental evergreen tree, fifth in importance among the timber
trees of North America now, although at one time it was the most important.

The delicate, graceful, soft green foliage of the white pine is unsurpassed by that
of any other hardy northern tree except possibly the hemlock. In the fall it drops its
three-year-old needles like many other evergreens, but the foliage that remains stays
a soft green throughout the long winter months. In fact, the normal green of white
pine foliage year in and year out makes this tree one of the most valuable for
background foliage in any landscape planting, be it large or small.

White pine may grow 10 feet in ten years and 25 feet in twenty years if it is in
good soil. Young trees are dense and often pyramidal in habit, but the older the tree

*The fastigiate form of the
eastern white pine* (Pinus
strobus).

grows the more picturesque it becomes—with flat top and a missing branch here and there until at a ripe old age these trees are the most conspicuous (and beautiful) in almost any landscape.

Easily transplanted, the white pine also withstands shearing, but this must be done in just the right way. On close inspection of any branch of white pine, it will be noticed that the needles are not distributed evenly along the current year's growth but are bunched near the tip. There is a portion of every twig with no needles. This is the place not to cut. Every snip with the pruning shears should be in the middle of the twig where needles are, leaving some of the needles on the twig. At the base of these, new buds will quickly form. If, on the other hand, the cut is made where there are no needles, then that part of the twig will die back to the previous year's growth. This is a rather important sidelight on pruning or shearing white pine, for when not done properly, pruning this tree can do more harm than good.

Currants of many types carry the dread white pine blister rust, the reason there is considerable legislation regulating the transport of five-needled pines and currants as well.

Fortunately for the small property owner, white pine can be restrained by proper pruning and so will not grow out of scale. For landscape work on small properties, in parks along major highways, and for many other purposes, the white pine is one of the best and most serviceable evergreen trees in eastern North America.

Pinus sylvestris   75'   Zone 2   Scotch pine

* HABIT: open, pyramidal while young but round-topped and irregular when old
* BARK: red on older trunks and branches
* FOLIAGE: stiff, twisted evergreen, bluish green needles, 2 in a bundle, ¾–3" long
  HABITAT: Europe to Siberia
  INTRODUCED: probably colonial times
  VARIETIES:

    'Argentea' *(Silver Scotch pine)*—leaves are a pronounced silvery color

    'Fastigiata' *(Pyramidal Scotch pine)*—columnar and narrow in habit, about the narrowest of any of the pines

    'French Blue'—foliage a brighter blue than other varieties, with the color retained throughout the winter

    'Watereri'—a slow-growing, densely pyramidal form with steel blue needles, almost as high as it is wide when young

Although a valued timber tree in Europe and extensively planted as a timber tree in America, it has not proved successful. As an ornamental it is valued for its bluish green foliage and very picturesque open habit at maturity, as well as its red trunk and older branches. It cannot be considered a good shade tree, but for displaying unique form and color among the pines it is outstanding. Many horticultural varieties have appeared as is so often the case, especially with native European plants that have been cultivated for centuries. The varieties *rigensis* (with very red bark) and 'Watereri' are the only ones being grown to any extent in this country, but there is a beautiful specimen of the variety 'Fastigiata' growing in Durand-Eastman Park, Rochester,

New York. It would seem that there might be an opportunity in this country for some of the other varieties so cherished in Europe.

Pinus thunbergii   90'   Zone 5   Japanese black pine

HABIT: dense, spreading, often pendulous branches
* FOLIAGE: stiff, open, evergreen, dark green needles, 2 in a bundle, 3–5″ long
HABITAT: Japan
INTRODUCED: 1855

The best pine, possibly the best evergreen, for planting along the seashore in the northeastern United States is the Japanese black pine. It has done very well on Nantucket and Martha's Vineyard, where other plants have failed, for it withstands seashore conditions and even a small amount of saltwater spray. Its large, grayish white terminal buds distinguish it from some of the other pines. The Japanese have trained this type into many grotesque forms. Even naturally it grows rather irregularly, but young, vigorous plants should find many uses in seaside gardens. Better pines are available for better growing conditions.

Pinus torreyana   45'   Zone 8   Torrey pine

HABIT: spreading and ascending branches but open
* FOLIAGE: evergreen needles, 5 in a bundle, 8–12″ long
HABITAT: southern California

This tree is of merit only in dry situations in southern California where better pines will not grow. In good soils, other trees certainly should be selected.

Pinus virginiana   45'   Zone 4   Virginia pine, Scrub pine

HABIT: open, branching, sparse, often with very wide top, stiff
* FOLIAGE: evergreen, 2 needles in a bundle, 1¼–3″ long
HABITAT: eastern United States

This tree is not an ornamental and is used only for planting in poor, dry soils where other pines will not grow.

Pinus wallichiana (syn. *P. excelsa, P. griffithii*)   150'   Zone 5
                                                               Himalayan pine

* HABIT: graceful, wide-spreading, dense
* FOLIAGE: soft textured, evergreen, blue-green needles, 5 in a bundle, 5–7″ long
HABITAT: Himalayas
INTRODUCED: 1827

A beautiful, fast-growing, wide-spreading tree that eventually may have a spread of 40 to 50 feet. It seems to do best in sandy loam but has been seriously injured in the Arnold Arboretum during the past years by winter cold and severe winds. The long, drooping, blue-green needles give it a graceful appearance. It does well in the vicinity of Philadelphia and of Seattle, where the climate and growing conditions seem to be exactly to its liking. This is a large tree, but where space is available to display it properly, it is an excellent pine to use.

Pistacia chinensis   50′   Zone 9   Chinese pistache

* FRUIT: small, red, in dense clusters; sexes separate
      EFFECTIVE: fall
  HABIT: broad-rounded, short trunk
  FOLIAGE: beautiful, fine textured, male trees more dense
* AUTUMN COLOR: red and orange
  HABITAT: China
  INTRODUCED: 1921

First introduced into America by that intrepid plant explorer for the U.S. Department of Agriculture, Frank L. Meyer, it is akin somewhat to *Rhus* or *Sophora.* It is slow-growing, effective on small properties, and withstands both heat and drought. The seed yields an oil used in cooking, and the Chinese have been known to boil the leaf buds and eat them. It is free of insect pests and diseases, which is an added advantage. The species *P. vera,* yielding the edible pistachio nuts of commerce, is frequently grafted or budded on roots of this Chinese species. In Florida this species has performed very well as a shade tree.

Pittosporum eugenioides   40′   Zone 10   Tarata pittosporum

* HABIT: oval-shaped, sometimes columnar, sometimes pyramidal
* FOLIAGE: evergreen, yellowish green
* HABITAT: New Zealand

This is probably used more as a shrub than as a tree in the warmer areas of the country since it does well under shearing.

Pittosporum rhombifolium   80′   Zone 10   Diamondleaf
                                                pittosporum

  FRUIT: bright orange berries, in large clusters
      EFFECTIVE: midwinter
  HABIT: symmetrical, rounded
* FOLIAGE: glossy, evergreen leaves, 3–4″ long
  HABITAT: Australia

A good tree for parkway planting in the southwestern United States where it is hardy; one of the most popular street trees in Santa Barbara, California.

⇥≫ *PLATANUS*

Sycamore lace bug causes a white peppered effect on the upper surface of the leaves. Spray with malathion as soon as the young leaves unfurl. Also, scales should be controlled.

Anthracnose produces black areas on the leaves and causes them to show dead, crisp areas, especially in cool, wet weather. Spray with copper sulfate or ferbam for effective control.

x Platanus acerifolia   100'   Zone 5   London plane tree

FRUIT: in pendulous, ball-like clusters, with 2, rarely 3, in a cluster
    EFFECTIVE: fall and winter
HABIT: wide-spreading branches, open
* BARK: exfoliating in flakes, underbark light colored, often yellowish
FOLIAGE: large, coarse, maplelike leaves, 5–10" wide
HYBRID ORIGIN: *P. occidentalis x P. orientalis*
ORIGINATED: probably before 1700

This tree is very resistant to the twig blight so troublesome to our native *P. occidentalis.* It grows with a tall, straight trunk, the older trees sometimes having trunks over 20 feet in circumference. Both this species and *P. orientalis* are easily clipped and have been grown as clipped screens and arbors, both in this country and abroad. However, their coarse leaves and vigorous growth seem to detract from their use in this way, especially since there are other materials of much finer texture available. It is of interest to note that the young twigs of both these European plane trees are densely covered with hairs at first, which are gradually shed during the summer. Sometimes a nasal irritation is brought about by these hairs when they are abundant in the summer. As a street tree, both this species and the Oriental plane tree are planted annually by the thousands.

Platanus orientalis   90'   Zone 6   Oriental plane tree

FRUIT: in pendulous, ball-like clusters, 3 or more in a cluster
    EFFECTIVE: fall and winter
HABIT: thick trunk, broad rounded head, open
* BARK: exfoliating in flakes, underbark greenish white
FOLIAGE: large, coarse, maplelike leaves, 4–8" wide

HABITAT: southeastern Europe, Asia Minor
INTRODUCED: colonial times

This species is much less susceptible to the serious twig blight disease so troublesome to the native sycamore, *P. occidentalis.* It has been planted as a shade tree since ancient times and grows almost as large in size as the London plane tree. The native *P. occidentalis* can usually be distinguished from this and *P. acerifolia,* in that the latter have two or more balls of fruit in a cluster while *P. occidentalis* has only one. This Oriental species, if let alone, will frequently grow with several trunks from the base and reach a great old age, some trees in England being said to be three hundred and even four hundred years old. This compares favorably with similar trees of *P. occidentalis* in Pennsylvania and Maryland known to have been growing in William Penn's time (1632). As street trees these are in great demand and have been widely used. However, they do grow large, and unless placed on large avenues or along highways with plenty of room, they will grow too big to serve their purpose properly. This can become a very important problem, for overly large street trees growing in cramped situations can become very costly to maintain properly.

Platanus racemosa   120′   Zone 7   California plane tree

FRUIT: in pendulous, ball-like clusters, 2–7 in a cluster
    EFFECTIVE: fall and winter
HABIT: usually several trunks of picturesque form, open, irregular
* BARK: exfoliating
FOLIAGE: coarse, maplelike leaves
HABITAT: southern California

Of value chiefly in the warmer climates for its irregular, often gnarled habit of growth. It is susceptible to blight but is frequently used nevertheless.

Podocarpus elongatus   70′   Zone 10   Fern podocarpus

FRUIT: fleshy, purplish, 1/3″ long
    EFFECTIVE: fall
HABITAT: dense
* FOLIAGE: evergreen, fine-textured leaves, 2″ long and ⅛″ broad
HABITAT: South Africa

Fern podocarpus is used only in the subtropical areas of the country.

Podocarpus macrophyllus   60′   Zone 7   Yew podocarpus

FRUIT: fleshy, purplish, ½″ long
    EFFECTIVE: fall
HABIT: horizontal branches, pendulous branchlets

* FOLIAGE: dense, evergreen, narrow, needlelike (similar to yews but larger), dark
        green, 4″ long
HABITAT: Japan
INTRODUCED: 1804

This tree has foliage similar to the yews except that the needles are longer and wider.
It is grown from North Carolina southward, making a popular hedge plant in this
country as well as in Tokyo Gardens where it is clipped into many different shapes.
This is the most common of the podocarpus species in America at this time.

Poncirus trifoliata   35′   Zones 5–6   Hardy-orange

* FLOWERS: very fragrant, white, 2″ in diameter
        TIME: late April
FRUIT: yellow, like a small orange, 2″ in diameter
        EFFECTIVE: fall
  HABIT: open and rather indefinite, thorny
FOLIAGE: open, deciduous, leathery, dark green
HABITAT: North China, Korea
* INTRODUCED: 1850

The hardy-orange is frequently used as a hedge in the South because of its dense
growth and prominent spines and also because it will withstand shearing well. Its
small, white flowers, faintly reminiscent of orange blossoms, do not remain effective
very long, but its leathery, dark green leaves and its small, bitter-tasting oranges are
its chief ornamental characteristics, while the dense growth, too, is of importance.
Hardy in protected places as far north as Boston, it can be depended on to weather
all winters south of Philadelphia. It is a unique plant, not among the best of ornamental specimens but nevertheless serviceable in some situations (especially in acid soils
where it grows well), and once established in the right situation it proves to be a
vigorous grower. It is not worth much as a shade tree or as a street tree because its
large thorns and fruit could easily prove a traffic hazard. No serious insect pests or
diseases.

⇛ *POPULUS*

In the past, poplars have entered into America's landscape plantings on a
wide scale, chiefly because they are vigorous growers. Some were used
widely in street tree plantings in our larger cities merely because they grow
well under adverse conditions. However, it soon became known that they
are voracious feeders; roots lifted sidewalks and street paving, and have
entered and seriously clogged water pipes and sewers, causing considerable

damage to such installations. Because of this they have become unpopular in recent years, and many cities have an ordinance against planting them along city streets.

Incidentally, the best method of controlling roots in the sewer is to allow 5 pounds of copper sulfate crystals dissolved in water to go down the drain slowly and flush no more wastage down for several hours. This might be done once a month until free flowage occurs. Four 1-pound applications per year should be sufficient to keep the roots killed. This also applies to killing the roots of elms and willows clogging local sewers.

Then, too, these trees are weak-wooded and brittle and break very easily during heavy snow- and windstorms. The Lombardy poplar, long valued for its columnar, upright habit, had been a good plant in landscape work until it was found that mature trees frequently developed a trunk canker at maturity for which there is no adequate cure. As a result, trees were carefully tended for years, only to die back at the top when they were finally beginning to prove effective for their habit. Also, broken branches and wounds on trunks may develop in serious "bleeding" cankers that are difficult to cure. This, combined with the fact that its flowers and fruit are of little ornamental value and frequently become a nuisance, have been responsible for the poplar's gradual disappearance from the landscape picture in areas where other trees can be grown.

Poplars are very rapid growers and therefore can be used as "fillers" until better trees become well established. Some, such as the white poplar *(P. alba),* withstand very dry growing situations and so can be used in parts of the Midwest where few other ornamentals can adapt to the trying growing conditions. The commercial grower likes to include them in his catalog because they are very easy to propagate and in good soil make a salable tree in one year's time. In fact, dormant cuttings can be put in the soil outdoors in the spring and with a reasonable amount of water can be expected to root in place. Not all species will respond to this treatment. People interested in growing wood for paper pulp have been experimenting with these trees for many years and have found that branches with flower buds from male and female trees can be brought into the greenhouse in early February, placed in water, the flowers forced to open and the female plants pollinized, and seed will set at once. This seed can then be sown and a small seedling will result that same year. Some of the hybrids so formed have been known to grow as much as 21 feet in two years' time. Consequently, there will always be a demand for poplars.

Twelve species are recommended here for specific uses. Their universal shortcomings should always be kept in mind and, when possible, plants with better ornamental qualifications should be chosen. For specific purposes or for use in certain areas with poor growing conditions, they may have their place.

One of the common pests of poplars and willows on the home grounds is the poplar curculio, the grub that tunnels in the twigs and branches, causing them to break or leaving conspicuous scars. Cutting out and spraying with methoxychlor in midsummer is suggested. The cottonwood leaf beetle develops three or four broods annually, and its black grubs will skeletonize poplar leaves. Malathion is effective. Poplar leaf hopper also may become very abundant. Malathion, diazinon, or methoxychlor should be applied where necessary. Additionally, the poplar is a favorite host of oyster shell scale, and poplar and other borers may damage older trees. Leaf-eating caterpillars such as tussock moth worms, spiny elm caterpillar, gypsy moth, and poplar tent-maker are minor pests that can be controlled by sprays of methoxychlor or malathion.

European canker causes split bark, dead branches, and excessive watersprouts. Lombardy poplar is most susceptible to this. Careful pruning and removal of infected trees are recommended, but thorough dormant sprays with lime sulfur have been helpful. Rust, scab, leaf curl, and anthracnose infect various species but seldom require control.

Populus alba   90'   Zone 3   White poplar

HABIT: irregular, rather open
* BARK: whitish gray
* FOLIAGE: upper side of leaves grayish green, lower side white and very pubescent, making an interesting color contrast
AUTUMN COLOR: red to reddish but not too pronounced
HABITAT: Europe, western Siberia
INTRODUCED: colonial times?
VARIETIES:

  nivea (Silver poplar)—leaves especially white on undersurface
  'Pyramidalis' *(Bolleana poplar)*—columnar in habit, probably originating in the wild about 1841
  'Richardii' *(Richard's white poplar)*—upper surface of leaves dull yellow; many plants with yellow leaves make inferior landscape specimens but this, with its white undersurface, seems to be a rather colorful combination and not objectionable.

The white poplar makes a good specimen where there is room for growing it properly, for it is a wide-spreading tree. It is the only poplar with lobed leaves (at least on vigorous shoots) and a downy undersurface. Its tendency to have red autumn color, even though it is not as pronounced as in the maples and some other trees, is a point in its favor for fall display. This excellent columnar variety is a good substitute for the Lombardy poplar and is not as susceptible to the trunk canker that mars the Lombardy poplar at maturity. It can well be considered one of the most ornamental of the columnar trees.

Populus balsamifera   90′   Zone 2   Balm of Gilead

HABIT: large, wide-spreading branches
FOLIAGE: rather open
HABITAT: origin unknown
INTRODUCED: prior to 1800?

This tree is very wide-spreading and is often confused with *P. tacamahaca.* Unless a wide-spreading tree is desired, this might well be omitted from consideration.

x *Populus berolinensis*   75′   Zone 2   Berlin poplar

* HABIT: ascending branches, almost columnar in habit
* FOLIAGE: open, bright green
HYBRID ORIGIN: *P. laurifolia x P. nigra* 'Italica'
ORIGINATED: prior to 1870

The Berlin poplar, a very hardy tree, is recommended for areas where the winters are very cold and the summers very hot, such as on the great prairie areas of the western part of North America. It does not compete well with better ornamental trees available for eastern planting.

x *Populus canadensis eugenei*   150′   Zone 4   Carolina poplar

HABIT: wide-spreading, open
FOLIAGE: coarse, glossy leaves
HYBRID ORIGIN: *P. deltoides x P. nigra*
ORIGINATED: about 1832 in France

This poplar must be mentioned here because it has been so widely used in the past. However, it is *not* recommended for use. In fact, many communities have passed legislation prohibiting its use as a street tree because its roots are sufficiently vigorous to seek out water pipes and drains, making their way into them and quickly clogging them. It is a "dirty" tree, dropping catkins, bud scales, and leaves at various times of the year. It is also weak-wooded, like all poplars, and twigs are continually breaking and littering streets and lawns. There are many superior trees that should be used in its place. The original tree, nearly one hundred years old, was measured a number of years ago at 150 feet in height and 38 feet in trunk circumference at base.

Populus fremontii   90′   Zone 7   Fremont cottonwood

HABIT: large, wide-spreading branches
FOLIAGE: loose, open, coarse
HABITAT: California, Arizona

This is recommended only for the dry, alkaline soils of the southwestern part of the country where it is difficult to get any trees to grow. Another species, *P. wislizeni,* has been used for similar purposes in Texas and New Mexico.

Populus lasiocarpa   60'   Zone 5   Chinese poplar

HABIT: rounded head, open
* FOLIAGE: leaves large (6–10"), bright green with red midrib and petiole
HABITAT: central and western China
INTRODUCED: 1904

One of the most beautiful poplars but still not a tree to use in preference to beeches, oaks, and maples.

Populus maximowiczii   90'   Zone 4   Japanese poplar

HABIT: wide top, open branching
BARK: grayish
FOLIAGE: rather coarse, dull green
HABITAT: Japan
INTRODUCED: before 1890

This very beautiful poplar is recommended here because it is the first of the poplars to unfold its leaves in the spring. This characteristic, combined with its 2½–5-inch-long leaves, light-colored bark, and vigorous habit, gives it qualities that might be desired under certain circumstances.

Populus nigra 'Italica'   90'   Zone 3   Lombardy poplar

* HABIT: columnar, dense
FOLIAGE: dense, leaves very wide at base
ORIGINATED: before 1750 as a clone of *P. nigra,* which is a native of Europe and western Asia
INTRODUCED: 1784

This commonly planted tree is not recommended except possibly as a very short-lived tree. As it matures, it often acquires a canker disease in its upper branches and trunk for which there is no cure, and this of course utterly destroys its symmetry. There are other columnar poplars that are almost as fast growing, and other columnar trees that, although they may not grow as tall as the Lombardy poplar, are more permanent. Consequently, avoid using this tree or use it as a quick-growing temporary screen, to be removed after a more permanent screen has had time to become thoroughly established.

Populus simonii   50′   Zone 2   Simon poplar

* HABIT: rather narrow, dense
   FOLIAGE: small, bright green leaves
   HABITAT: northern China
   INTRODUCED: 1862
   VARIETY:
        'Fastigiata' *(Pyramidal Simon poplar)*—narrowly pyramidal in outline, not exactly columnar but nearly so

A handsome poplar that has been used in ornamental plantings in America. Its light green foliage, rather narrow habit, and vigorous growth are its prime qualities. The fastigiate variety makes a good substitute for the Lombardy poplar, although it is not as columnar in habit. The extreme hardiness of the species is another very important attribute that should be emphasized.

Populus tremula erecta   50′   Zone 2

* HABIT: fastigiate
   ORIGIN: Sweden, 1926

Found in the forests of Sweden, this upright European aspen is grown in America, but further trial is necessary to prove whether it will be a smaller substitute for the Lombardy poplar.

Populus tremuloides   90′   Zone 1   Quaking aspen

   HABIT: loose and open
* BARK: gray to white
* FOLIAGE: leaves small but attached by flat, weak petioles, causing the leaves to move in the slightest breeze
* AUTUMN COLOR: yellow
   HABITAT: North America, coast to coast

The quaking aspen is probably the most widely distributed tree in nature on the North American continent. It should not be considered as a specimen tree because it is too loose and open. Planted in groups or groves, however, or in natural wooded areas, it really comes into its own. There is no sight more beautiful in the Rocky Mountains (or anywhere else for that matter) than a mountainside covered with these trees in their full autumn regalia. Although it does grow nearly 100 feet tall, it is frequently encountered much smaller than this, for it is one of the first trees to sprout up after fire has destroyed a coniferous forest. Usually the larger the tree, the whiter the trunk, and the more susceptible to diseases and breakage from storms.

Prosopis glandulosa   50′   Zone 8   Honey mesquite

FLOWERS: yellowish orange, in racemes; attractive to bees
    TIME: November
HABIT: loose, irregular top; short trunk
FOLIAGE: feathery bright green
HABITAT: southwestern United States

This tough-wooded, slow-growing, drought-resistant tree will not withstand temperatures much below zero.

⇒⇒ *PRUNUS*

The cherries, apricots, plums, and peaches constitute a large group of trees native in the northern temperate regions of the world and range in size from the 15- to 20-foot Oriental double-flowering cherries to the more than 90-foot height of our native black cherry. They are mostly small to medium-sized trees, of particular interest because of their early spring flowers. The flowers of the Asiatic species and varieties appear in early spring before the leaves and are usually borne profusely; those of the native American types and European types bloom a little later, the flowers appearing with the leaves. It is these European and American natives that have very small flowers in racemes, while the Asiatic types have much larger flowers in clusters or sometimes borne singly or in twos. Many of the flowers are single, either pink or white, but there is that very important group of double-flowered Asiatic cherries without which our spring displays would look sad indeed.

Since this group bears its flowers comparatively early in the season, its fruit also appears early, when the leaves are fully developed. As a result, many of them are completely hidden and so have little landscape value. They are red before they ripen, then turn blue or black at maturity, when they are quickly eaten by the birds. The double-flowered cherries, of course, do not bear fruit.

A few of these trees have autumn color, and those few should be used and recommended, for this brings them into the select group of trees that are of interest two seasons of the year. In addition, several have interesting, shiny bark (typical of many cherries), and this is of great ornamental value, especially in the winter landscape. In fact, some of the species have three seasons of interest for this very reason.

The flowers range in size from the small ¼-inch-diameter type appearing in racemes on the bird cherries to the giant 2½-inch-diameter size of some of the double-flowered peaches and Oriental cherries. Each one has a special use in the landscape.

There are some two hundred species of *Prunus,* probably many more varieties—a great many have little ornamental value when compared with some of the best in the list following. Over 150 species and ornamental varieties are being grown by the nurseries of America, and about the same number are being grown in the collection of the Arnold Arboretum. In 1959, Professor George Cochran of Utah State College found by mail survey that over six hundred different *Prunus* species, varieties, and hybrids were being grown in the various collections and arboretums of the United States and Canada.

One group of ornamentals might be used as an example of what has been done with these plants. The ornamental flowering peaches (not the commercial varieties) have been valued for some time. Over seventy-five have been named in the past, and about a third of this number are currently being grown by the nurseries of the country. Some of these double-flowered varieties are certainly conspicuous when they are in bloom, but at best they are short-lived and the methods of keeping them in good growing conditions are unknown to most gardeners. Varieties offered now are not the same ones offered ten years ago, and undoubtedly they will not be the same ten years hence. In other words, new varieties are continually being accepted and older ones are being discarded.

As a group, the *Prunus* are susceptible to various troubles affecting other rosaceous plants, chiefly borers and scale. Canker worm and other leaf-eating insects seem to like the foliage to such an extent that it should be sprayed with malathion once every year when the new growth begins in order to keep such pests under control. The cherries as a whole are susceptible to various virus diseases that unfortunately are becoming more and more destructive in certain parts of the country each year. It is because of this that no *Prunus* can now be imported from overseas. Also, some of the large *Prunus* collections are hopelessly infested with virus. Propagation material, if distributed from such collections, tends to make a confusing situation only worse.

The *Prunus* are all of comparatively easy culture but should have full sun in order to bloom their best. Because of the much publicized planting around the Tidal Basin in Washington, D.C., the opinion has been expressed that the cherries, at least, must be planted near water. This conception is erroneous. Most of the group are short-lived trees normally but will grow in any good soil with a normal supply of soil moisture. In cold areas, sun scald of the trunks of some species takes its toll in cold winters, and heavy winds, snowstorms, or ice storms can always be expected to cause some damage to the branches because they split very easily. Consequently, fifteen to twenty years is a normal life expectancy for them as a group, but some species, such as *P. serotina,* will live considerably longer.

Prunus amygdalus   24′   Zone 6   Almond

* FLOWERS: pink and white, 1–2″ in diameter
      TIME: February or March
  HABIT: bushy
  FOLIAGE: dense
  HABITAT: western Asia, northern Africa
  INTRODUCED: colonial times
  VARIETIES:
       'Albo-plena'—the flowers are double and white
       'Nana'—this is a compact, dwarf form grown in California
       'Pendula'—the branches of this form are pendulous
       'Roseo-plena'—the flowers are double and pink

This is mentioned merely because it blooms very early in the spring. Other than this it might very well be overlooked since flowering peaches have been developed to a greater extent than the almond.

Prunus armeniaca   30′   Zone 5   Apricot

* FLOWERS: single, white or pinkish, 1″ in diameter
      TIME: late April
  FRUIT: yellowish red cheek, 1¼″ in diameter
      EFFECTIVE: early summer
  HABIT: rounded head
  FOLIAGE: loose, open
  HABITAT: western Asia
  INTRODUCED: before 1875
  VARIETIES:
       'Ansu'—the flowers of this old-fashioned variety are a flushed pink
       'Charles Abraham'—this is popular in California, with deep red flower buds
       and double, deep pink flowers. It was brought over from China and named
       after the San Francisco nurseryman who imported it. It remains in bloom
       longer than other varieties.

This hardy apricot blooms early in the spring before its leaves appear. In some areas in the northern United States, the flowers appear so early that they are killed by late frosts. As an ornamental tree, it is not one of the best choices for this very reason. However, many planters are trying to grow certain clones of it, such as 'Scout,' 'Henderson,' 'Zing,' and others. In order to ensure proper pollination, several clones should be grown in close proximity to each other.

This is the apricot so much grown in southern California and other areas on the West Coast. There are many varieties grown in those areas especially for their fruit. All things considered, however, this apricot is an inferior ornamental plant that might easily be replaced by better trees. Its chief value is, of course, economic. The Japanese apricot, *P. mume,* is better for flowering purposes.

Prunus avium 'Plena'   60'   Zone 3   Double-flowered mazzard
                                                        cherry

* FLOWERS: double, white, 1½" in diameter with as many as 30 petals
       TIME: early May
HABIT: dense, tall, and pyramidal
FOLIAGE: dense, rather coarse
INTRODUCED: before 1878

The common mazzard cherry *(P. avium)* is a native of Europe and has been planted for centuries there (and in America as well) for its fruit. Nurseries in America also use it as an understock on which to graft other cherries, and undoubtedly there are seedlings of this species growing over wide areas of the United States. Everything considered, however, it does not make an outstanding ornamental specimen because the flowers are single and white, lasting only a few days, and then it has little value as an ornamental for the rest of the year.

The double mazzard cherry, on the other hand, is valuable because of its double, white flowers, 1½ inches in diameter, with as many as 30 petals. It blooms in early May (before most of the double-flowered Oriental cherries), and because they are double, the flowers remain effective a week to ten days. Because of its hardiness it can be used in areas where the double-flowered Oriental cherries are not hardy. This variety has been known and grown for at least two and a half centuries.

Several varieties of the mazzard cherry that are supposedly being grown in Europe are not in cultivation in the United States as far as I know. They are the clones 'Asplenifolia,' the leaves of which are delicately cut; 'Fastigiata,' an upright, columnar form of the species; 'Nana,' a shrubby dwarf form; and 'Rubrifolia,' with reddish leaves.

x Prunus blireiana   24'   Zone 5   Blireiana plum

* FLOWERS: double, light pink, 1" in diameter
       TIME: early May
HABIT: rounded, dense branching
* FOLIAGE: reddish purple (actually garnet-brown on the Royal Horticultural Society's Colour Chart)
HYBRID ORIGIN: *P. cerasifera* 'Atropurpurea' x *P. mume*
ORIGINATED: 1895

If double flowers are desired, with fewer fruits and longer bloom, this hybrid or some of its clones might be desirable in place of the other purple-leaved plums *(P. cerasifera* vars.). The foliage is about the same color as the others and just as effective. The variety *moseri* has been grown a great deal, but its flowers are slightly smaller and for this reason it might be discarded. This, like other purple-leaved plums, needs considerable pruning to keep it in good growing condition. It is not as vigorous in growth as the pissard plum and has been recorded as having foliage slightly lighter than it, but as they grow side by side in the Arnold Arboretum the foliage color seems to be identical. Its purplish red fruits are not effective merely because they are approximately the same color as the foliage.

Prunus campanulata   24′   Zone 7   Taiwan cherry

* FLOWERS: single, rose-colored, 1″ in diameter
     TIME: early spring
  FRUIT: red
     EFFECTIVE: early summer
* HABIT: small, bushy tree, dense branching
  FOLIAGE: lustrous
  HABITAT: Japan, Taiwan
  INTRODUCED: 1899

In southern and central California, where this cherry grows well, it blooms two weeks before any of the others.

Prunus caroliniana   20–40′   Zone 8   Carolina cherry-laurel

  FLOWERS: small, cream-colored, in short racemes
     TIME: February to April
  HABIT: dense
* FOLIAGE: glossy, evergreen leaves, 2–4″ long
  FRUIT: black, shining berries, ½″ long, sometimes persisting for a year
  HABITAT: South Carolina to Florida and Texas
  VARIETY:
     'Compacta'—a form apparently being offered in California because of its more
        compact habit of growth

This is a variable plant but serviceable in gardens throughout the southeastern United States and in southern California, chiefly for its evergreen leaves. Flowers and fruits are not effective, but because it withstands shearing it is used as a hedge and also as a specimen plant.

Prunus cerasifera '**Atropurpurea**' (syn. *P. pissardi*)   24′   Zone 4
                                                            Pissard plum

  FLOWERS: pink, ¾″ in diameter
     TIME: late April
  HABIT: upright, dense branching
* FOLIAGE: reddish purple (actually garnet-brown on the Royal Horticultural Soci-
        ety's Colour Chart)
  HABITAT: originally found in Iran
  INTRODUCED: about 1890
  OTHER VARIETIES OF *P. cerasifera:*
     '**Hollywood**'—this is unique since the foliage first appears green as it opens,
        then turns a deep purple
     '**Nigra**' *(Black myrobalan plum)*—the foliage color of this clone is very dark
        purple, slightly darker than that of 'Atropurpurea,' and is retained through-
        out the summer. The flowers are single, pink, and ⅝″ in diameter.

'Pendula'—the branches of this are pendulous; apparently it is being grown in California

'Thundercloud'—first offered by Housewearts Nursery of Woodburn, Oregon, in 1937. It is supposed to be the best of these varieties for retaining its deep purple foliage color during the summer.

'Vesuvius'—the leaves are large and deep purple, one of the most colored of the varieties. It seldom blooms, but this is no defect since the pink bloom of these purple-leaved varieties is ineffective, to say the least. This was a Luther Burbank introduction before 1929.

Prunus cerasifera itself is not a needed ornamental tree. Its several purple-leaved varieties are, however, greatly in demand in certain areas primarily because of their reddish purple foliage that remains so colored throughout the entire growing season. The species is considerably variable; many varieties and clones have appeared on the market. 'Thundercloud' is one clone that has done well and might be recommended. The fruits of most are edible but small and not effective from a landscape point of view. The double-flowered *P. blireiana* is better than any *P. cerasifera* varieties in flower, and the double flowers last longer on the tree.

From the standpoint of purple foliage I have tried to detect marked differences among our plants at different times of the year but have failed to do so. In fact, I have grown a series of *P. cerasifera* 'Nigra' plants side by side with a similar series of *P. blireiana* 'Newport,' treated them with different fertilizers over a period of several years, and failed to see any differences in the leaf color, which remained a reddish purple throughout the spring, summer, and fall.

All these plums seem to withstand the hot, often dry summers of the Chicago area very well. They need constant pruning to correct a bad habit of cross branching. They are small, compact, and colorful over a long period and hence are of interest to a large group of small property owners. If grown in the full sun they develop their leaf color to its vivid hue, but in shade or partial shade they are not nearly as colorful.

Prunus cerasus   30′   Zone 3   Sour cherry

* FLOWERS: single, white, ¾–1″ in diameter
          TIME: early May
   FRUIT: red to blackish cherries
          EFFECTIVE: early summer
   HABIT: rounded, open
   FOLIAGE: light green
   HABITAT: western Asia, southeastern Europe
   INTRODUCED: colonial times
   VARIETY:
          'Rhexii' *(Rhex sour cherry)*—with double, white flowers, 1½″ in diameter

Usually grown for its fruits but listed here because of its extreme hardiness, it is one of the hardiest of the Asiatic cherries. Its double-flowered variety 'Rhexii' is therefore usable much farther north than most double-flowering cherries except the double-flowered form of *P. avium*. It has been noted that this is one of the few fruit trees suitable for growing in shaded locations.

Prunus conradinae 'Semiplena'   30'   Zone 6   Double
                                                          conradina cherry

* FLOWERS: fragrant, double, white to pale pink, 1″ in diameter, in clusters
        TIME: mid-May
   FRUIT: egg-shaped, red, 1/3″ long
        EFFECTIVE: early summer
   HABIT: rounded
   FOLIAGE: dense
   ORIGINATED: in the garden of Collingwood Ingram, Benenden, Kent, England,
        before 1925

This is highly valued in England because of its very early flowers, often by early March, and is more desirable than the species since the flowers remain effective longer.

x Prunus 'Hally Jolivette'   15'?   Zone 5

* FLOWERS: pink buds; double, white, flowers 1¼″ in diameter
        TIME: early May
   HABIT: rounded, dense branching
   FOLIAGE: fine texture
   HYBRID ORIGIN: *P. subhirtella x P. yedoensis* crossed back on *P. subhirtella*
   ORIGINATED: 1940 by Dr. Karl Sax of the Arnold Arboretum, Boston, Massachu-
        setts

This hybrid has merit because its very double flowers do not open all at once but open consecutively over a ten- to twenty-day period. This gives it considerable ornamental value. It also blooms very early in life, usually when only two years old, and has a dense, rounded habit similar to *P. subhirtella.* Its exact mature height is not yet known, but it is very shrubby and may reach 15 feet.

x Prunus hillieri 'Spire'   25'   Zone 5

* FLOWERS: single, soft pink
        TIME: late April
* HABIT: pyramidal (25' high by 8' across)
   AUTUMN COLOR: red
   HYBRID ORIGIN: *(P. incisa x P. sargentii)*
   INTRODUCED: about 1935 by Hillier Nursery Co., Winchester, England

A comparatively new tree, proving very popular in England. Well worthy of further trial.

Prunus incisa 'Pendula Alba' 20′ Zone 6 White weeping Fuji cherry

FLOWERS: single, white, less than ½″ across, borne in profusion
    TIME: early spring
HABIT: pendulous branches
AUTUMN COLOR: orange-red
HABITAT: Japan

A delicate, small tree with drooping branches, but its flowers do not last very long.

Prunus laurocerasus 18′ Zones 6–7 Cherry-laurel

FLOWERS: small, white, in upright racemes 2–5″ long
    TIME: late spring
FRUIT: small, black berries
    TIME: late summer
* FOLIAGE: glossy, evergreen leaves, 4–6″ long
HABIT: rounded as a tree, often grown as a shrub
INTRODUCED: colonial times, native of Europe

Prunus laurocerasus, *the popular evergreen cherry-laurel of the South.*

VARIETIES:

   'Rotundifolia'—with dense foliage, best of the group for making hedges
   schipkaensis—hardiest form, almost up to Boston, Massachusetts. More or less
   shrubby.

This serviceable plant stands shearing well and is often used as a hedge or windbreak,
with smaller leaves than the species. An excellent plant in the South. Occasionally it
grows as a small tree.

Prunus lusitanica   6–60′   Zone 7   Portugal laurel

* FLOWERS: white, ½″ in diameter, in racemes 10″ long
        TIME: May
   FRUIT: purplish cherries
        EFFECTIVE: summer
   HABIT: bushy with dense branching
* FOLIAGE: dense, evergreen, glossy leaves, to 5″ long
   HABITAT: Spain, Portugal
   INTRODUCED: early colonial times

An extremely serviceable, glossy-leaved evergreen for southern gardens that may
grow into tree form or be confined as a shrub. As an evergreen background or clipped
hedge, it has many uses.

Prunus maackii   45′   Zone 2   Amur chokecherry

* FLOWERS: small, white, in racemes 2–3″ long
        TIME: mid-May
   HABIT: rounded, dense branching
* BARK: brownish yellow, flaking
   FOLIAGE: dense
   HABITAT: Korea, Manchuria
   INTRODUCED: 1878

This differs from the other bird cherries in forming its flower clusters on the previous
year's growth, not the current year's, and is ornamental because of its bright-colored
bark that peels off in thin strips like that of the birch. Also, it is among the hardiest
of trees. It should be considered only for areas with unusually low winter temperatures.

Prunus maximowiczii   48′   Zone 4   Miyama cherry

* FLOWERS: single, white
        TIME: late May
   HABIT: rounded, dense branching

FOLIAGE: dense
* AUTUMN COLOR: scarlet
HABITAT: Korea, Manchuria
INTRODUCED: 1892

The brilliant autumn color of this tree makes it one of the few Oriental cherries of ornamental interest two seasons of the year.

Prunus mume   30′   Zone 6   Japanese apricot

* FLOWERS: fragrant single, pink
    TIME: early May
HABIT: rounded head
FOLIAGE: loose, open
HABITAT: Japan, China
INTRODUCED: 1844
VARIETIES:

    'Albo-plena' *(Double white Japanese apricot)*—flowers double, white, early flowering; introduced 1934

    'Alphandii'—has double, pink flowers

    'Dawn'—has large, double, shell pink flowers; was first introduced in 1925. It is one of the late-blooming varieties.

    'Rosemary Clarke'—a variety with large, fragrant, semidouble, white flowers, each with a red calyx; named by W. B. Clarke, San Jose, California, in 1938

Most of the flowering apricots belong in this group. They are similar to the flowering peaches but are slightly less hardy, hence have a more limited use. Usually these are small trees, considerably under the 30 feet given as the height of the species. Many varieties found in nurseries are unnamed seedlings of this species; to avoid disappointment, it might be well to observe them in flower in the nursery before selection.

Prunus nipponica   18′   Zone 5   Nipponese cherry

* FLOWERS: single, white to pale pink
    TIME: late April
* HABIT: bushy, dense branching
FOLIAGE: dense
* AUTUMN COLOR: yellow, orange to crimson
HABITAT: Japan
INTRODUCED: 1915

This ornamental cherry of dense habit has much to recommend it for general planting, and it might possibly be preferred to some of the other cherries because of its foliage, which turns a brilliant yellow to orange autumn color.

x Prunus 'Okame'   24'   Zone 7

* FLOWERS: deep pink
       TIME: spring
  HYBRID ORIGIN: *P. incisa x P. campanulata*

From the garden of Collingwood Ingram in southern England, this tree is spectacular
in bloom. The flowers are fully effective for almost three weeks.

Prunus padus   45'   Zone 3   European bird cherry

* FLOWERS: fragrant, small, white, in drooping racemes 3–6" long
       TIME: early May
  FRUIT: small, black cherries, ¼" in diameter
       EFFECTIVE: July
  HABIT: open
  FOLIAGE: rather open
  HABITAT: Europe, northern Asia, Japan, Korea
  INTRODUCED: colonial times
  VARIETIES:
       'Commutata' *(Harbinger European bird cherry)*—individual flowers ½" in diam-
          eter and blooms nearly three weeks before other varieties
       'Plena' *(Double European bird cherry)*—flowers large and double, remaining in
          flower longer than any other variety; one of the best varieties
       'Spaethii' *(Bigflower European bird cherry)*—flower clusters somewhat pendu-
          lous; one of the better varieties in the collections at Arnold Arboretum
       'Watereri' *(Longcluster European bird cherry)*—this has proved the best single-
          flowered variety in Europe, with racemes of blossoms 8" long

The European bird cherry is superior to our native *P. virginiana* as an ornamental
because the flowers and fruits are larger, it has better foliage, and it is less susceptible to attacks from tent caterpillars. Particularly, it is conspicuous as one of the first
trees to produce leaves in the spring, an important trait that has earned it much
praise.

Prunus pensylvanica   36'   Zone 2   Wild red cherry, Pin cherry

  FLOWERS: small, white, in short racemes or clusters
       TIME: early May
* FRUIT: small, red cherries, ¼" in diameter
       EFFECTIVE: late August
  HABIT: open
  BARK: shining, red
  FOLIAGE: open, fine textured
* AUTUMN COLOR: red
  HABITAT: eastern and central North America

This cherry is short-lived and should not be used as a specimen, but it proves splendid on the border of woodlands or actually in the woodlands. It is beautiful in early spring when in full flower (when the leaves are only half grown) and again when the fruit is colored a brilliant red. The birds eat the fruit readily and are responsible for distributing the tree over a wide area. This is one of the first "nurse" trees to appear after certain hardwood forests are cut over, and although it does not live long, it nevertheless yields ample shade until the longer-lived young trees of other species become fully established.

Prunus persica   24′   Zone 5   Peach

* FLOWERS: single, pink, 1–1½″ in diameter
        TIME: late April
FRUIT: red or yellow peaches
HABIT: rounded
FOLIAGE: dense
HABITAT: China
INTRODUCED: early colonial times (probably before 1696)
VARIETIES:

    'Double White'—the flowers are double and pure white

    'Early Double Red'—this has double, red flowers appearing before the other varieties

    'Helen Borchers'—originated and selected by the W. B. Clarke Nursery, San Jose, California, in 1936. Valued because of its clear pink flowers, 2½″ in diameter, which keep well.

    'Iceberg'—also introduced by W. B. Clarke in 1939. The flowers are white and it blooms very early.

    'Late Double Red'—a late double, red-flowering variety

    'Peppermint Stick'—another of W. B. Clarke's introductions (1933) and valued because of its double, white flowers that are mottled with pink stripes. This is similar to, if not identical with, 'Versicolor,' introduced by the German nursery of Spaeth in 1889. It is obvious that W. B. Clarke was actively introducing new ornamental varieties of this species thirty years ago, some of which are still popular.

    'Royal Redleaf'—with reddish leaves. There are probably others in the trade with reddish leaves also. The leaves first appear a brilliant dark red, later turning a bronze-green.

    'Weeping Double Pink'—pendulous branches and double, pink flowers

    'Weeping Double Red'—pendulous branches and double, red flowers

The common peach is colorful enough where it is grown commercially; when in bloom in large orchards it attracts many people. One can hardly visualize the peach used as a specimen lawn tree, however, for there are many other ornamentals far superior to it in many ways. Often enough, one tree is used in the rear of the grounds or near the vegetable garden, chiefly planted for its fruit. The peach is troubled with several diseases and insect pests and is particularly troubled with borers in the trunk. Because of this it should be planted only when provision will be made to control such pests persistently and completely.

Because the hazards in growing these peaches are not well known, there is a demand for the ornamental varieties. There have been nearly seventy-five of these named in recent years, a third of them being offered for sale by nurseries today. But it is a changing list; those varieties grown ten or fifteen years ago have mostly been replaced by other varieties, and those grown today may be unpopular in the future. It is impossible for me to select "the best" in this ever-changing group. I have not seen many of them, nor can we keep them alive for long periods in the Arnold Arboretum where we have repeatedly tried to test them properly.

The ornamental peaches are best in those areas along the East and West coasts where commercial peach production is a major operation. Of some twenty-five being grown commercially today, those listed above seem to be the most popular.

The varieties are mentioned here because many people, after seeing a small tree or branch in bloom, visualize an entire 20-foot tree covered with the blooms. Unfortunately, in the majority of cases, these large, flowering varieties make very poor trees. They are weak and easily susceptible to the inroads of pest troubles. They might better be treated as shrubs, kept heavily pruned, and so relegated to a hidden part of the garden. They should be pruned immediately after flowering in such a way as to force out much new growth, for it is only on this new growth that flower buds will be formed for the next year. The more vigorous the growth, the better the blossoms. Hence, in order to have profuse blooms the following year, the majority of flowering branches are cut back after blooming is completed. Plants treated this way are rather unsightly for some time afterward.

These trees have colorful and large flowers but require special care and culture in order to produce good ones. Because of this they are not considered good specimens but rather plants to be forced in a particular way to produce proper blooms.

Prunus sargentii   75′   Zone 4   Sargent cherry

* FLOWERS: single, deep pink, 1¼″ in diameter
         TIME: late April
* HABIT: dense, upright but rounded top
  BARK: typical cherry bark, dark and lustrous
  FOLIAGE: dense
* AUTUMN COLOR: red
  HABITAT: Japan
  INTRODUCED: 1890
  VARIETY:

> 'Columnaris'—this columnar form of the Sargent cherry was first noted in the Arnold Arboretum in 1914. Many scions have been distributed from it throughout the United States. A younger tree, now about 25′ tall, is only 8′ in diameter, but of course it will grow wider as the tree grows older. It has all the fine qualities of the Sargent cherry except that it is columnar in habit.

Probably the finest of all the cherry trees, both as an ornamental and as a timber tree (it has been used in Japan a long time for its excellent timber). The oldest tree in America, propagated from the first seed introduced into this country in 1890, was growing in the Arnold Arboretum but had to be taken down some time ago after being badly smashed during a severe summer storm. This species is a standard tree, far more hardy than most Oriental cherries, and is covered with single, deep pink flowers in the early spring. As soon as these fall, the young foliage begins to appear a very colorful bronze, later turning green as the leaves mature. It is one of the few cherries to have a vivid red autumn color, and of course its bark is of interest all winter.

This makes a splendid specimen tree, possibly a little too large for the small property, but where there is room for it on the home grounds, in parks, or as a street tree, it makes a perfect ornamental for beauty as well as dense shade.

Prunus serotina   90'   Zone 3   Black cherry, Rum cherry

* FLOWERS: single, white, in drooping, terminal racemes
      TIME: late May
* FRUIT: small, black cherries, but effective while red
      EFFECTIVE: August
* HABIT: partly drooping branches
* FOLIAGE: dense, lustrous, peach-shaped leaves
  HABITAT: eastern and central North America
  VARIETY:
      pendula (Weeping black cherry)—with fully pendulous branchlets; a very graceful form

This is certainly the best of the native American species of *Prunus* for ornamental planting. Only one other, the pin cherry *(P. pensylvanica),* has been added to the recommended group. This black cherry, with its long, lustrous, peachlike leaves, slightly pendulous branches, and dense foliage, is an excellent tree for general foliage purposes. The small, white flowers, in profuse 4–5½-inch-long racemes, are followed by conspicuous red fruit, eventually turning black. Very few large trees of this species are left standing in the East now, for its wood has been highly prized in furniture-making since colonial times.

Prunus serrula   30'   Zone 5

  FLOWERS: single, white
      TIME: early May
  HABIT: wide-spreading, often with several trunks
* BARK: brilliant, glossy red
  FOLIAGE: open
  HABITAT: western China
  INTRODUCED: 1908

The best of all the cherries as far as ornamental bark is concerned—the brilliant, lustrous, dark red color of this bark makes the tree of interest throughout the year, especially during the winter. It is very difficult to find commercially.

Prunus serrulata—most varieties   20–25′   Zones 5–6   Oriental cherry

* FLOWERS: single and double, white to pink, ½–2½″ in diameter
       TIME: early to mid-May
HABIT: low trees, usually upright
FOLIAGE: coarse
HABITAT: cultivated in Japan for centuries

Most of the cultivated varieties of Oriental cherries found in Japanese and Chinese gardens have been relegated to this species. The Japanese have named over 120 varieties, but only about 50 are probably grown in this country; many of these are barely distinguishable one from the other by the average gardener. Most are small trees (under 30 feet in height), although the species itself reaches 75 feet in height. They have proved very popular in America, and many featured plantings of them have been made on the East and West coasts.

The flowers are either single or double, white or pink, but most appear before the leaves or with them. Some of the varieties have fragrant flowers, and other things being equal, it is these varieties that certainly should be given preference over those without fragrant flowers. This is a very important factor.

There has long been a controversy concerning the best type of understock on which to graft these varieties. *Prunus sargentii* was highly recommended for a long time. William H. Judd, formerly propagator at the Arnold Arboretum for over thirty years, decided after long experience with both *P. sargentii* and *P. avium* that the latter was superior as an understock. It always "works" better than *P. sargentii,* and this has been borne out by others, including R. E. Horsey, formerly of the Rochester Park Department.

The recommended varieties are not all among the hardiest of the Oriental cherry group. In his excellent publication "The Oriental Flowering Cherries" (U.S. Department of Agriculture, Circular 313, March 1934), Paul Russell lists the following five as the hardiest:

     P. sargentii
     P. serrulata 'Fugenzo'
     P. serrulata 'Kwanzan'
     P. serrulata 'Shirofugen'
     P. subhirtella

Russell also divides the varieties of *P. serrulata* and other species into the following general groups, and those recommended here are listed accordingly:

     Trees with pendulous branches—*P. subhirtella pendula*
     Trees with fastigiate branches—*P. serrulata* 'Amanogawa'
     Trees with spreading or upright branches (none recommended here)
     Trees with flowers greenish yellow—*P. serrulata* 'Gyoiko,' 'Ukon'
     Trees with flowers white, single or nearly so—*P. serrulata* 'Jo-nioi,' 'Taki-nioi,' 'Washin-o'
     Trees with flowers white, semidouble or double—*P. serrulata* 'Shirotae'

Trees with flowers pink, single or nearly so (none recommended here)
Trees with flowers pink, semidouble or double—*P. serrulata* 'Botan-zakura,'
'Kwanzan,' 'Shogetsu,' and *P. sieboldii*

This classification shows the variation that is evident among the varieties of this interesting species.

VARIETIES:

'Amanogawa'—the only truly fastigiate Oriental cherry worth growing. Usually not over 20′ tall, flowers 1¾″ in diameter, semidouble, light pink, and fragrant. The varietal name means "milky way," an indication of its floriferous blooms. David Fairchild is credited with first introducing this variety from Japan in 1906. It is interesting to note that a very high percentage of the seedlings of this tree are identical with the mother plant in form and flowers.

'Botan-zakura'—a small tree with spreading or upright branches. The flowers are semidouble, pale pink, often 2″ in diameter, with 6–15 petals, and fragrant. When it is possible to grow some of these Oriental varieties that are truly fragrant, it would seem that those that are not might be discarded.

'Fugenzo'—this popular variety is also found in nursery catalogs under the names 'James H. Veitch' and 'Kofugen.' The Japanese name translated means "goddess on a white elephant." The flowers are as much as 2½″ in diameter, rosy pink fading to a light pink, double, with about 30 petals, blooming at about the same time as 'Kwanzan.' It is rather wide-spreading in habit.

Paul Russell, in his excellent, above cited work on the Oriental flowering cherries, notes that this variety was known to the Japanese five hundred years ago and is still widely planted. It is often confused with 'Shirofugen,' but the flowers of this last variety fade.

'Gyoiko'—the Japanese name means "imperial yellowish costume," appropriate since the flowers are actually yellowish green. This variety is certainly unusual but not objectionable, and adds considerable interest to every flowering collection in which it appears. It grows about 20′ tall, the flowers are semidouble and about 1½″ in diameter, with about 15 petals. The variety 'Ukon' is similar but the flowers are slightly larger.

'Jo-nioi'—E. H. Wilson, who knew the Oriental cherries very well, claimed that this variety was the most fragrant of all—reason enough why it should prove popular. The flowers are mostly single, white, and about 1½″ in diameter. It is upright and slightly spreading in habit, reaching a mature height of about 18′. It is similar to 'Taki-nioi' but differs slightly in habit.

'Kwanzan'—probably the most popular and the most hardy of all the double-flowered Oriental cherries. The double, deep pink flowers are 2½″ in diameter and have 30 petals. They are borne on a fairly upright growing tree about 12–18′ tall. The young foliage, as it first appears, is a bright reddish copper color, adding considerably to the colorful display of this tree in early spring. Probably the best display is at Washington, D.C., along the Tidal Basin, where nearly two hundred trees of this one variety are growing.

'Sekiyama'—the correct name for 'Kwanzan,' which has been used so long that it is doubtful it will be dropped now

Of the many Japanese cherries, this variety, Prunus serrulata *'Kwanzan,' has proved to be one of the most popular, with its fine, double, pink flowers.*

'Shirofugen'—often called 'White Goddess,' this has double, pink flowers up to 2½″ in diameter which quickly fade to white as the flowers mature. The young foliage, like that of 'Kwanzan,' is bronze, turning green by the time it is fully mature.

'Shirotae'—with double or semidouble, pure white flowers, often called the finest of all the double, white Oriental cherries. Its name means "snow white." The flowers are 2½″ in diameter and fragrant. The petals (about 12) are slightly ruffled, giving the flowers a pleasing appearance. (There is, however, no double white with as many petals as 'Kwanzan.')

'Shogetsu'—considered by some the handsomest of the double-flowered cherries. The tree grows about 15′ tall, is broad, and flat-topped. The flowers are double (about 30 petals), very pale pink, often with a white center, and are up to 2″ in diameter.

'Sieboldii'—this double, pink-flowered cherry was once considered a species but has been placed as a variety of *P. serrulata* and so it is considered here. Certainly its bloom and form, as it has grown in the Arnold Arboretum, would indicate this. The flowers are about 1¼″ in diameter and appear in early May, at the same time as other double-flowered forms of *P. serrulata.* Certainly it is as hardy as 'Kwanzan.'

'Taki-nioi'—the Japanese varietal name means "fragrant cascade." This tree seldom grows over 12' tall and blooms at about the same time as 'Kwanzan.' The flowers are single and white but very fragrant, up to 1¼" in diameter.

'Ukon'—the pendulous flowers are semidouble and a very pale yellow color. The young foliage of this tree is also bronze as the leaves begin to unfurl, and at the time of bloom this forms a very beautiful color combination.

'Washin-o'—has single, white flowers, 1½" in diameter, that are very fragrant. It grows about 20' tall with wide-spreading and upright branches.

Prunus subhirtella   30'   Zone 5   Higan cherry

* FLOWERS: single, light pink, 1½" in diameter
    TIME: late April
* HABIT: rounded, dense branching
  FOLIAGE: small, fine textured
  HABITAT: Japan
  INTRODUCED: 1894
  VARIETIES:
    autumnalis—the semidouble, pink flowers of this autumn-flowering cherry are ¾" in diameter, and during a warm fall some of the flowers may bloom. On

The Higan cherry (Prunus subhirtella), *with its single, light pink flowers, is one of the earliest Oriental cherries to bloom.*

the other hand, if the weather is cold, none may bloom until the following spring. It is one of the best of this species because its semidouble flowers remain effective for a longer period of time.

pendula *(Weeping Higan cherry)*—the most popular variety of the Higan cherries, with gracefully pendulous branches and single, pale pink flowers. It was first introduced to America from Japan about 1862.

'Rosy Cloud' *(Plant Patent #4540)*—a small, spreading, upright tree, with many double flowers that remain on the tree a week longer than the single-flowered varieties. Originated by the Princeton Nurseries, Princeton, New Jersey.

'Wayside Pendula'—a small tree with single, deep pink flowers that eventually fade to white and pendulous branches

'White Fountain'—has pendulous branches reaching to the ground and single, white flowers. Reaches 15' tall.

'Yae-shidare-higan'—many nurseries incorrectly list this plant as *Prunus subhirtella pendula plena.* The tree has pendulous branches and the small, pink flowers are double—hence it is effective longer than *P. subhirtella pendula.* When seedlings of the weeping Higan cherry are planted, variations do occur among the seedlings, and this accounts for many of the names occasionally appearing that are given to describe these variations. The six varieties mentioned here are the most important ones of *P. subhirtella.*

This is one of the earliest of the Oriental cherries to bloom (always before the leaves appear) and one of the most floriferous as well. The gracefully weeping variety *(pendula)* was probably the first one to come to this country. The old Ellwanger and Barry Nursery of Rochester, New York, listed it in their catalog in 1846. The species itself varies considerably in the form and color of the flowers, giving rise to such ill-named freaks as "P. subhirtella ascendens pendula rubra flore plena."

Prunus virginiana 'Shubert'   30'   Zone 2

FLOWERS: small, single, white, in terminal racemes
      TIME: mid-May
HABIT: pyramidal
FOLIAGE: dense, green at first, then changing to reddish purple
INTRODUCED: by Oscar H. Will Nurseries of Bismarck, North Dakota, about 1950

Unlike most other trees with colored foliage, the leaves of this tree appear green at first but then in early June quickly change to dark reddish purple and remain this color the rest of the growing season. The process is usually just the reverse on other trees. This is an interesting and colorful tree, very easily grown and certainly hardy over a wide area of the northern United States and Canada.

Prunus yedoensis   48'   Zone 5   Yoshino cherry

* FLOWERS: slightly fragrant, single, white to pink, 1" in diameter
      TIME: late April

* HABIT: flat-topped, bushy
  FOLIAGE: dense
  HABITAT: cultivated in Japan
  INTRODUCED: 1902
  VARIETIES:

> 'Afterglow' *(Plant Patent #5750)*—originated by Princeton Nurseries, Princeton, New Jersey. This is a seedling of 'Akebono,' with rich, simple, rose-pink flowers (much deeper than *P. yedoensis*) that bloom in late April. It grows rapidly, forming a float top at maturity.

> 'Akebono'—selected in 1920, named and introduced about 1925 by W. B. Clarke Nursery, San Jose, California, as a softer pink-flowering tree than the species. The synonym, under which some nurseries list it, is 'Daybreak.'

> 'Perpendens'—with irregularly pendulous branches

It is this species that constitutes the majority of the famous tree plantings about the Tidal Basin in Washington, D.C., where about nine hundred were planted in 1912 as part of the cherry collection presented by the mayor of Tokyo to the city of Washington as a gift of friendship. To do their best they should be planted 30 to 40 feet apart, which precludes their extensive use on the small property. Although often considered a hybrid, they will breed true from seed. It is widely planted in Tokyo, where over fifty thousand trees of this one species were growing a few years ago. It is quick-growing, rather short-lived, and like most other *Prunus,* is best displayed by planting in front of some dense evergreens, for the flowers appear very early, before the leaves. This species was first introduced into America by the Arnold Arboretum. One of the most floriferous of all Oriental cherries, it can be grown from seed or cuttings, or grafted on *P. avium* as the understock.

Pseudolarix kaempferi (syn. *P. amabilis*)   120'   Zone 5   Golden
                                                                    larch

* FRUIT: unusual cones borne upright on the upper side of the branches
          EFFECTIVE: summer and early fall, the cones falling apart by late October
* HABIT: very broad and pyramidal with horizontal branches, open
  FOLIAGE: open, deciduous needles, 1½–2½" long
* AUTUMN COLOR: golden yellow
  HABITAT: eastern China
  INTRODUCED: 1854

The golden larch is one of the most beautiful exotic trees. Originally found by Robert Fortune as ornamental pot plants in China; eleven years later he discovered it growing naturally in a monastery garden. Unfortunately, it has never become popular in America, possibly because it is not a tree for the small garden since trees even up to 30 to 40 feet are almost as broad as they are tall! Also, it is likely that seed sources, especially in this country, are very limited. Our trees have a good crop of seed only about every three or four years. On large estates or in parks it can quickly become a beautiful specimen, interesting because of its beautiful foliage throughout the spring and summer. In the late summer, when the cones begin to mature, these too are attractive, and in the fall its beautiful golden yellow color is outstanding even though it is of short duration. Its unique habit of growth and wide-spreading horizontal branches add to its beauty throughout the winter months. As far as I know (it has been growing in the Arnold Arboretum since 1891) it has no serious insect pests or diseases, another very important factor in its favor.

Pseudotsuga menziesii (syn. *P. taxifolia)*   300'   Zones 4–6
                                                                Douglas-fir

* FRUIT: pendulous cones, 2–4½" long
     EFFECTIVE: fall and winter
* HABIT: densely pyramidal, branching horizontal
* FOLIAGE: dense, evergreen needles
  HABITAT: Rocky Mountains, Pacific Coast
  VARIETIES:
     'Compacta'—compact, conical form, short needles
     glauca—this is the Rocky Mountain form, hardy in Zone 4 and the best form

Native to the northwestern part of the United States, the Douglas-fir (Pseudotsuga menziesii) *is a popular and valuable ornamental evergreen tree.*

for northern gardens. This type is more compact, with slightly more ascending branches than the species. Foliage bluish green.

'Pendula'—pendulous branchlets

viridis—the form typical of the West Coast regions and not as hardy as variety *glauca*

Second only to yellow pine in the volume of lumber produced annually, the greater part of these trees are in Washington, Oregon, and northern California. It is the slower-growing form found in the mountains of Colorado and surrounding mountain states that constitutes the hardy ornamental tree of northern gardens. F. L. Skinner of Dropmore, Manitoba, Canada, had a form hardy under his very trying conditions in Zone 2. The coastal form is not nearly as hardy. Both forms vary considerably as to general outline, color of foliage, and habit because few of these are grafted and most are grown from seed. On the West Coast where moisture is sufficient the tree will grow 35 feet in twenty-five years, which is rather rapid for an evergreen. The needles remain on the tree a considerable time after it is cut, allowing it to be used for Christmas trees in large numbers where it is native. Also, it withstands pruning and shearing well and so can be used in hedges. About the only serious pest it has, in eastern gardens at least, is a white mealy bug that is easily controlled by spraying with malathion.

It is readily distinguished from all other evergreens by its unique pendulous cones, its long, pointed, terminal buds with many scales, and its soft needles. The Douglas-fir can be considered one of our best native evergreen ornamental trees, not superior to the hemlocks, possibly, but certainly well up near the top of the list.

Pterocarya fraxinifolia   90'   Zone 5   Caucasian wingnut

FLOWERS: female catkins 12–20" long
    TIME: early spring
* FRUIT: drooping racemes of light green, winged nuts
    EFFECTIVE: summer
HABIT: wide-spreading, open
* FOLIAGE: handsome compound, dark green leaves, 8–24" long
HABITAT: Caucasus to northern Iran
INTRODUCED: 1850

This peculiar and interesting tree is not common but has considerable interest during the summer at a time when most other trees are uninteresting because of its long racemes of fruits. It is closely related to *Carya* and *Juglans* and requires moist soil. The more tender species, *P. stenoptera,* also makes fast growth and is used in California on poor soils as a substitute for *Ailanthus altissima.* No serious pests.

Pterostyrax hispida   45'   Zone 5   Fragrant epaulette tree

* FLOWERS: fragrant, creamy white, in pendulous panicles 4½–9" long
    TIME: June

HABIT: open head; slender, spreading branches
FOLIAGE: open, coarse
HABITAT: Japan
INTRODUCED: 1875

This is an interesting tree, unusual because of its pendulous flower panicles but very difficult to find commercially. It should not be used in preference to more easily obtained trees, but it does make an out-of-the-ordinary specimen. No serious pests.

⇥⟫ *PYRUS*

The pears are not outstanding ornamental trees. When they are planted in orchards and home gardens for their fruit, they must be persistently cared for since most of them, unfortunately, are very susceptible to fire blight disease. This is probably the greatest scourge in the growing of this particular fruit. Other pests also trouble these trees.

As a result of this, only three species have been recommended. *Pyrus calleryana* and *P. ussuriensis* are the least susceptible to the blight, and a cultivar of one of the species has been tried successfully for street tree work. The third species, *P. salicifolia,* is suggested because it has a graceful habit and interesting foliage, but it can be severely cut back by fire blight disease. Everyone is familiar with pear trees as they flower in early spring, and they are beautiful. On the whole, the effort necessary to keep them in good growing condition is not worth the time and trouble. Fruit growers in certain areas of the country may find it profitable to battle these problems on a large scale, and of course many experiment stations have long-range studies dealing with them.

Pyrus calleryana   30'   Zone 4   Callery pear

* FLOWERS: white, 1" in diameter
          TIME: early May
FRUIT: russet-colored, about ½" long
HABIT: more or less pyramidal
FOLIAGE: dense
* AUTUMN COLOR: red to glossy scarlet
HABITAT: China
INTRODUCED: 1908
VARIETIES:
          'Aristocrat'—dark green leaves with wavy margin, thornless

'Bradford'—has been selected from seedlings grown from seed collected by Frank Meyer in China in 1918 and grown at the U.S. Department of Agriculture Plant Introduction Station in Glenn Dale, Maryland. It was named in honor of F. C. Bradford, former director of the station. This vigorous tree does not have spines. Test plantings of this clone have been made in Maryland with good results and, according to Dr. John L. Creech, it has survived better under the variable soil conditions of this planting than the 'Kwanzan' cherry.

'Capital'—narrow, columnar form, glossy, rich green leaves of leathery texture, reddish purple in autumn. Introduced by the National Arboretum.

'Chanticleer'—fine upright, pyramidal form, narrower than 'Bradford,' thornless

'Fauriei'—pleasing pyramidal outline, lustrous, dark green foliage that produces autumn color (yellow to red) earlier than 'Bradford' and drops its leaves earlier. Grows to about 40'.

'Redspire' *(Plant Patent #3815)*—rapid-growing, narrowly upright with leathery dark green foliage, turning shades of purple and red in the fall. Originated by Princeton Nurseries, Princeton, New Jersey. Grows to about 40'.

'Whitehouse'—deciduous, less robust than 'Bradford,' purple-red fall coloring

The only reason the Callery pear is mentioned at all is that it is the least susceptible to fire blight and so has earned a place for itself in fruit tree breeding, even though it is less hardy than *P. ussuriensis.* If a pear tree is not needed, certainly there are better ornamentals than the varieties listed above.

Pyrus salicifolia   24'   Zone 4   Willowleaf pear

FLOWERS: white
    TIME: mid-May
FRUIT: about 1″ long, of no value
* HABIT: slender, almost pendulous branches
* FOLIAGE: graceful, silvery gray, leaves willowlike
HABITAT: southeastern Europe to western Asia
INTRODUCED: 1780 (England?)
VARIETY:
    'Pendula' *(Weeping willowleaf pear)*—deciduous with spreading crown of gracefully drooping branches; leaves gray-green

In England this has been listed as the most ornamental of the pears because of the silvery white young foliage and graceful habit of the tree itself. As the leaves mature they become greener on the upper surface. In our experience this tree has been very susceptible to fire blight, but where this disease is not a serious hazard, the willowleaf pear does have merit as an ornamental.

The willowleaf pear (Pyrus salicifolia) *has pendulous branches and graceful, silvery gray leaves.*

Pyrus ussuriensis   50'   Zone 3   Ussurian pear

* FLOWERS: white, 1½" in diameter
        TIME: early May
   FRUIT: greenish yellow, 1½" long, not effective
   HABIT: more or less pyramidal
   FOLIAGE: dense
* AUTUMN COLOR: glossy scarlet
   HABITAT: northeastern Asia
   INTRODUCED: 1855

Chiefly of merit for its vigorous, dense growth, good foliage, and brilliant autumn color, this tree is the hardiest of all pears. Its fruits are practically worthless, however, and certainly are not ornamental, although varieties of it are cultivated in Korea, Manchuria, and northern China. Of course it has been used in breeding experiments with pears, but apparently pears are susceptible to a "black-end disorder" when worked on this species as an understock. As a flowering tree the Ussurian pear is the best of the pears because the flower buds are frequently tinged pink and open gradually to white. It is suggested here only because it is the hardiest of the pears and is one of the least susceptible to fire blight. If a pear is not needed, certainly there are better ornamentals than either this or *P. calleryana.*

→≫ *QUERCUS*

The oaks are among the most dependable of our ornamental trees. Some are native in almost all but the arid regions of North America. Thirty-two are recommended here (twenty-six species and six varieties), although forty or more are listed as being grown commercially in American nurseries and offered for sale. Undoubtedly there are still others that are used locally where they are native. The members of this genus are valued for their sturdy growth, many for their brilliant autumn color, some for their evergreen leaves, and most of them for their large size or the definite shapes they take at maturity.

Unlike the willows, their wood is strong and they do not split easily in summer storms or as a result of winter's snow and ice. Some live to a great old age, the live oaks of the South certainly being in this group, some of these having trunks as much as 35 feet in diameter, breast high, and having a branch spread of well over 100 feet. Seven of the species *(agrifolia, chrysolepis, engleriana, ilex, laurifolia, suber,* and *virginiana)* have evergreen leaves, five of these being native in the South.

It is interesting to note that of the twenty-six species recommended here, three are native in the Orient, five are native in Europe, and the rest are native in North America. The European species have no autumn color, as is the case with many European natives, but most of the rest of the species have excellent fall color.

Only four of the entire group have a mature height under 50 feet, most of the others growing to be 75 feet or more in height. All in all, this is a group of truly big trees, and few should be given space in the very small garden. They may grow satisfactorily for a while, but sooner or later they grow out of proportion to such a small area. As specimen shade trees in large lawns and parks and as street trees, this group includes some of the best types available from all parts of the world for growing in North America today.

Unfortunately, the oaks are susceptible to various disease and insect troubles. They are a preferred host of the gypsy moth, which may defoliate the tree in about two weeks. Two or three annual defoliations kill many trees. Hairy brown egg masses are laid on bark or nearby but can be killed by painting with creosote. The large, striped, hairy caterpillars feed in early summer. The dirty white female moths with black angular lines on wings have a heavy brown body and cannot fly. Spraying with methoxychlor or malathion is necessary to prevent defoliation. Canker worms in the spring and the orange-striped oak worm in late summer are the primary leaf eaters. Several gall insects make conspicuous galls, such as oak-apple, wool sewer, and oak-bullet on the leaves. Gouty oak gall wasps form rough, lumpy galls on the twigs and branches on scarlet and red oaks, and are very unsightly. Infested twigs should be cut promptly. Other gall insects and leaf miners seldom require control. Small twigs with leaves still attached that fall to the ground in midsummer may have been infested by the oak twig pruner, which tunnels in the twig, causing it to break, especially from wind. The worm is in the fallen twig, which should be promptly burned. The pit-making oak scale, so named because it lives in a depression in the bark, is especially injurious to white oak. Sprays of dormant oil have been used effectively.

Oak wilt is a serious disease of black and red oaks, especially in the Midwest. Infected leaves turn black and curl upward, and eventually the tree will die. The disease is spread by root grafts and insects. Infected trees should be destroyed, and oak should not be replanted nearby. Anthracnose curls the leaves of white oak inward and spots the leaves of black and red oak along margins and veins. Spraying with zineb, ferbam, or thiram controls this and other leaf spots. Shoestring root rot often causes the death of weakened trees. The inside of loose bark is covered with black, stringlike threads. It commonly lives on dead stumps and roots in the woods. Small ornamental trees can be treated with dinocap according to directions.

Quercus acutissima   45′   Zone 6   Sawtooth oak

* HABIT: very wide-spreading branches, rounded head
  FOLIAGE: chestnutlike, lustrous, dense
  HABITAT: China, Korea, Japan
  INTRODUCED: 1862

An excellent specimen of this exotic tree is growing on the grounds of the U.S. Department of Agriculture Plant Introduction Station at Glenn Dale, Maryland. This tree needs plenty of space for lateral development because it grows nearly as broad as it does high.

Quercus agrifolia   90′   Zone 9   California live oak

* HABIT: rounded head, spreading branches
* FOLIAGE: evergreen, hollylike
  HABITAT: California

This tree is used chiefly near the California coast, where it is native.

Quercus alba   90′   Zone 4   White oak

* HABIT: broad, rounded head, wide-spreading branches
* FOLIAGE: dense
* AUTUMN COLOR: purplish red to violet-purple
  HABITAT: eastern United States

The "mighty oak" is significantly exemplified in the white oak, for massive specimens 150 feet high and some as much as eight hundred years old have been recorded. Older specimens are almost perfectly rounded in outline and usually blessed with thick and sturdy horizontal branches. The white oak is difficult to transplant because of a very strong tap root, and when compared with the red oak, it is rather slow in growth, two reasons that some look upon it with disfavor. Its wide-spreading branches, usually spaced far apart, make it possible to string electric wires through it easily with a minimum of disfiguring pruning. Also, the dead leaves frequently remain on the tree a good part of the winter. Hence, it makes an excellent specimen tree, needing plenty of room (80 feet or more) in which to mature properly. Where fast growth is essential, other trees might be substituted, but for majestically mature beauty no tree can surpass a well-grown white oak.

Quercus bicolor   60'   Zone 3   Swamp white oak

HABIT: narrow, round-topped, open head
FOLIAGE: dense
AUTUMN COLOR: yellow-brown to red
HABITAT: eastern and central North America

This is an excellent tree for moist or wet soils, somewhat similar to *Q. alba,* but the leaves are coarser and the tree itself is not as refined.

Quercus cerris   100'   Zone 6   Turkey oak

HABIT: broadly pyramidal
FOLIAGE: open with small, fine-textured, dark green leaves
HABITAT: southern Europe, western Asia
INTRODUCED: 1735

An interesting ornamental tree with leaves 2–4 inches long, comparatively small for the oaks. One of the faster-growing oaks but apparently not doing well north of the southern New England coast.

Quercus chrysolepis   60'   Zone 7   Canyon live oak, Golden-cup
                                                              oak

* HABIT: wide-spreading head, often pendulous branchlets
* FOLIAGE: evergreen
  HABITAT: West Coast

This oak is often considered the most beautiful of the oaks native in California, but planted only in that region as an ornamental.

Quercus coccinea   75′   Zone 4   Scarlet oak

* HABIT: open and round-topped head
   FOLIAGE: rather lustrous but open
* AUTUMN COLOR: brilliant scarlet
   HABITAT: eastern and central United States
   VARIETY:
       'Splendens' *(Knaphill oak)*—foliage slightly more glossy than species

Many might consider this tree of secondary importance to some of the other oaks for one very important reason: it is hard to transplant. Possibly it should not be recommended. Arborists often say they have more difficulty moving it than most trees. It must be said in its favor, however, that it grows naturally over nearly a third of the United States and has a loosely open habit which most of the oaks (especially *Q. palustris* and *rubra)* do not. Its lustrous foliage and brilliant autumn coloration make it attractive for all types of landscape use. It should be given the greatest care when it is being transplanted.

Part of the Veteran's Highway on the outskirts of Boston was planted with the scarlet oak in the central strip (it is a four-lane highway), where the trees necessarily have little room, and the pin oak on either side of the roadway where they have been given plenty of room—an interesting way of using these two species in parkway planting. The scarlet oak is more open, gives less shade, and in parkway planting is certainly easier to see through since the branching is not as dense as in the pin oak.

Quercus engleriana   30′   Zone 7   Engler's oak

   HABIT: rounded head
* FOLIAGE: evergreen leaves, 3–7″ long
   HABITAT: central and western China
   INTRODUCED: 1900

Because of its small size and evergreen foliage, this might be worthy of trial where larger evergreen oaks thrive.

Quercus falcata   75′   Zone 5   Spanish oak, Southern red oak

* HABIT: rounded head but upright, with stout, spreading branches
   FOLIAGE: rather open
   AUTUMN COLOR: dull orange to brown
   HABITAT: southeastern United States

Growing over a wide area of the southeastern United States, the Spanish or southern red oak grows as far north as New Jersey and Pennsylvania. Surprisingly enough, this tree is perfectly hardy in the Arnold Arboretum where a specimen 75 feet tall with a trunk 2 feet in diameter has been doing well for over seventy-five years. Since it is a native, it has been used frequently in landscape planting.

Quercus garryana   90′   Zone 6   Oregon white oak

HABIT: rounded head, ascending branches
FOLIAGE: dense, similar in size and shape to that of *Q. alba*
HABITAT: West Coast

This white oak is the most important oak for timber purposes on the Pacific coast. As an ornamental it is used only within its habitat and does well on dry or gravelly soils.

Quercus ilex   60′   Zone 9   Holly oak, Holm oak

HABIT: rounded head, broad spread
* FOLIAGE: dense, fine-textured, evergreen leaves, 1½–3″ long and 1″ wide
HABITAT: southern Europe
INTRODUCED: colonial times

The holly oak has been a popular tree in southern Europe for centuries and has proved itself one of the best of the evergreen oaks, especially in plantings near the seashore where the atmosphere is continually moist. It can be clipped easily into various forms and makes an excellent shade tree. The leaves are variable in shape, about 1 inch wide. This tree, however, has the bad habit of dropping the previous year's foliage in late spring, making the lawn underneath unsightly for some time. This can be circumvented easily, of course, by planting a ground cover underneath in which such falling leaves can settle without being conspicuous.

Quercus imbricaria   75′   Zone 5   Shingle oak

* HABIT: pyramidal while young, round-topped when old, open
* FOLIAGE: lustrous, laurel-like, often remaining on the tree far into the winter
* AUTUMN COLOR: yellowish to russet
HABITAT: central United States

When well cared for and well grown, the shingle oak can easily be one of the most beautiful of all the oaks. Its leaves are similar in size and shape to those of the mountain-laurel, and a lustrous dark green on the upper surface. After turning a rich yellow to russet in the fall, the leaves may remain on the trees all winter long. This is amenable to shearing and makes excellent hedges, especially the larger sizes for windbreaks and screens. Even though a native of the Ohio Valley, it is unfortunately difficult to find in commercial nurseries.

Quercus kelloggii   90′   Zone 7   California black oak

HABIT: open, rounded head, stout, spreading branches
FOLIAGE: dense
HABITAT: Oregon to California

This tree does well in dry, sandy, or gravelly soils on the West Coast and is supposed to live to a ripe old age of two hundred to three hundred years.

Quercus laurifolia   60′   Zone 7   Laurel oak

HABIT: dense, round-topped
FOLIAGE: semi-evergreen, lustrous, dark green
HABITAT: southeastern United States

This tree is used considerably as a street tree in the southern United States.

Quercus libani   30′   Zone 5   Lebanon oak

* HABIT: rounded
* FOLIAGE: deciduous to semi-evergreen; leaves 2–4″ long
HABITAT: Syria, Asia Minor
INTRODUCED: 1855

A handsome, small tree, with small, regularly toothed, narrow leaves that look at a distance like the leaves of a willow. This is one of the smallest leaved of all the oaks growing in the Arnold Arboretum in Boston. It has been highly recommended in England and should find considerable use in American gardens.

Quercus marilandica   30′   Zone 6   Blackjack oak

HABIT: irregular, stout branches
FOLIAGE: leathery, glossy
AUTUMN COLOR: brown or yellow
HABITAT: eastern and central United States

This slow-growing tree is well adapted for planting on poor, dry, sterile soil. At maturity it is only a small tree and can hardly be considered a tree until after ten to fifteen years of growth. It has splendid foliage but should be considered for planting only in poor soil situations where more ornamental oaks would not grow.

Quercus nigra   75′   Zone 6   Water oak

HABIT: conical or round-topped, slender branches
FOLIAGE: fine-textured, small leaves
HABITAT: southeastern United States

A tree frequently used in the Southeast, it is apparently very easily transplanted and makes a good street tree where it is hardy; frequently used in the South on moist to wet soils.

Quercus palustris   75'   Zone 4   Pin oak

* HABIT: pyramidal with drooping branches, dense branching
* FOLIAGE: fine textured
* AUTUMN COLOR: scarlet
  HABITAT: central and mideastern United States
  VARIETY:
>   'Crownright' *(Plant Patent #2936)*—with a narrow, sharply pyramidal head, lower branches do not weep downward as do those of the species. Originated by Princeton Nurseries, Princeton, New Jersey.

This is one of the most picturesque of the oaks because of its peculiar habit of growth. The upper branches are upright, the middle branches are horizontal, and the lower branches are pendulous, giving the tree a beautiful pyramidal outline. The limbs are small, not massive as in the white oak, but are numerous, and mature foliage is very dense. Usually found in nature in moist bottom lands, the pin oak is easily moved because of its fibrous root system (it has no tap roots) but is sometimes rather difficult to grow in a location where the soil is alkaline. It is one of the few trees in the East that show a chlorotic condition of the foliage when the soil is not just right. This condition is quickly cured (though often only temporarily) by spraying soluble iron salts on the foliage or injecting them into the tree trunk itself.

   This tree makes an excellent specimen as a lawn tree but should never be used as a street tree unless it is placed at least 20 feet from the roadway. It is certainly a mistake to plant it as close to the road as a red oak, for instance, since the pendulous limbs obstruct traffic. These are cut off and before long the limbs that were horizontal begin to acquire a pendulous habit, and then these too must be removed. It seems that there are always hanging branches to be cut out of a pin oak when it is not given sufficient room for normal lateral growth. Allowed to grow naturally with sufficient space so its pendulous branches can sweep the ground, there is no more beautiful or graceful tree.

Quercus phellos   50'   Zone 5   Willow oak

* HABIT: round-topped to conical, dense branching
* FOLIAGE: fine textured
  AUTUMN COLOR: yellowish
  HABITAT: eastern seaboard, Gulf states

The willow oak has what is perhaps the finest foliage texture of any, with leaves 2½–5 inches long, narrow, and pointed at both ends more or less like those of a willow tree, and the side branches are slender like those of the pin oak. It is included here for this reason and because it is used widely for ornamental planting and as a street tree throughout its native habitat, one of the principal reasons being that it is easy to transplant because of shallow roots.

Quercus prinus (syn *Q. montana*)   90'   Zone 4   Chestnut oak

HABIT: dense, rounded head
FOLIAGE: dark green
AUTUMN COLOR: dull orange
HABITAT: eastern North America

The chestnut oak is a good tree for planting in rather dry, rocky soil but is probably surpassed in beauty by other oaks in good soil. Nevertheless it is superior to *Q. muhlenbergii* because of its better foliage and so can be included here especially for planting in rather dry situations.

Quercus robur   75–150'   Zone 5   English oak

HABIT: open, broad head, short trunk
FOLIAGE: rather open
HABITAT: Europe, northern Africa, western Asia
INTRODUCED: colonial times
VARIETIES:
> '**Asplenifolia**' *(Spleenwort English oak)*—deeply cut, fernlike, fine-textured
>   leaves
> '**Atropurpurea**' *(Purple English oak)*—leaves dark purple
> '**Concordia**' *(Golden oak)*—leaves are a bright yellow, especially when they first
>   appear in the spring. In very hot sun, however, the leaves may scorch.

An old specimen of the English oak (Quercus robur) *in Wales.*

'Fastigiata' *(Pyramidal English oak)*—columnar in habit with form similar to that of the Lombardy poplar. An excellent ornamental—a great majority of the seedlings raised from acorns sown from this tree have the same columnar habit as the parent.

Over 110 other varieties have been named. Widely planted in Europe, many varieties of this species have been noted. It is not entirely satisfactory in the Arnold Arboretum. Large trees will grow sometimes a foot in trunk diameter, and then will die suddenly within a year, due to no apparent cause other than unsuitable climate or winter cold. It is widely distributed in American gardens, and the fastigiate variety is even more popular. Like many a native European plant, this tree does not have a vivid autumn color since the leaves drop off late in the fall while still green. *Quercus petraea* is very similar but does better in drier soils and holds its leaves longer in the fall.

Quercus rubra   75′   Zone 3   Red oak

* HABIT: broad, round-topped when old, pyramidal when young
* FOLIAGE: dense, usually lustrous
* AUTUMN COLOR: red
HABITAT: northeastern and central North America

The red oak is one of the most popular of all the oaks for ornamental planting. It transplants easily, something that cannot be said of all oaks, and grows vigorously. It withstands city conditions, is clean in habit, and makes one of the best street or avenue trees we have. Botanists have arbitrarily distinguished a variety, *maxima,* as being larger and more widely distributed, but for ornamental purposes it is certainly identical with the species. The red oak is the most rapid-growing of all the oaks and certainly worthy of consideration for landscape planting.

Quercus suber   60′   Zone 7   Cork oak

* HABIT: round-topped head, short trunk, massive branches
* FOLIAGE: small, fine-textured, evergreen leaves
HABITAT: southern Europe, northern Africa
INTRODUCED: colonial times

Thomas Jefferson was probably one of the first Americans to realize the merits of the cork oak, but it was not until about 1858 that some of the first successful cork oak plantings were made from seed distributed by the U.S. Department of Agriculture. This tree is ornamental because of its large branches, rounded habit, and evergreen foliage. Because of the fact that the United States uses in excess of 150,000 tons of cork annually, most of it imported from the Mediterranean region, American sources were scrutinized rather carefully during World War II. Many mature cork oaks were found in perfect condition in this country. One of these trees yielded 1,050 pounds of cork when its bark was stripped off.

As the result of an extensive cork-planting program conducted by the Crown

The bark of a cork oak
(Quercus suber) *about one*
hundred years old.

Cork and Seal Co. of Baltimore, Maryland, and certain state and federal agencies, thousands of trees have been set out during the past few decades. There are now well over one hundred thousand cork oaks growing in the United States, chiefly in California and the southern states as far north as Baltimore County, Maryland.

The outer bark is first stripped off the tree when it is about fifteen years old and then at seven- to twelve-year intervals thereafter for at least one hundred years or more. The inner living cambium tissue is not injured in this process. The grade of cork improves for the first three strippings and remains fairly uniform thereafter. The virgin bark must be removed before the high-grade cork is produced.

Cork trees require full sun and seem to thrive in semiarid soil. The economic interest in this new American-grown crop, combined with the fact that the tree does have good ornamental possibilities, should give the planting of cork trees momentum in those regions of the South peculiarly adapted to its growth, where winter temperatures do not fall below zero and average rainfall approaches amounts equal to those in the cork-growing areas of Spain and Portugal.

Quercus variabilis   75′   Zone 5   Oriental oak

HABIT: fairly open but still yields good shade
BARK: yellowish gray, deeply furrowed, decidedly corklike
FOLIAGE: dull green, similar to that of *Castanea crenata*
HABITAT: northern China, Korea, Japan
INTRODUCED: 1861

This tree is of particular interest because of its outer bark, which is very corklike. In fact, in some regions of China the bark does have economic value, supplying a poor grade of cork. This cork layer is only about ½ inch thick, however, and the chances are the tree will have little economic use in any country where *Q. suber* can be grown in the warmer regions.

Quercus velutina   100–150′   Zone 4   Black oak

* HABIT: rounded and dense
* FOLIAGE: lustrous, dark green
* AUTUMN COLOR: red
  HABITAT: eastern and central United States

This species is not frequently planted as an ornamental tree, probably because its deep tap root makes it difficult to transplant, especially in the larger sizes. The branching system is not as rugged as that of *Q. alba,* nor is it as wide-spreading, but it is one of the largest growing of all the hardy northern oaks. The inner bark is yellow and the terminal winter buds pubescent, the chief means by which it can be distinguished from *Q. rubra.* If lustrous leaves and tremendous height are desired, this certainly is the species to use. Otherwise, some of the other species might do as well.

Quercus virginiana   60′   Zone 7   Live oak

* HABIT: very wide-spreading, nearly horizontal branches
* FOLIAGE: evergreen in the southern part of its range, deciduous only near its
      northern limits, fine textured
  HABITAT: southeastern United States

This massive oak is one of the most impressive sights of the coastal gardens of the southeastern Gulf states. One of the largest trees on record has a trunk circumference of 39 feet and a spread of 132 feet even though it is only 55 feet high. The leaves are comparatively small and narrow (about 2–5 inches long) and are usually ever-green. Near its northern limit in Virginia, however, the leaves are often deciduous. The typical habit of one of these trees is easily twice as broad as it is high and densely rounded in outline.

It is easily transplanted when young and has long been popular in the South as a shade and street tree. In Texas it has withstood temperatures of 10°F below zero without any injury to the wood, although the leaves have been killed.

Quillaja saponaria   60'   Zone 10   Soapbark tree

FLOWERS: white, ½" in diameter
    TIME: spring
HABIT: open
* FOLIAGE: evergreen, open, lustrous
HABITAT: Chile

The soapbark tree is sometimes used as an ornamental in southern California, especially because of its evergreen foliage.

Ravenala madagascariensis   30'   Zone 10   Madagascar
                                                          traveler's tree

* HABIT: upright palm, open, like a huge fan
FOLIAGE: coarse but picturesque, leaves often 15' long
HABITAT: Madagascar

This striking and unusual tree, closely related to the banana, is used only in subtropical areas for striking effect. The common name comes from the fact that it stores a palatable watery fluid at the base of the leaves that can be used as a substitute for water where this is not available to the weary traveler. Its peculiar fanlike shape sets it apart from other trees.

Rhamnus davurica   30'   Zone 2   Dahurian buckthorn

* FRUIT: shiny red to black berries, ¼" in diameter
    EFFECTIVE: fall
HABIT: indefinite
* FOLIAGE: lustrous
HABITAT: north China, Manchuria, Korea
INTRODUCED: 1817

This is not a particularly desirable ornamental, but it is a vigorous grower in almost any normal soil. The lustrous green leaves and fruit, which attract many kinds of birds, are about its only important characteristics.

Rhododendron maximum   12–36'   Zone 3   Rosebay
                                                      rhododendron

* FLOWERS: rose-colored to purple-pink, spotted olive-green to orange
    TIME: late June
HABIT: rounded and irregularly open
* FOLIAGE: evergreen, dark green leaves, 5–10" long
HABITAT: eastern North America

VARIETIES:
> *album*—white flowers
> *purpureum*—deep pink to purple flowers

This native species is perhaps the hardiest of all the evergreen rhododendrons, and certainly the tallest and most treelike of those hardy in the North. Its flowers are not as large as those of *R. catawbiense* but are free of the objectionable magenta color. They appear after the leaves of the current year's growth are well opened. The new foliage hides the flower clusters to a considerable degree. The rosebay rhododendron, then, is of value for its hardiness, its tall habit of growth, and its long leaves, but when flowers alone are considered, many species and hybrids are far more satisfactory. It requires semishade to do well and is frequently used in gardens in the northern United States merely as part of an evergreen shrub background for more ornamental plants. Seldom is it used in gardens as a tree, although it sometimes reaches tree proportions in its native habitat. There are many other rhododendrons that grow to tree size, but not until very recently have these been introduced to America. Nearly thirty have been noted as trees, one *(R. giganteum)* described as the tallest of all, reaching 90 feet in height in its native habitat. These are still so rare in America, however, that none have grown to tree size and so will not be considered here.

⇥⋙ *ROBINIA*

Many trees and groves of black locust have been ruined by the locust borer. Large scars in the bark, crooked branches, and exit holes of the beetle are characteristic of this intruder. Control measures have not been developed, but spraying with methoxychlor in late summer when the beetles are active should be helpful. Putnam scale attacks black locust, and locust leaf miners make large blotch mines where the orange-colored larvae live for three or four weeks. Sprays of malathion are effective.

On small trees the main trunk and branches may show distinct swelling caused by the locust twig borer. The reddish yellow borer emerges through a conspicuous exit hole in the gall. Cutting and burning the infested twigs while the borer is still in them is suggested.

x Robinia 'Idaho'   40'   Zones 3–4

* FLOWERS: pealike, dark reddish purple, in pendulous clusters
       TIME: early June
  FRUIT: dry pods
  HABIT: open

FOLIAGE: open, compound leaves
ORIGIN: a hybrid of unknown origin

This tree has a mixed hybrid parentage, but it is not a variety of *R. pseudoacacia.* It is being used in landscape work especially in the Midwest and is valued for its flowers, which are the darkest reddish purple of any of the *Robinia* group. It undoubtedly has the same drawbacks from borers and leaf miners as does *R. pseudoacacia,* hence should be used only in areas where those insects are not major pests. Like the other locusts, it does well on poor, dry soils where better trees seem to have a difficult time.

Robinia pseudoacacia   75'   Zone 3   Black locust

* FLOWERS: fragrant, pealike, white, in pendulous clusters
         TIME: early June
FRUIT: dry pods
HABIT: few, open branches, upright
FOLIAGE: open
HABITAT: eastern United States
VARIETIES:

'Decaisneana' *(Decaisne locust)*—flowers light rose-colored
dependens—pendulous branchlets
'Semperflorens' *(Perpetual black locust)*—flowers throughout the summer
'Umbraculifera' *(Umbrella black locust)*—branches form a dense, rounded head

There are at least three types, some with single, straight trunks, others with irregular trunks, and still others with a fan-shaped habit of branching. Locusts are valued for their late spring flowers (after the foliage is fully developed) and for their ability to grow in poor, sterile, and dry soils. They are legumes and do have small nitrogen nodules on their roots; their small, stipular thorns are omnipresent and rather effective in vigorous, young growth.

Like many other native trees, they are frequently planted throughout their native habitat, but there are two serious pests that frequently disfigure them, namely, the locust borer and the locust leaf miner. The borer, once it gets into the trunk and large branches, can create much havoc and seriously reduce the vigor and beauty of the tree. Control is difficult once the borers are inside the trunk.

The locust leaf miner, once it becomes established, can skeletonize the foliage of the entire tree or even groves of them in the late summer. This can be controlled by spraying the foliage with poison at the proper time. The point to remember is that in areas where these pests are known to be prevalent, locusts are going to require persistent maintenance care in order to be satisfactory ornamental trees. The shade they yield is practically negligible.

Roystonea regia   70'   Zone 10   Royal palm

* HABIT: palm tree
FOLIAGE: graceful
HABITAT: Cuba, southern Florida

This is the most graceful of the palms planted in the southeastern United States. The lower leaves droop and the central leaves are upright, always swaying gracefully in any breeze. The trunk is swollen slightly in the center and then tapers gracefully above and below. A typical tree in the subtropical part of Florida, it is very popular because of its plumelike leaves, which are uniquely suitable to avenue planting in the tropics.

Sabal palmetto   90′   Zone 8   Palmetto

* HABIT: palm with tufted growth of leaves at top of trunk
  FOLIAGE: coarse, fan-shaped
  HABITAT: North Carolina to Florida

This is the tree the Seminole Indians of the Florida Everglades call the "cabbage palmetto" because it affords timber for the construction of their houses, fiber for tying things, leaves for thatching roofs, and the young buds taste like cabbage when cooked. It is the dried leaves of this palm that are cut and distributed so widely in religious services on Palm Sunday. The fanlike leaves are 5 to 6 feet long and 7 to 8 feet across, partially divided into long, narrow segments. Of course if the terminal bud is removed, the tree dies. This tree is typical of the landscape of the southeastern coastal sections of the United States, and it is used for ornamental and street tree planting as well. The palmetto is one of the hardiest of the palms.

⇢≫ *SALIX*

There are over three hundred species of willows in the northern temperate regions of the world, some of them trees and many shrubs. A few trees are ornamental and are listed here, but there are many characteristics common to this group that should be thoroughly understood before any one is selected for planting. Many are extremely difficult to identify—even the expert taxonomist throws up his hands in despair when confronted by a pile of herbarium specimens for determination. They have hybridized a great deal so that many hybrids have occurred only to further confuse the identification picture.

In the first place, the flowers of most willows (except the so-called pussy willow) are not ornamental. The sexes are separate, the male catkins occurring on one tree, the female catkins on another. Incidentally, this does not make the identification of the species any easier. As a rule, the foliage is of a fine texture, and most of the leaves might be considered "small." The species are twiggy in habit, with many fine branches continually in motion in almost any breeze.

As a group they flourish in moist situations, and here is where they are best used in gardens. Because of their affinity for water, however, their roots readily seek out openings in drains or sewers and quickly clog them as easily as those of the Carolina poplar (see page 367). The weeping willows, in particular, have become associated with plantings by ponds, and of course the shrubby types are frequently found in nature in moist soils. All can be readily propagated by cuttings.

The wood of all willows is very weak and cracks easily. This is one of the most important reasons that they should not be used as street or avenue trees. It has been done, probably in many places, but the cost of maintenance far outstrips any possible value added to real estate when such plantings are made.

In many areas, willows are troubled with several serious diseases and with insect pests as well, both important reasons that they require much maintenance. Over one hundred different insects have been noted to feed on willows. Insecticides such as malathion, methoxycholor, and dormant oil, and fungicides such as captafol and dinitrocresol should be used at the proper times to help control some of these pests.

All in all, willows should be planted only in moist situations where vigorous growth and corresponding good foliage is assured, and only after the serious consideration of other kinds of trees that might be used to take their place. For this reason, only nine willow tree species have been suggested for possible consideration here. Many more could have been included, but the fewer that are planted, especially along public rights of way, the less expense to everyone responsible for their care.

Admittedly, there is nothing as beautiful and graceful, in the northern part of the country at least, as a well-grown weeping willow. As will be noted in the following discussions, some may prove superior to others, but certainly there is no other tree like the weeping willow for northern planting. A careful selection should be made from among the four types of weeping willows suggested, in order to best fit the situation under consideration.

The weeping willows have been considerably mixed in the nurseries and gardens of this country for well over fifty years and probably will continue to be. It is unfortunate that they have become confused, particularly in the trade, for they can be distinguished one from the other in most cases, even in the nursery row when they are nothing more than rooted cuttings. Since some are hardier than others and some make better weeping specimens than others, it would seem advisable for all commercial growers to work up correctly named stock.

A study of these plants was begun at the Arnold Arboretum a number of years ago when three different nurseries had sent in material for identification during one week. Material of these weeping types was requested from twenty of the leading nurseries in the East and the Midwest, then lined out in the nurseries of the Arnold Arboretum and grown for several years. This study pointed out the great confusion concerning nomenclature that now exists, since at least a third of the specimens we received were misnamed.

It is unfortunate that the Babylon weeping willow, for some reason or other, has become accepted in the minds of many people as the only weeping willow. As a matter of fact, several types of weeping willows are being grown in the trade under the name of *S. babylonica,* and it must be admitted that there are actually six willow trees in this category. The Babylon weeping willow is hardy in only about the lower third of the United States. In more northern areas the hardier species should be grown.

The most hardy is the golden willow *(S. alba* 'Tristis,' often incorrectly termed *S. vitellina pendula).* Of the remaining four, one is a native of China and probably not much distributed in this country *(S. matsudana pendula),* and the other three are hybrids, each having *S. babylonica* as one of its parents. It is this affinity that is causing the confusion in identification.

Salix sepulcralis (often termed *S. salamoni)* is the least pendulous of the three *S. babylonica* hybrids and so is not recommended here as one of the truly "weeping" willows. The Thurlow weeping willow *(S. elegantissima)* and the Wisconsin weeping willow *(S. blanda)* are both grown and recommended, but the latter is probably the less desirable since, in mature specimens, its branchlets are not as long as are those of the Thurlow weeping willow.

Of all these, the most pendulous are *S. babylonica, S. alba* 'Tristis,' and *S. elegantissima,* easily distinguishable one from the other. *Salix matsudana pendula* is probably not distributed much in America, and *S. sepulcralis* is the least pendulous of all. The Wisconsin weeping willow is a very popular one also because of its good growth and lustrous leaves.

In order to assist in the identification of the four weeping willows here recommended, the following key is offered. It does not always prove accurate, but at least it may help to assist in the proper identification of these very closely related species:

1. One-year-old twigs definitely yellow and pendulous, red very little if any on upper side of young twigs, young leaves hairy above and below
. . . . S. *alba* 'Tristis'
   2. Young twigs yellowish green and reddish on upper side, leaves less than ⅝ inch in width and glabrous; branchlets very pendulous—one-year-old rooted cuttings grow almost prostrate on the ground, petiole ⅜ inch long. . . . . S. *babylonica*
      3. Twigs distinctly green, growth much more upright, leaves ⅝–⅞ inch in width and glabrous
         a. Leaves lustrous above, one-year-old twigs reddish to brown
. . . . S. *blanda*
         b. Leaves not lustrous above, one-year-old twigs green
. . . . S. *elegantissima*

Salix alba   75′   Zone 2   White willow

HABIT: loose, open, spreading branches
FOLIAGE: fine textured
AUTUMN COLOR: yellow
HABIT: Europe, northern Africa to central Asia
INTRODUCED: colonial times
VARIETIES:

'Chermesina' *(Redstem willow)*—twigs bright red

'Tristis' *(Golden weeping willow)*—extremely hardy, this is a gracefully beautiful tree in its own right, hardy throughout the northern United States and southern Canada. It is available in the trade erroneously under three different names, *S. vitellina pendula,* "Niobe," and *S. alba* 'Tristis.' Old, established trees in the Arnold Arboretum do not have branches "sweeping the ground," but some of the younger trees, planted in good soil about Boston, are 25′ tall, have branches that are definitely pendant for at least 15′, and these do "sweep the ground." Dr. L. H. Bailey noted a *S. babylonica aurea,* which name may have been picked up from an incorrect listing in a nursery catalog or introduced from Europe many years ago. Certainly if there were a form of *S. babylonica* with pendulous yellow twigs, it would be practically impossible to tell it from *S. alba* 'Tristis.'

E. H. Wilson has suggested that possibly there are two forms of *S. blanda,* one with yellowish shoots called "Niobe." It is apparently certain that there are two forms of yellow-twigged weeping willows in the trade,

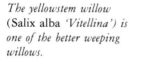

The yellowstem willow (Salix alba *'Vitellina') is* *one of the better weeping* *willows.*

even though our best taxonomic botanists classify them both under *S. alba* 'Tristis.' One has much longer pendulous branches than the other.

'Vitellina' *(Yellowstem willow)*—with yellow twigs

This can be considered one of the best of the upright willows for landscape planting. Most willows (except the weeping varieties) are not recommended for planting because of their weak wood and susceptibility to attacks, and rather severe ones, from several serious diseases and insect pests. Consequently, for special locations, such as by the water or where the varieties with colored winter twigs seem desirable, this species could be used.

Salix babylonica   30′   Zone 6   Babylon weeping willow

* HABIT: long, pendulous branches
* FOLIAGE: fine textured
  HABITAT: China
  INTRODUCED: 1730

This is the best of the weeping willows, and where it is hardy it should be given first choice. The specific name was first given it by Linnaeus when it was found in the region of the Euphrates River in Babylon, but botanical exploration centuries later proved that it was a native of China. Apparently it is another of those plants like *Syringa persica* that were deposited along the old trade route from China to Egypt. It has been a popular tree for centuries, being very much in the public eye about 1823 when Napoleon, exiled to the island of St. Helena, used to sit under one and contemplate his better days. In fact, he loved this particular specimen so much that he was buried under it, and cuttings from it were later in great demand all over the world.

    Being a willow, it is naturally a fast-growing and weak-wooded tree, easily susceptible to breakage from ice or snow. It is not hardy in New England where it is frequently tried, only to winter-kill miserably during the first really hard winter that strikes it. When propagated from cuttings it can be distinguished easily from other willows for the first year or two, for it lies almost prostrate on the ground.

x Salix blanda   40′   Zone 4   Wisconsin weeping willow, Niobe
    weeping willow

* HABIT: wide-spreading head, long, pendulous branchlets
* FOLIAGE: fine textured
  ORIGIN: *S. babylonica* x *S. fragilis*
  INTRODUCED: before 1830?

Probably a clone of the same cross as *S. elegantissima,* the true Wisconsin weeping willow is probably the less desirable specimen because its pendulous branches are only half as long as those of the Thurlow weeping willow, although more lustrous. Whether or not the term "Niobe" is a synonym is a matter for much discussion.

E. H. Wilson has remarked that there were two forms of *S. blanda,* "one with yellowish twigs called Niobe." Whether or not this is true, all specimens of "Niobe" that I have been able to acquire from many nursery sources have proved to be *S. alba* 'Tristis.' As previously noted, possibly there are two clones of this variety.

Salix caprea   27'   Zone 4   Goat willow

* FLOWERS: small, composite heads or catkins, about 1″ long; sexes separate
     TIME: March
HABITAT: Europe to northern Asia and northern Iran
INTRODUCED: early colonial times

This species is the best of the "pussy willows" because it has the largest catkins. The sexes in willows are separate, and the male of this species has those long, fluffy, gray catkins that eventually sprout many bright yellow stamens as they mature. The catkins of the female plant eventually have greenish pistils that are not nearly as pretty as those of the male. This willow is a vigorous shrub or small tree of little interest the rest of the year, but the catkins come so early in the season that there may be room in the large garden for this plant to serve just this one purpose. Larger catkins are frequently obtained by cutting the plant to the ground every three years, thus forcing it into vigorous growth. The native *S. discolor* of the United States is also common in woods and swampy places over the eastern United States, but its catkins are smaller than those of *S. caprea.*

Salix elaeagnos   45'   Zone 4   Elaeagnus willow

HABIT: slender-branched, rounded head
* FOLIAGE: feathery, grayish
AUTUMN COLOR: yellow
HABITAT: southern Europe, Asia Minor
INTRODUCED: before 1850

This tree is interesting because of its feathery, grayish foliage. However, where this characteristic is wanted, the true *Elaeagnus angustifolia* might better be used since it is not as susceptible to attack from pests.

x *Salix elegantissima*   40'   Zone 4   Thurlow weeping willow

* HABIT: long, pendulous branchlets
FOLIAGE: fine textured
ORIGIN: unknown, possibly *S. babylonica* x *S. fragilis*
INTRODUCED: about 1860

The Thurlow weeping willow is the best substitute for the Babylon weeping willow in the North. Although the pendulous branches are not as long as those of *S.*

babylonica, they are twice as long as those of *S. blanda.* This latter species does have lustrous leaves, lacking in the Thurlow weeping willow. Other than these two differences, these weeping willows are very much alike; both probably have the same parents.

Salix matsudana 'Tortuosa'   30'   Zone 4   Corkscrew willow,
                                                  Contorted willow

* HABIT: branches twisted or contorted
FOLIAGE: leaves 2–3½" long
HABITAT: China, Korea
INTRODUCED: 1923

Cuttings of this peculiar willow were received by the Arnold Arboretum in 1923 direct from China. When all the leaves have fallen the peculiar "corkscrew" effect of the branching is most evident, but when the leaves are fully developed, it is hidden. Of garden interest only for this unique characteristic.

The corkscrew, or contorted, willow (Salix matsudana *'Tortuosa') is of interest only when all the leaves have fallen and its branches can be seen in outline.*

Salix pentandra   60'   Zone 4   Laurel willow

HABIT: rounded
* FOLIAGE: lustrous, dark green leaves about the size of those of the mountain-laurel
HABITAT: Europe
INTRODUCED: colonial times?

This is one of the best of the willows for ornamental planting, especially because of
its lustrous, dark green foliage and its shiny, brownish twigs. When subjected to the
ravages of insect attack, which is a failing of most willows, it appears as the most
dilapidated tree in the garden or along the highway, but cared for properly, it makes
an excellent specimen.

The laurel willow has been used occasionally as a street tree. This is a mistake,
for all willows are in the "high maintenance" group of trees that require costly
spraying and pruning every year in order to look good.

x Salix **'Prairie Cascade'**   50'   Zone 2

BARK: golden
FOLIAGE: glossy
HYBRID ORIGIN: *S. blanda x S. pentandra*

A very good, hardy, weeping willow from the Marden Research station in Manitoba,
Canada.

Sambucus coerulea   45'   Zone 5   Blueberry elder

* FLOWERS: small, yellowish white, in large, flat clusters, 7" in diameter
           TIME: late June
* FRUIT: blue-black but whitened by a heavy bloom
           EFFECTIVE: late summer
HABITAT: West Coast of the United States and Canada

The fruit of this plant has a whitish blue appearance that is most attractive and makes
this popular for planting on the West Coast. It is very vigorous and when cut back
it may grow as much as 3 to 12 feet in one year. However, as a tree, the wood is weak
and susceptible to breakage in severe storms.

Sapium sebiferum   40'   Zone 9   Chinese tallow tree

* FRUIT: milky white seed adhering to central part of capsule long after it is open
           EFFECTIVE: fall
HABIT: spreading, unsymmetrical trunk divided into several large branches
FOLIAGE: light, lustrous green, poplarlike

AUTUMN COLOR: deep red and yellow
HABITAT: China, Japan

With the general ornamental aspects of a poplar, the Chinese tallow tree has been planted in the southern part of the Gulf states and in lower California. The Chinese use the waxy coating around the seeds for making candles and soap. This tree is remarkably free of insect pests and diseases and is adaptable for planting in a wide variety of soils.

Sassafras albidum (syn. *S. officinale)*   60'   Zone 4   Sassafras

FRUIT: bluish black berry, under ½" in diameter, with a red stalk
    EFFECTIVE: early fall
* HABIT: short, sparsely spaced branches, long trunk
FOLIAGE: irregularly shaped, often like one- or two-fingered mittens
* AUTUMN COLOR: brilliant orange to scarlet
HABITAT: eastern and northeastern United States

The sassafras is widely distributed, familiar to most people interested in native trees because of its irregular, mitten-shaped leaves, their aromatic odor when crushed, and brilliant autumn coloration. The sexes may be separate, some trees having both staminate and pistillate flowers on the same tree and in still others the flowers may be perfect. The tree often grows in poor, gravelly soils and is rather difficult to transplant, at least when it is large. When it grows in groups, as it often does on the border of woodlands or along old fence rows, it tends to be narrow and upright, but grown individually out in the open it makes a fine tree. The oil of sassafras is distilled from the roots and the bark, and it was from these that sassafras tea was made by the early settlers. Mostly free of serious pests.

Schinus molle   40'   Zone 9   California pepper tree

* FRUIT: red berries in abundant clusters
    EFFECTIVE: fall
HABIT: wide-spreading branches, rounded top
FOLIAGE: feather-shaped, compound leaves, 9" long
HABITAT: Peru

The California pepper tree is an excellent highway or street tree in California and widely planted there. Sturdy in growth, the pendant branchlets often reach the ground, and in rather arid conditions it seems to thrive even though given little attention on poor soils. It is susceptible to black scale (it is banned near orange orchards in some sections for this reason) and has the bad reputation for dropping litter on well-kept lawns; otherwise it is a fine plant.

Schinus terebinthifolius   40′   Zones 9–10   Brazil pepper tree

* FRUIT: small, bright red
       EFFECTIVE: winter
  HABIT: rounded
* FOLIAGE: attractive, evergreen, compound, 4–8″ long
  HABITAT: Brazil

This tree is used chiefly in Florida as a lawn or avenue tree and is often called the "Christmas-berry tree" because its fruits are conspicuous in midwinter for quite some time. It grows well and very rapidly in dry areas.

Sciadopitys verticillata   120′   Zone 5   Umbrella pine

FRUIT: cones 3–5″ long
       EFFECTIVE: fall

An excellent evergreen ornamental, the umbrella pine (Sciadopitys verticillata) *is one of the best for its dark green foliage.*

* HABIT: densely pyramidal, often narrow
* FOLIAGE: evergreen, dark green needles, 3–5″ long
  HABITAT: central Japan
  INTRODUCED: 1861

This very beautiful tree, easily grown and not susceptible to any serious disease, is valued for its dense habit and very dark green foliage, especially while young. Twenty to thirty of the needles are arranged in whorls about the twigs, somewhat similar to the arrangement of ribs of an umbrella, from which it gets its common name. These needles remain on the tree two to three years before falling off, and one of its good points is that it keeps its lower branches for a long time and so makes a splendid lawn specimen. Although growing tall in Japan, it is rather slow-growing in this country, and plants fifty years old in the Arnold Arboretum are still only 25 feet tall. It should have good soil and not be planted in hot, dry situations. No serious pests.

Sequoia sempervirens   365′   Zone 7   Redwood

* HABIT: narrow, open, straight, massive trunk
* FOLIAGE: evergreen, open, somewhat like that of hemlock
  HABITAT: southern Oregon, California

In its native habitat along the West Coast, the redwood is outstanding because of its massive beauty. Here giant trees measuring up to 365 feet in height grow in groves so dense that sunlight seldom filters through. The trunks may measure as much as 75–85 feet in circumference. The bark is very thick and dense, serving as an excellent insulation against fire and disease. The wood is red and solid, used considerably for furniture and the exterior and interior finishing of houses. The small needles remind one very much of those of hemlocks. These are the tallest trees on the North American continent, and considerable work has been done in order to preserve certain groves north of San Francisco along the "Redwood Highway" to prevent them from being destroyed for their lumber.

Sequoiadendron giganteum (syn. *Sequoia gigantea*)   300′   Zone 6
Giant sequoia

* HABIT: narrow, open, straight, massive trunk
* FOLIAGE: evergreen, open
  HABITAT: California

The giant sequoias are among the oldest trees in the United States, some often estimated to be three thousand to four thousand years old. These do not grow quite as tall as the redwood, but they grow greater in trunk diameter. The General Sherman Tree of Sequoia National Park in California—estimated to be nearly four thousand years old—is 37 feet in diameter at its base and 17 feet in diameter at 120 feet above the base, the largest tree in bulk of trunk, at least in North America. This is the hardier of the two sequoia species. The most northern tree on the East Coast is a splendid

70-foot specimen at Bristol, Rhode Island. Other trees have been grown, one reaching 60 feet in height on Cayuga Lake in central New York, only to be killed outright by the severe winter of 1933–34. They have never permanently survived in the Arnold Arboretum although they have been tried many times. This is not a tree for the small garden!

Sophora japonica   75'   Zone 4   Japanese pagoda tree

* FLOWERS: pealike, white, in large, pyramidal, upright clusters
        TIME: August
    HABIT: rounded, wide-branching
    FOLIAGE: rather open, compound leaves, somewhat like those of the locust
    HABITAT: China, Korea
    INTRODUCED: 1747
    VARIETIES:

    'Fastigiata'—fastigiate habit
    'Pendula' *(Weeping Japanese pagoda tree)*—with pendulous branches, seldom flowering but frequently used as a formal specimen
    'Princeton Upright' *(Plant Patent #5524)*—attractive, shiny foliage, blooming from late July to late August, with creamy white flowers. Highly resistant to twig dieback and bark canker. Tolerant to drought and high pH soils that turn many oaks and maples yellow. Originated by Princeton Nurseries, Princeton, New Jersey.
    'Regent' *(Plant Patent #2338)*—large, oval crown, bearing large, pyramidal trusses of pealike, white flowers in July and August. Grows faster than other seedlings of this species and is free of pests. Originated by Princeton Nurseries.

This is a good shade tree with alternate compound leaves dark green in color. The common name comes from the fact that it is frequently used around Buddhist temples in the Orient. It is also used considerably there as a wide-spreading street tree, possessing several desirable qualities. It blossoms in late summer, with large, pyramidal clusters of pealike, yellowish flowers that are most conspicuous. A yellow dye is made from the flowers and buds merely by baking them in an oven until they turn brown and then boiling them in water. It is the last of the larger trees to bloom in the fall and so is greatly valued as an ornamental. One excellent quality is its apparent ability to withstand city conditions, certainly an attractive trait. Old trees have much the same general rounded habit as the white ash. The yellowish pods, following the flowers, frequently remain on the tree all winter. A desirable large tree, it should be used considerably more than it is. It is troubled with canker, twig blight, powdery mildew, and leaf hoppers. Canker and twig blight should be cut out and burned; powdery mildew should be sprayed with bordeaux mixture; and leaf hoppers should be sprayed with malathion as soon as they appear, and affected parts should be cut and burned.

Sophora tetraptera   40'   Zone 9   New Zealand sophora

* FLOWERS: pealike, golden yellow, in racemes 4–8″ long
     TIME: May
* FOLIAGE: evergreen to semideciduous; leaves pinnately compound, 1½–4½″ long
    HABITAT: Chile, New Zealand
    INTRODUCED: 1772 (England)

One of the most conspicuous flowering trees grown in the subtropical areas of the United States. The peculiar four-winged fruit pods, excellent flowers, and its ability to grow in sandy soils make it popular where it proves hardy.

⇶ SORBUS

There are about sixty species and varieties of *Sorbus* growing in the Arnold Arboretum, but not all of them are of outstanding ornamental interest. In fact, only about fifteen different species and varieties are being grown by American nurseries. However, the European gardener and the commercial grower as well apparently think more highly of them, for sixty-four different ones can be found by searching European nursery catalogs—in fact one English nursery lists forty-five.

These trees are native throughout the northern temperate regions of the world. Perhaps the most commonly planted in America is the European *S. aucuparia,* which has been popular here since colonial times and grows vigorously. There are several native American species that are just as good and might be used a great deal more than they are at present. Some of the white fruiting Asiatic types present variation in the fall, and the most recent introduction, at present a plant going under the name of *S. cashmiriana,* shows promise of being one of the most ornamental of all.

The mountain-ashes are excellent ornamental trees except for one serious drawback. In some parts of the country, especially the East, they are frequently seriously infested with borers near the base of the trunk; these borers materially weaken the trees and eventually may kill them. The old-fashioned method of probing for the borers with a wire is time-consuming but feasible.

On small properties one or two trees frequently can be used, but the property holders should never plant them unless they are fully cognizant of the borer problem and will take steps to control it continuously. Once treatment is forgotten or omitted for a year or two, borers can get into the trunk and have sufficient time to destroy it completely. A large tree, grown and carefully cared for during a period of fifteen to twenty years, is a beautiful thing, and its quick loss due to short neglect is most disheartening. These things should be kept in mind when using the mountain-ash, especially in the East. On the West Coast, in Seattle and Portland, there are many fine streets lined with mountain-ash, apparently unaffected by the ravages of the borer. Gardeners in this area are most fortunate!

All *Sorbus* are susceptible to San Jose scale, sometimes to sun scald of the trunk and larger branches, and fire blight can be a very serious problem. Diseased branches should be cut and burned. Also, *Sorbus* seem to grow better in limestone soils than in strictly acid soils—a rather important observation.

Aside from these defects, the *Sorbus* group has good specimen trees to offer. The leaves of some are simple *(S. alnifolia)* but most are compound. The flowers are small, white, and produced in large, flat clusters like those of some viburnums or Queen Anne's lace. The brilliant orange to red fruits (about ¼ inch in diameter) appear in large clusters about 3 to 5 inches in diameter and remain colorful for weeks.

Looking them over more carefully, the Korean mountain-ash *(S. alnifolia)* and Kashmir mountain-ash *(S. cashmiriana)* have about the largest individual flowers of any, between ¾ and 1 inch in diameter. In fact, the latter has flower buds tinged a pale pink and the flowers open tinged blush pink, making them outstanding when observed closely.

Sorbus hybrida, S. folgneri, and *S. aria* species have leaves that are white tomentose underneath, so much so as to be of considerable ornamental value. Some of the varieties are of fastigiate habit, and while the tree is young and under about 20 feet in height, such plants make excellent specimens. Older plants, however, will crack and break up, so that these fastigiate forms should be considered for only short service.

Fruits of the different species vary in size and color between red, orange, and yellow. Some have fruits that are slightly brownish and are not recommended for ornamental use. However, the foliage of many will turn a rich yellow to orange to sometimes reddish, and this makes them stand out as excellent specimens in the fall.

The Korean mountain-ash appears to be the least affected by borers, hence it would seem that this species might be widely used. The flowers are borne in great numbers, and I think it might be considered best in this respect. Then, too, the leaves are simple and not compound, making for finer texture of the foliage, and the autumn color is a brilliant orange to scarlet.

New "hybrids" have been imported from abroad, such as 'Apricot Queen,' 'Kirsten Pink,' 'Red Copper Glow,' 'Upright Yellow,' and 'White Wax.' It is too early to tell much about these—whether they are good new clones or whether new names have been coined for old varieties.

All in all, the mountain-ash is not one of our best ornamental trees. Certainly its pests are sufficiently numerous to prevent it from being used widely as a street tree. As an ornamental here and there, however, especially for fall display when it can be grown in the full sun where it does best and not in partial shade, it will add a colorful spot of interest to almost any planting.

Sorbus alnifolia   60′   Zone 4   Korean mountain-ash

* FLOWERS: small, white, in flat clusters; single flowers often as much as ¾″ in diameter
     TIME: late May
* FRUIT: scarlet to orange berries, ⅜″ in diameter
     EFFECTIVE: fall
  HABIT: pyramidal and upright while young, rounded at maturity, dense branching
* BARK: smooth and gray, very much like that of the beech
  FOLIAGE: dense, lustrous, bright green leaves, not compound
* AUTUMN COLOR: orange to scarlet
  HABITAT: Japan, central China, Korea
  INTRODUCED: 1892

This is one of the most successful of the flowering trees introduced by the Arnold Arboretum from Japan, and it requires practically no attention. It makes a truly beautiful specimen, dense and well rounded from top to bottom. Why it is not better known and grown I do not know. It certainly is deserving, particularly as a tree at its best during the autumn months when fruit and foliage coloration are pronounced. A splendid tree, it might easily be considered the best of the mountain-ashes and the least susceptible to borer attack in our experience in Boston. Well worth growing as a vigorous (and eventually a rather large) specimen. The smooth, gray bark is a truly outstanding ornamental asset, for in this respect this tree is almost as good as a beech, especially in winter. Least susceptible of all *Sorbus* to borer injury.

Sorbus aria   45′   Zone 5   White beam mountain-ash

  FLOWERS: small, white, in flat clusters 2–3″ in diameter
     TIME: late May
* FRUIT: scarlet-red berries, ⅓–½″ long, specked with brownish dots
     EFFECTIVE: fall
  HABIT: rounded, rather open
  FOLIAGE: leaves not compound, 2–4″ long, handsome bright green above and covered with a feltlike, white pubescence beneath
  AUTUMN COLOR: reddish
  HABITAT: Europe
  INTRODUCED: before 1830?
  VARIETIES:
     'Aurea'—often considered the best of the yellow-leaved *Sorbus* varieties
     majestica (Majestic white beam mountain-ash)—formerly called *decaisneana,* this variety's red fruits are as much as ⅝″ in diameter. It has simple leaves that

are as much as 7″ long. This is considered the most conspicuous variety of this species. It is excellent for growing in alkaline soils but does well in acid soils also.

This is a common tree in Europe and in England, where it does very well on the chalk cliffs and other limestone soils. The fruit is most colorful but is unfortunately quickly eaten by the birds as soon as it is ripe. A splendid ornamental, not seen much in gardens in this country but certainly worthy of being grown more. It is especially desirable (but not in areas where much smoke or soot is in the atmosphere) because of the pubescent, white undersurface of the leaves, giving the foliage a delightful contrasting color.

Sorbus aucuparia   45′   Zone 3   European mountain-ash, Rowan
tree

* FLOWERS: small, white flowers, in flat clusters 3–5″ in diameter
    TIME: late May
* FRUIT: bright red berries, ¼″ in diameter, in large clusters
    EFFECTIVE: fall
  HABIT: erect while young, spreading and gracefully open at maturity
  FOLIAGE: rather open, compound leaves
* AUTUMN COLOR: reddish
  HABITAT: Europe to western Asia
  INTRODUCED: early colonial times
  VARIETIES:

    'Asplenifolia' *(Cutleaf European mountain-ash)*—the leaflets doubly serrate, a graceful clone
    beissneri—a graceful variety with pinnately lobed leaflets; leaf petioles and branchlets bright red
    'Black Hawk'—distinct columnar habit, with dark green leaves that resist sun scald and large fruit clusters in summer. Zone 2.
    edulis (Moravian rowan)—fruit slightly larger than that of the species and used for preserves in Europe. Native of Czechoslovakia.
    'Fastigiata' *(Upright European mountain-ash)*—upright in habit of growth
    'Pendula' *(Weeping European mountain-ash)*—with pendulous branches, not particularly graceful
    xanthocarpa—with yellow fruits

By far the most popular of the mountain-ashes in North America, this has been grown and admired since colonial times and is even naturalized in Alaska. Its conspicuous flowers, bright colored fruit, and autumn color make it of considerable interest for several seasons of the year. Like most other members of the *Sorbus* group, it is very susceptible to borers, especially low on the trunk. Unless the borer problem is not meticulously prevented, the mountain-ash should not be grown in avenues or in large numbers where the elimination of a few trees might destroy the general effect. (See discussion under *Sorbus* on page 421.)

Sorbus cashmiriana   40'   Zone 4   Kashmir mountain-ash

* FLOWERS: flower buds blush pink; flowers tinged pink, single flowers ¾" in diameter
  TIME: late May
* FRUIT: white, often tinged pink, ⅜" in diameter; fruit stalks pink to red
  EFFECTIVE: early fall
  HABIT: pyramidal
  FOLIAGE: compound leaves
  AUTUMN COLOR: red
  HABITAT: Himalayas
  INTRODUCED: Arnold Arboretum, 1949

This tree introduced from England has great ornamental possibilities both for its flowers and its fruit. Some consider it merely a variety of *S. tianshanica,* but the plant in the Arnold Arboretum has been perfectly hardy for the twenty-five years it has been growing there. It is vigorous in growth, well worthy of a trial wherever mountain-ashes are grown.

Sorbus decora   30'   Zone 2   Showy mountain-ash

  FLOWERS: small, white, in flat clusters 2–4" in diameter
  TIME: late May
* FRUIT: bright red berries, nearly ½" in diameter, in clusters
  EFFECTIVE: early fall
  HABIT: shrubby tree
  FOLIAGE: compound leaves usually with about 15 leaflets
  HABITAT: southeastern Canada, northeastern United States
  VARIETY:
  'Nana'—a compact-growing type worthy of further trial. Introduced to America by the Arnold Arboretum from Geo. Jackman & Sons, Ltd., Woking, England, in 1957.

This tree has larger and more conspicuous fruit than its close relative, *S. americana,* hence is better for ornamental use.

Sorbus discolor   30'   Zone 5   Snowberry mountain-ash

  FLOWERS: small, white flowers, in flat clusters
  TIME: late May
* FRUIT: small, white berries, ⅜" in diameter, in clusters
  EFFECTIVE: fall
  HABIT: rounded, open
  FOLIAGE: compound leaves, with 11–17 leaflets, rather open
* AUTUMN COLOR: red

HABITAT: northern China
INTRODUCED: 1883

The plant growing in the Arnold Arboretum has white fruit but several descriptions of this species by reliable botanists seem to be confused as to the color, listing it variously from yellow to pink. Of course it may well be that it varies considerably in this respect.

Sorbus folgneri   24'   Zone 5   Folgner mountain-ash

FLOWERS: small, white, rather inconspicuous, in many-flowered clusters about 4" in diameter
    TIME: late May
* FRUIT: red berries, ½" long, in clusters
    EFFECTIVE: fall
HABIT: variable but usually with gracefully spreading branches
FOLIAGE: leaves single (not compound), 2–3" long, dark green above but woolly tomentose and white below
* AUTUMN COLOR: russet-red
HABITAT: central China
INTRODUCED: 1901
VARIETY:
    'Pendula' *(Weeping Folgner mountain-ash)*—with pendulous branches, not particularly graceful

This species can be considered even handsomer than *S. alnifolia,* although it is a considerably smaller tree. The fruit is slightly egg-shaped and its habit of growth is very graceful. It is particularly interesting because of the woolly, white undersurface of the leaves, which adds an element of considerable interest, especially in the wind. Also, it may well be that red spider and certain other insects damaging the undersurface of the leaves of *Sorbus* in general are held in considerable check by the woolly surface of the leaves of this particular species.

x Sorbus hybrida 'Fastigiata'   36'   Zone 4

FRUIT: red, about ½" in diameter
    EFFECTIVE: fall
HABIT: narrow, fastigiate
FOLIAGE: unusually compound leaves, sometimes only pinnately lobed, sometimes cut nearly to the midrib
HABITAT: central Europe
HYBRID ORIGIN: *S. aucuparia x S. intermedia*

Merely listed here because of its narrow habit.

x *Sorbus hybrida* 'Gibbsii'   36'   Zone 4

* FRUIT: coral-red
    EFFECTIVE: fall

Similar to the species except for its beautifully colored fruit, so it might be used in place of the variable hybrid species to produce more uniform plants.

Sorbus sargentiana   30'   Zone 6   Sargent mountain-ash

* FLOWERS: white, borne on white, tomentose flower stalks
    TIME: late May
* FRUIT: scarlet, ⅕" in diameter
    EFFECTIVE: early fall
* FOLIAGE: compound, 8–12" long, with 7–11 leaflets; white tomentose beneath
  HABITAT: western China
  INTRODUCED: 1908

The chief ornamental value is the white tomentose condition of the undersurface of the leaves, flower stalks, fruit stalks, and even young twigs.

Sorbus tianshanica   15'   Zone 5

* FLOWERS: white, nearly ¾" in diameter
    TIME: late May
* FRUIT: bright red, in clusters 3–5" in diameter; individual fruits about ⅓" in diameter
    EFFECTIVE: early fall
  HABIT: shrub to small tree
* FOLIAGE: lustrous, dark green
  HABITAT: Turkestan
  INTRODUCED: 1895

Listed here merely because of its potential use in small gardens, especially in restricted areas.

Sorbus vilmorinii   18'   Zone 5   Vilmorin mountain-ash

* FLOWERS: white
    TIME: late May
* FRUIT: bright red, but these may turn nearly white at maturity, ¼" in diameter
    EFFECTIVE: early fall
* HABIT: shrub to small tree, about as high as it is wide
* FOLIAGE: 3–5½" long, about the smallest of the mountain-ash group, with up to 31 leaflets, each slightly under 1" long

HABITAT: western China
INTRODUCED: 1889

Another small mountain-ash for the small garden, considered one of the best of the smaller types.

Spathodea campanulata   70'   Zone 10   Bell flambeau tree

* FLOWERS: cup-shaped scarlet flowers, on short, terminal racemes, 4" long
        TIME: winter
  FRUIT: dry capsules, 8" long, 2" wide
        EFFECTIVE: winter
  HABIT: erect
* FOLIAGE: evergreen in Florida but deciduous in parts of California, leaves compound, may be 2' long
  HABITAT: tropical Africa

This is a most conspicuous tree in flower, a vigorous grower, and seems to do best in fertile, well-drained soil, but it will not survive the frosted areas.

The Korean stewartia (Stewartia koreana) *has mottled bark that is of ornamental interest the entire year.*

Stewartia koreana   45'   Zone 5   Korean stewartia

* FLOWERS: white, 3″ in diameter, with yellow conspicuous stamens
      TIME: July
* HABIT: pyramidal, dense
* BARK: flaking, varicolored
  FOLIAGE: dense
* AUTUMN COLOR: orange-red
  HABITAT: Korea
  INTRODUCED: 1917

Smaller growing than *S. pseudo-camellia* but with larger flowers and just as interesting winter bark, Korean stewartia is very difficult to find in gardens. The conspicuous, early summer flowers make it a useful small tree for bloom when few trees are in flower. The striking bark, irregularly flaking off in pieces—the older, darker bark on the outside of the trunk breaking off to disclose the inner, lighter colored bark beneath it—is somewhat similar to the bark of the sycamore or *Pinus bungeana.*

It is unfortunate that this excellent specimen is extremely difficult to find in nursery catalogs because it has been flourishing in the Arnold Arboretum, where it

The Korean stewartia blooms in July.

has been perfectly hardy ever since 1917 when it was first introduced. All stewartias are difficult to transplant so it is recommended they be grown in containers in the smaller sizes and transplanted to the garden only when the permanent place has been definitely decided upon. Not many pests.

Stewartia pseudo-camellia   60'   Zone 5   Japanese stewartia

* FLOWERS: cup-shaped, white, 2½" in diameter
       TIME: early July
  HABIT: pyramidal
  FOLIAGE: bright green
  AUTUMN COLOR: purplish
* BARK: flaking bark on older branches and trunk
  HABITAT: Japan
  INTRODUCED: 1874

The flower is very similar to that of a single camellia, to which all stewartias are closely related, hence the specific name of this species. The flaking bark is more colorful than that of the other stewartias, being red and peeling off in large flakes. It is difficult to discard any stewartia, for they bloom several weeks in the summer at a time when few woody plants are in flower. However, this species has the smallest flowers of any. Another tree species, *S. chinensis* from China, also has cup-shaped flowers, 2 inches in diameter, and is hardy in Zone 6.

Styrax japonica   30'   Zone 5   Japanese snowbell

* FLOWERS: pendulous, bell-shaped, white, about ¾" in diameter
       TIME: early June
  HABIT: very wide-spreading branches, flat top, often twice as wide as it is high
  FOLIAGE: fine textured
  HABITAT: China, Japan
  INTRODUCED: 1862
  VARIETY:
       'Pink Chimes'—with pale pink flowers, 2½" in diameter, branches somewhat
       drooping. Grows to about 20' in Zone 5. A good but rare specimen.

This wide-spreading shrub or tree, rather dense, with graceful, small, pendulous, waxy white flowers in early June, makes an excellent specimen because of its curving horizontal branches and fine dark green leaves. The interesting thing about the blooms of this plant is that they appear after the leaves are fully developed, but the leaves are firmly held on the upper side of the branches and the pendulous flowers are clearly evident on the underside of all the small twigs and branches so that their effect is not dimmed by the foliage at all. Few if any pests.

Styrax obassia   30'   Zone 6   Fragrant snowbell

* FLOWERS: fragrant, white, ¾" in diameter, produced in terminal racemes 6–8" long
      TIME: early June
HABIT: dense, ascending branches
FOLIAGE: large, coarse leaves, 3–8" long
HABITAT: Japan
INTRODUCED: 1879

It is unfortunate that the flowers of this handsome tree are partly hidden by the large leaves, but even with this slight defect the tree is an excellent ornamental in flower. I have never observed any autumn coloration of the foliage. Few if any pests.

Symplocos paniculata   35'   Zone 5   Asiatic sweetleaf

* FLOWERS: fragrant, small, white, in small clusters
      TIME: late May
* FRUIT: bright blue berries, ¼" in diameter
      EFFECTIVE: October
HABIT: shrubby, wide-spreading, with dense branches
FOLIAGE: open
HABITAT: Himalaya Mountains to China and Japan
INTRODUCED: 1875

This tall, wide-spreading, dense shrub or small tree is chiefly of merit for its bright, pale blue berries about ¼ inch in diameter, but they do not remain on the plant more than a week after they have reached the peak of their color. The profuse, small, white flowers are fragrant, but these too do not remain effective long. Because of these short periods of interest it is better to use other plants for growing in the limited space of the small garden. On large estates or in parks, where space is available for unique plants, this might be a good selection. No serious pests.

Syringa reticulata (syn. *S. amurensis japonica*)   30'   Zone 4
                                                      Japanese tree lilac

* FLOWERS: small, creamy white, in large pyramidal heads sometimes 6" high
      TIME: mid-June
HABIT: pyramidal, rather open
* BARK: cherrylike bark on trunk and older branches
FOLIAGE: leaves larger than those of the common lilac, almost coarse
HABITAT: Japan
INTRODUCED: 1876

This Japanese lilac can be grown with a single trunk and is of special value because of the late bloom of the flowers. The shiny, cherrylike bark is interesting in the winter, the large leaves and conspicuously vigorous habit is striking in the spring and summer, and the large, pyramidal, creamy white flower clusters make it an outstanding plant, either as a specimen or in a group as a screen or windbreak. The variety differs from the species in being more treelike in habit, taller, and slightly later to flower. It is susceptible to borers and scale infestations, which must be kept in check if it is to be a well-grown plant. For this reason it should not be used as a street tree where annual maintenance and close surveillance are necessities. This is the only native Japanese tree that F. L. Skinner can grow in the severe climate of Dropmore, Manitoba, Canada.

Taxodium distichum   150'   Zone 4   Common bald cypress

HABIT: narrowly pyramidal while young, broadly rounded at maturity
FOLIAGE: deciduous, needlelike, very open
HABITAT: southeastern and south central United States
VARIETY:
     'Pendens'—with pendulous branchlets

This beautiful tree, hardy as far north as Boston where there is a specimen 80 feet tall in perfect condition, has foliage somewhat like that of hemlock but is deciduous. The foliage appears late in the season—in fact it is the last tree to send out its leaves in the Arnold Arboretum in Boston. In nature it is found in swampy areas, and of course is famed for its "knees" or large, woody growths coming up from the roots, sometimes as much as 6 feet tall. Its wood is highly valued for its great water-resisting properties, for it will not rot, even when standing in water for long periods of time. Because of its light, feathery foliage, it cannot be considered a good shade tree, and because of its great height it is not a good tree for the small property. In parks or large estates it makes a distinctive specimen. Pests include twig blight, wood decay, spider mites, and gall-forming mites.

⇥≫ *TAXUS*

The yews are the darkest green of all evergreen shrubs and trees and, without question, the most striking. They flourish in many kinds of soils and withstand clipping and pruning, thus making perfect hedges and screens as well as excellent specimens. Their fleshy, bright red fruits are conspicuous during the fall. It is fortunate that they are represented by a large number of varieties ranging in size and shape so that they can be used for a number of garden purposes.

The yew has been known and valued for centuries, records having shown that pieces of wood of the English yew, *T. baccata,* have been found under glacial deposits in England.

Two principal species provide the ornamental varieties for American gardens—*T. cuspidata,* the Japanese yew, and *T. baccata.* There are yews in England that must be a thousand years old, their trunk circumferences being at least 30 feet. Robin Hood and his Merry Men used stout cudgels made from yew, as were their long bows and cross-bows. Even before this, spears were made from this sturdy wood, one having been dug from underneath a peat-deposit bog in England and estimated to be over three thousand years old.

These excellent evergreens are rather slow in growth when compared with deciduous trees, with wood that is hard and close-grained. The yews resemble each other so much that a few botanists have suggested in the past that there is only one species, *T. baccata,* and that all other yews are merely geographical varieties of this.

Poisonous properties of the yews have been recorded since early times. Caesar wrote that Cativolcus, king of the Eburones, poisoned himself by drinking the juice of the yew. The toxic material is probably an alkaloid named taxine, a heart depressant, present in the leaves and to a lesser extent in the twigs and bark. Although many cases of cattle poisoning have been reported where cattle eat the foliage of *T. brevifolia,* there are instances where the branches have been lopped off in the pasture with no ill effects. While the seed or stone in the fruit is poisonous, the fleshy pulp of the fruit, the only part of the plant that might be eaten by humans, is not.

Many a yew has failed to produce the decorative, colorful fruit and therefore caused disappointment. This is because the sexes are separate, the staminate flowers on one plant, the pistillate flowers on another. Both are necessary to ensure fruiting. One staminate plant is sufficient for every six or eight pistillate or fruiting plants. If a specimen-fruiting plant is desired, it can be placed in the spot with the staminate plant nearby in an inconspicuous or partly hidden location. If a group of fruiting plants is desired, the staminate plant may be hidden in the center of the group and kept fairly inconspicuous by clipping.

Of course the female plant can be identified in fruit, but the sexes can be distinguished one from the other at other times of the year as well—in fact, a greater part of the growing season. The flowers are open for a very short time only in the early spring, when the identification of the sexes is easy. However, the staminate flower buds of the yew are rounded and hang from the underside of the terminal year's growth. The pistillate flower buds are smaller, not nearly as obvious, and very definitely pointed. These differences are marked and easily noted. With little practice one can be proficient at telling these apart.

There are over one hundred species and varieties of yews being grown in the United States, although not all are available from nurseries. Of the seven species grown, the Chinese yew, *T. chinensis,* and the Pacific yew, *T. brevifolia,* are little seen in cultivation and are not recommended here.

The English yew is the least hardy. Although certain varieties—with some winter protection—can be safely grown as far north as Boston, *T. baccata* is not dependably hardy north of New York. Since it has been carefully grown for hundreds of years, it is only natural to expect that a number of forms have originated and have been propagated. The Japanese species has been grown extensively outside Japan for less than half a century, and consequently comparatively few varieties of it are to be found in commercial nurseries in this country up to this time.

In the Old World the English yew is widely distributed from England to North Africa and western Asia. It grows as a tree, from 30 to 60 feet high, with needles usually two-ranked and blunt at the end. Over fifty varieties have been named, but some are difficult to obtain in this country and several are closely similar. The yews are all comparatively slow-growing but particularly well adapted for hedges and topiary work. In England topiary work has been a hobby with gardeners for centuries, and many splendid examples of painstaking pruning are to be seen about the countryside there.

In all probability the most famous variety of the English yew is *T. baccata stricta,* popularly called the "Irish yew." Two pistillate trees were found on a farm in Ireland about 1780, differing from the ordinary English yew in having several leaders all densely upright in habit of growth. Even the needles on the twigs were arranged differently from the English yew, distributed around all sides of the twig rather than being two-ranked in a flat spray. It is from cuttings of these two trees that the Irish yew has been propagated. It is highly valued for its upright habit of growth and is excellent for formal planting.

Another popular variety is the Westfelton yew, *T. baccata* 'Dovastoni,' a tree with an erect trunk, horizontal branches, and pendulous branchlets. This plant makes an excellent specimen. It was first raised in Shrewsbury, England, in 1777, and has long been a popular form. It may be of interest to know that there is a form with yellow foliage.

Not all varieties of the English yew are trees. For instance, the variety *adpressa* is a wide-spreading, low shrub with needles only half as long as those of the species. Fortunately, this variety is a fruiting form. The spreading English yew, *T. baccata repandens,* is a low, almost prostrate form, grown considerably in the northern United States, where it is apparently more hardy than any other variety of English yew. If clipped and restrained, it may grow 3 feet or so in height, with the young branchlets decidedly pendulous. If allowed to grow unrestrained, it becomes very prostrate in habit and literally creeps along the ground.

The Japanese yew, *T. cuspidata,* was first introduced into this country in 1861 by Dr. George R. Hall, a doctor who practiced medicine in the foreign settlement of Shanghai for a number of years. Later he became interested in collecting plants in both China and Japan, and in sending them back to the United States. This plant has shown its good qualities time and again, and now is being grown by the majority of American nurseries. It has proved itself hardy under trying winter conditions; although not foolproof, it can be grown where many other evergreens cannot.

The nomenclature of the varieties of this plant is still greatly confused. In Bailey's *Cyclopedia* published in 1917, and in numerous other articles written before and since that time, it has been pointed out that *T. cuspidata* is a tree. Hence, the variety erroneously listed in many nursery catalogs as *T. cuspidata capitata* actually is *T. cuspidata.* However, this misunderstanding of names has probably been augmented by the fact that there is a variety of *T. cuspidata* that has spreading, upright branches, forming a low center, and in cross section looks broadly V-shaped. Practically every nursery has it and practically every nursery calls this *T. cuspidata.* To alleviate confusion, this form has been named *T. cuspidata expansa.* It is readily known that when seed of *T. cuspidata* is sown, many interesting seedlings will appear, varying considerably in shape and height, and a certain proportion of them will have this desirable spreading, upright shape.

Fortunately, these dignified evergreens are comparatively free of serious pests. Occasionally an old plant may be attacked by the strawberry root weevil and the needles will begin to drop. Often this can be controlled by the use of poison baits for the beetles, and pyrethrum sprays on the ground for the grubs that do the damage.

For specimens, for hedges, for backgrounds, for any one of many uses, the yews are excellently well suited, and because of their large number and variety of shapes and sizes, it is not exaggeration to say that there is a yew for every garden where evergreens can be grown.

Taxus baccata   60'   Zone 6   English yew

* FRUIT: fleshy, single-seeded, red berry; sexes separate
       EFFECTIVE: fall
HABIT: pyramidal, dense branching
* FOLIAGE: evergreen, lustrous, dark green needles
HABITAT: Europe, northern Africa, western Asia
INTRODUCED: early colonial times
VARIETIES:
     'Aurea'—yellow leaves
     'Dovastoni' *(Westfelton yew)*—upright in habit with horizontal branches and dark green foliage
     'Elegantissima' *(Elegant English yew)*—vigorous, wide-spreading bush with main branches mostly horizontal with young foliage striped yellow
     'Erecta' *(Broom yew)*—upright in habit but much wider in growth than Irish yew
     'Lutea'—yellow fruit
     stricta (Irish yew)—rigidly columnar and upright in habit, one of the most picturesque of all varieties

Over fifty varieties of the English yew have been listed, and the above are perhaps
the most prominent of the tree types.

Taxus cuspidata   50'   Zone 4   Japanese yew

* FRUIT: fleshy, red berries
     EFFECTIVE: fall
  HABIT: pyramidal, dense branching
* FOLIAGE: evergreen, dark needles
  HABITAT: Japan, Korea
  INTRODUCED: 1855
  VARIETIES:
     'Columnaris'—more narrow than 'Pyramidalis' but faster growing. Red ber-
     ries. Zone 5.
     'Pyramidalis'—erect, columnar

The Japanese yew is one of the best narrow-leaved evergreens for ornamental purposes. Many varieties are being grown in this country chiefly as shrubs. (See discussion under *Taxus* concerning the popular commercial variety *T. cuspidata capitata* on
page 435.)

Topiary figures sheared out of a golden-leaved form of yew.

x Taxus media   40′   Zone 4   Intermediate yew

* FRUIT: fleshy, one-seeded, red berry
     EFFECTIVE: fall
  HABIT: broadly columnar to narrowly pyramidal, dense branching
* FOLIAGE: evergreen needles
  HYBRID: *T. cuspidata x T. baccata*
  INTRODUCED: about 1900
  VARIETIES:
     'Anthony Wayne'—fast growing, wide, and columnar, with light green new foliage and red fruit
     'Hicksii'—upright, with red fruit and dark green needles; an old-fashioned favorite

About 1900 a new species of yew originated as a result of a cross between the English and Japanese yews. T. D. Hatfield, superintendent of the famous Hunnewell Estate in Wellesley, Massachusetts, had grown a number of seedlings that were given the specific name of *T. media*. This hybrid is broadly pyramidal, frequently has a central leader, and grows into tree form. The hardy qualities of the Japanese yew and the ornamental qualities of the English yew are merged in this plant to give an excellent ornamental evergreen.

⇉ *THUJA*

The arborvitae as a group are evergreen trees with flat, scalelike leaves, two of the species, at least, being quite variable, with many different varieties, mostly shrubby. The four species recommended here are trees and grow in more or less dense pyramids of foliage, at least while they are young. The American arborvitae and its forms seem to require considerable atmospheric moisture or they will not do well at all. The same is true of the Oriental arborvitae. The other two seem to grow better where there is less moisture in the atmosphere, but even these cannot be depended upon in dry situations.

There are some forms of these arborvitae with colored foliage, but these are not at all satisfactory in the winter, for their leaves frequently turn a sickly yellowish or brownish color. The same is true even of *T. occidentalis* under certain conditions. The other three species maintain their foliage in rather good condition throughout the winter, reason enough why they are valued as evergreens.

It should be emphasized here again that all evergreens drop some of their leaves every year, usually in the fall, and arborvitae are no exception. There is no cause for alarm when dead leaves are observed on these plants in the fall of the year when the leaves of all deciduous plants are colorful.

Browning of the foliage may develop at other times of year, and when this happens the cause should be quickly determined. As a group they are sometimes infested heavily with red spider, but this can be controlled if caught before it does too much damage. In general arborvitaes are pest-free, but occasionally they are also susceptible to infestations of leaf blight, juniper blight, arborvitae aphid, arborvitae leaf miner, and mealy bugs. Then, too, the inner leaves may turn brown and drop in the fall. Spraying with diazinon or malathion can help.

As a group, then, and as trees, these plants are to be considered slow-growing evergreens, rather stiff in habit, with foliage not nearly as soft in texture as that of the pines and hemlocks. As trees they are used primarily as stiff accent points in the landscape.

Thuja occidentalis   60′   Zone 2   American arborvitae

HABIT: almost columnar
* FOLIAGE: evergreen, flat, scalelike
HABITAT: eastern North America
VARIETIES:

  'Douglasii Pyramidalis' *(Douglas arborvitae)*—dense, broadly columnar
  'Elwangeriana'—yellow foliage. Zone 6.
  fastigiata—more narrow and columnar than other varieties, with very short lateral branches
  'Hetz Wintergreen'—very narrow, upright, fast growing; grows to about 60′. Zone 4.
  'Lutea'—often termed the 'George Peabody' arborvitae of years ago, this is the best of all the colored foliage forms of the American arborvitae growing in the Arnold Arboretum. It originated in Geneva, New York, before 1873, grows tall and pyramidal, and is one of the very few of the many colored forms of this species to keep its good color throughout the full growing season and into the fall.
  'Nigra' *(Dark American arborvitae)*—broad, upright, growing to 50′. Dark green needles. Zone 4.
  'Sherwood Column'—narrow, upright, with fan-shaped foliage. Grows to 50′. Zone 4.

This native species has many slow-growing forms that are mostly shrublike in character. They are often used in foundation plantings and seem to do best in areas with considerable atmospheric moisture. In nature these trees are always found in moist woods, often near or beside water. The species and most of the varieties have the undesirable trait of turning brownish in the winter, sometimes markedly so, hence it fails to give a display of good green foliage when it is needed most. This is especially true of those forms with colored foliage—the reason that none is recommended here.

Thuja orientalis   50'   Zone 6   Oriental arborvitae

* HABIT: pyramidal, open
* FOLIAGE: evergreen, lustrous, scalelike, usually arranged in planes, the edges of
    which face the outside of the plant
  HABITAT: northern China, Korea
  INTRODUCED: before 1737
  VARIETIES:
      'Baker' *(Baker Oriental arborvitae)*—foliage bright green; seems to withstand
      hot, dry locations

This is a very popular evergreen with many garden varieties that vary in habit and
color of foliage. The species is a graceful and symmetrical tree, easily distinguished
from other *Thuja* species because its fruits or cones have characteristic hooks on them.
In China, at New Year's celebrations, sprays of this fragrant evergreen are used to
symbolize long life and happiness. One of the more commonly used evergreens
throughout the South, this has many shrub forms. Subject to bag worm and red spider
mites. Spray with malathion in early summer.

Thuja plicata   180'   Zone 5   Giant arborvitae

* HABIT: pyramidal, narrow
* FOLIAGE: evergreen, lustrous, scalelike
  AUTUMN COLOR: bronze
  HABITAT: Alaska to northern California and Montana
  VARIETY:
      atrovirens—foliage very dark green

This arborvitae is the best for northern gardens because its foliage does not turn
brown in the winter as does the foliage of most of the *T. occidentalis* varieties.
Commercial growers in the northeastern United States have learned that it is necessary to use seed collected from plants high in the mountains of Montana and Utah
since plants grown from seed collected on the West Coast have not proved hardy in
the East. The giant arborvitae is a splendid tree, large or small, and can be kept
restrained at almost any height by proper clipping.

Thuja standishii   40'   Zone 5   Japanese arborvitae

* HABIT: spreading branches, broadly pyramidal
* FOLIAGE: evergreen, scalelike
  HABITAT: Japan
  INTRODUCED: 1860

This handsome tree is considerably more spreading in habit than the arborvitae native
to America and hence of value for this characteristic. The foliage does not turn brown
in the winter as does that of *T. occidentalis*. However, the winter foliage of *T. plicata*
is superior, at least in New England.

Thujopsis dolabrata   45'   Zone 6   Hiba false arborvitae

HABIT: pyramidal
* FOLIAGE: evergreen, lustrous, dense, somewhat similar to that of arborvitae
HABITAT: Japan
INTRODUCED: 1861

The Hiba false arborvitae is somewhat similar to the arborvitae and develops into a beautiful, dense tree when grown in good soil with plenty of moisture. It is of no particular merit in preference to the arborvitaes.

⇥≫ *TILIA*

The lindens are among the best of our shade trees, especially the exotic species. They are widely used for ornament as specimens and they are especially valued as street trees. The seven that are most commonly used can be differentiated one from the other in the following ways:

    1. †Leaves large (3–6 inches long) and coarse, tree of open habit
. . . . *T. americana*
        2. Leaves silvery pubescent beneath, very distinct
            3. petioles shorter than half the leaf blade. . . . . *T. tomentosa*
            3. petioles longer than half the leaf blades . . . . *T. petiolaris*
                4. Leaves 2–5 inches long, tree of dense habit
                    5. Brown hairs in axils of veins on undersurface of the
                       leaves . . . . *T. cordata*
                    5. Leaves shiny above. . . . . *T. euchlora*
                    5. Leaves slightly hairy on both sides . . *T. platyphyllos*
                    5. Leaves very thin in texture, much more so than any
                     of the others. . . . . *T. europaea, T. vulgaris*

These lindens are the street trees of the Northern Hemisphere, highly valued in Europe as well as America. Some of the species are better than others for this purpose, but all have been used. Lindens have slightly heart-shaped leaves that are unequally developed at the base. They have small, pendulous flowers in early summer that are not especially ornamental but are deliciously fragrant. The round, hard fruit, borne on a unique leafy bract, remains on the tree until winter, and the seeds often take two years to germinate.

———
†Read down. If the specimen does not meet the first characteristic, try the next in sequence, and so on to the end. This is merely a suggestive key of some merit, but only for the amateur. For positive identification see some precise botanical key in an accepted botanical text.

It has been our experience here in the Arnold Arboretum, where different lindens have been growing side by side for half a century, that the European species are the more vigorous and handsome trees. The American lindens have coarse leaves and do not have good color late in the season, turning brownish. The Asiatic lindens are not much better. The European lindens, on the other hand, keep their color, and occasionally the leaves even turn yellow before they fall.

As street trees they are superb, but they must be sprayed occasionally with malathion since leaf-eating insects feed voraciously on their foliage. As specimens, there are few trees superior to the silver linden or the gracefully beautiful pendant silver linden. All lindens should be known to those responsible for selecting trees for planting since they are such highly valued and serviceable foliage trees.

A word should be said about the common European linden, *T. vulgaris* or *T. europaea.* Years ago this was widely planted in Europe and Great Britain but is not as good an ornamental as some of the other species. It should not be recommended. Mature trees are continually throwing up suckers at the base which must be cut off, and it also seems to be the species most susceptible to infestations of plant lice.

Linden borer is a serious pest of young trees, often causing the trunk and limbs to break because of the large cavities they create in their tunneling. The olive-green beetles, about ¾ inch long with long antennae and four black spots near the center of the wing covers, are active in late summer and fall. Spraying at this time with methoxychlor gives protection. Mulberry white fly may become abundant on lindens and require sprays of malathion. Linden is also a favorite host of the oyster shell scale. Japanese beetles also attack lindens, and elm span worm and white marked tussock moth worms may become epidemic, requiring emergency spraying with methoxychlor.

Among several leaf diseases, anthracnose is the most destructive. Browning of the leaves inward from the margin is characteristic of its onset. Spraying with ferbam or thiram when the buds break and again when the leaves are about half grown is suggested.

Tilia americana 'Fastigiata'	90'	Zone 2	Pyramidal American linden

HABIT: narrowly pyramidal

This variety of the American linden does have merit even though the leaves are slightly larger than some of those of the European species.

Tilia cordata	90'	Zone 3	Littleleaf linden

FLOWERS: small, yellowish to whitish, rather inconspicuous but unusually fragrant
    TIME: early July
* HABIT: densely pyramidal
* FOLIAGE: dense, compact, giving perfect shade, leaves 1½–3" long
HABITAT: Europe
INTRODUCED: probably early colonial times

VARIETIES:

'Greenspire'—originating before 1953, this tree was patented September 5, 1961 (#2086) by William Flemer III, of Princeton Nurseryman's Associates, Princeton, New Jersey. It grows with a single, straight trunk and radially produced branches, making a good clone of this important species. It is widely sold for street tree planting.

'Handsworth'—scions of this were obtained from the Royal Botanic Gardens, Kew, England, by the Arnold Arboretum in 1952. The one-year-old twigs are a beautiful light yellow-green. Small trees of vigorous growth are outstanding in the winter. This originated in the Handsworth Nursery, near Sheffield, England, according to Mr. Campbell of Kew.

'Pyramidalis'—with a widely pyramidal habit

'Swedish Upright'—this clone was collected in Sweden in 1906 by Alfred Rehder of the Arnold Arboretum. During its fifty-eight years of growth here, it has grown 35 feet tall with a diameter of branch spread of 12 feet. The lateral branches are borne at right angles to the trunk, more or less regularly, while the lower branches dip gracefully toward the ground. Its narrowly upright habit and short side branches make this tree outstanding among the lindens. Named and registered by the Arnold Arboretum, September 18, 1963.

Over fifteen other varieties have been named. Usually a slow-growing small tree, considerably under the mature height at which it is sometimes seen in Europe. It is the last of the lindens to flower, with heart-shaped leaves often broader than they are long, very dark green above, and pale beneath. Because of its dense habit and tightly pyramidal form it makes an excellent shade and street tree. The foliage is of finer texture than the much larger leaved native, *T. americana,* and so it is valued. If a fast-growing street tree is desired, however, one of the other lindens might best be used. This, like some of the other lindens, has grown unusually well under adverse city conditions, making it one of the best street trees for urban conditions. Also, this species is growing as far north as Dropmore, Manitoba, Canada, demonstrating its ability to withstand low temperatures very well and making it the hardiest of the lindens recommended here.

x Tilia euchlora   60'   Zone 4   Crimean linden

FLOWERS: small, yellowish, rather inconspicuous but very fragrant
    TIME: early July
* HABIT: graceful, somewhat pendulous branches
* FOLIAGE: dense, glossy, bright green leaves, 2–4" long
HYBRID ORIGIN: *T. cordata x T. dasystyla?*
VARIETY:

'Redmond'—introduced by the Plumfield Nurseries of Fremont, Nebraska, in 1927. It was named for C. M. Redmond, who discovered it growing in his garden in Fremont in the early 1920s. The parent tree is now nearly 50 feet tall and is densely pyramidal in habit. It is stated that this is adapted to growing well in many situations. Certainly it has met with much popularity in the Midwest. Probably a variety of *T. americana.*

One of the best of the lindens, it should be used more than it is. A graceful tree with glossy, bright green foliage and fairly vigorous growth, it has many good points for use as a shade tree. The branches are only slightly pendulous, but it makes an excellent specimen or street tree.

Tilia mongolica   30′   Zone 4   Mongolian linden

FLOWERS: small, yellowish, rather inconspicuous but very fragrant
    TIME: mid-July
* HABIT: graceful and pyramidal
FOLIAGE: leaves 1½–3″ long
HABITAT: China, Mongolia
INTRODUCED: 1880

This small tree is graceful and worthy of further trial because of its small leaves, reddish branchlets, and general good looks.

Tilia petiolaris   75′   Zone 5   Pendant silver linden

FLOWERS: small, yellowish, rather inconspicuous but very fragrant
    TIME: mid-July
* HABIT: drooping branches forming a narrow head
* FOLIAGE: leaves silvery white underneath, on long petioles, fluttering about in the
    smallest breeze, about 2–4½″ long
HABITAT: probably southeastern Europe
INTRODUCED: 1840

Closely related to the silver linden *(T. tomentosa)* but considered more exquisite because of its pendant branches. It is too bad this beautiful specimen tree is not grown more in America. Its very distinct weeping habit and lovely leaves, which are downy white underneath, make it the most beautiful and graceful of all the lindens for specimen use. Bees seem to find the flowers either narcotic or actually poisonous, as they can be found in large numbers on the ground under such trees. Also, because of the dense pubescence on the undersurface of the leaves, this tree should not be grown in urban areas where there is a large amount of smoke, for soot and dust collect and make them rather unsightly. But in the open, away from sooty areas, this is without question the most beautiful of the lindens, particularly adapted for use as a specimen shade tree.

Tilia platyphyllos   120′   Zone 3   Bigleaf linden

FLOWERS: small, yellowish, rather inconspicuous but very fragrant
    TIME: early July
* HABIT: rounded to pyramidal in outline
* FOLIAGE: leaves 2–5″ long and as wide, dense, somewhat coarse in texture

HABITAT: Europe
INTRODUCED: colonial times
VARIETIES:

> *aurea*—with young twigs and yellow branches
> 'Fastigiata' *(Columnar bigleaf linden)*—narrow and columnar in habit
> 'Laciniata'—with irregularly lobed leaves; a considerably smaller tree than the
> species
> 'Rubra'—young twigs red. There is a variety in European nurseries under the
> name of *T. platyphyllos corallina,* but this is a synonym of 'Rubra.'

Over twenty other varieties have been named. Possibly not as commonly grown in this country and Europe as *T. cordata,* it is still a shapely tree and does not produce the swollen burls on which sprout so many shoots, as does the common linden. The leaves are the largest of any of these recommended European lindens, making it somewhat coarse in texture.

Tilia tomentosa   90'   Zone 4   Silver linden

FLOWERS: small, yellowish, rather inconspicuous but very fragrant
    TIME: mid-July
* HABIT: broad, compact, pyramidal, dense
* FOLIAGE: leaves green above, white and pubescent below, about 2–4" long
HABITAT: southeastern Europe to western Asia
INTRODUCED: colonial times

Over a dozen varieties have been named. This is another outstanding specimen tree with erect branches, lacking the pendulous habit of *T. petiolaris* but nevertheless a beautiful tree in its own right. Its very definite outline makes it appear as if it has been clipped, and its beautiful leaves, which are white underneath, are always of interest. When the leaves are blown in the wind and the undersurfaces are clearly seen, this tree is striking indeed. Here again, however, because of the pubescence, these trees should not be grown where there are large amounts of dust and soot. It has been reported that the flowers of this tree are in some way injurious to bees.

Torreya nucifera   75'   Zone 5   Japanese torreya

FRUIT: a greenish plumlike ovoid, 1" long, ripening the second season; the seed is
    edible
* HABIT: pyramidal, often ovoid head with spreading branches
* FOLIAGE: yewlike
HABITAT: Japan
INTRODUCED: about 1860

Very similar to yews in habit and leaf, the Japanese torreya is frequently confused with them. This is the hardiest of the three species. *Torreya californica,* the California nutmeg, might be used where native in California, and *T. taxifolia* (called the stinking cedar because the foliage has a disagreeable odor when crushed) in Florida, where it is native. These torreyas are found infrequently in gardens, but they have merit where hardy, especially *T. nucifera* since it grows farther north than the others in areas where evergreens are most desirable winter plants.

Tristania conferta   60'   Zone 10   Brisbane box

BARK: reddish brown
FOLIAGE: leathery, evergreen
HABITAT: Australia

An interesting tree, somewhat similar to the madrone; appropriate for only the warmest parts of the country. It should be pruned occasionally to prevent the leaves from forming at the tips of the branches. The flowers and fruit are not particularly conspicuous.

→»» *TSUGA*

The hemlocks easily can be considered the most graceful and beautiful of the narrow-leaved evergreen trees, but they will grow only in areas where water is abundant the greater part of the year. Native on both sides of the continent, the species of the West Coast *(T. mertensiana* and *T. heterophylla)* do not grow well in the East. The Canada hemlock *(T. canadensis),* native in the eastern and northeastern United States, is the most diversified of the species, with many variants showing differences in foliage, habit, and method of growth. The Carolina hemlock *(T. caroliniana)* makes just as good an ornamental, perhaps doing slightly better than its northern relative in the cities, and the dense, dark green Japanese hemlock *(T. diversifolia)* should be grown a great deal more than it is. All have profuse small, pendulous cones, but these are not always produced every year.

All are easy to transplant, provided, of course, they are planted in good soil; all withstand and even thrive under stiff shearing. Hemlocks do not grow well in the city. The leaves of the Canada hemlock remain on the tree three or four years, those of the Carolina hemlock a year longer. In view of the excellent ornamental qualities of the Japanese hemlock, it should be noted that needles sometimes appear on eight- to ten-year-old wood. This is why their foliage appears so dense. Although all species withstand shade, they grow best in full sunlight.

Spruce mite is often more destructive to hemlock than to other evergreens, and hemlock scale causes heavy needle drop when abundant. Use malathion in midsummer. Black vine weevil and the smaller strawberry root weevil feed on hemlock roots in the grub stage and may wilt or kill the tree. Treat the soil around the roots with malathion. Hemlock looper, which has defoliated and killed many acres of forest trees, is occasionally found on ornamental trees. Spray with carbaryl.

Hemlocks are susceptible to three types of rust that also live on azaleas, rhododendrons, hydrangeas, and poplars; they will form orange pustules on the needles. If a rust is prevalent, remove any host plants nearby and spray in early summer with ferbam. Botrytis tip blight may kill new shoots in cool damp weather. No control is yet known.

→≫ FOLIAGE KEY TO THE HEMLOCKS
Native or Available in North America

Needles borne singly, leaf bases persistent . . . . *Picea and Tsuga*
1. Needles narrowed at base to form distinct petioles . . . . . . *Tsuga* species
This character must be clearly interpreted. Sometimes when the needle of a spruce is pulled off, a small portion of the twig bark also comes off, looking like a petiole unless observed with a lens. The needles of all spruces are without petioles, their leaf blades being attached directly to the twig.
    2. Needles with white lines on undersurface only, cones less than 2 inches long.
        3. Needles noticeably blunt and notched at tip
            4. One-year-old branchlets pubescent . . . . *T. diversifolia*
                (Japan) Zone 5
            4. One-year-old branchlets glabrous. . . . . *T. sieboldii*
                (Japan) Zone 5
        3. Needles not noticeably notched at end but rounded
            4. Many of the needles on vigorous one-year-old shoots wider at the base than at the tip, that is, gradually tapering from base to tip; needles mostly two-ranked, in one plane, and with a very fine serrulate margin (when examined with a lens); cones ¾ inch or less in length. . . . . . *T. canadensis*
                (Nova Scotia and eastern United States) Zone 4
            4. Majority of needles on vigorous one-year-old shoots not tapering but about as wide at the base as at the tip; needles in several planes about twig; needle margin of *T. caroliniana* entire and *T. heterophylla* is serrulate (when examined with a lens). Cones longer than ¾ inch.
                5. One-year-old twigs orange-brown, cones 1–1½" long
                . . . . *T. caroliniana*
                    (southeastern United States) Zone 4
                5. One-year-old twigs pale yellowish brown; cones ¾–1 inch long. . . . . *T. heterophylla*
                    (Alaska to Idaho and California) Zone 6

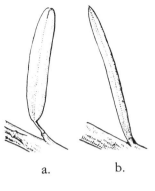

a.   b.

FIGURE 13

The needle of (a) a hemlock with a petiole and (b) a spruce without a petiole.

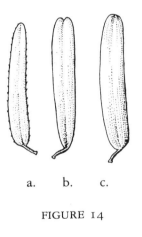

a.   b.   c.

FIGURE 14

The needles of (a) Tsuga canadensis *(the very fine serrulate margin can be seen only with a lens), (b)* T. sieboldii, *and (c)* T. caroliniana.

2. Needles with white lines on upper and lower surfaces, cones 2 inches or more in length .... *T. mertensiana*
(Alaska to Idaho and California) Zone 5

Tsuga canadensis   90′   Zone 3   Canada hemlock

* HABIT: long, slender, horizontal to sometimes drooping branches, forming a pyramidal head
* FOLIAGE: dense, evergreen needles
  HABITAT: northeastern North America
  VARIETIES:

'Bradshaw'—originated at Kingsville Nurseries, Kingsville, Maryland. Makes a perfect pyramid of growth, dense and with a wide base. More compact than 'Hiti.'

'Dawsoniana'—slow-growing, compact, dark green; originated at Wellesley, Massachusetts, about 1920. Is broader than it is high.

'Fremdii'—a more dense specimen at 30' than *T. compacta;* found in Rye, New York, in 1887. Densely pyramidal. Better than *T. atrovirens,* for the needles are more radially arranged.

'Globosa'—dense and rounded, as broad as it is high; named in 1887

'Kingsville'—narrow, fastigiate clone; one 18' foot tall tree is only 3½' wide at base

'Macrophylla'—originating in France before 1891, has leaves slightly longer and wider than the species

'Pendula' *(Sargent hemlock)*—probably the most popular form at this time because it has been available for nearly seventy-five years. This is a particularly graceful plant, two or three times as broad as it is tall, round, and moundlike in habit of growth with slightly pendulous branches. Four plants were originally found in the woods near Beacon, New York, before 1870 and were named after Henry W. Sargent, the neighbor of General Joseph Howland who found them.

'Pomfret'—faster growing than 'Fremdii,' but dense and pyramidal in habit

taxifolia—with yewlike foliage, selected in Vermont about 1928

'Westonigra'—introduced by Weston Nurseries, Weston, Massachusetts, about 1948 for its very dark green foliage

Many other varieties are named and available, but it takes years and years of growth for the respective merits of the clones to be evaluated. The Canada hemlock is without question one of our best ornamental evergreens either as a specimen or grouped as a serviceable screen or background. It should always be one of the first evergreen trees to consider for planting within its hardiness limitations.

Charles Sprague Sargent, who knew all the trees of North America thoroughly, used to say that no other conifer surpassed the hemlocks in grace and beauty. This is true fifty years later, although many exotic trees have been introduced in the meantime. Particularly is this true of *T. canadensis* and *T. caroliniana.*

The Canada hemlock grows over a wide area of the northeastern United States, whereas the Carolina hemlock is confined to a comparatively small area of the mountains of southwestern Virginia and Georgia, at the same time being perfectly hardy over the same range as *T. canadensis.* The foliage of the Canada hemlock tends to be flatter than that of its southern relative.

The Indians made a paste from the bark of *T. canadensis* by first boiling and then pounding it, using this for poultices with antiseptic properties. It is definitely not poisonous. (The poisonous "hemlock" of ancient times, a potion drunk by Socrates, was a species of herb *[Conium]* somewhat similar and related to our common wild carrot.)

At least nine trees have been reported in the Philadelphia area that are estimated to have been alive when William Penn first came up the Delaware River over 250 years ago. An old stump was reported in New York State a number of years ago that had eight hundred annual growth rings, but no trees of this great age are known to be alive today.

Because of its wide habitat, over fifty variants of this species have been noted and described. Some vary only slightly from others, but they do vary in habit, size, and foliage. Not all are readily available in the trade by any means, but at least eighteen of them are. They range in height from one dwarf variety ('Minuta'), which grows only about ½ inch a year (a twenty-year-old plant being only 6 inches tall), to the standard trees of the forest.

It may be of interest to note that these variants were generally grouped into the following classes by John C. Swartley in a very intensive study he made during graduate work at Cornell University about 1938:

Broadleaf	*Prostrate*
Bushy globe	*Pygmy*
Cinnamon	*Pyramidal*
Dense	*Slender*
Dwarf pyramidal	*Sparseleaf*
Fastigiate	*Spreading*
Globe	*Twiggy*
Golden	*Weeping*
Largeleaf	*Whitetip*
Littleleaf	*Yewlike*

These groups might be reduced still further by the home owner who is interested in only a few of the most striking forms to: upright, dense slow-growers; dwarf; weeping; leaf variants (form); and leaf variants (color).

A graceful tree in its own right, the Canada hemlock can be maintained at only 3 to 4 feet indefinitely by judicial pruning. Pruning or clipping in this way, it makes one of the best possible hedges. The advantages of using either the Canada or Carolina hemlock in the hedges are that these plants can be pruned in a stiffly rigid shape if desired, or the hedge can be allowed to grow in a delightfully informal fashion. This is done by clipping in a general mounded form and allowing the long, graceful shoots to grow for a year or even two without additional clipping. Then they must be pruned back hard in the early spring or the plant will soon grow out of shape. Thus the planting serves the dual purpose of formal hedge one year and informal hedge the next.

Tsuga caroliniana   75'   Zone 4   Carolina hemlock

* HABIT: compact, pyramidal tree, often with somewhat pendulous branches
* FOLIAGE: dense, evergreen needles
  HABITAT: mountains of southwestern Virginia to Georgia

The Carolina hemlock is one of the best all-purpose evergreen trees. It grows naturally into a standard tree, yet it can be sheared and clipped and forced to grow into any shape. Everything said above in favor of the Canada hemlock applies to this species as well. The needles are slightly whorled around the twigs, apparently one

The Carolina hemlock (Tsuga caroliniana) *is a fine ornamental tree, useful in many ways.*

of the reasons the tree can withstand the smoke and dust in city gardens better than its northern relative, *T. canadensis.* It can be used to make splendid hedges.

Tsuga diversifolia   90′   Zone 5   Japanese hemlock

* HABIT: pyramidal, with horizontal branches
* FOLIAGE: very dense, evergreen needles
  HABITAT: Japan
  INTRODUCED: 1861

Like most hemlocks, this tree has a pyramidal outline. It usually grows with several trunks, sometimes almost as a shrub, and because it is rather slow-growing, it makes a neater, smaller tree than some of the other hemlocks. It is the first of the hemlocks to produce new leaves in the spring and is apparently the only one that produces (or holds) needles on eight- to ten-year-old twigs.

Tsuga heterophylla   200′   Zone 6   Western hemlock

* HABIT: short, pendulous branches, making a narrow, pyramidal head
* FOLIAGE: evergreen needles
  HABITAT: north Pacific coast

A humid climate and moist soil are needed for this tree. In these conditions it grows rapidly. It does not do at all well in the eastern United States, probably because the atmosphere is not sufficiently moist. It seems to do best on the western slopes of the Cascade Mountains at altitudes between 1,500 and 3,500 feet and grows very well in shaded situations. This very stately tree is the tallest of the eight species of hemlocks.

⇢≫ ULMUS

With six elm species native in the United States, five species native in Europe (and many varieties), and several more species native in Asia, the identification of these shade trees is rather difficult. The elm is, and always has been, a standard shade tree in America, and even though it is threatened with partial or complete destruction by various diseases, it is doubtful whether the gardening public will stop planting them.

Unfortunately, over the period of time they have increased in popularity in this country, disease and insect infestations have plagued them. Although many an arborist will not admit it, these trees require more spraying (and pruning) than most other groups of trees. The ginkgo, as an example, requires practically no spraying and pruning. This does not mean that the ginkgo is a "superior" ornamental by any means, but the necessity of spraying elms to keep them in good condition is something that should be kept in mind.

It is not up to any one individual to categorically state that elms should or should not be grown at the present time. Over two hundred clones have been named in Europe and America. Each individual planter and grower will have to determine the viability of planting elms after thoroughly investigating the local situation concerning the possibility of disease and its effective control.

This is not the place to discuss the Dutch elm disease. Its history is well known to most, and the current situation concerning its inroads on the elms, both locally and nationally, should also be commonly available information. Suffice it to say here that *U. pumila, U. parvifolia,* and *U. carpinifolia* 'Christine Buisman' and 'Bea Schwarz' are the only elms reported as resistant to the disease by the plant pathologists in the United States Department of Agriculture who have been working with this problem for years. *Zelkova serrata* may be advertised as "immune" by those who have it for sale, but it is still listed by the above department as merely resistant and only to the same extent as are both *U. pumila* and *parvifolia.*

All elms are susceptible to several insect pests and diseases so that annual spraying is a necessity. Elms have no flowers or fruits that are ornamental, merely a yellow autumn color (none at all in most of the European elms)— reddish in the case of *U. parvifolia.* Also, all elms are gross feeders, making it difficult to get plants to grow properly underneath them.

With these obvious drawbacks and with the Dutch elm disease a constant threat, elm planting should be carefully assessed. We have valued them for their varying forms. If they have no particular *form* or *shape,* then under the circumstances, why plant them? There are certainly better trees that might be used instead.

Elms should be planted only where it is a foregone conclusion that they will receive the best of *annual* care. Intelligent pruning, spraying, and fertilizing should be counted on as insurance against diseases, and only partial insurance at that, since even some of the best-kept trees eventually succumb.

All elms are easily transplanted, having fibrous roots, and grow vigorously. They respond well to surface applications of fertilizers.

→» SIMPLE KEY TO THE ELMS

The following key is offered as an aid to the identification of elm species on the basis of foliage characters. More exact keys have been made in which the flowers and fruits are used, but many an amateur is confronted with the perplexing problem of identification when flowers and fruits are not available. Every one of the elm species varies greatly, and to make a key using only one or two characteristics is not very satisfactory. Therefore, this key is not infallible, but it may serve its purpose to many who are perplexed concerning the identification of these trees.

In using the key, merely go to the first number. If the statement there applies to the specimen, go to the next higher number until the tree is identified. If the statement there does not apply, proceed to the following group headed by the same number and proceed as above.

It should be noted that this key does not take into consideration the varieties of these species, many of which can be identified by their form alone. Also, and this is very important, it should be noted that *U. japonica, laevis,* and *plotii* are not common in America except in botanical collections, and that other species, such as *U. thomasii* and *serotina,* are used infrequently in landscape work. A knowledge of these facts should make this key much more usable.

The elms are so variable that it is likely they will continue to be difficult to identify. These notes and suggestions are offered merely as aids to those interested in this group of trees.

1. Corky ridges or wings on younger branches
  2. Leaves simply serrate . . . . *U. crassifolia*
  2. Leaves doubly serrate
    3. Young twigs glabrous or nearly so
      4. Wings usually two and opposite . . . . *U. alata*
      4. Wings several, not necessarily opposite, flowers in spring; not native . . . . *U. carpinifolia suberosa*
      4. Wings several, not necessarily opposite, flowers in fall; native . . . . *U. serotina*
    3. Young twigs pubescent
      4. Tree irregularly columnar . . . . *U. thomasii*
      4. Tree not irregularly columnar; oval or rounded in outline
        5. Leaves 2–3 inches long, wings occasionally . . . . *U. procera*
        5. Leaves 3–4¾ inches long, wings occasionally . . . . *U. japonica*
1. Leaves three-pointed at tip or occasionally so, branches not corky
  2. Mature branches reddish brown, hairy while young; leaves occasionally with one or two extra points at apex . . . . *U. glabra*
  2. Mature branches pale yellowish or grayish brown, glabrous or nearly so when young; most of the leaves three-pointed at apex . . . . *U. laciniata*
1. Leaves simply or almost simply serrate, ¾–2¾ inches long
  2. Leaves often nearly equal at base, many leaves showing indications of double serration, young branches pubescent or glabrous, stipules broad, flowers in spring . . . . *U. pumila*
  2. Leaves usually unequally rounded at base, young branches pubescent, stipules linear, flowers in fall . . . . *U. parvifolia*
1. Leaves doubly serrate
  2. Young branches glabrous
    3. Leaves 2¾–6 inches long
      4. Leaves usually twice as long as wide, no conspicuous axillary tufts of hair . . . . *U. americana*
      4. Leaves less than 1½ times as long as wide, usually with conspicuous tufts of hair in axils of veins on undersurface of leaves; considerably variable . . . . *U. hollandica*
    3. Leaves 1¼–3¼ inches long
      4. Petioles ¼–½ inch long, leaves 2–3 inches long, smooth above . . . . *U. carpinifolia*
      4. Petioles less than ¼ inch long, leaves 1¼–2¼ inches long, slightly scabrous above . . . . *U. plotii*
  2. Young branches pubescent
    3. Leaves often glabrous beneath . . . . *U. americana*
    3. Leaves pubescent beneath
      4. Leaves 2–3 inches long . . . . *U. procera*

    4. Leaves longer
        5. Leaves often widest at middle, 4–8 inches long
            6. Branchlets gray to light brown, buds covered with rusty brown hairs . . . . . . *U. rubra (fulva)*
            6. Branchlets dark brown, buds without rusty brown hairs, leaves sometimes showing a tendency to be three-pointed at tip . . . . *U. glabra*
        5. Leaves usually widest above middle, 2½–4¾ inches long
            6. Leaves scabrous and pubescent above, corky wings on branches occasionally . . . *U. japonica*
            6. Leaves usually glabrous above, very unequal at base . . . . *U. laevis*

Ulmus americana   120′   Zone 2   American elm

* HABIT: vase-shaped, widely arching branches
   FOLIAGE: open

The American elm (Ulmus americana), *with its vase-shaped branching, should not be used anymore until a remedy is found for the devastating Dutch elm disease.*

HABITAT: central and eastern North America

The American elm has been without question the most popular shade tree in North America. Its unique vase-shaped form is not to be found in any other tree growing in this country, native or exotic. It is closely associated with the earliest gardens in America, and many a century-old monarch is pointed out by local citizens as being rich in local history.

Because of its wide distribution and its universal use in this country, several varieties have been noted, especially narrow, columnar types. The typical form is arching, but some trees have more pendulous branches than others, and some are "feathered" down the trunks with numerous small side shoots.

There is no ornamental tree like the American elm. It makes an excellent lawn specimen, for its lofty branches allow much air circulation underneath, and although they supply excellent shade, the widely arching branches do not obstruct views from houses. This wide-arching habit is not evident in young specimens and varies materially when the trees are grown from seed. Propagating elms asexually may be more tedious but certainly results in more uniform specimens.

The elms in general, and *U. americana* in particular, are susceptible to more disease and insect troubles than any other tree. Now that Dutch elm disease and phloem necrosis disease seriously threaten most elms, it seems advisable to limit the planting of the American elm. It may be that at some time in the future some good control may be found for these tree-killing diseases, but until that time comes, the planting of the American elm should be done with discretion, and certainly only after thoroughly considering the selection of all other possible tree types.

Ulmus carpinifolia   90'   Zone 4   Smoothleaf elm

* HABIT: variable, many forms
FOLIAGE: bright green
HABITAT: Europe, western Asia
INTRODUCED: before 1850

A variable species with several very interesting varieties. Usually it has a single trunk with slender branches, forming a pyramidal head. Some of these varieties offer excellent material for small-scale planting, especially for use along narrow streets.

Ulmus glabra   120'   Zone 4   Scotch elm, Wych elm

HABIT: wide-spreading, rather open
FOLIAGE: coarse
HABITAT: Europe, western Asia
INTRODUCED: colonial times

A rather popular tree, especially the varieties, but it should be pointed out that the elm leaf miner will riddle this tree before it will touch most of the other elms. Consequently, preventive sprays should be put on these trees in sufficient time to forestall the inroads of this very destructive insect. The species itself is certainly no better an ornamental than *U. americana.*

Ulmus parvifolia   50′   Zone 5   Chinese elm

* HABIT: round-topped
* BARK: mottled and often exfoliating in irregular spots, exposing a much lighter colored bark underneath
* FOLIAGE: dense, small leaves, 1–2″ long
  AUTUMN COLOR: reddish to purplish
  HABITAT: China, Korea, Japan
  INTRODUCED: 1794

Frequently confused with the Siberian elm *(U. pumila)*, the true Chinese elm is a better ornamental. The leaves are dark green, remaining on the tree long into the fall. The flowers appear in the fall, not in the spring as do those of *U. pumila,* and the beautiful bark of older trees makes them of considerable ornamental interest throughout the entire year. In the warmer temperate regions of China and Japan the leaves are evergreen, but in southern California a special clone has been used widely for this reason and given the varietal name 'Pendens.' It is remarkable for its wide-spreading branches that frequently are pendulous and touch the ground. This variety, easily reproduced by cuttings, is surviving as a small tree in the Arnold Arboretum but has not been tried sufficiently long to prove its hardiness in the North. It has been noted in the Japanese-beetle area around Philadelphia that where the Siberian and Chinese elms were growing side by side, the beetles would practically defoliate the former and hardly touch the latter until other food became scarce. The true Chinese elm is fast-growing, an excellent ornamental, and well worth more use in American gardens. It might be used as a temporary or permanent screen or to provide quick growth, and as a permanent tree in the landscape it has considerably more merit, in the East and South at least, than does *U. pumila.*

Ulmus procera (syn. *U. campestris*)   120′   Zone 5   English elm

HABIT: oval or oblong head, often wide-spreading
FOLIAGE: dense
HABITAT: England, western Europe
INTRODUCED: colonial times

The English elm, formerly called *U. campestris,* has been widely planted in America since colonial times. It withstands city conditions better than most other elms but of course lacks the desirable vase-shaped habit of *U. americana.* The foliage remains on the tree about two weeks longer in the fall than does that of the American elm.

Ulmus pumila 75′ Zone 4 Siberian elm

HABIT: rounded head, rather open
* FOLIAGE: fine-textured, small leaves, ¾–2¾″ long
HABITAT: eastern Siberia, northern China
INTRODUCED: 1860

Widely publicized and offered as the "Chinese" elm, this native of Siberia has been much overplanted. It is not a tree to plant indiscriminately in any garden. In the very dry areas of the Great Plains or on dry banks where other trees will not grow, it has merit. Because of its rapid, vigorous growth it will make a quick screen but may not grow old gracefully. Seedlings do vary and some have much better form than others. One type, named 'Coolshade,' has proved much stronger-wooded in Missouri ice storms and because of this is being propagated asexually. It is slower in growth and much denser than the species in habit. The foliage is darker green, and all in all this clone appears to be superior to the species in many ways. The Siberian elm is hardier than *U. parvifolia* and is one of the four elms currently resistant to the Dutch elm disease. (The others are *U. parvifolia* and *U. carpinifolia* 'Bea Schwarz' and 'Christine Buisman.') In the eastern United States, at least, the Siberian elm should not be considered an ornamental tree but a service tree for certain specific purposes. There are many other trees that will better serve as ornamentals than this.

Umbellularia californica 75′ Zone 7 California-laurel

* HABIT: dense, rounded head
* FOLIAGE: evergreen, lustrous, green leaves, 2–5″ long, aromatic when crushed
HABITAT: California to Oregon

A handsome evergreen tree used on the West Coast as a street, park, and garden specimen tree of considerable merit. One of the largest of the species is known as the "Laurel of San Marcos" near Santa Barbara, California, being 82 feet in height with a spread of 104 feet (according to Maunsell Van Rensselaer, formerly of the Santa Barbara Botanic Garden), at an estimated age of two hundred to three hundred years old. The wood is very hard and has been used for making house rollers, and the aromatic leaves have been used in flavoring soups. A truly ornamental specimen, this native American tree is worthy of considerable planting where it is hardy.

Vaccinium arboreum 27′ Zone 7 Farkleberry

FLOWERS: small, waxy, white
   TIME: summer
FRUIT: blue berries
   EFFECTIVE: early fall
* FOLIAGE: evergreen leaves, 2″ long
HABITAT: southeastern United States

The farkleberry is grown as an evergreen in the South where its lustrous green leaves and diminutive, waxy, white flowers promote its value as a garden ornamental.

Viburnum lentago   30′   Zone 2   Nannyberry

* FLOWERS: white, in flat clusters
        TIME: late May
* FRUIT: black berries, in flat clusters
        EFFECTIVE: fall and winter
* AUTUMN COLOR: purplish red
    HABITAT: eastern United States

A native, vigorous viburnum that makes a dense mass; if allowed, the branches of old plants will arch over and rest on the ground, often taking root. It is useful as a background and screen, and is used mostly as a shrub although it can be trained to grow in tree form and is very effective on the edges of woodlands. The fruit is valued by the birds as a winter food. Its shiny green leaves and splendid fall color add to its usefulness. No serious pests.

Viburnum prunifolium   15′   Zone 3   Blackhaw

* FLOWERS: white, in flat clusters
        TIME: mid-May
* FRUIT: blue-black berries, in flat clusters
        EFFECTIVE: fall
* AUTUMN COLOR: shining red
    HABITAT: eastern United States

Often this plant has been recommended as a substitute (in form) for some of the hawthorns. Sometimes it is grown as a small tree with a single trunk. The fruit has been used for making preserves since colonial times, and in certain areas strains have been selected particularly because the fruit is large and palatable. Its fruit grows to ½ inch long, about the largest on any viburnum, and it is produced in great profusion. An excellent plant as a specimen or for massing; no serious pests.

Viburnum rufidulum   30′   Zone 5   Southern blackhaw

* FLOWERS: creamy white, in flat clusters
        TIME: late May
* FRUIT: dark blue berries, in clusters
        EFFECTIVE: fall
    FOLIAGE: lustrous green leaves
* AUTUMN COLOR: red
    HABITAT: southeastern United States

The southern counterpart of *V. prunifolium,* it need be grown only in the South where its northern relative is unavailable. No serious pests.

Viburnum sieboldii   30'   Zone 4   Siebold viburnum

* FLOWERS: creamy white, in flat clusters
        TIME: late May
* FRUIT: red to black berries on red fruit stalks, in flat to rounded clusters
        EFFECTIVE: summer
  HABIT: rounded, often rather open
* FOLIAGE: rugose, lustrous, dark green foliage
  AUTUMN COLOR: red
  HABITAT: Japan
  INTRODUCED: 1880

If I were to choose only one viburnum for my garden, I think it would be this because of the splendid long (6-inch) leaves, its very desirable branching habit that results in rounded masses of foliage interspersed with open areas where light and shadow add much interest, and also because of its colorful fruit. Although these are black at maturity, they remain unripe and bright red for several weeks in the summer, and even after they turn black and fall off or are eaten by the birds, their red fruit stalks remain another three or four weeks to give color to the plant at a time when the fruit of other shrubs is not sufficiently ripened to be colorful. As a specimen plant it is the best of the viburnums, for the northern United States at least.

Washingtonia robusta   90'   Zone 10   Mexican Washington
                                                                          palm

* HABIT: fan-shaped foliage, only at top of trunk
  FOLIAGE: coarse
  HABITAT: Mexico

A slender palm with a long trunk; leaves fan-shaped and drop off the stem at maturity. It is used a great deal in plantings on the southern California coast.

Yucca brevifolia   40'   Zone 7   Joshua tree

FLOWERS: greenish white, 2" long, in 12" panicles
HABIT: rounded, trunk often 15' long
FOLIAGE: evergreen leaves, to 9" long
HABITAT: southwestern United States

Only used in dry, hot desert areas.

Zelkova carpinifolia   75′   Zone 6   Elm zelkova

HABIT: ovoid to oblong head, dense branching
BARK: peels off in flakes
FOLIAGE: medium to fine textured
AUTUMN COLOR: red
HABITAT: Caucasus
INTRODUCED: 1760

Slow-growing and long-lived, this may prove as good as *Z. serrata* as an elm substitute. It has no main trunk but a number of branches from the base and is certainly worth further trial in America, where it is used very little at present.

Zelkova serrata   90′   Zone 5   Japanese zelkova

* HABIT: round-topped, short trunk, many ascending branches
FOLIAGE: medium to fine textured

The Japanese zelkova
(Zelkova serrata) *has
interesting bark and makes
an admirable substitute for
the American elm.*

AUTUMN COLOR: yellow to russet
HABITAT: Japan
INTRODUCED: about 1860
VARIETIES:

'Green Vase' *(Plant Patent #5080)*—with a vase-shaped habit similar to that of the American elm. Taller and not as broad as 'Village Green' and twice as fast-growing. Autumn color orange. Grows well on city streets. Originated by Princeton Nurseries, Princeton, New Jersey.

'Village Green' *(Plant Patent #2337)*—has the good vase shape of the American elm. Highly resistant to Dutch elm disease and leaf-eating insects, as well as the bark beetle. It must be propagated by grafting. Originated by Princeton Nurseries.

Somewhat similar to a small-leaved elm, Japanese zelkova has wide-spreading branches and is quite graceful in habit. Its primary use is, of course, as a shade tree. It is closely akin to the elm; in fact, it is often used as an understock on which to graft certain types of elm and has been recommended for the root understock on which the Dutch-elm-disease-resistant clone 'Christine Buisman' is root-grafted.

This tree might be accepted as one of the best substitutes for the American elm since it is closer in shape to the elm than is any other tree, and it grows very fast. It is also resistant to the Dutch elm disease. The rare Chinese species *Z. sinica* does not have this elm habit. The *Zelkova* yields the highest priced lumber of Japan, where it is used for lacquerware, trays, and high-grade furniture. This species has proved very satisfactory in the British Isles, where some excellent, very tall specimens have been grown, often with many small trunks instead of one short trunk.

Ziziphus jujuba   30'   Zone 7   Common jujube, Chinese date

FRUIT: datelike, dark red to black, up to 1″ long, edible
   EFFECTIVE: September and October
HABIT: spiny, open
FOLIAGE: open
HABITAT: southern Europe, Asia

The common jujube is not particularly ornamental, but it has been found to withstand heat, drought, and alkaline soils in the southwestern United States, and these would be the reasons for growing it in areas where other trees prove difficult. It is cultivated for its edible fruit in the Mediterranean and is available from commercial concerns in America.

APPENDIX 1:

Secondary Tree List

-»»

The following trees are among the host of plants grown in this country that should not be grown until the better types recommended have first been tried. They should not be considered "discards" entirely since under certain circumstances or under certain growing conditions, they may possibly do as well as the recommended types. However, the majority of these species and varieties differ only slightly from the recommended plants or are decidedly inferior to them and so can be omitted from consideration, especially where space is a limiting factor. Persons responsible for planting large numbers of trees along streets or highways would do well to consider only the recommended trees for such plantings.

There have been several reasons for placing these trees in a secondary list. Many planters will not agree with the following lists or the reasons for placing certain trees in a secondary list. The time for the research necessary in making this list will have been worthwhile if it merely impresses gardeners with the fact that some trees are more useful in our gardens than others, and time and space should not be given to trees with inferior qualities. The gardener will undoubtedly want to make his or her own list and can well start by critically examining this one.

The numbers after the trees represent the reasons for placing them in this group. They are as follows:

1. The tree is not superior to the varieties given in the recommended list. Many trees are practically identical, from a landscape viewpoint, differing merely in more pubescence on the leaf, a slightly different type of leaf margin, fruit that may be only slightly different in shape, size, or pubescence—many factors, but in the garden such plants look alike and serve identical purposes. Such minor differences do not seem sufficient to clutter up our nurseries and gardens with plants of many different names.

Also included in this group are some hybrid species that may vary considerably. It is much better to plant asexually propagated named clones of such species, with known ornamental characteristics.

2. The tree has inferior flowers to those in the recommended list.

3. The tree has inferior fruit to those in the recommended list.

4. The tree has poor foliage. Included are many variegated-leaved trees and those with so-called golden leaves, but actually many of these prove very difficult to grow and may look good for only a very short period. The "golden"-leaved evergreens (most of them at least) are outstanding examples of trees that look disreputable throughout the winter months. It would seem that such trees should be avoided or used only after serious consideration has been given to better trees.

5. Evergreens with poor winter foliage. If an evergreen does not appear at its best in the winter, it should be given up in preference to one that does.

6. The tree has a poor habit of growth.

7. The tree is usually troubled with an insect pest or disease.

8. The tree cannot be located in the nurseries and arboretums of this country. So many times we run across interesting varieties described in botanical texts that are impossible to locate in nurseries. Upon investigation it is shown that many such varieties are represented only by herbarium specimens, in some cases only the original ones from which they were first named. No such plants have been included in the recommended list.

9. The tree or one of its parts is poisonous.

Abies alba & vars. 1
  amabilis 1, 6
  balsamea & vars. 1, 6, 7
  borisii-regis 1
  bornmulleriana 8
  cephalonica & vars. 1
  chensiensis 1
  cilicica & vars. 1
  concolor aurea 1, 4
    'Globosa' 4
    'Lowiana' 1, 6
    'Pendula' 1
    'Wattezii' 1, 4
  delavayi 8
  ernestii 8

  fabrii 1, 8
  fargesii 8
  faxoniana 1, 8
  firma 1
  forrestii 8
  fraseri 1, 6
  georgei 8
  grandis 1
  holophylla 1
  homolepsis tomomi 1, 6
    umbellata 1
  insignis & vars. 8
  lasiocarpa & vars. 1
  magnifica shastensis 1
  mariesii 1, 8

marocana 8
nebrodensis 8
nephrolepis 1
nordmanniana & vars. 1
numidica & vars. 1, 8
pindrow & vars. 8
pinsapo
  'Pendula' 1, 6
recurvata 1, 8
sachalinensis & vars. 1, 6, 8
sibirica 1, 6, 8
squamata 8
sutchuenensis 1
veitchii nikkoensis 1
veitchii olivacea 1
venusta 1, 8
vilmorinii 8
Acacia longifolia floribunda 1
Acer buergerianum integrifolium 1, 2, 3
  b. ningpoense 1, 2, 3
  campestre 'Albo-variegatum' 2, 3, 4
    hebecarpum 1, 2, 3
    leiocarpum 1, 2, 3
    'Schwerinii' 2, 3, 4
    tauricum 1, 2, 3
  cappadocicum 1
  cissifolium 1
  crataegifolium 1, 2, 3
  diabolicum 1, 4
  dieckii 2, 3, 4
  distylum 1, 2, 3
  durettii 1, 2, 3
  franchettii 1, 2, 3
  glabrum douglasii 1, 2
  glabrum torreyi 1, 2
  grandidentatum 1, 2, 3
  grosseri & vars. 1, 2
  heldreichii & vars. 1, 2
  henryi 1, 2, 3
  hyrcanum 1, 2, 3
  leucoderme 1, 2, 3
  mayrii 2, 4
  micranthum 1, 2, 3
  miyabei 1, 2, 3
  mono & vars. 1, 2, 3
  negundo californicum 1
    texanum 1

oblongum & vars. 1, 2, 3
oliverianum 1, 2, 3
palmatum—since at least eighty varieties of this species are now being grown in the United States, at least half or more should be in this Secondary List. The best have already been recommended, pages 126–29.
platanoides 'Argutum' 1, 2, 3
  'Aureo-marginatum' 2, 3, 4
  'Columnare' 1
  'Crispum' *(cucullatum)* 2, 3, 4
  'Fassen's Black' 1, 4
  'Goldsworth Purple' 1, 4
  'Greenlace' 1, 4
  'Improved Columnar' 1, 2, 3
  laciniatum 2, 3, 4
  'Natorp' 1, 2, 3
  'Olmstead' 1
  'Palmatifidum' 1
  'Royal Red' 1
  rubrum 1, 4
  'Schwedleri' 1, 2, 3
  'Stollii' 1, 4
  'Variegatum' 1, 4
pseudoplatanus corstorphinense 1, 4
  'Euchlorum' 1
pseudoplatanus 'Flavo-variegatum' 1, 4
  'Leopoldii' 1, 4
  'Nizettii' 4
  'Prinz Handjery' 4
  tomentosum 1
  'Tricolor' 4
  'Variegatum' 1, 4
pseudo-sieboldianum 1
rubrum drummondii 1
  'Doric' 1, 8
  'Gerling' 1, 8
  pallidiflorum 1
  'Schlesingeri' 1
  tomentosum 1
  trilobum 1
rufinerve 1
saccharinum & vars. 1, 3, 6
  over sixty clonal names have been given to this species.

saccharum glaucum 1, 2
  rugelii 1, 2
  schneckii 1, 2
  senecaensis 1, 2
  sieboldianum & vars. may have value
  tegmentosum 1, 2, 3
  tetramerum & vars. 1, 2, 3
  trautvetteri 1, 2
  truncatum 1, 2, 3
  velutinum 2, 3, 4
  zoeschense 1, 2, 3
Aesculus arnoldiana 1, 2, 3, 7
  bushii 1, 3, 4, 7
  californica 1, 2, 3
  carnea 'Pendula' 1, 3, 4, 6, 7
  chinensis 1, 2, 3
  discolor & vars. 1, 2
  dupontii & vars. 1, 2
  glabra leucodermis 1, 3, 4, 7
    monticola 1, 3, 4, 7
    'Pallida' 1, 3, 4, 7
    sargentii 1, 3, 4, 7
  hippocastanum & most vars. except
    'Baumannii' 1, 2, 3, 7
  hybrida 1, 2, 3, 4, 7
  indica 1
  marylandica 1, 2, 3, 4, 7
  mississippiensis 1, 2, 3, 4, 7
  mutabilis & vars. 1, 2, 3, 4
  neglecta & vars. 1, 2, 3, 7
  octandra & vars. 1, 3, 7
  parviflora serotina 1, 3, 7
  pavia 1, 3, 4, 7
  sylvatica 1, 2, 3
  turbinata 1, 3, 4, 7
    pubescens 1, 3, 4, 7
  wilsonii 1, 3, 4, 7
  woerlitzensis & var. 1, 2, 3
Ailanthus vilmoriniana 1, 4, 6
Alnus aschersoniana 1, 3, 7
  cremastogyne 1, 3, 8
  elliptica 1, 3, 4
  glutinosa—most vars. except
    'Laciniata' 1, 3
  hirsuta 1, 3
  japonica 1, 3, 7
    arguta 1, 3, 7
  maritima 1, 3

nitida 1, 3
oblongifolia 1, 3
orientalis 1, 3, 8
rugosa & vars. 1, 3
sinuata 1, 3
subcordata 1, 3
tenuifolia & var. 1, 3
Amelanchier arborea & var. 1, 3
  asiatica 1
  canadensis nuda 1
  grandiflora 'Rubescens' 1
Aralia chinensis 1, 2
  spinosa 1, 2
Bumelia lanuginosa 1, 2, 3
Betula albo-sinensis septentrionalis 1, 3
  caerulea 1, 3
  caerulea-grandis 1, 3
  concinna 1, 3, 8
  coriacea 1, 3, 8
  corylifolia 1, 3
  costata 1, 3, 8
  ermanii 1, 3, 7
  globispica 1, 3, 8
  grossa 1, 3
  lenta 'Laciniata' 3, 8
  luminifera 1, 3, 8
  lutea 1, 3, 7
  medwediewi 1, 3, 8
  microphylla 1, 3, 8
  papyrifera—most vars. are no better
    than the species 1, 3
  pubescens 1, 3, 6, 8
  raddeana 1, 3, 8
  schmidtii 1, 3
  turkestanica 1, 3, 8
  utilis 1, 3, 8
Callitris robusta 1
Camellia japonica—many vars. 1
Caragana arborescens 1, 2
Carpinus betulus 'Albo-variegata' 1, 4
    'Aureo-variegata' 1, 4
    'Carpinizza' 1
    'Cucullata' 1, 4
    'Marmorata' 1, 4
    parva 1, 4
    purpurea 1
    'Quercifolia' 1, 6
    'Variegata' 1, 4

cordata & var. 1
eximia 1
fargesiana 1
henryana 1
laxiflora 1
   macrostachya 1
orientalis 'Calcarea' 1
   'Grandiflora' 1
turczaniovii 1, 4
   ovalifolia 1, 4
Carya aquatica 1, 2, 3
   brownii 1, 2, 3
   carolinae-septentrionalis 1, 2, 3
   cathayensis 1, 2, 3, 8
   glabra megacarpa 1, 2, 3
   laciniosa 1, 2, 3
   laneyi 1, 2, 3
   lecontei 1, 2, 3
   myristicaeformis 1, 2, 3
   ovalis & vars. 1, 2, 3
   ovata fraxinifolia 1, 2, 3
     halesii 1, 2, 3
     nuttallii 1, 2, 3
   pallida 1, 2, 3
   texana & vars. 1, 2, 3
Catalpa bignonioides koehnei 1, 4
   bungei 1, 2, 4
     heterophylla 1, 2, 4
   fargesii 1, 4
     duclouxii, 1, 4
   hybrida 1, 4
     japonica 1, 4
     purpurea 1, 4
   ovata 1, 2, 4
     flavescens 1, 2, 4
Castanea—most species except *C.*
   crenata & *C. mollissima* 1, 2, 7
Celtis biondii 1, 8
   caucasica 1, 8
   cerasifera 1, 8
   douglasii 1
   glabrata 1, 8
   julianae 1, 8
   koraiensis 1, 7
   labilis 1, 6, 8
   occidentalis & vars. 1, 7
   pumila 1
   reticulata 1, 8

tournefortii 1
Cephalotaxus drupacea 1, 2, 4
   fortuni 1, 2, 4
Cercidiphyllum japonicum sinense 1
Cercis canadensis plena 2
Chaenomeles sinensis 2, 3, 7
Chamaecyparis lawsoniana
   'Darlyensis' 1
   'Fraseri' 1
   'Krameri' 1, 4
   'Lycopodoides' 1, 4, 6
   'Silver Queen' 1, 5
   'Smithii' 1
   'Wisselii' 1, 4, 6
   obtusa 'Aurea' 5
     'Keteleeri' 1
   pisifera 'Aureo-variegata' 1, 4, 5
   plumosa 'Argentea' 1, 4, 5
     'Flavescens' 1, 4, 5
     'Sulphurea' 1, 4, 5
   thyoides 1, 4, 6
Chionanthus retusus 1
   virginicus maritimus 1
Cladrastis platycarpa 1
   sinensis 1
   wilsonii 1
Clerodendron trichotomum fargesii 1
Cornus coreana 1
   florida 'Prosser' 1, 2
     'Rose Valley' 1, 2
   kousa viridis 1, 2
   officinalis 1
   walteri 1
Corylus chinensis 1, 6
   colurna grandulifera 1
   tibetica 1
Crataegomespilus species 1, 6
Crataegus—most species other than
   those recommended on pages
   210–19. Over five hundred
   species and varieties have been
   tested at the Arnold Arboretum.
Cryptomeria japonica 'Lobbii' 1
   j. sinense 1, 6
Cupressus arizonica 1
   a. 'Bonita' 1
   sempervirens indica 1
     lutea 1, 4

variegata 1, 4
Cydonia oblonga 1, 2, 6, 7
Diospyros lotus 1, 3
Erythea armata 1
Eucommia ulmoides 1, 4, 6
Eugenia smithii 1
    e. uniflora 1
Euonymus bungeana 1, 2, 3, 7
  europaea 2, 3, 7
    angustifolia 2, 3, 4, 7
    atropurpurea 2, 3, 7
    'Atrorubens' 1, 2, 7
    'Aucubaefolia' 1, 4, 7
    'Chrysophylla' 1, 2, 7
    'Coccinea' 1, 2, 7
    japonica 'Argenteo variegata' 2, 4
      'Aureo-variegata' 2, 4
      'Pyramidata' 2, 8
      'Viridi-variegata' 2, 4
    lanceifolia 1, 2
    latifolia 1, 4, 7
    maackii 1, 2, 3
    oxyphylla 2, 8
    sanguinea brevipedunculata 1, 2
      camptoneura 1, 2
Euptelea polyandra 1, 2, 3
Fagus crenata 1
  engleriana 1
  grandifolia caroliniana 1
    pubescens 1
  japonica 1
  longipetiolata 1
  lucida 1
  orientalis 1
  sylvatica 'Albo-variegata' 1, 4
    'Cristata' 1, 4
    'Latifolia' 1, 4
    'Luteo-variegata' 1, 4
    'Quercoides' 1
    'Tricolor' 1, 4
    'Zlatia' 1, 4
Fontanesia species 1, 2, 3, 4
Forestiera species 1, 2, 3, 4
Fraxinus angustifolia 1, 2
  anomala 1, 2
  biltmoreana 1
  caroliniana & var. 1, 2
  chinensis & vars. 1, 2

elonga 1, 2
excelsior 'Argenteo-variegata' 1, 2, 4
  'Asplenifolia' 1, 2
  'Aureo-pendula' 1, 2, 4
  'Aureo-variegata' 1, 2, 4
  'Crispa' 1, 2, 4
  'Diversifolia' 1, 2
  'Erosa' 1, 2
  horizontalis 1, 2
  'Spectabilis' 1, 2
floribunda 1, 2
griffithii 1, 2
hookeri 1, 2
longicuspis 1, 2
lowellii 1, 2
mandshurica 1
nigra 1
numidica 1, 2
obliqua 1, 2
ornus juglandifolia 1, 2
  rotundifolia 1, 2
oxycarpa 1, 2
pallisae 1
pennsylvanica 1
  acubaefolia 1, 2, 4
  subintegerrima 1, 2
platypoda 1, 2
potamophila 1, 2
pubinervis 1, 2
quadrangulata 1
raibocarpa 1, 2
retusa & var. 1, 2
rotundifolia & var. 1, 2
syriaca 1, 2, 6
texensis 1
tomentosa 1, 8
velutina coriacea 1, 8
xanthoxyloides & vars. 1
Ginkgo biloba aurea 1, 4
  b. variegata 1, 4
Gleditsia aquatica 1, 2, 3
  caspica 1, 2, 6
  delavayi 1, 2, 8
  ferox 1, 2, 8
  heterophylla 1, 2, 8
  japonica 1, 7
  macracantha 1, 2, 8
  sinensis & var. 1, 2

texana 1, 2, 6
triacanthos 'Calhoun' 1, 2, 3
  'Millwood' 1, 2, 3
Halesia carolina dialypetala 1
  c. mollis 1
  diptera 1, 2
  monticola vestita 1
Hippophae salicifolia 1, 2
Hovenia dulcis 2, 3
Ilex aquifolium—many vars.; see pages
  249–50 for some of the best—1
  dipyrena & var. 1
  macropoda 1, 2, 3
  opaca—many vars. depending on
    hardiness and adaptability (see
    pages 252–54)
  pedunculosa continentalis 1
  purpurea 1
Jacaranda acutifolia 1
Juglans—most sp. and vars. except
  those recommended (see pages
  255–57)
Juniperus chinensis 1
  coxii 1, 8
  deppeana pachyphlaea 1
  formosana 1
  monosperma 1, 4, 6
  occidentalis 1
  recurva 8
  thurifera 8
  utahensis 1
  virginiana 'Albo-spica' 4, 5
    aurea 4, 5
    chamberlaynii 1, 4
    cinerascens 1, 4, 5
    'Nevin's Blue' 1, 4, 5
    plumosa 1, 4, 5
    'Smith' 1, 4
    'Triomphe d'Angers' 1, 4
    'Variegata' 4, 5
  wallichiana 1, 4, 5
Keteleeria davidiana 8
Koelreuteria formosana 1, 2
Laburnocytisus adami 4, 6, 8
Laburnum alpinum autumnale 1
  anagyroides & vars. 1, 2
Larix gmelina & vars. 1, 6
  griffithii 1

lyallii 1, 6
marschlinsi 1
mastersiana 1
occidentalis 1
pendula 1
potaninii 1
sibirica 1, 6
Liriodendron chinense 1
  tulipifera integrifolium 1
  'Obtusilobum' 1
Maackia chinensis
Macludrania hybrida 1, 2, 3
Maddenia hypoleuca 1
Magnolia ashei 1
  biondii 1
  cylindrica 1
  delavayi 1
  highdownensis 1
  kewensis 1
  kobus & var. 1, 2
  loebneri 1, 2
  obovata 1
  officinalis 1, 4
  proctoriana 1, 2
  pyramidata 1, 2
  sargentiana 8
  slavinii 1
  soulangiana 'Amabilis' 1, 2
    'Candolleana' 1
    'George Henry Kern' 1, 2
    'Lennei Alba' 1, 2
    'Norbertiana' 1, 2
    purpurea 1, 2
    'Spectabilis' 1, 2
    'Triumphant' 1, 2
  sprengeri elongata 1
  tripetala 1
  virginiana australis 1
  wilsonii taliensis 1

Malus—reasons for listing these here
are explained below:

Flowers: fade badly	Ff
average bloom	Fav
Fruit: alternate bearer	FrA
green	FrG
too large	FrL

not especially ornamental	FrN
Susceptible to fire blight	FB
Susceptible to cedar rust	CR
Susceptible to apple scab	s
Not especially ornamental	N
Similar to others	S
Inferior to others	I
For extreme hardiness only	H

'Abundance'	Ff
'Alexis'	Ss
'Almey'	FrA, s
'Ames'	N
'Amisk'	FrA, Ff
'Amsib'	N
'Amur'	S
'Anaros'	FB
angustifolia	FrG, CR
pendula	FrG, CR
'Arctic Dawn'	H
'Arrow'	Ss
astracanica	N
'Athabasca'	FrA, Fav
baccata	
'Columnaris'	S
himalaica	S
'Big River'	H
'Boone Park'	FrG, S
bracteata	FrG, CR
'Brier'	FrL
'Cal Trio'	N
'Calros'	FB
'Carmel'	FrL, N
'Cashmere'	N
'Cathay'	N
'Centennial'	FrL
'Cheal's Crimson'	N
'Cheal's Golden Gem'	FrN, s
'Chilko'	FrA
'Colonel Lee'	S
'Columbia'	FrL, s
coronaria	FrG, CR
dasycalyx	FrG, CR
elongata	FrG, CR
'Cowichan'	I, s
'Crimson Brilliant'	FrA, s

'Dakota Beauty'	I
'Dartmouth'	FrL
'Dauphin'	I
dawsoniana	S
'Delite'	I
'E. H. Wilson'	I
'Early Strawberry'	FrL
'Elise Rathke'	N, FrA
'Elk River'	FrG
'Ellwangeriana'	S
'Erie'	FrA, s
'Exzellenz Thiel'	FrA, s
'Fairy'	FrA
'Florence'	FrL
florentina	N
formosana	N
'Frau Luise Dittmann'	FrA
fusca	FrA, N
levipes	FrA, N
'Garnet'	FrL
'Geneva'	FrL, s
'George Eden'	FrL
'Gibb'	N
'Gibb Golden Gage'	FrL
glabrata	FrG, CR
glaucescens	FrG, CR
gloriosa	FrA
'Gold'	I
'Golden Anniversary'	I
halliana	FrN
spontanea	FrA, N
hartwigii	FrA
'Helen'	I
'Henrietta Crosby'	FrA, FrN, s
heterophylla	FrG, CR
'Hillier Crab'	S
honanensis	N
'Hopa'	s
'Hyslop'	FB
ioensis	FrG, CR
fimbriata	FrG, CR
palmeri	FrG, CR
spinosa	FrG, CR
texana	FrG, CR
'Irene'	I, s
'Ivan'	S
'Jay Darling'	S
'Joan'	FrA, s

'John Downie'	FrA	*rinkii*	FrA, s
kansuensis calva	N	*pumila*	FrG
'Kerr'	FrL	*apetala*	FrG
'King's Crab'	FrG	*niedzwetzkyana*	FrA, FrI, s
'Kinsmere'	I	*paradisiaca*	FrG
'Kit Trio'	FrL	*translucens*	I
'Kola'	FrG, L	'Purple Wave'	S
lancifolia	FrG, CR	*purpurea*	Ff
'Laxton's Red'	Ff	'Aldenhamensis'	FrA, s
'Lee Trio'	FrL	'Eleyi'	FrA, s
'Lonedale'	S	*kornicensis*	Ff
'Lyman Prolific'	I	'Quaker Beauty'	FrG
magdeburgensis	FrN	'Quality'	H
'Magnus'	FrL	'Queen's Choice'	I
'Martha'	N	'Radiant'	S
'Martha-Dolgo'	S	'Red River'	FrL
'Mary Currelly'	Fr, FrA	'Red Silver'	S
'Mathews'	FrL, FrA	'Red Tip'	FrG, FrL
'Meach'	I	'Redfield'	I, s
micromalus	FrA, N	'Redflesh'	FrA
'Midnight'	H	'Redford'	FrA
'Milo'	S	'Rescue'	H
'Montreal Beauty'	FrG, s	'Robin'	FrL
'Morton'	FrG	*rockii*	N
'Mrs. Bayard Thayer'	I	'Rondo'	FrL
'Muskoka'	FrA, I	'Rosilda'	FrL, s
'Nancy Townsend'	I	'Rudolph'	S
'Nevis'	FrG	*sargentii*	I
'Nipissing'	FrA, FB	'Saska'	S
'Oakes'	I	'September'	FrL
'Olga'	FB	'Severn'	I
'Oporto'	Ff	*sieboldii*	I
'Orange'	FrL	*sikkimensis*	N
'Osman'	FB	'Silvia'	FB
'Pattie'	FrL	'Simcoe'	Ff, FrA
'Peachblow'	S	'Snowcap'	S, H
'Pink Eye'	FrN	*soulardii*	FrG, CR
'Pink Giant'	I	'Soulard'	FrG, CR
'Pioneer Scarlet'	S	*spectabilis plena*	I
'Piotosh'	FrL	'Strathmore'	FrA, s
platycarpa	FrG, CR	'Striped Beauty'	N
hoopesii	FrG, CR	*sublobata*	N
prattii	N	'Sugar Crab'	FrL
'Printosh'	FB	'Sugog'	FrA, FrL, FB
'Profusion'	I	'Sundog'	Ff
prunifolia	FrN, s	'Sutherland'	H
'Fastigiata'	FrN, s	*sylvestris*	FrL
'Pendula'	FrN, s	*plena*	N

'Tanner'   N
'Thomas'   S
'Thomas Roland'   I, s
'Timiskaming'   FrA
'Tomiko'   Ff
'Toshprince'   FrL
'Trail'   FrL
'Transcendent'   FB
transitoria   N
trilobata   N
tschonoskii   N
'University'   S
'Veitch's Scarlet'   FrL
'Virginia Seedless'   I
'Wabiskaw'   I
'Wakpala'   FrL
'Wamdesa'   FrL
'White Fox River'   H
'Whitney'   FB
'Wickson'   FrL
'William Anderson'   I
'William Sim'   FrA, S
'Winter Gold'   I
'Wisley Crab'   Ff
'Wynema'   FrG, FrA, FrL
'Young America'   FrL
yunnanensis   N
    veitchii   N
'Zaza'   S
'Zita'   FrL
'Zumi'   I
Mespilus germanica 1, 2, 3
Morus australis 1, 2, 3
    nigra 1, 3
    rubra 1, 3
Nemopanthus mucronatus 2, 3, 4
Nyssa aquatica 1
    ogeche 1
    sylvatica biflora 1
Ostrya carpinifolia 1, 2
    japonica 1, 2
    knowltonii 1, 2, 8
    virginiana glandulosa 1, 2
Parrotiopsis jacquemontiana 1, 2, 3
Paulonia tomentosa lanata 1
    t. pallida 1, 2
Phellodendron chinense 1
    c. glabriusculum 1

japonicum 1, 6
lavallei 1
piriforme 1, 6
sachalinense 1
Photinia davidsoniae 8
villosa sinica 1, 7
Picea abies argentea 1, 4, 5
    a. 'Argenteo-spica' 1, 4, 5
    'Aurea' 1, 4
    chlorocarpa 1
    'Cincinnata' 1, 6
    'Cupressina' 1
    'Erythrocarpa' 1
    'Finedonensis' 1, 4
    'Inversa' 1, 6
    'Monstrosa' 1, 6
    'Pendula' 1, 6
    'Viminalis' 1, 6
    'Virgata' 1, 6
asperata vars. 1
aurantiaca 1, 4
bicolor & vars. 1, 8
brachytyla & vars. 1
glauca albertiana 1
    'Aurea' 1, 4
    'Parva' 1, 6
    'Porsildii' 1, 8
glehnii 1
jezoensis & vars. 1
likiangensis & var. 1
mariana 1, 6
    'Beissneri' 1, 6
    'Ericoides' 1, 4
maximowiczii 1, 4, 6
meyeri 1
montigena 1
moseri 1
notha 1
obovata & vars. 1
orientalis 'Aureo-spicata' 1, 4
polita 1
pungens 'Aurea' 1, 4
    'Compacta' 1, 4
    viridis 1
purpurea 1, 6
retroflexa 1, 6
rubens 1, 6
    virgata 1, 6

schrenkiana 1
spinulosa 1, 6, 8
torano 1, 6
Pinus albicaulis 1
armandi 1
attenuata 1
ayacahuite 8
cembra vars. 1
cembroides & vars. 1
densiflora 'Aurea' 1, 4
echinata 1, 6
edulis 1
excelsa 1
glehnii 1
griffithii 1
halepensis vars. 8
heldreichii & vars. 1
holfordiana 1
massoniana 1
montezumae 8
nigra caramanica 1
   cebennensis 6
   'Monstrosa' 1, 6
   'Pendula' 6
palustris 1, 6
poiretiana 1
pungens 1, 6
sabiniana 1, 6
schwerinii 1
serotina 8
strobus 'Contorta' 1, 6
sylvestris *'Aurea'* 1, 4
   engadinensis 1
   'Hamata' 1
   lapponica 1, 6
   'Parviflora' 1
   'Pendula' 1, 6
   rigensis 1
   scotia 1
tabulaeformis & var. 1
taeda 1
thunbergii 'Aurea' 1, 4
   'Oculus-draconis' 1, 4
   'Variegata' 1, 4
yunnanensis 1
Pittosporum undulatum 1
Planera aquatica 1
Platanus acerifolia kelseyana 1, 4

a. hispanica 1
   suttneri 1, 4
occidentalis 7
   glabrata 7
orientalis cuneata 1
   digitata 1
Populus acuminata 1, 3
a. 'Glenmore' 1
adenopoda 1, 3
angulata 1, 3
   cordata 1, 3
angustifolia 1, 3
arizonica 1, 3
canadensis 1, 3
   aurea 1, 3, 8
   erecta 1, 3, 8
   marilandica 1, 3
   regenerata 1, 3
   serotina 1, 3, 8
candicans 1, 2, 3
canescens 1, 3
cathayana 1, 3
deltoides 1, 3
grandidentata 1, 3, 6
heterophylla 1, 3
koreana 1, 3
laurifolia 1, 3
macdougalii 1, 3
nigra 1, 7
   betulifolia 1, 3, 6
   elegans 1, 3, 6
   thevestina 1, 3, 6
palmeri 1, 3
petrowskyana 1, 3
pruinosa 1, 3
pseudograndidentata 1, 3
purdomii 1, 3
rasmouskyana 1, 3, 8
robusta 1, 3
rotundifolia 1, 3
sargentii 1, 3
sieboldii 1, 3
suaveolens 1, 3
szechuanica 1, 3
tacamahaca 1, 3
texana 1, 3
tomentosa 1, 3
tremula 1, 3

davidiana 1, 3
villosa 1, 3
tremuloides vancouveriana 1, 3
trichocarpa 1, 3
tristis 1, 3
wilsonii 1, 3
yunnanensis 1, 3
Prunus alabamensis
alleghaniensis 1, 2
americana 1, 2
x *amygdalo-persica*
amygdalus amara 1, 2
angustifolia 1, 2
dulcia 1, 2
fragilia 1, 2
'Purpurea' 1, 2
'Sativa' 1, 2
angustifolia 1
apetala 1
armeniaca 'Pendula' 1, 2, 6
'Variegata' 1, 2, 4
australis 1, 2, 8
avium 1
bicolor 1, 2, 8
blireiana 'Moseri' 1,2
'Othello' 1
bokhariensis 1, 2, 8
buergeriana 1
ceramus 1, 2, 8
cerasifera 1, 4
divaricata 1, 2
'Elegans' 1, 4
'Hessei' 1, 4
lindsayae 1, 2, 8
'Newport' 1, 2
'Othello' 1, 2
purpusii 1, 4
woodii 1, 2
cerasoides 1, 2, 8
conradenia 1, 2, 8
cornuta 1, 2, 8
cyclamina 1
dasycarpa 1
davidiana 1, 3, 6
dielsiana 1, 2, 8
discadenia 1, 2, 8
domestica 1
x *fontanesiana* 1, 2

grayana 1, 2, 8
hortulana 1
incisa 1, 3
serrata 1, 3
insititia 1
juddii 1
kansuensis 1, 2, 8
lanata 1, 3
laucheana 1, 3
litigiosa 1, 2, 8
lobulata 1, 2, 8
lyonii 1, 2, 3
macradenia 1, 2, 8
mahaleb 1
mandshurica 1, 3
mexicana 1, 2
meyeri 1, 2
mira 1
munsoniana 1
padus 'Aucubaefolia' 1, 4
'Leucocarpos' 1
'Parviflora' 1, 2
'Pendula' 1, 2
'Pubescens' 1
pensylvanica saximontana 1, 2
persica 1
alba 1
'Aurora' 1
'Blushing Bride' 1
'Clara Meyer' 1
'Coccinea Plena' 1
dianthiflora 1
'Double Crimson' 1
'Double Maroon' 1
'Duplex' 1
'Early Red' 1
'General Bei' 1
magnifica 1
'Mandarin' 6
pyramidalis 1
rubro-plena 1
'San José Pink' 1
sanguinea 1
versicolor 1
'Woodside' 6
pilosiuscula 1, 2, 8
pleiocerasus 1, 2, 8
pseudoarmenica 1, 2, 8

reverchonii 1
rivularis 1, 2, 8
rufomicans 1, 2, 8
salicina 1
sericea 1, 2, 8
serotina cartilaginea 1
   montana 1
   phelloides 1
serrulata—many vars. except those
   recommended (see pages
   384–87)
simonii 1
slavinii 1
spinosa 1
ssiori 1, 2, 8
subcordata 1
subhirtella 'Ascendens' 1, 2
umbellata 1
virens 1, 2, 8
virginiana 1, 7
wilsonii 1, 2, 8
yedoensis 'Perpendens' 1, 2
Ptelea trifoliata 1, 2, 3, 7
Pterocarya hupehensis 1, 2, 3
Pteroceltis tatarinowi 1, 2, 3
Pterostyrax corymbosa 1
Pyrus betulaefolia 1, 3, 7
bretschneideri 1, 3, 7
calleryana dimorphophylla 1, 3
   graciliflora 1, 3, 7
   tometella 1, 3
communis 1, 3, 7
   cordata 1, 3, 7
   pyraster 1, 3, 7
   sativa 1, 3, 7
elaeagrifolia 1, 3, 7
kawakami 6
nivalis 1, 3, 7
pashia 1, 3, 7
phaeocarpa 1, 3, 7
pyrifolia 1, 3, 7
regelii 1, 3, 7
serrulata 1, 3, 7
ussuriensis hondoensis 1, 3, 7
   ovoidea 1, 3, 7
Quercus alba latiloba 1, 2, 3
a. repanda 1, 2, 3
aliena 1, 2, 3

acuteserrata 1, 2, 3
arkansana 1, 2, 3
baronii 1, 2, 3
bebbiana 1, 2, 3
benderi 1, 2, 3
borealis flabellata 1, 2, 3
brittonii 1, 2, 3
bushii, 1, 2, 3
calliprinos 8
capesii 1, 2, 3
castanaefolia & vars. 1, 2, 3
cerris ambrozyana 1, 2, 3
   austriaca 1, 2, 3
comptonae 1, 2, 3
dalchampii 1, 2, 3
deamii 1, 2, 3
dentata & vars. 1, 4, 6
durandii 1, 2, 3
ellipsoidalis 1, 2, 3
exacta 1, 2, 3
frainetto 1, 6
glandulifera 6
gunnisonii 6
haas & vars. 1, 2, 3
hartwissiana 1, 2, 3
heterophylla 6
hickelii 1, 2, 3
hillii 1, 2, 3
hispanica & vars. 1, 2, 3
iberica 1, 2, 3
ilex—most vars. 1, 2, 3
ilicifolia 1, 4, 6
inermis 1, 2, 3
infectoria 1, 2, 3
laevis 1, 2, 3
leana 1, 2, 3
leptophylla 1, 2, 3
liaotungensis 6
lobata 1, 2, 3
ludoviciana & var. 1, 2, 3
lusitanica 8
lyrata 1, 4, 6
macnabiana 6
macranthera 1, 2, 3
macrocarpa 1, 4, 6
   olivaeformis 1, 2, 3
macrolepis 1, 2, 3
michauxii 1, 2, 3

aria longifolia 1
  'Lutescens' 1
arnoldiana 1
aucuparia 'Dirkeni' 1, 4
  intergerrima 1
  rossica 1
commixta 1
domestica 1, 3
dumosa 8
esserteauiana 1
glomerulata 1
gracilis 1, 3
helenae & vars. 1
hupehensis & vars. 1
hybrida 1
  'Meinichii' 1
intermedia & vars. 1
japonica & vars. 2
keissleri 3
latifolia 1
matsumurana 2
meliosmifolia 3
mougeotii 3
pallescens 3
pohuashanensis 1
prattii & vars. 6
reflexipetala 1
rehderiana 1
rufo-ferruginea 1
sargentiana warleyensis 1
serotina 1
splendida 1
thuringiaca 1
torminalis 1, 3
umbellata 1
wilsoniana 8
Staphylea species 1, 2, 3, 6
Stewartia monadelpha 1, 2
  serrata 1
Syringa amurensis 1, 2
Taxodium ascendens 1, 6
Taxus baccata 'adpressa aurea' 2, 4, 5
  b. linearis 1, 2
    variegata 2, 4, 5
  brevifolia 1, 6
  chinensis 1, 6
  hunnewelliana 1

Tecoma stans 2, 3
Thuja occidentalis 'Alba' 1, 4, 5
  o. 'Albo-spicata' 1, 2, 4
  aurea 2, 4, 5
  'Aureo-variegata' 2, 4, 5
  'Columbia' 1, 2, 4
  'Douglas Golden' 1, 2, 4
  filicioides 1, 2
  filiformis 1, 4, 5
  'Lutescens' 2, 4, 5
  'Pendula' 1, 2, 6
  pulcherrima 2, 5
  'Reid' 1, 2
  semperaurea 2, 4, 5
  spiralis 1, 2, 6
  variegata 1, 2, 4
  'Vervane' 1, 2
  'Waxen' 2, 5
orientalis argenteo-variegata 2, 4
  aurea 2, 4
  'Beverleyensis' 2, 4
  conspicua 2, 4, 5
  'Elegantissima' 2, 4
  flagelliformis 2, 4
  'Kallay Gold' 1, 2, 4
  'Semperaurescens' 2, 4
plicata elegantissima 1, 2, 4
  pendula 1, 2, 6
  variegata 1, 2, 4
  zebrina 1, 2, 4
Tilia americana 1, 4, 7
  a. ampelophylla 1, 4, 7
  dentata 1, 4, 7
  macrophylla 1, 4, 7
  amurensis 1, 6
  caroliniana 1, 4
  cordata ascidiata 1
  dasystyla 1
  europaea & var. 1, 6
  flaccida 1, 4
  flavescens 1
  floridana 1
  henryana 1
    subglabra 1
  heterophylla 1
    michauxii 1
  insularis 1, 6
  japonica 1

mandshurica 1
maximowicziana 1, 4
miqueliana 1
moltkei 1
monticola 1
neglecta 1, 4
oliveri 1
paucicostata 1
platyphyllos vitifolia 1
tuan 1
    chinensis 1
Tsuga canadensis albo-spica 1, 2, 4
   c. 'Argentea' 1, 2, 4
     atrovirens 1, 2, 4
     aurea 1, 2, 4
     gracilis 1
     microphylla 1, 2, 4
     parvula 1, 2, 4
     pyramidata 1
     sparsifolia 1, 2, 4
     'Variegata' 1, 2, 4
   chinensis 1
   dumosa 1
   heterophylla argenteo-variegata 1, 2, 4
   mertensiana & vars. 1
   sieboldii 1
   yunnanensis 1
Ulmus alata 1, 2, 3, 7
   americana vars. 7
   bergmanniana 1, 2, 3, 7
   carpinifolia cornubiensis 1, 2, 3, 7
     'Dampieri' 1, 2, 3, 4, 7
     gracilis 1, 2, 3, 4, 7
     italica 1, 2, 3, 7
     'Propendens' 1, 2, 3, 7

     'Suberosa' 1, 2, 3, 6, 7
     'Variegata' 1, 2, 3, 4, 7
     'Webbiana' 1, 2, 3, 4, 7
   crassifolia 1, 2, 3, 7
   davidiana 1, 7
   densa x *pumila* 'Androssowii' 1, 7
   fulva 1, 2, 3, 4, 6, 7
   glabra atropurpurea 1, 6, 7
     'Camperdownii' 7
     'Cornuta' 1, 2, 3, 7
     'Crispa' 1, 2, 3, 4, 7
     'Exoniensis' 1, 7
     'Lutescens' 1, 2, 3, 4, 7
     'Monstrosa' 1, 6, 7
     nitida 1, 2, 3, 4, 8
   x hollandica & vars. 1, 2, 3, 7, 8
   japonica 1, 2, 3, 7
   laciniata 1, 2, 3, 6, 7
   laevis 1, 2, 3, 7
   macrocarpa 1, 7
   parvifolia vars. 7
   plotii 1, 2, 3, 7
   procera—most vars. except
     'Viminalis' 1, 2, 3, 7
   pumila arborea 1, 7
   rubra 1, 2, 3, 4, 7
   serotina 1, 2, 3, 7
   thomasii 1, 2, 3, 6, 7
   wilsoniana 1, 7
Viburnum cylindricum 2, 3
Xanthoceras sorbifolium 1, 2, 3
Zanthoxylum americanum 1, 2, 3
   schinifolium 1, 2
   simulans 1, 2

APPENDIX 2:

One Hundred Tree Champions

→≫≫

The American Forestry Association has been keeping a file of the largest (as of 1988) recorded specimens of American tree species, a most interesting file now containing 725 Big Tree Champions recorded with the trunk circumference (breast-high), spread of the branches, height, and location of each tree. Ninety-nine of these are listed below. These recorded "giants" can be expected to be superseded, but a glance through the list might prove of interest.

SPECIES AND YEAR OF LAST MEASUREMENT	GIRTH (INCHES)	HEIGHT (FEET)
ALDER		
Red *(Alnus oregana)* 1979	245	104
White *(A. rhombifolia)* 1984	145	37
APPLE		
Common *(Malus pumila)* 1986	141	70
ARBORVITAE		
Oriental *(Thuja orientalis)* 1982	100	59
ASH		
Oregon *(Fraxinus latifolia)* 1975	263	59
White *(F. americana)* 1983	304	95
ASPEN		
Bigtooth *(Populus grandidentata)* 1980	140	102
Quaking *(P. tremuloides)* 1982	122	109
BALD CYPRESS		
Common *(Taxodium distichum)* 1981	644	83

SPECIES AND YEAR OF LAST MEASUREMENT	GIRTH (INCHES)	HEIGHT (FEET)
BEECH		
American *(Fagus grandifolia)* 1984	222	130
BEEFWOOD		
Horsetail *(Casuarina equisetifolia)* 1968	207	89
BIRCH		
Canoe *(Betula papyrifera)* 1979	217	93
River *(B. nigra)* 1987	188	90
Yellow *(B. alleghaniensis)* 1983	252	76
BITTERNUT *(Carya cordiformis)* 1987	174	120
BOX-ELDER *(Acer negundo)* 1984	216	98
BUCKEYE		
Ohio *(Aesculus glabra)* 1984	146	144
BUCKTHORN		
Cascara *(Rhamnus purshiana)* 1980	109	27
BUTTERNUT *(Juglans cinerea)* 1987	222	80
CALIFORNIA-LAUREL *(Umbellularia californica)* 1978	501	88
CAMPHOR TREE *(Cinnamomum camphora)* 1977	368	72
CATALPA		
Northern *(Catalpa speciosa)* 1984	239	98
CEDAR		
Incense *(Calocedrus decurrens)* 1969	462	152
CHERRY		
Black *(Prunus serotina)* 1984	222	93
Sour *(P. cerasus)* 1972	119	68
CHESTNUT		
American *(Castanea dentata)* 1987	193	69
CHINABERRY *(Melia azedarach)* 1967	222	75
CHINKAPIN		
Giant *(Castanea pumila)* 1986	135	115

SPECIES AND YEAR OF LAST MEASUREMENT	GIRTH (INCHES)	HEIGHT (FEET)
COCONUT *(Cocos nucifera)* 1979	60	92
COFFEE-TREE		
Kentucky *(Gymnocladus dioicus)* 1985	212	78
COTTONWOOD		
Eastern *(Populus deltoides)* 1984	373	132
CUCUMBER TREE *(Magnolia acuminata)* 1985	293	75
CYPRESS		
Arizona *(Cupressus arizonica)* 1977	226	73
Monterey *(C. macrocarpa)* 1975	333	97
DOGWOOD		
Flowering *(Cornus florida)* 1986	70	40
Pacific *(C. nuttallii)* 1986	169	60
DOUGLAS-FIR *(Pseudotsuga menziesii)* 1975	545	202
ELM		
American *(Ulmus americana)* 1985	284	125
FALSE CYPRESS		
Nootka *(Chamaecyparis nootkatensis)* 1979	452	120
FIR		
Red *(Abies magnifica)* 1972	320	180
White *(A. concolor)* 1972	335	192
HACKBERRY		
Common *(Celtis occidentalis)* 1987	162	97
HAWTHORN		
Black *(Crataegus nigra)* 1973	114	33
Downy *(C. mollis)* 1972	105	52
HEMLOCK		
Canada *(Tsuga canadensis)* 1979	224	123
Carolina *(T. caroliniana)* 1972	139	88
Western *(T. heterophylla)* 1987	270	241
HICKORY		
Shagbark *(Carya ovata)* 1984	132	153

SPECIES AND YEAR OF LAST MEASUREMENT	GIRTH (INCHES)	HEIGHT (FEET)
HOLLY		
American *(Ilex opaca)* 1987	135	62
HONEY-LOCUST		
Common *(Gleditsia tricanthos)* 1985	216	115
JUNIPER		
Alligator *(Juniperus deppeana)* 1962	355	57
Western *(J. scopulorum)* 1983	480	86
LARCH		
Western *(Larix occidentalis)* 1980	233	175
LINDEN		
American *(Tilia americana)* 1987	249	122
LOCUST		
Black *(Robinia pseudoacacia)* 1974	280	96
MADRONE		
Pacific *(Arbutus menziesii)* 1984	408	96
MAPLE		
Bigleaf *(Acer macrophyllum)* 1977	419	101
Norway *(A. platanoides)* 1985	288	65
Red *(A. rubrum)* 1984	222	179
Silver *(A. saccharinum)* 1982	276	125
Sugar *(A. saccharum)* 1984	269	91
MOUNTAIN-ASH		
American *(Sorbus americana)* 1979	80	62
European *(S. aucuparia)* 1987	123	43
MULBERRY		
White *(Morus alba)* 1982	276	55
OAK		
Black *(Quercus velutina)* 1985	293	97
Canyon live *(Q. chrysolepis)* 1984	404	72
Live *(Q. virginiana)* 1976	439	55
Northern red *(Q. rubra)* 1987	364	66
Pin *(Q. palustris)* 1986	214	130
White *(Q. alba)* 1986	414	107
OSAGE-ORANGE *(Maclura pomifera)* 1986	300	64

SPECIES AND YEAR OF LAST MEASUREMENT	GIRTH (INCHES)	HEIGHT (FEET)
PALM		
California fan *(Washingtonia filifera)* 1978	100	89
PAPER-MULBERRY		
Common *(Broussonetia papyrifera)* 1987	164	40
PEAR		
Common *(Pyrus communis)* 1972	117	75
PECAN *(Carya illinoinensis)* 1980	231	143
PERSIMMON		
Common *(Diospyros virginiana)* 1972	146	60
PIGNUT *(Carya glabra)* 1985	157	190
PINE		
Eastern white *(Pinus strobus)* 1984	202	181
Jeffrey *(P. jeffreyi)* 1984	307	197
Sugar *(P. lambertiana)* 1967	384	216
Western white *(P. monticola)* 1984	414	157
POPLAR		
Balsam *(Populus balsamifera)* 1986	163	138
REDBUD		
Eastern *(Cercis canadensis)* 1987	139	41
RED-CEDAR		
Eastern *(Juniperus virginiana)* 1986	190	62
Western *(J. scopulorum)* 1977	150	55
REDWOOD *(Sequoia sempervirens)* 1972	629	362
SASSAFRAS *(Sassafras albidum)* 1982	253	76
SEQUOIA		
Giant *(Sequoiadendron giganteum)* 1975	998	275
SOURWOOD *(Oxydendrum arboreum)* 1968	77	118
SPRUCE		
Engelmann *(Picea engelmannii)* 1970	290	179
Sitka *(P. sitchensis)* 1987	673	206

The giant redwoods
(Sequoiadendron
giganteum) *of northern
California are several
thousand years old.*

SPECIES AND YEAR OF LAST MEASUREMENT	GIRTH (INCHES)	HEIGHT (FEET)
SWEET-GUM *(Liquidambar styraciflua)* 1986	278	136
TAMARACK *(Larix laricina)* 1983	143	92
TREE OF HEAVEN *(Ailanthus altissima)*	238	64
TULIP TREE *(Liriodendron tulipifera)* 1986	374	146
TUPELO		
Black *(Nyssa sylvatica)* 1987	238	102
WALNUT		
Eastern black *(Juglans nigra)* 1983	271	122
WILLOW		
Black *(Salix nigra)* 1987	377	109
YELLOWWOOD		
American *(Cladrastis lutea)* 1987	276	72

Glossary

→≫

acicular: shaped like a needle

anther: the pollen-bearing part of a stamen

apetalous: without petals

axil: the upper angle formed by a leaf or branch with the stem

axis: the main stem or central support of a stem

bract: a much reduced leaf, particularly the small or scalelike leaves in a flower cluster or associated with the flowers

branchlet: a division of the branch

calyx: the outer perianth of the flower; the collective term for sepals

capsule: a dry fruit of more than one carpel, opening at maturity

carpel: one of the units composing an ovary or pistil

catkin: a deciduous spike of unisexual, apetalous flowers

chlorotic: lacking in chlorophyll; such plants or parts of plants are usually sickly and yellowish

clone: a group of plants composed of individuals produced vegetatively from a single original plant; clones differ from races and strains in that they will fail to come true from seeds. Examples of this are the Concord grape and Baldwin apple.

coarse: consisting of large or rough parts

columnar: having the shape of a column

compact: arranged in a small amount of space; of dense habit *compound:* composed of two or more similar parts united into one whole; *compound leaf:* one divided into separate leaflets

conical: cone-shaped, as in the young form of many spruces

cordate: heart-shaped; usually referring to the base of the leaf

cultivar: a cultivated variety

deciduous: (of a tree) having leaves that drop in winter

digitate: see *palmate*

dioecious: with staminate (male) and pistillate (female) flowers on different plants

double (flowers): flowers that have more than the usual number of petals, colored sepals, or bracts

elliptical: having the outline of an ellipse, broadest at the middle and narrower at each end

exfoliate: to peel off in shreds or thin layers, as bark from a tree

exudate: exuded matter, oozing out of a cut plant part

fastigiate: with close and erect branches, as in the Lombardy poplar

fibrous: (of roots) having no prominent central axis and branching in all directions

floriferous: flower-bearing, usually in the sense of abundantly flowering

glabrous: not hairy but smooth

glaucous: covered with a bloom, a bluish white or bluish gray powder

inflorescence: the flower cluster

key (that is, winged key): a winged fruit, as in maples; see *samara*

leader: the primary or terminal shoot of a tree

legume: a seed vessel or pod of the pea or bean family

midrib: the central vein or rib of a leaf

node: the place on a stem that normally bears a leaf or leaves

nutlet: diminutive nut

open pollinate: pistils free to open air, allowing the pollen to be blown by the wind

orbicular: circular, rounded in outline

ovate: having an outline like that of a hen's egg

palmate: radiately lobed or divided with three or more veins arising from one point

panicle: a compound, usually loose flower cluster, longer than it is broad

pedicels: the stalk of a flower or fruit when in a cluster

pendulous: more or less hanging or declined

perfect (in flowers): having both functional stamens and pistils on the same plant; bisexual

petiole: leaf stalk

pinnate (leaf): compound, with the leaflets placed on each side of a midrib; feather-like

pistil: the seed-bearing organ of a flower consisting of the ovary, style, and stigma

pistillate: having a pistil and no stamens; female

polygamous: bearing unisexual and bisexual flowers on the same plant

pome: a fleshy fruit such as the apple or the pear

prostrate: lying flat on the ground

pubescent: covered with short, soft hairs

pyramidal: broadest at the base, tapering apically; pyramid-shaped

raceme: a simple inflorescence of stalked flowers on a more or less elongated axis

resinous: secreting a sticky substance

rosaceous: flower similar to that of a rose

rugose: wrinkled

samara: an indehiscent winged fruit not opening along regular lines

scabrous: rough or gritty to the touch; rough pubescent

scalelike: resembling a scale

scion: a slip or shoot used for grafting

semidouble (flowers): flowers that have partly changed into double flowers, with the inner stamens perfect and the outer stamens petal-like

sepal: a division of the calyx

serrate: saw-toothed, with the teeth pointing toward the apex of the plant part

serrulate: serrate with fine teeth

sheath: a tubular envelope, such as the lower part of the leaf in grasses

single (flowers): flowers that have only a single row of petals, colored sepals, or bracts

sport: a sudden deviation in plant growth starting from a bud or seed

stamen: the pollen-bearing organ of a flower

staminate: having stamens and no pistil; male

stipular: having stipules at the base of the leaves

stipule: the appendage at the base of the petiole, usually one on each side

stoma or *stomate:* a "breathing" pore in the epidermis of the leaf leading into an intercellular space communicating with the internal tissue through which gases are exchanged

terminal: at the tip or distal end

ternate: in threes

tetraploid: having a chromosome number four times the monoploid number

tomentose: dense, woolly pubescence

trifoliate: with a leaf of three leaflets

truss: a compact flower or fruit cluster

umbel: an inflorescence with pedicels or branches arising at the same point and of nearly equal length

understock: plant roots or stem on which a scion is attached by grafting

upright: having the main axis perpendicular

weeping: dropping conspicuously; pendant

whorl: the arrangement of three or more structures arising from a single node

winged nut: see *samara*

Index

→>>>

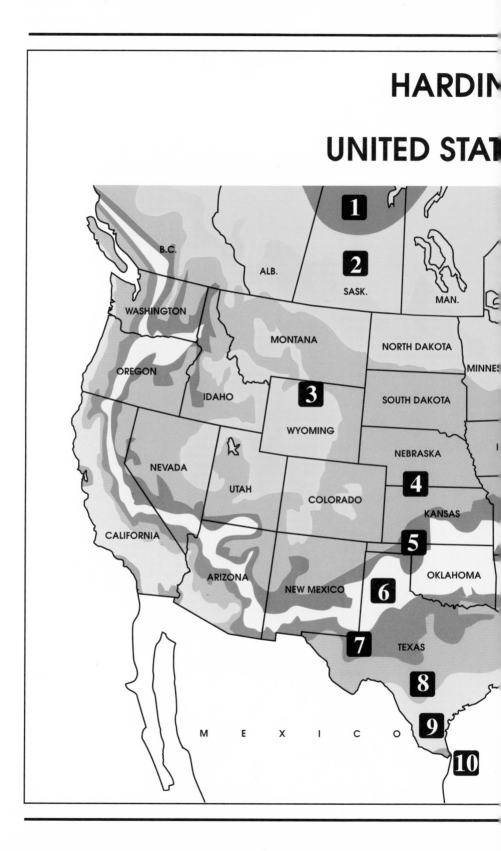